Dear Dr Kate &
Thanks for he[l]
change the world

A Poor and Merciful Church

A Poor and Merciful Church

The Illuminative Ecclesiology of Pope Francis

Stan Chu Ilo

ORBIS BOOKS
Maryknoll, New York 10545

ORBIS BOOKS
Maryknoll, New York 10545

Fathers and Brothers
MARYKNOLL™

Founded in 1970, Orbis Books endeavors to publish works that enlighten the mind, nourish the spirit, and challenge the conscience. The publishing arm of the Maryknoll Fathers and Brothers, Orbis seeks to explore the global dimensions of the Christian faith and mission, to invite dialogue with diverse cultures and religious traditions, and to serve the cause of reconciliation and peace. The books published reflect the views of their authors and do not represent the official position of the Maryknoll Society. To learn more about Maryknoll and Orbis Books, please visit our website at www.maryknollsociety.org.

Library of Congress Cataloging-in-Publication Data

Names: Ilo, Stan Chu, author.
Title: A poor and merciful church : the illuminative ecclesiology of Pope
    Francis / Stan Chu Ilo.
Description: Maryknoll, NY : Orbis Books, [2018] | Includes bibliographical
    references and index.
Identifiers: LCCN 2017040793 (print) | LCCN 2017047677 (ebook) | ISBN
    9781608337316 (e-book) | ISBN 9781626982659 (pbk.)
Subjects: LCSH: Church. | Francis, Pope, 1936- | Catholic Church—Doctrines.
    | Christianity—Africa.
Classification: LCC BX1746 (ebook) | LCC BX1746 .I39 2018 (print) | DDC
    262/.02—dc23
LC record available at https://lccn.loc.gov/2017040793

To the eternal memory of my father,
His Royal Highness, Igwe Vincent Onyekelu Ilo, 1933–2016,
a great servant of God, teacher, and ideal Father who with my mother,
Lolo Igwe Rose Ilo,
created in our family and community a model of a society
animated by love, mercy, compassion, and solidarity
especially for the poor and the marginalized.
This was my first image and model of
an illuminative church sustained by a healthy and transformative
culture of deep human, cosmic, and spiritual encounters.

Contents

Acknowledgments

I did not set out to write a book on Pope Francis. However, over the last four years, I was invited to speak or write about issues in the Catholic Church, African Christianity, church and development, and on Pope Francis. It was through these conferences, research projects, and book events that the ideas in this book were formed, tested, and refined. It was in these encounters that I started to hear those encouraging words that continue to ring in my ears that these ideas need to be made available to a wider audience. Many people played important roles in this journey.

I thank Agbonkhianmeghe Orobator, SJ, who convened and led a three-year research project on theology, religion, and society in Africa where I was able to make three different presentations on the church in Africa and on Pope Francis. The feedback from my fellow African theologians, practitioners, and church leaders, and from Orobator himself, enriched this book.

Sister Rosemary Nyirumbe has been a close friend and conversation partner for the last four years. She has remained a role model for me and an inspiration to millions of people in Africa and the world through her courageous sacrifice in rescuing over four thousand abducted girls in Northern Uganda and giving them hope and a new life at St. Monica's in Gulu, Northern Uganda. I am grateful for her friendship and that she found time in her numerous commitments and travels to read through this work.

I thank Kurt Appel and Ikenna Okafor, both professors at the University of Vienna, Austria, for inviting me to the Pope Francis Conference in 2015, where I was able to test the idea of "illuminative ecclesiology" and gained much insight from leading Catholic theologians from Europe, North America, and Latin America on this topic.

I am grateful to Matthew Shadle, the editor of the Catholic Social Ethics section of the Political Theology blog for inviting me to write a review of *Amoris Laetitia* soon after its publication. His feedback on my essay helped me develop those ideas further for this book.

I thank Paulinus Odozor of University of Notre Dame for his friendship and encouragement and for the invitation to speak at the conference on the Future of African Theology in Rome, where again I was able to share some of the ideas in this book on cultural pluralism and the hermeneutics of multiplicity in the teaching of Pope Francis.

I want to express my profuse gratitude to the following senior colleagues and friends who read this manuscript in part or in whole and who through conversation and written reviews helped refine my argument and improve my methodology and style, and who gave helpful suggestions and sources to enrich the content: Laurenti Magesa, Elochukwu Uzukwu, Bill Cavanaugh, Michael Budde, Emmanuel Katongole, Bradford Hinze, and Sister Mary Sylvia Nwachukwu, DDL. All my colleagues at the Center for World Catholicism and the Department of Catholic Studies at DePaul University have been supportive and have provided me with an ideal family environment where I could flourish.

To Father Ken Simpson and the clergy and staff at St. Clement's parish, Chicago, I remain ever grateful. Father Bill Tkachuk, John Hoffman, Bill Killeen of St. Francis Xavier Parish La Grange, and Father Jim Blazek of St. Maria Goretti Parish Schiller Park, Father Collins Ekpe, CM, Father Idara Otu, and Father Richard LoBianco, I thank you for being sources of light in the world.

I wish to acknowledge the lessons which I have learned—some of which are recounted in this book—from all our women and agents in our social justice ministries in Kenya, Uganda, Central African Republic, Burkina Faso, and Nigeria. I would like to mention especially the following: Rose Egolet, Nancy Graham, Catherine Ekalam, Rose Kantiono, Sara Dunn, Chiamaka Igboayaka, Irene Kyompaire, Flora Samba Pasquereau, Ekwy Odozor and Mama Rose.

I am grateful to Cardinal Anthony Okogie, Cardinal John Onaiyekan, Cardinal Blaise Cupich, Archbishop Ignatius Kaigama, Professor Dezie Chibuko, Bishop Hiiboro Kissala, Bishop Anthony Gbuji, Bishop Matthew Kukah, Bishop John Okoye, Paul Bere, SJ, Professor Lilian Dube, Father Barry Eneh, Father Jan Kolodynski, Janet Cloud Mose, and Professor Kathleen Skerrett for their inspiration and encouragement for my scholarship, publication and priestly life.

And to Jim Keane and Robert Ellsberg at Orbis, thanks for believing in this project.

Special thanks are due to my mum, Lolo Igwe Rose A. Ilo for always being there for me.

My father, His Royal Highness, Igwe Vincent O. Ilo, Ohabuenyi of Achi, died before I could finish this project. He has always remained my greatest fan, motivator, and inspiration. I am sure that he continues to watch me, our family and clan as our Great Ancestor. I dedicate this book to his eternal memory.

Introduction

Come Be My Light!

Nor does the light of faith make us forget the sufferings of this world. How many men and women of faith have found *mediators of light* in those who suffer! So it was with Saint Francis of Assisi and the leper, or with Blessed Mother Teresa of Calcutta and her poor. They understood the mystery at work in them. In drawing near to the suffering, they were certainly not able to eliminate all their pain or to explain every evil. *Faith is not a light which scatters all our darkness, but a lamp which guides our steps in the night and suffices for the journey.* To those who suffer, God does not provide arguments which explain everything; rather, his response is that of *an accompanying presence, a history of goodness which touches every story of suffering and opens up a ray of light.* In Christ, God himself wishes to share this path with us and to *offer us his gaze so that we might see the light within it* (Heb 12:2).

—Pope Francis, *Lumen Fidei*, 57

One of the most lasting images of Pope Francis, one which profoundly touched many people when it was beamed out to the world on the news, was his encounter with Vinicio Riva. Vinicio suffers from the genetic disease neurofibromatosis, a condition that has left him disfigured and covered from head to toe in noncontagious, itchy, sore-like growths. His aunt Caterina Lotto fears that Vinicio and his sister Morena will have to live in a care home when she dies because there will be no one to look after them at home. Vinicio and his sister, in addition to this painful and lacerating disease, also suffer from learning difficulties and cannot leave their home without being helped and accompanied by their aunt. When Pope Francis saw Vinicio in the audience, seated in a wheelchair, he deliberately went to him, embraced him, held him tightly to himself for what seemed like ages, and covered him with kisses.

In an interview that Vinicio granted to the *Daily Mail*, a London-based newspaper, he recalled the impact of this meeting in these words:

> His hands were so soft. And his smile was so clear and open. But the thing that struck me most is that there has not been thinking about whether or not to hug me. I'm not contagious, but he did not know. But he just did it: he caressed me all over my face, and as he did I felt only love. It was like being in paradise.

He went on to speak about this moment of mutual encounter and intimacy in this way:

> First, I kissed his hand while he, with the other hand, caressed my head and wounds. Then he drew me to him in a strong embrace, kissing my face. My head was against his chest his arms were wrapped around me. It lasted just over a minute, but to me it seemed like an eternity.

Vinicio recalled that for him the meeting with Pope Francis, though lasting for only a few minutes, was a turning point in his life and marked a new beginning. Vinicio's wounds did not suddenly disappear. However, the encounter was life-giving and grace-filled; it was deep, intimate, and heartfelt. As a result of this meeting, Vinicio felt a new experience of God's love, a new irruption of light in the darkness of his life, and a new experience of healing and recovery. As he recalled telling his aunt as they left St. Peter's Square, "Here, I leave my pain behind."[1]

Vinicio is a representative image of our wounded world in need of healing and the touch of God. Like Vinicio, there are many people in the world today carrying physical and spiritual wounds; like Vinicio, who spoke with pain about how people often avoided contact with him, there are millions of people in the world who feel isolated, alienated, and abandoned because of their race, color, religion, sexuality, gender, sex, nationality, ethnicity, and other forms of identity. There are people in our churches who feel rejected by fellow Christians and pastors because they are considered sinners and unworthy of God's blessing. However, in touching Vinicio and allowing Vinicio to touch him, Pope Francis showed the healing power of a genuine encounter between people. Through a simple but meaningful one-minute encounter he showed that physical and spiritual wounds and the burdens that many people carry today in our world can be healed through a genuine act of love. There is healing and hope in the world because people can enter into other people's wounds, and in doing so bring a new reality even in the midst of darkness.

---

[1]*Daily Mail*, November 19, 2013, www.dailymail.co.uk,

Vinicio became an instant celebrity because such acts of kindness and compassion shown by Pope Francis are the kind of light that the world is looking for in the darkness surrounding us. Darkness surrounds the world when people hide in their own small worlds, comfort zones, and behind crumbling identity walls. The world wishes to see such visible and concrete signs as the pope's gesture in our churches, because they are illuminative paths that lead people to God. The encounter with Vinicio is one of the many examples of how the culture of encounter has defined the ministry of Pope Francis.

Every Wednesday and in most trips outside Rome, Pope Francis is seen in the company of the marginalized, migrants, prisoners, ex-priests and nuns, and victims of clerical sexual abuse, among many others. He also embraces the powerful and the mighty of this world, but his preferential company with the poor and the vulnerable is so evident. According to Elisabetta Piqué:

> A smiling pope greets the personalities who have come to occupy privileged positions in the audience—but later he also finds time to comfort the sick, the suffering, the strangers. That's when you can see him truly in his element, authentic, while he greets countless anonymous sick people, some in wheelchairs. He devotes more time to them than to the powerful of the earth; he hugs them and lets himself be hugged, warmly, which inspires applause. . . . In a few minutes he changes their lives and makes them feel happy, he makes them understand that it is true, that God exists, that God is love and mercy.[2]

This culture of encounter is not only with human beings, but also with the world of nature, politics, and social media.[3] The culture of encounter is not only a movement from the Roman center to the periphery, but the discovery of Rome in the margins through a decentering from Rome and a recentering of the church in the margins. However, the church is not to be narrowed to the acts of popes, bishops, priests, and religious; everyone everywhere can illuminate the world with the light of Christ. This culture of encounter is a starting point for understanding the praxis of the kind of church that Pope Francis is bringing about today following the example of Christ. The theology of this way of being church is what I wish to share in this book through what I have called illuminative ecclesiology of Pope Francis.

When we look at the words and deeds of Pope Francis since the beginning of his papacy, it is obvious that he has quietly changed Catholic ecclesiol-

---

[2]Elisabetta Piqué, *Pope Francis: Life and Revolution* (Chicago: Loyola Press, 2014), 188.

[3]Massimo Faggioli, *Pope Francis: Tradition in Transition* (New York: Paulist Press, 2015), 15–16.

ogy. The Francis effect is now the new narrative of the Catholic Church, with all the positive consequences it brings in realizing the mission of the church in the world. Pope Francis has accomplished so much in so short a time that even celebrities like Elton John have called Pope Francis "a miracle of humility in an era of vanity."[4] Elton John called Pope Francis his "hero" because Pope Francis is "a compassionate, loving man who wants everybody to be included in the love of God." The famed singer concluded in the special Italian edition of *Vanity Fair* (which, like *Time Magazine*, had nominated Francis as the Person of the Year for 2013) that "his beacon of hope will bring more light than any advancement of science, because no drug has the power of love."[5]

The *Economist*, in its April 19, 2014, edition titled "The Francis Effect," offered three key strategies which any CEO of a failing company could learn from how Pope Francis handled the church's problems since he took office from Benedict XVI. The first was *concentrating on the core competence of the church, which is serving the poor*: Francis has refocused his organization on one mission: helping the poor. According to the *Economist*:

One of the first decisions was to forsake the papal apartments in favor of a boarding house which he shares with 50 other priests and sundry visitors. He took the name of a saint who is famous for looking after the poor and animals. He washed and kissed the feet of 12 inmates of a juvenile detention center. He got rid of the fur-trimmed velvet capes that popes have worn since the Renaissance, swapped Benedict's red shoes for plain black ones and ignored his fully loaded Mercedes in favor of a battered Ford. . . . This poor-first strategy is also aimed squarely at emerging markets, where the potential growth is greatest but competition fiercest.

A second approach was *brand repositioning by changing the way the message is communicated*. Francis has prioritized deeds over words, but when he uses words they are so poignant and so loaded with meaning not simply because of their pithy and cryptic nature but because they are embodied in and sacramentalized through his actions.

The third strategy was *restructuring the church*. Elements of this restructuring included reforming the Vatican bank, creating the G8, making the procedures for the synod of bishops more participatory, shaking up the membership of the Vatican department that picks bishops, naming more

---

[4] John Allen Jr., *Against the Tide: The Radical Leadership of Pope Francis* (Ligouri, MO: Ligouri Press, 2014), 21.

[5] *Christian Post*, July 10, 2013, www.christianpost.com.

cardinals from the ends of the earth against the practice of populating that elite body with Italians and other Europeans, trimming the tug of careerism in the church by restricting the use of the title of "monsignor" to priests over the age of sixty-five, and publicly rebuking the curial cardinals, archbishops, priests, and staff on their spiritual diseases, which he warned were undermining the mission of God.[6]

By the time Pope Francis was elected on March 13, 2013, there was a general feeling that we were reaching the end of an era in the Catholic Church and that the Holy Spirit was calling the church to a new beginning. Indeed, by 2011, I had already developed an outline of a book to define the historical outline of this dying era. I intended to title the book *Catholicism at the End of an Era*. Many other theologians, including Popes John Paul II and Benedict XVI, began to talk about a crisis in the church, an anthropological crisis and a crisis of faith.[7] There was also, as Gregory Baum wrote, a struggle within the church on how to deal with cultural and religious pluralism and the new challenges of social change.[8] Many questions began to emerge: What kind of ecclesiology could effectively deal with the questions of inclusion and exclusion in the church, and the need for a strong central authority, but one with openness and respect for vibrant and dynamic local churches?[9]

What emerged toward the twilight of the last millennium and into the new as a response to some of these questions, especially in the United States, was what Richard Gaillardetz calls "a program of Catholic neo-triumphalism and magisterial activism that is doomed to failure."[10] However, all these have changed because Pope Francis is leading the church to find new answers to old questions, posing questions which people never raised in the church until now, and calling for a listening church that seeks answers to questions through multiple roads less traveled.

Francis is redefining Catholicism for good!

Pope Francis is quietly toppling an old framework and the leftover of a dying Christendom which had persisted in Roman Catholicism since Pope Pius IX. He has quietly changed the tone of the message and the style of

---

[6]Allen, *Against the Tide*, 8–9.

[7]Michael H. Crosby, *Repair My House: Becoming a "Kindom" Catholic* (Maryknoll, NY: Orbis Books, 2012), 44–63.

[8]See Gregory Baum, *Truth and Relevance: Catholic Theology in French Quebec since the Quiet Revolution* (Montreal: McGill-Queens University Press, 2014), 38–42, 178–84.

[9]See Dennis M. Doyle, "Gerard Mannion's Ecclesiology and Postmodernity," in *Ecclesiology and Exclusion: Boundaries of Being and Belonging in Postmodern Times*, ed. Dennis M. Doyle, Timothy J. Furry, and Pascal D. Bazzell (Maryknoll, NY: Orbis Books, 2012), 7–17. See also Gerard Mannion, *Ecclesiology and Postmodernity: Questions for the Church of Our Time* (Collegeville, MN: Liturgical Press, 2007), 6–16.

[10]Richard R. Gaillardetz, *An Unfinished Council: Vatican II, Pope Francis, and the Renewal of Catholicism* (Collegeville, MN: Liturgical Press, 2015), 139–40.

leadership at the Vatican. Although he has not substantially altered the content of that message, which is often seen as conservative, Eurocentric, and resistant to the exigencies of history and social change, he is chipping away at its foundations through a new hermeneutic of multiplicity and inclusion. In doing this, he has fundamentally and radically shifted the priorities and practices of the Catholic Church on such core issues as power and authority in the church with regard to service and discipleship, pastoral leadership, financial management of the resources of the church, and recognition of the diversity of gifts and talents in the whole of the people of God.

Indeed, Pope Francis has opened the doors to the voices of the marginalized in the church—women, the poor, homosexual persons, the so-called dissenters and rebels who were excluded in the past. Indeed, under Pope Francis, the biblical image of the church as the net of the Lord Jesus containing all kinds of fish has become true (see John 21–11). Francis is bringing about a new experience of Catholicism as a poor and merciful church.

The church of Pope Francis is one where saints and sinners, divorced and separated Catholics, as well as those who have been denied communion, have hope for acceptance and are lovingly encouraged to follow the illuminative path which makes us whole. It is a church in which non-Catholic Christians and people of other religions and people of no faith are seen as friends to be embraced, and not infidels to be pitied or aliens to be avoided. Francis has given expression to the full meaning of Catholicism as universality with the appointments of cardinals from every corner of the earth, a greater commitment to collegiality and synodality, through, for instance, the administration of the church through an international Council of Cardinals with a representative from every continent. He has also through his words and deeds shown an openness to greater dialogue in the church and openness to hearing the Word of God spoken through people of other faiths. Pope Francis has given greater prominence to the voices of the Global South.

When I left my home country of Nigeria sixteen years ago to study in Rome, my father made one request of me: When you return for holidays from Rome, please bring me Holy Water from the fountain at St. Peter's Square. Like many ordinary Catholics, he did not want to be bothered with the politics or battles in Rome, or with ideological or dogmatic Catholicism, or even the fundamentalist thinking that still persists in the church and holds that the church cannot make mistakes or that when decisions are made by a pope or a bishop, that it cannot be reversed in the light of new evidence or new reality.[11] Many Catholics in Africa, like my father, cherish

---

[11] This kind of thinking, the *dictatus papae,* goes back to Pope Gregory VII, whose statements among others included that a sentence passed by the pope may not be modified by anyone and that he alone can modify the sentences of other people. See Marco Politi, *Pope Francis among the Wolves: The Inside*

their spiritual connection with Rome. What they wanted for themselves, their children, and grandchildren, is a deeper encounter with the mysteries of divine love revealed in Christ, and the "grace of greater things" through a culture of encounter in the church which brings about communion with God, and friendship with men and women of goodwill from all the corners of the earth.

For many Catholics today, there is still that idyllic image of Catholicism as a bastion of spiritual strength, a reliable source for creedal certainty in a world ideologically awash with diverse theological, moral, and spiritual standpoints. Most Catholics take pride in their church—for better or for worse—as the gold standard of Christian orthodoxy. However, Catholicism for those outside of it, and more so for those inside of it, remains a cultural heritage which can never be contained in one vessel, historically, theologically, spiritually, and otherwise. Catholicism is much more than a single narrative or a homogenous sociological form without cultural and spiritual differentiation. Catholicism is like a deep ocean, with many tributaries. There should be a place for everyone in this family. However, not all Catholics accept this account of Catholicism or embrace this vision.

This is why the antinomies of inclusion and exclusion continue to be a challenge to Catholicism. Whatever perspectives one admits in the cultural discourse in Catholicism today, by 2013 the times seemed appropriate for the emergence of new prophets: such men and women who will lift our gaze beyond the imprisoning certainties about the things we do not know, or the pride of an ecclesial mind-set that seeks to provide definitive answers to indefinite questions and mysteries that reveal to us what it means to be human in an infinitely boundless cosmos.

The challenge facing Catholics today is the need to forge a new Catholic imagination. It is a summons to creative appropriation of the rich and boundless treasures of the church to meet the challenges of the times. It calls for courage and hope to embrace fully the reforms and renewal already begun with Vatican II to make the church truly a light to the nations. This is the time of prophets, who like sentinels on the mountaintop point the church and the world to new paths.

Many people see Pope Francis as such a prophet. He demonstrates that it is possible for Catholicism to find a new way of being church. Pope Francis is pointing to new paths for meeting the challenges of today in fidelity to the God of surprises and renewal whose Holy Spirit leads us to new truths and brings wholeness through the mediation of the Love of God incarnate in the Son. He is also leading the church to leave behind the remaining baggage of Christendom. Many discerning Catholics fear, however, that the forces of

---

Story of a Revolution, trans. William McCuaig (New York: Columbia University Press, 2015), 63.

monocultural Catholicism may be too strong for new prophetic witnesses to help find new pathways for the church. They point as evidence to justify theirs fears to the growing opposition to the pope and internal dissent among the College of Cardinals, and the discordant doctrinal and pastoral tunes being played by bishops even from the same countries and regions on some of the fundamental questions of marriage, divorce, annulment, remarriage, same-sex relations, relationships with people of other faiths and other denominations, liturgical practices, and priestly and religious lives, among others.

Many Catholics, therefore, worry that Pope Francis faces pushback by the more conservative wing of the church's leadership, a hidden power play in the Vatican and in local churches, and resistance from those who were benefiting financially until now from the financial mismanagement at the Vatican Bank.[12] Others fear that Pope Francis's changes may be rejected by his successor since he has not changed any article in the canon law or the *Catechism of the Catholic Church*, those foundational documents of the church. There is significant unease among both progressives and conservatives in the Catholic Church on the future of Catholicism after Pope Francis. There is also palpable confusion after the publication of *Amoris Laetitia* on the position of the church on some of the issues about marriage, family life, annulment, polygamy, and same-sex unions, among many other contested moral issues. The synods of 2014 and 2015 revealed the theological and ideological fault lines in Catholicism in the era of Francis. They also point to the persistent and unresolved questions of faith and morals, institution and charism, innovation and tradition on the fundamental teachings and pastoral practices of the Catholic Church, which may not be resolved in this papacy or the next.

There is the need then to give some theological, biblical, historical, and patristic account of what one sees as operative in the ecclesiology of Pope Francis. This will help answer the question as to what kind of church is emerging through the papacy of Pope Francis and whether the changes that have been introduced will outlive him. Providing such a foundation, hopefully, will offer some helpful answers to questions that I often hear in conferences, seminars, in universities, parishes and chanceries and among Vatican officials, priests, bishops, laity and religious alike: Is it not too much or even too precarious to expect the reform of a 1.2 billion strong church to rest on the weak shoulders of an aging eighty-year-old pope? Is Catholicism

---

[12]See Politi, *Pope Francis among the Wolves*; Gianluigi Nuzzi, *Merchants in the Temple: Inside Pope Francis's Secret Battle against Corruption in the Vatican*, trans. Michael F. Moore (New York: Henry Holt, 2015). Perhaps the strongest of such a rejection of Pope Francis is a work that challenges the validity of his election as pope—Antonio Socci, *Non é Francesco: La chiesa nella grande tempesta* (Milan: Arnoldo Mondadori Ediore, 2014).

going to be lost as many people know it as a result of the papacy of Francis?

I think that the cultural bereavement of many Catholics should not simply be of a doctrinal and dogmatic fortress that may wither with the reforms introduced by Pope Francis. I think what should be grieved is the loss of the renewing fire of the Holy Spirit that will be smothered if the church does not open itself to the gift of prophecy from the Holy Spirit, whose wind blows wherever and whenever it pleases. Faith entails among other things, stepping into uncharted territory in humble obedience to the God whose plans are better and bigger than our historically constructed approximation of divine revelation in our claims, doctrines, and laws.

WHY ANOTHER BOOK ON POPE FRANCIS?

There are many books written about Pope Francis, and more will be written. However, this book is different from earlier books because it takes up a theological construction of the ecclesiology of this papacy and its implications for world Catholicism and Christianity beyond Pope Francis. I wrote this book because I wanted to give a theological explanation to what I see in the practices and priorities of Pope Francis since he became the Bishop of Rome. Pope Francis employs some expressions and manifestations of a model of ecclesiology that has been forgotten in the church, but which has been latent since the time of Jesus Christ. I call it *illuminative ecclesiology*.

Another reason for this book is that in the light of the paradigm shift that I see in Pope Francis, I want to move the theological conversation from a fascination about him or the now famous "Francis effect" to a deeper theological dialogue on the praxis and limitations of his approach to church and society. This dialogue is first about what kind of dynamic ecclesiological models and praxis are emerging from Pope Francis's actions and words. Second, it is a dialogue about how continuous or discontinuous this ecclesiology is to other models of the church that have been discussed and experimented on in previous papacies since the Second Vatican Council. I also look at how illuminative ecclesiology confronts the challenges and opportunities opening up to the church more than fifty years after Vatican II. I explore in this work how this way of being church has roots in the traditions and scripture and why I am convinced that it will outlive Pope Francis.

This book is, therefore, not simply another book on Pope Francis. It is a book about the church, which Pope Francis serves. It is a book about the church that Pope Francis is helping people to see more clearly. Though this book is inspired by Pope Francis, it looks at the movement before Pope Francis, and the directions in which the church will be moving beyond Pope Francis. Because there have been some uncritical assumptions that Pope

Francis's papal ministry lacks theological depth, this book is a theological narrative of a way of being church of which Pope Francis is an exemplary though imperfect model.[13]

A third reason for writing this book is that I want to locate Pope Francis within an ecclesiological model that has been present in the history of the church since the time of the Lord Jesus Christ. This model, which I call *illuminative ecclesiology*, is a way of being church which answers this question: *What form of witnessing and proclamation can someone experience in every instance of the life of Christians and in the priorities and practices of churches and their leaders which points to Christ and shows the face of the world to God and the merciful, loving and compassionate face of God to a wounded world?*

The form of witnessing in its identity and mission, which the church assumes at every given point in history that answers this key question, is what I have termed illuminative ecclesiology. This form of the church emerges from its Trinitarian origin, which gives the church its inner identity and external mission. This Trinitarian origin specifies the features and mission of the church which is the bearer of the light of Christ, and it discovers this light in the people of God in a diversity of expressions and manifestations.

In other words, illuminative ecclesiology is that form of witnessing and proclamation that can be experienced as a transformative encounter with the Lord Jesus Christ by all—Christians and non-Christians—through the priorities and practices of the church. This form makes the church and is made by the church, because both the identity and mission of the church as light are inseparable. Everyone is capable of bearing the light of Christ and sharing the same light with everyone. Through this form of witnessing and proclamation, the people of God are offered the gift of the welcoming, merciful, loving, and compassionate face of God, and the people of God through the ministry of the church offer God's liberating and transformative love, healing and grace to a wounded world.

This form of proclamation and witnessing is open to all people in their different stations and situations in life, especially the poor and the wounded.

---

[13]Bronwen Catherine McShea in an article titled "Pope Francis as Historian" is very damning in her judgment about Pope Francis's lack of theological depth when she writes, "Now Francis, we know, is not the professorial pope that Benedict has been. Neither is he an historian by training or even by vocation; his focus in school as a young man was chemistry, and later as a Jesuit teacher he focused on literature and psychology. He has had a busy administrative, pastoral, and politically freighted clerical career since that time. So, in fairness, we cannot expect him to speak with exceptional precision on historical themes, even where these touch on present-day ecclesial matters" (www.firstthings.com).

Massimo Faggioli argues that Pope Francis is more concerned by a spiritual vision than a theological vision, which should not be seen as a lack of theological depth or insight, but rather a very sophisticated social Catholicism, "with a subtle and complex vision of 'modernity', and more multifaceted than that of the promoters of a simplistic return to an idealized past." See *Pope Francis: Tradition in Transitions,* 78.

Through this form, the church cherishes and presents to God every day the multiple faces of a wounded humanity in its search for meaning and salvation. This form of witnessing and proclamation is that of a poor and merciful church. The structures, laws, rituals, liturgies, and pastoral plan of churches are thus relative instruments, which consistently must lead to this fundamental form as concrete praxis and channels for realizing the identity (poor) and mission (mercy) of the church as salt and light. This form, emerging as a gift from the Trinity, reflects a light that has all the properties of the Triune God: participation of all in the life of God and in the life of one another, solidarity in the joys and sorrows of everyone, mutual participation and sharing in the life of God and in the lives of one another, respect and reverence for diversity, and openness to inclusion through a radical openness to each other, service from all and to all, and unity of essence and diversity of action through which the gifts of each become more manifest for the realization of the reign of God in history.

Illuminative ecclesiology is shown in this book to contain four moments in the witnessing and proclamation of the Good News. These four moments are a culture of encounter and accountability, the art of accompaniment, a vulnerable mission, and transformation through a spirituality of action. Everything that happens in the life of the Christian community—liturgy, service, pastoral and social ministry—must reflect these four moments in order to be true to the Trinitarian form through which the church becomes salt of the earth and light of the world.

Each moment begins with the experience of poverty both in the church and in the world represented by the wounds or sins in the lives of individuals, both members and nonmembers of the visible church. Each moment brings healing and grace through the mercy of God. Each moment is Trinitarian in nature because the identity and mission of the church at each moment is always rooted in its Trinitarian origin. These moments are not successive or chronological; they are points of encounter through which the church assumes the form of mercy and poverty in order to show the face of God to the world and show the faces of people in the world to God. It is in this mutual reflection of faces as in a mirror that the church becomes an authentic and credible witness to the presence of God as light in the world. In these moments salvation becomes an event in history.

Illuminative ecclesiology starts from a culture of encounter, which is an openness to all human and cosmic realities in their beauty and complexity. This is because Jesus as the New Temple of the Lord is present among the people of God wherever they are gathered in the name of God. Jesus has taken the place of the Temple in Jerusalem and by the presence of the Holy Spirit, the Lord has made Jerusalem present everywhere and available to everyone as the site of God's meeting with God's people.[14] The culture of encounter presupposes that everything is a contact point for meeting God— including sin and the wounds, joys, and sorrows of all people. Thus deep and open encounter with people and the world is the pathway for following the Lord to human and cosmic fulfillment.

The culture of contact also emerges as a response to the light of Christ, which is always present even in the darkest moments of life. However, it shines brightest in the broken world of the poor and those on the margins. The poor, the sick, sinners, and the rejected of society are bearers of the hidden light of Christ. It is only in entering into a deeper encounter with them that the light of God can shine in the world. The church is a bearer of the light, which it sees first in the hidden light of the poor and the wounded; it is also illumined by the glory of the Lord which it received first as a wounded and sinful church. Every moment of encounter in the church bears the light of Christ in the logic of grace and in the economy of salvation. These two points of light are mediated to the church through a culture of encounter with the Word of God proclaimed in the church and through the poor, by the sacramental and pastoral life of the church, by divine worship, and social ministry.

The idea of "illumination" came to me as I read *The Light of Faith* and *Amoris Laetitia.* What immediately struck me was that Pope Francis used the word "light" more than fifty times in these documents. Even though some might argue that the first encyclical of Pope Francis, *The Light of Faith,* draws from an unfinished draft of an encyclical by Pope Benedict XVI, Victor Manuel Fernández argues that Pope Francis received some help in developing some points, but "what we can say is that the contributions received from other people were subsidiary because the voice that comes across is undoubtedly from him alone."[15]

Indeed, anyone who paid attention to some of the earliest speeches of Pope Francis will notice that the use of the word "light" was constant in his description of the church and how the beautiful illuminative path must emerge through the culture of contact in the church. In his first Holy Thursday celebration of the Chrism Mass, he preached about the anointing of the people in these words:

A good priest can be recognized by the way his people are anointed: this is a clear proof. When our people are anointed with the oil of

---

[14]Yves Congar, *The Mystery of the Temple,* trans. Reginald F. Trevett (Westminster: Newman Press, 1962), 246.

[15]Victor Manuel Fernández, *The Francis Project: Where He Wants to Take the Church* (New York: Paulist Press, 2016), 15–16.

gladness, it is obvious: for example, when they leave Mass looking as if they have heard the good news. Our people like to hear the Gospel preached with "unction"; they like it when the Gospel we preach touches their daily lives, when it runs down like the oil of Aaron to the edges of reality, when it brings light to moments of extreme darkness, to the "outskirts" where people of faith are most exposed to the onslaught of those who want to tear down their faith.[16]

The same use of "light" is found in his speeches to the leadership of the Latin American Episcopal Council (CELAM) on July 27 and 28, 2013, to the Brazilian Conference of Bishops, in which he proposes the need for a church that accompanies the people in the night into which their flight has led them so that they can see the light. Accordingly, Pope Francis states:

We need a Church unafraid of going forth into their night. We need a Church capable of meeting them on their way. We need a Church capable of entering into their conversation. We need a Church able to dialogue with those disciples who, having left Jerusalem behind, are wandering aimlessly, alone, with their own disappointment, disillusioned by a Christianity now considered barren, fruitless soil, incapable of generating meaning.

Pastors of the church should, he proposes, be close to their people and have the smell of sheep because it is through this closeness that they can bring light to the heart of the people.

Bishops must be pastors, close to people, fathers and brothers, and gentle, patient and merciful. Men who love poverty, both interior poverty, as freedom before the Lord, and exterior poverty, as simplicity and austerity of life. Men who do not think and behave like "princes." Men who are not ambitious, who are married to one church without having their eyes on another. Men capable of watching over the flock entrusted to them and protecting everything that keeps it together: guarding their people out of concern for the dangers which could threaten them, but above all instilling hope: so that light will shine in people's hearts.

The centrality of illuminative ecclesiology became so clear to me when I reread the Dogmatic Constitution of the Second Vatican Council on the Church, *Lumen Gentium,* in the light of what I was noticing in Pope Fran-

---

[16]Pope Francis, *The Church of Mercy: A Vision for the Church* (Chicago: Loyola Press, 2014), 93.

cis. I was fascinated by the strong emphasis on theological aesthetics in Pope Francis, which has a direct inspiration from the first line of *Lumen Gentium*—namely, the culture of encounter, touching the other, being with people, finding God in the simplest and darkest realities, touching the flesh of Christ by touching the poor, seeing the light of Christ in the midst of suffering, pain, and poverty.

As young seminarians, studying theology in my home country of Nigeria, we were required to write summaries of four major documents of Vatican II (*Sacrosanctum Concilium, Lumen Gentium, Gaudium et Spes, Dei Verbum*). We were also required to choose and develop what we considered as the key to understanding each document. It struck me over eighteen years ago that the organizing theme for understanding *Lumen Gentium* was the first article. The first paragraph of this Constitution reads:

> Christ is the light of humanity; and it is, accordingly, the heartfelt desire of this sacred Council, being gathered together in the Holy Spirit, that by proclaiming his Gospel to every creature (cf. Mk 16:15), it may bring to all men that light of Christ which shines out visibly from the Church. Since the Church, in Christ, is in the nature of sacrament—a sign and instrument, that is, of communion with God and of unity among all men—she here purposes, for the benefit of the faithful and of the whole world, to set forth, as clearly as possible, and in the tradition laid down by earlier Councils, her own nature and universal mission.

I wrote what was judged to be a good paper then, but I lacked the historical and theological resources to develop further this illuminative ecclesiology which I saw in the text.

As I continued my theological study, I wondered why no theologian or pastor has seen this first article as the key to the ecclesiology of Vatican II: Christ is the light of humanity, and the church proclaiming the gospel to every creature has a mission of bringing to all people that light which must shine visibly in the church. However, as Pope Paul VI in *Ecclesiam Suam* (sec. 70) taught on the missionary outreach of the church, the light can also be found within history, through contact with people: "The world will not be saved from outside. Like the Word of God who became man, we have to some extent to assimilate the forms of life of those to whom we want to take the message of Christ without claiming privileges that will put us at a distance from others."[17] What is the form of this light? Where can

---

[17]See Yves Congar, "Moving Toward a Pilgrim Church," in *Vatican II by Those Who Were There*, ed. Alberic Stacpoole (London: Geoffrey Chapman, 1986), 130.

we find this light in the church and in the world? How does this light shine visibly in the church as a result of its Trinitarian origin and identity? What practices and priorities of the church can manifest this light in its saving mission? The other images in *Lumen Gentium*—the church as people of God, church as communion, church as sacrament, church as temple of the Holy Spirit, and church as Body of Christ—seemed to me then as well as today as ways of understanding the identity and mission of a church which is salt and light. The church is, for instance, communion or people of God because it receives light from Christ and brings light to the world through its proclamation of and witnessing to the gospel. If the church does not bring this light to the world and does not discover it in the world, especially in the faces of a wounded humanity, it cannot be a communion or a sacrament of salvation. Nor can it be a people of God if the lives of God's pilgrim people are surrounded permanently with darkness and gloom. Salvation is the light that emerges at the center of the wounds of humanity, and the grace that leads the believer in the illuminative path to the eschatological future that God wills. These images in *Lumen Gentium* then are only commentaries and manifestations of the daily performances of Christians and their communities that must bring the light of Christ visibly to the ends of the earth.[18]

Why has this theme of light not been developed as an ecclesiological model even when the African bishops chose this as the theme of the Second African Synod? The reason for this forgetfulness can only be appreciated through an exploration of the key issues in the development of Catholic ecclesiology since Vatican II. It is through this historical understanding that one can see how Pope Francis unifies in his papacy the sometimes conflicting, sometimes contested, and sometimes complementary images and models of the church since Vatican II. Illuminative ecclesiology is thus a key for liberating Catholic ecclesiology from a fixed model or image of the church and a preoccupation with defining the church according to our own sociological templates and cultural narratives. It invites the church to contemplate beauty and light in the concrete context of encounter. It is a way of understanding the identity and mission of the church as the community of God's people gathered in the name of the Lord in multiple sites of human-divine encounters in order to be a point of light in the world and mediate the light of Christ in history.

The fundamental question then is not about the identity of the church, but rather our fidelity to that identity. The church is not reducible to the decisions, thoughts, and performance of one person, a pope, a council,

---

[18]For a succinct explanation of these images see Richard R. Gaillardetz, *The Church in the Making: Lumen Gentium, Christus Dominus, Orientalum Ecclesiarum* (New York: Paulist Press, 2006), 41–51.

or synod, a bishop, layperson, priest, or religious. The gift of the church includes all these persons, but it is much more. The church is a gift from the wounded side of the Lord, which is beyond the style, preference, or pastoral predilection of a pope. The church is the form of Christ's form as light in the world, which our daily actions, pastoral strategies, practices, and priorities make manifest rather than generate.

What is often lacking in many ecclesiological images of the church, especially after Vatican II, is a certain fundamentalism to a particular form or shape of the church, which is often dictated by ideological posturing, oppositional, and polarizing theological categories and images. What emerges is a poorly developed theological aesthetics or a neglect of the searching or seeing eyes that need to be purified by the tears that should flow when we behold the wounds of the Lord and the wounds in our lives and in our neighbors. This calls for humility and a fruitful reflection on bended knees on the gift of the church in history. Thus, the idea of a church, which we want, and a church, which is relevant to our context, has given an unlimited bandwidth to theological exploration and experimentation on the question of what the church is. At the same time, it has created a wedge between different theologians and regional bodies, churches and denominations on dialogue about how we can enter into the mysteries of the gift of the church.

Particularly in Africa, where the momentum of Christian expansion has given rise to new religious movements and new ecclesial communities with appeals to autochthonous spiritual values in Africa and a commitment in some cases to ecology and poverty eradication, new questions arise. These questions emerge as to how structures and forms of being church dictated by a confluence of specific cultural and historical factors are to be defined as definitive for churches everywhere. What then is Catholic or Christian in these irruptions of the Holy Spirit and in churches that are emerging from the *payatas* in Philippines or the slums of *Kibera* in Nairobi or the *favelas* of Rio? The development of ecclesiologies, especially in world Catholicism, needs to assume a sense of humility and a new lens for seeing where God is present shining the light of Christ at the margins. This is what is very important in Pope Francis's ecclesiology: it is an ecclesiology that is more interested in where the church is, rather than who the church is. It is in the location of the church that we can find its identity, and interestingly it is in such obscure locations that the light of Christ shines the brightest.

In what follows in this introduction, I briefly examine the methodological issues in ecclesiology in order to give an outline of how Pope Francis's approach to ministry and mission in the Catholic Church has quietly changed Catholic ecclesiology and mapped a new path for the future of Catholicism.

THE THEOLOGY OF CHURCH: THE TWO WAYS

In Protestant and Catholic theologies of the church, there are broadly speaking two main approaches: an ecclesiology from above and an ecclesiology from below. The first is essentialized, metaphysical, and often presented as the image of a transcultural church heavily grounded in dogmatic and apologetic categories. The second approach is practical and historical, grounded in social analysis, and the daily experiences of people and praxis.

The claim of ecclesiology from above is that the form and structure are gifts that the church received from the Most Holy Trinity in history. The church is called to preserve, defend, protect, discover, live, celebrate, and perpetuate this form until all is returned to God at the consummation of time. In this light, there is some DNA or trademark, which specifies the identity and mission of the church, which transcends space and time, and specific realization of the church in particular local churches. Every local instantiation of the church is but a particular reflection of the selfsame church in its archetypical form, which must reflect the ecclesial genetics or family traits in order to be authentically Catholic, apostolic, one, and holy.[19]

Those who inhabit this theological domain see the church as an ahistorical subject, a revealed truth with an essentialist or transcendentalist identity and mission. The mission of such a church as it crosses different cultural, historical, and spiritual frontiers does not change in content; rather it might change in expression. Particularly in the Catholic Church, the pastoral ministry of local churches is to be pursued through a centralizing and synchronic prototype that seeks and receives answers and approval from the Roman center for all things Catholic even in those pastoral challenges that are specific to particular churches.

The church's teachings and precepts for those in this camp will be absolute, definitive, and unchanging on faith and morals. The data for reflection for theologians in this camp are the same but varied in terms of whether the reflection should proceed from Trinitarian, biblical, pneumatological, Christological, eschatological, or missionary foundation with regard to the origins, identity, and mission of the church. They all proceed from an aprior-

---

[19]The question of the autonomy and identity of local churches vis-à-vis the authority of Rome is still a source of tension in the Catholic Church. It is a question of contextualization and communion in a Catholic faith that is still weighed down by a synchronizing church authority at the center. This was a prominent debate between Cardinal Walter Kasper and the then Cardinal Ratzinger. The debate led to the publication of two books by both prelates (Walter Kasper, *Leadership in the Church: How Traditional Roles Can Serve the Christian Community Today* [New York: Crossroad, 2003], and Joseph Ratzinger, *Called to Communion: Understanding the Church Today* [San Francisco: Ignatius Press, 1991]) defending their opposing positions on whether the center has priority over the local.

istic notion of church. It is from this standpoint of believing and presenting the truths of the Catholic Church in its self-identity as a unique assembly of God's people, and in what it teaches as definitive and irreformable that every aspect of ecclesiology is presented and defended. This touches every aspect of the life of the church: the biblical foundation of ecclesiology and ministry in the church; the hierarchical structure of the church and an all-male celibate priesthood, the marginal place of the laity in the church, the conditions for reception of the sacraments and the form and effects of the sacraments, and authority in the church. How these are interpreted and presented by successive popes or bishops at the Roman center or in the dioceses and parishes may vary, but the structure that informs this approach of a top-down ecclesiology remains the same in all models of ecclesiology as presented by Avery Dulles.[20]

Bishops who are liberal may give less emphasis to the institutional model. They sometimes may offer a token to women by allowing them to serve at Mass at Episcopal ordination, as I witnessed in Chicago during the installation of Cardinal Cupich. They may seek a greater participation of the priests and laity in the decision-making process and run an open, transparent, and accountable church. However, the local church or the universal church rests within this pyramidal top-down structure on the decision of a few celibate men and their chosen ones.

In the light of these, the progressive steps taken in a diocese by one bishop or the reform initiated by one pope could be wiped away in a month or two by a conservative successor. This is because the structure in most cases has given unlimited authority to a single individual or a single office. Therefore, what is decisive here in this top-down approach is not the institutionalization of power or the liberality with which power and service are shared in the church, it is on the claims and legitimization to accession to power by the few men who occupy such positions. It is also about how the rank-and-file Catholics often accept this structure as something that is a form of revelation rather than a historically conditioned pattern and shape that grew out of specific historical context of faith and life. In this light, Claudio Carvalhaes describes an interesting dilemma which Pope Francis and all bishops who are looking for a new ecclesiology face:

> On one hand, he [Pope Francis] will show fantastic pastoral care and offer a public voice of transformation in the world, but will continue to be faithful to an institution that keeps its money, land, privileges and hierarchical monopolies that often strangle the voice of the poor. Will he do this by keeping the church's current balance of power and its structures, homilies, paternalism and voluntarism that will remodel

---

[20]See Avery Dulles, *Models of the Church*, Expanded Edition (New York: Image/Doubleday, 2002).

the whole structure with more of the same and not provide for a real break with the system? Or will he instead break with the system by employing anti-imperialist ways of thinking and living, feminist, queer economic movements of transgression, autonomous labor movements, anti-hierarchical horizontal grassroots social organizations, and new base communities connected through networks such as the *via campesina.*[21]

A top-down approach to ecclesiology raises some fundamental questions: Should ecclesiology start with making a prejudgment about the daily faith and cultures of the people prior to encountering those cultures with regard to an idealized notion of church? Furthermore, should ecclesiology be descriptive, naming these daily realities in the light of the unfolding of revelation in history? Should ecclesiology be a critical examination of how local churches mirror the DNA of the universal church defined narrowly through its central Roman interpretations and canonical prescriptions? Should it be about the ordering of sacramental life of the church and its conformity to norms set in former times? Which official teaching should be given greater resonance in the missionary and evangelical priorities and activities of local churches, and what criteria are to be used for making a judgment on fidelity to the gospel and discipleship?

Here one is faced with important challenges about understanding the task of ecclesiology. This involves among other things the need to make a distinction, as Neil Ormerod proposes, between how people live their lives in the church, pastoral practices, and teaching authority, and how the faithful and theologians reflect on them. These two are not equivalent; what theologians say about the church and what the magisterium teaches may not necessarily reflect how the people live out the faith. There is always, as most Christians will admit, a gap between some of the teachings of the church and the writings of theologians and what happens in the pews. There is also the need to constantly put in focus this gap between theological judgment on how people live their lives as Christians and in the church and the ecclesiologies being proposed by the church and/or by theologians. In many instances, there is a tripartite structure of meaning: the teaching of the magisterium of the church on faith and life; the multiple writings of the theologians, which may draw from this or diverge from it; and the daily experiences of faith or actual faith of Christians, which may not be identified explicitly in these other two levels.

---

[21]Claudio Carvalhaes, "Which Liberation Theology? Pope Francis and the Choice of Theologies of His Papacy," in *Pope Francis in Postcolonial Reality: Complexities, Ambiguities and Paradoxes*, ed. Nicolas Panotto (N.p.: Borderless Press, 2015), 36–37.

Another concern is the question of how people live the faith on a day-to-day basis in fidelity to the official teaching of the church or through appeal to other forms of validation outside of these canons. In other words, what is necessary for salvation, and how do churches embody patterns and models that can bring about salvation for God's people? How does one account in any model of ecclesiology for the everyday experiences of Christians? How can one determine what is essential to the form of the church and what is variable in considering some contested questions—marriage, sexuality, gender, celibate clergy/religious, ministry, the hierarchical structure of the church, the papacy, leadership in the church, and so on? The final question posed by a top-down approach to ecclesiology is on how adequate is the response of the magisterium of the church to new questions, cultural, and religious diversity, and contested versions of development and modernity in charting the path for the church's mission in history, especially in the context of the cultural pluralism of the world today?[22]

The other approach, an ecclesiology from below, adopts an approach heavily influenced by the social sciences, human experience, ethnography, and cultural contexts. This approach has been popularized through two significant works by John Milbank[23] and Clodovis Boff.[24]

The approach of an ecclesiology from below proceeds through an immersion in the context of the faith of the people; it seeks to understand and interpret their daily challenges, pains, hopes, and dreams as central to the mission of the church. Indeed, proponents of this approach argue that the church is found in no other place outside of this social context and that salvation can only be mediated in and through the stories of the actual faith of people. In a sense, for those who read the identity and mission of the church this way, every ecclesiology emerges through a process of negotiation of identity and mission in what Bernard Lonergan calls "progressive self-constitution." This is part of the unfolding of the gifts of the Holy Spirit; hence every instantiation of faith carries within it seeds of God's revelation.

For those in this camp, morality and spirituality are open structures to be worked out through fidelity to what God has revealed in the past and its appropriation today, through entering into the new revelations of God's presence in diverse contexts of faith and life. For theologians and church leaders who reflect on the church from this standpoint, ecclesiology should provide a portrait and illuminative text of multiple modes of being and

---

[22]See, for instance, Neil Ormerod, *Revisioning the Church: An Experiment in Systematic Historical Ecclesiology* (Minneapolis: Fortress Press, 2014), 5.

[23]John Milbank, *Theology and Social Theory: Beyond Secular Reason* (Cambridge, MA: Blackwell, 1991).

[24]Clodovis Boff, *Theology and Praxis: Epistemological Foundations* (Maryknoll, NY: Orbis Books, 1987).

acting as the community of faith gathered in the name of the Lord and convoked by the Holy Spirit. Every ecclesiology is dynamic and open to the surprises of the Holy Spirit in the mysterious movement of history. It is in this diversity of living the faith that God provides illumination to the city of God and offers new and diverse pathways for witnessing to the redeeming and liberating message of the gospel.

People who approach ecclesiology from this standpoint pay particular attention to the participation of every member of the community in the life of the church. They are also interested in the process, and context of believing and acting in the name of the Lord, and social, cultural, and historical forces and reflective practices in the shaping of Christian imagination and Christian witnessing for transforming the world.

The fundamental challenge for this approach is about how to establish that the multiplicities of expression share common elements that could identify any community as Christian. A further challenge is to show that particular Christian communities share some family traits with each other.

The other challenge is about the distinctive theological foundation of every ecclesiology. The Christian community is called together by God as a people and is given an identity as God's people through its Trinitarian origin. The question is whether ecclesial tribalism may hamper the Christian mission of uniting God's scattered people.

Theologians who adopt these two approaches do not come to the data for their reflection from the same epistemological starting point. However, from a Catholic ecclesiological perspective, all theologians, pastors, laity, clergy, and the hierarchy who are involved in developing theologies of the church claim that they are faithful to the spirit and text of Vatican II and the sources of faith. However, sometimes the interpretations and application of the spirit of Vatican II to the life and structure of the church display an unbridgeable gulf. This is at the heart of the crisis of ecclesiology in the Catholic Church which seems to be widening with the strong resistance and the pushback being experienced in the church, especially since the Synod on the Family (2014 and 2015) and the publication of *Amoris Laetitia*.

For those theologians who do ecclesiology from above, the text is always the revealed truth of salvation—including the biblical evidence, the claimed continuity with the apostolic, Patristic, and historical traditions on the mystery, nature, and identity of the church.[25] However, for those who do ecclesiology from below, empirical, experiential, critical, and practical approaches and a praxis-orientation are usually the necessary first steps.

---

[25]Pedro Rodriques, "Theological Method for Ecclesiology," in *The Gift of the Church: A Textbook on Ecclesiology in Honor of Patrick Granfied, OSB*, ed. Peter Phan (Collegeville, MN: Liturgical Press, 2000), 135–42.

The text for theological reflection for this group could be as diverse as the conditions of the poor, the stories of hope and survival after personal or communal tragedies, the alienation of many who are excluded from communion, the search of people in high places for a sanctuary of peace and rest where they can listen to and discern the voice of God. What is important is that every ecclesiology must be history, that is, it must emerge from and be concerned with how the stories of people in their diversities of faith all come together in the unfolding of God's kingdom in time and beyond time.

What is evident in this brief survey of these two broad methods is that even though *Lumen Gentium* opened the door for creativity and dynamism in developing diverse approaches to ecclesiology, the battle for the interpretation and appropriation of a satisfactory ecclesiology which celebrates the richness and diversity of the communities of faith gathered in the name of the Lord around the world has not ceased. *Lumen Gentium* moved Catholic ecclesiology beyond its Tridentine transcultural and ahistorical reading and application of the four marks of the church—unity, catholicity, apostolicity, and holiness. According to Richard Gaillardetz:

> The council members recognized the reductive and atrophied state of theological reflection on the church found in the dogmatic manuals of the nineteenth and early twentieth centuries. Consequently, the council's reflections on the church took the form not of some normative systematic treatise but of a recovery of the theological breadth and depth of the Catholic tradition with particular attention to neglected theological perspectives from the Christian heritage of the first thousand years.[26]

I propose that Pope Francis offers an approach that is capable of leading today's church to the realization of the spirit of the Second Vatican Council.

METHODOLOGY AND OVERVIEW

The primary texts for this book are the writings and speeches of Pope Francis, especially on the aspects of ecclesiology and Catholic social teaching in *Lumen Fidei, Evangelii Gaudium, Laudato Si,* and *Amoris Laetitia.* I have relied on these as primary texts and have made a serious effort not to use commentaries and texts on these documents. In addition, I have also used some of Pope Francis's speeches at his weekly audiences, homilies, and interviews, as well as the Aparecida document, to illuminate his words

---

[26] Richard R. Gaillardetz, *Ecclesiology for a Global Church: A People Called and Sent* (Maryknoll, NY: Orbis Books, 2011), xviii.

or interpret his deeds. I have tried to allow these texts to speak for themselves, while employing the hermeneutics of multiplicity in drawing out the intelligibilities in these texts and their relevance to the development of illuminative ecclesiology. I have enriched my explication of Pope Francis's ecclesiology by drawing from conversations in African Christianity about the present state of the Catholic Church and how illuminative ecclesiology offers a praxis for a social mission in Africa. I believe that the best way to try out some of the moments and praxis of illuminative ecclesiology is to place them in the context of the continent where the church is growing exponentially, but also where God's people are held on the Cross of suffering, but are filled with hope. Africa becomes, in my thinking, a representative model of how the praxis of illuminative ecclesiology can bring about human and cosmic flourishing and mediate the graces and life of God for integral salvation in the world.

I have engaged the voices of many Africans in this work. Most important, I have relied on the stories from ordinary Africans in their daily realities. I have been involved in international charities in five African countries for the last fifteen years, working to discover, develop, and build on the assets of African women. I thus draw from my own personal involvement in such Catholic charities as Chalice Canada, Canadian Samaritans for Africa, IG-Welt Austria, Catholic Health Association of USA, Kijiji Cha Upendo Women's group in Kibera, Nairobi, Grace for Rural Orphans and Widows (Uganda), Adu Achi Women Multi-purpose micro-credit co-operative union (Nigeria), and Espérance et Solidarité pour Le Centrafique (ESCA).

Working with the poor locally in six different African countries (Kenya, Uganda, Central African Republic, Nigeria, Burkina Faso, and Cote d'Ivoire) and with a number of international organizations has been the best immersion for me into the exhilarating rich world of a poor and merciful church. It has also taught me that the future belongs to the poor because they are the best witnesses to the gospel of hope and the transformative presence of faith; they are the bearers of the true light that shines in the darkness. They also teach me that they are the best suited to find answers to the problem of poverty. My theology or ecclesiology will make no sense to the poor if it does not emerge from their stories as a source and model for reversal of the unacceptable history dotted by structural violence and structures of sin. The actual faith, which I have witnessed among the courageous women of Africa in the field of social ministry, has spoken to me deeper than any theological seminar or writings. This is why the analysis of the moments of illuminative ecclesiology that I present in this book is filled with stories from the field of the social mission that I have been part of or which I have learned about from my colleagues and friends. The work is also enriched by the ethnographic accounts taken in Central African Republic after the visit of Pope Francis in November 2015. This ethnography is aimed at finding out through the narratives of everyday life in Central African Republic how Pope Francis's visit has helped change the face of this country as it recovers from many years of failed leadership and war.

One other thing that will become evident to the readers of this book is that this work is grounded in strong biblical, theological, and sociohistorical foundations. My approach to writing a theology of church is to begin by harvesting the stories of the poor and the stories of the traditions and practices of faith in the long history of the church across different cultures and spiritual zones with a view to seeing the constant and changing patterns of the footprints of God in history. I also pay special attention to different ways in which the mysteries of faith are celebrated. I follow seriously the local processes that emerge as people, driven by their Christian faith, make sense of life by creating alternate sites of hope through a praxis that emerges from and leads back to agency and performance. This, in my thinking, is the best way of entering into the story of God's great deeds in history.

I am able as much as possible to be faithful to the cultural knowledge from local contexts of faith and life, and to be in touch with the diverse faith experiences of the church. These offer me the phenomenological basis for doing a transformational theology that is then put in conversation with biblical revelation, the life of the church across the ages, the witness of saints and sinners within the church, and the documentation of these experiences in the theological writings of experts and practitioners. All these help me give a good portrait of faith and life and its various forms of emergence as the message of the gospel crosses different cultural and spiritual frontiers in the era of world Christianity. Through this approach, I write myself, as it were, or I write my Christian faith and about a church to which I belong. What I write here is my story. Largely, it is limited by my own narration of this experience and how these stories shape my understanding of the church. In this sense, every ecclesiology is both a personal Christian autobiography and an ecclesial prosopography.

However, my first person narrative is also significant because here I am also telling the story of the church as Africans do through stories of people's everyday experiences. Faith as narration of where "God happens" in the community is the way I grew up hearing about Jesus. It was in the communal experience—in the exuberant dance and joyful rendition of all the parts of the Mass, in song—that I began to feel, touch, and see the church as a living and dynamic reality. This experience was not simply something which took place in the church or when we gathered for catechetical instruction for *uka mgbede* (Sunday evening service and benediction), it was a diffuse actual faith enacted, renewed, and celebrated in daily practices, in the airplane, or bus, in *tuku tuku* (tricycle), and in the farms. The reason Pope Francis made so much impact in his short visit to Africa was that he naturally connected with the African sense of community, the ordinariness of faith in its extraordinary expressions as forms of worship and patterns of assent, which stretch beyond ritual and structure. This was the cultural mediation of the ecclesial life that Pope Francis describes as the most memorable experience of his trip to Africa in 2015: "Africa was a surprise. God always surprises us but Africa surprises us too. I remember many moments, but above all, I remember the crowds. . . . They felt visited; they are so incredibly welcoming."

These are the cultural forms through which the faith was mediated to me. It was that communal experience which offers young and old the sense that faith and life cannot be separated; that the church cannot be separated from the daily lives of the people and that the community of faith is a place of encounter that is like an ever-expanding door into the sacred to which all are welcomed as in a village square. This idea of community, which believes that it is when we are participating in the life of everyone and of the cosmic world that abundant life from the Lord is fully available for everyone, is central to what I have written in this book. I realize more than ever that no matter the depth and range of my theological and pastoral formation, the original African experience of belonging to a community of faith, where everyone is welcomed, and where everyone is offered the inconceivable prospect of receiving the life and love of God, has stayed with me as an inner vision and light. That experience goes back to my life in Nigeria growing up in the 1970s after the civil war in my country, when our lives were saved by the humanitarian work of Caritas, for instance, which still sustains my scholarship and drives my methodology. This is why I have written this book from a first person perspective. I see these patterns and performance—of a first person narrative and experiential connection between faith and daily experiences—in Pope Francis. Those who are familiar with his writings will notice that he often speaks from a personal perspective and places a strong emphasis on a culture of encounter, which gives so much credibility and force to his proclamation and witnessing.

Those who are looking for a systematic development of an ecclesiology that will follow the established patterns of *de ecclesia* or which will be developed using the framework of *Lumen Gentium*, or canons of a Northern epistemology and structure of scientific discourse, may be disappointed. In the first place, Pope Francis's pastoral ministry cannot be narrowed to a single narrative or put into one box or systematic theology. It is an experimentation with the beauty and gifts of God in the church and in the world, which no one can fully articulate as a system or a model. We are being led to an openness to the surprises of the Holy Spirit, and we humbly trust and confide in the God who is within and beyond history and who leads us into the future eschatological fulfillment of God's reign.

Second, I am writing as an African Christian who grew up in an environment where stories, proverbs, metaphors, and symbolic language are the media for narrating what often is an imponderable mystery of human-divine encounters. The goal of the narrator is to release the full range of the course and content of the ebb and flow of life through the craft of speech and language. At the same time, the narrator must give the audience the freedom to work out the meaning of what is narrated and how it reveals the face of God, the community of the living, the living-dead, the not-yet-born, and the entire human and cosmic world. The story never manifests the complete horizon; the audience and those who will hear the story through the primary auditors will ultimately enrich the story through their own performance and re-telling of the story. This will be true of Pope Francis's legacy.

This book is, therefore, an invitation to a journey that will take you to different worlds which define a way of being church which should be present in every instance of the ecclesial life and Christian life. Pope Francis will be our guide in this journey. The stories from African Christians and African social reality and ecclesial life will offer the phenomenological data for engaging the teachings, words, and images which the papacy of Francis is offering the church and the world today and into the future, which God alone knows.

The book comprises this introduction, five main chapters, and a concluding chapter. In chapter 1, the meaning and theological aesthetics of illuminative ecclesiology in Pope Francis is developed by showing the features and images of the paradigm change which he has brought to both Catholic ecclesiology and the social mission of the church. I answer three central questions about this ecclesiology: Who is the church? What does the church do? Where is the church to be found? I show how this ecclesiology is in continuity with the teaching of the Second Vatican Council and why such a grounded theory of being church rooted in a culture of encounter is both a model and inspiration for facing the challenges and opportunities of faith and life in world Catholicism. Because I believe that Pope Francis has not introduced a new ecclesiology but rather a paradigm change which is helping the church to see clearly a central dimension of its identity and mission, I devote some time to demonstrating how this ecclesiology fits into the renewal of Catholic ecclesiology in the twentieth and twenty-first centuries. This will be accomplished by discussing the foundation given to this ecclesiology in the works of Yves Congar and Hans Urs von Balthasar, two significant theologians who, along with Romano Guardini, influenced Pope Francis's vision of the church. I conclude the chapter with a section on what Pope Francis's ecclesiology means for world Christianity.

Chapter 2 locates illuminative ecclesiology in Pope Francis within a larger tradition—Vatican II, biblical tradition, and historical/Patristic traditions. I demonstrate how this ecclesiology of a poor church is grounded in both the Trinitarian origin and mission that Vatican II's *Lumen Gentium* identified. Another foundation for the image of a poor church is demonstrated through a commentary on Saint James, which I chose as a key text for presenting a portrait of a major source and model of the poor-first policy of Pope Francis. I conclude the chapter by examining the early church's poor-first identity and mission. Here, I use the homilies of Saint John Chrysostom to show that what Pope Francis is calling the church to embrace today is central to the identity, features, proclamation, and witness of the church. Chrysostom serves as a model of seeing the continuity between the message of Pope Francis and that of the church through the ages.

In chapter 3, I answer the question: What is the praxis of illuminative ecclesiology? What will our churches look like if we embrace the priorities and practices modeled by Pope Francis? I begin the chapter by drawing the outline of three of the moments in illuminative ecclesiology: culture of encounter and accountability, the art of accompaniment, and vulnerable mission. The culture of encounter and accountability is grounded in the example of a moment of intimacy between Pope Francis and Vinicio. This is the first step to creating a community of the beloved and searching for light in the world and in people. The culture of encounter is presented as a praxis through which the church can discover and present the faces of everyone as in mirror to God because their gifts and needs are recognized and seen not as a deficit but as a blessing. This is so important in developing pastoral practices that will help address the exclusionary practices that have calcified in our church structures, especially racism, sexism, homophobia, fundamentalism, patriarchy, and intolerance of those who are seen to be sinners or far from God.

The second moment of illuminative ecclesiology, discussed in chapter 3, is the art of accompaniment that is presented as a praxis for journeying with those whom we have encountered, being touched by their stories, bringing healing to their wounds, and being healed ourselves by touching their wounds. These mutually self-mediating relations are modeled after the sacred dance of intimacy, solidarity, and respect between the three persons in the Trinity. Vulnerable mission, the third moment, is presented as the model of mission for the church, which not only accounts for everyone and accompanies everyone, but also proceeds from the experience of vulnerability and humility after the example of God who steps down to our level. It is also a praxis of encounter that wants us to move from our limited human horizon to the infinite horizon of God. Thus, vulnerable mission is presented as a praxis of transformation, and successive patterns of activities and practices that aim at giving agency to the people and giving voice to the voiceless and new life to those on the margins of society. I use the story of the heroic witness of Sister Namaika in Congo to show how these three moments look like in a concrete African social condition and in the experience of brokenness and pain in a particular context of social, political, and ecclesial life.

In chapter 4, I demonstrate how these three moments can come together in bringing transformation in the church and in the world and a spirituality of action and new life in Christ for the people of God. Drawing from my own experience of social ministry in Africa, and African social imagination, and illumined through the speeches of Pope Francis during his 2015 visit to three African countries, I develop the following important themes as essential to the social mission of a church which brings light in darkness, and receives light from the darkness by seeing beauty in the wounds of the world: (1) a model of social analysis in the African context; (2) a model for analysis of poverty, structures of sin and structural violence, and their devastating impact on the lives of the poor and in generating conflicts; (3) a commentary on why aid and interventionist approaches to African development is failing Africans and donors; (4) and how to reweave the social fabric in Africa through a new form of prophetic social ministry that begins with dialogue with the poor in Africa and dialogue with women in Africa. This is the only way to discover how local processes in Africa are giving birth to alternative communities of hope that are reversing the course of history and redefining the many defunct theories of development and social mission. Chapter 4 shows how such a dialogue with the poor in conversation with Catholic social teaching and new forms of Catholic social mission could be both a catharsis for people's faith and a guide for daily practices that help to bring about a new earth and a new heaven.

In chapter 5, I show how illuminative ecclesiology specifies the mission of the church of mercy to a wounded world. Here, I use the image of the Good Samaritan, wounded healer, and the church as a healing inn for the wounded to demonstrate how the church of mercy gives light to the people of God and finds light and mercy through touching the wounds of the world. I bring the teachings of Pope Francis on the church of mercy in conversation with the teachings of Pope John Paul II and biblical traditions to show the continuity of this central dimension of illuminative ecclesiology. I demonstrate how this approach to being church can meet some of the challenges and exclusionary practices in the Catholic Church. This is with regard to divorced and separated Catholics, annulment, clerical sexual abuse, the condition of ex-priests and ex-nuns, conflicts in the church and in the world, and healing of the hidden wounds that many people carry, and as result of which many have turned their back on God because of the sins and scandals that they see in the church. I also demonstrate how this praxis of mercy is helping African Christians confront the social challenges in Africa—refugee crisis, wars, famine, and ethnocentrism.

I conclude the book with some proposals on how Pope Francis's influence is giving birth to the renewal of Catholicism in Africa. These patterns and models that are emerging are often inchoate, but they contain the seeds for what I propose should take place in every Catholic community. I particularly emphasize in this conclusion the importance of prayer, placing God at the center of life, and the need for a new language of love, friendship, and dialogue in the church which is nonjudgmental and speaks of respect, healing, caring, compassion, and sensitivity to the suffering of others. These will help bring the face of God to people and present the faces of the world to God. They are thus shown to be signs of the new things that God promised to God's church as a sign of the unction of the Spirit and prophetic function of all of God's people.

My hope and prayer is that this book will help all Christians and church leaders to see their calling as that of giving light where there is darkness and helping others see light even when they are surrounded by darkness. In addition, I hope that theologians will find in this book some grains of an emerging theological aesthetics that will help the development of ecclesiologies that connect with the everyday experiences of people. Theologians, like the church, must be found in the everyday sites so that their writings will emerge from their belonging to communities of faith and so that varied human experiences will illumine theological reflection. This light is God's love, life, grace, and gift, which restores us to wholeness of being, and which animates the inner life of the church and the dynamics of its proclamation and witnessing in the world. Every Christian should see the possibility of light emerging in every contact with another and in the world of nature. The interconnectedness of everything, *Ubuntu,* defines our lives here on earth, reveals to us the images of the Trinity, and offers us a celebration of the life of God in our communities.[27] It is this interconnectedness that illuminative ecclesiology offers as the identity and mission of Christians and the church as light-bearers because they are Christ-bearers.

I conclude with a story of a famous light-bearer, Saint Mother Teresa, who like Pope Francis radiates the light that can illumine the darkness in people's lives through a genuine human and Christian encounter. Mother Teresa, during a trip to Australia, decided to visit the Aborigines in the reserves. She went with her sisters to visit a poor, elderly man who lived alone on an Aborigine reservation. He was probably in his mid-eighties. His home was disordered and dirty. Mother Teresa said to him: "Please let me clean your house, wash your clothes, and make your bed."

"I'm okay like this," he replied. "Let it be. Do not worry yourself."

---

[27]Richard Rohr and Mike Morrell, *The Divine Dance: The Trinity and Your Transformation* (London: SPCK, 2016), 56.

"You will be better if you allowed me to do your house cleaning," she persisted.

The man finally relented. As Mother Teresa cleaned his home and washed his laundry, she discovered a beautiful lamp covered with dust. Only God knows how many years had passed since he last lit it.

"Don't you ever light your lamp? Don't you ever use it?" asked Mother Teresa.

"No one ever comes to see me," he replied. "I have no need to light it. Who would I light it for?"

"Will you light it every night if the sisters came?" she asked.

"Of course," he said.

From that day on the sisters visited him nightly.

Two years passed, and Mother Teresa, back in Calcutta, received a message from the old man in Australia: "Tell my friend that the light she lit in my life continues to shine still."

It is fitting that Mother Teresa's collection of letters is titled *Come Be My Light*. It is the call of the church today, and it is the vocation of all Christians. How I wish that the whole world would be set aflame with the light of divine love, compassion, and kindness! How I wish someone wounded and broken can say that he or she is alive and joyful today because of the light lit in his or her life by a Christian or a Christian community. If this happens in small ways in our churches and homes, this book will have served its purpose. In addition, we do this not because Pope Francis has taught us to do so or shown us how to do it, but because it is the commandment of the Lord: You are the salt of the earth! You are the light of the world![28]

---

[28]Mother Teresa, *In the Heart of the World: Thoughts, Stories, and Prayers* (Novato, CA: New World Library, 2010), 30.

1

Illuminative Ecclesiology and Pope Francis

> The Christian can see with the eyes of Jesus and share in his mind, his filial disposition, because he or she shares in his love, which is the Spirit. In the love of Jesus, we receive in a certain way his vision.
>
> —Pope Francis, *Lumen Fidei*, June 29, 2013

> The Church is an institution, but when she makes herself a "centre," she becomes merely functional, and slowly but surely turns into a kind of NGO. The Church then claims to have a light of her own, and she stops being that "*mysterium lunae*" of which the Church Fathers spoke. She becomes increasingly self-referential and loses her need to be missionary. From an "institution" she becomes an "enterprise." She stops being a bride and ends up being an administrator; from being a servant, she becomes an "inspector." Aparecida wanted a Church which is bride, mother and servant, a facilitator of faith and not an inspector of faith.
>
> —Pope Francis, Address to the Leadership of CELAM,
> July 28, 2013

THE STARTING POINT OF ECCLESIOLOGY: THE LIGHT OF FAITH

When Pope Francis gave a special blessing to a little girl, Lizzy Myers, at a weekly audience in 2016, it did not make a big headline. However, for the Myers family from Ohio in the United States, this was a new experience of God's love and light. Lizzy had a rare condition called Usher Syndrome, which will make her lose her sight in the second decade of her life. Her parents wanted to give her as much experience with beauty as possible so that when she eventually loses her sight, she will, as they said, "have an inner illumination and a beautiful memory stored up to enrich her life." According to the family, Lizzy "was enthralled by the experience" of seeing the "big guy in the white hat," and she was profoundly touched.

We all are affected in different ways by powerful experiences, especially when we encounter genuine human love. The aspect of encounter with the other and entering into the sometimes "messy lives" of people is a constant in the ministry of Pope Francis. He gives a wonderful description of why such encounters constitute a light for the church and a light from the church in *Evangelii Gaudium*, 272: "Loving others is a spiritual force drawing us to union with God; indeed, one who does not love others 'walks in the darkness' (1 Jn 2:11), 'remains in death' (1 Jn 3:14) and 'does not know God' (1 Jn 4:8)." Benedict XVI has said that "closing our eyes to our neighbour also blinds us to God," and that love is, in the end, the *only light* that

> can always illuminate a world grown dim and give us the courage needed to keep living and working. When we live out a spirituality of drawing nearer to others and seeking their welfare, our hearts are opened wide to the Lord's greatest and most beautiful gifts. Whenever we encounter another person in love, we learn something new about God. Whenever our eyes are opened to acknowledge the other, we grow in the light of faith and the knowledge of God.

What is significant for me in this story, like many other stories about Pope Francis's encounters with people, is the extent to which the pope reached out to meet and greet this family when he learned of the story of Lizzy. There was the aspect of a deep encounter which was transformative because it grew from a deep desire to meet another human being at the point of her need. It was a personal and direct meeting of two hearts who were drawn by the love of God burning in their hearts. The image of the encounter with the pope as reported by Lizzy's parents was like "an inner illumination" that Lizzy will remember for the rest of her life. One can think of the powerful stories of the meeting between Jesus and Zacchaeus (Lk 19:1–10) and the meeting between Jesus and the woman by the well (Jn 4:1–42) in order to see how a deep and genuine encounter of love and concern between two people can be a moment of grace, transformation, and newness.

The kind of church that Pope Francis wishes to bring about is tender and caring, with a humble immersion in the lives of others, and a willingness to accompany people in the chaos and woundedess of their lives. It is a church that is wholly molded after the example of the poor man of Galilee who made himself all things for the sake of human liberation. In his famous TED talk speech, Pope Francis underlines this aspect of deep encounter as the key to the future of humanity, "'The future you': the future is made of 'yous'; it is made of encounters, because life flows through our relations with others. Quite a few years of life have strengthened my conviction that each and everyone's existence is deeply tied to that of others: life is not merely time passing by; life is about interactions."[1] The church exists to make possible the transforming encounter and meeting of peoples in diversities of situations through the love, life, and grace of God which it mediates in history.

Many people who come to churches wish to encounter Jesus in the Christian community. People are hungry for God and for love. Many people are thirsty for meaning and search for safety and comfort especially in our churches because they are looking for a light of hope in a world that is often tottering on the brink of despair in the face of evil, suffering, and violence. The question therefore arises: How can the encounter of people through our churches become an inner illumination for them, which leads them deeper into the mystery of divine love? In other words, what form of witnessing and proclamation can someone experience in our churches that points to Christ and shows the face of the world to God and the merciful, loving, and compassionate face of God to a wounded world? What I have termed "illuminative ecclesiology" is the form of witnessing by the church that answers this key question. It is a form of witnessing and proclamation that I see in Pope Francis.

In other words, illuminative ecclesiology is that form of witnessing and proclamation which can be experienced as a transformative encounter with the Lord Jesus Christ by all—Christians and non-Christians—through the priorities and practices of the church. It is also that form of proclamation and witnessing which is open to all people in their different stations and situations in life. Through this form, the church carries in its loving bosom and presents to God every new day the multiple faces of a wounded humanity in search of meaning and salvation. The structures, laws, rituals, liturgies, and pastoral plan of churches are thus relative instruments, which consistently must lead to this fundamental form as concrete praxis and channels for realizing the identity and mission of the church as salt and light.

Lizzy's meeting with Pope Francis is one of many inspirational stories of the encounters between persons and Pope Francis. These stories give us a concrete narrative for unpacking this form of being church central to Pope Francis's ministry, which is modeled after the example of the Lord Jesus Christ. This idea of the church as a place of encounter where we experience the powerful force of love, friendship, mercy, grace, and compassion through embracing one another is a good starting point for beginning the conversation on how the priorities and practices of our churches should lead

---

[1]Pope Francis, TED Talk, April 25, 2017, www.ted.com.

people to God, and place them in the comforting heart of the Lord Jesus Christ. It is a good image for beginning a theological account of illuminative ecclesiology modeled by Pope Francis for a world church.

When Pope Francis heard about the story of Lizzy, he expressed the desire to meet her personally, to spend some time chatting with her and her family, and to become a fellow traveler with Lizzy in her journey. Pope Francis takes human experience seriously because it is in the ordinary daily encounters with reality and with one another that we encounter God. Faith is mediated through our daily experiences. In addition, our daily experiences are sites where the beauty of God's grace and life comes in touch with our human condition. The experience of faith, which we receive as a gift of love from God, serves as the foundation of all things we say or do as Christians and in the church. Faith is a movement of love and intimacy from God to humans. It is also our movement of gratitude and humility drawn by love toward God, humans, and the entire cosmos, because we see and love in them what God sees and loves in them. Faith is the principle of joy and happiness that makes us light. As Joseph Ratzinger proposes,

> The ease of unbelief and the difficulty of belief lie on different planes. Unbelief, too, is a heavy burden, and in my opinion even more so than faith is. Faith also makes man light. This can be seen in the church fathers, especially in monastic theology. To believe means that we become like angels, they say. We can fly, because we no longer weigh so heavy in our own estimation. To become a believer means to become light, to escape our own gravity, which drags us down, and thus to enter the weightlessness of faith.[2]

There is a certain mutuality between us and God in the act of faith. This mutual journey between us and God opens our eyes to see God in all things and to see all things in the light of God. Faith gives us the prejudgment and anticipation of the good, the true, and the beautiful in every reality even before we encounter it. Faith is rooted in our inner desire for transcendence and for connection, and it moves the heart to the Other who is reflected in every reality and especially in the face of a brother or sister who is suffering, neglected, poor, or losing his or her way in life. Lizzy's family noted that even though she was very young, she had a deep faith in God, which she received through her deeply religious family. Before she met the pope, she already had a deep hunger for divine illumination. However, she needed a spark. Each of us by the gift of God we carry can always be a spark to ignite

---

[2]Joseph Ratzinger, *Salt of the Earth: The Church at the End of the Millennium* (San Francisco: Ignatius Books, 1997), 28.

the flame of love and life in another human being, especially the wearied soul and the empty spirit of those who feel that they are insignificant or unworthy of love.

This message is central to the teaching of Pope Francis. In his first encyclical, *Light of Faith*, he argues in the first part that the beginning of the Christian life is an illuminating faith which guides the Christian path from the past and the present into the future. His insight on the illuminative pathway of faith for Christians bears presenting in full:

> Here is an urgent need, then, to see once again that faith is a light, for once the flame of faith dies out, all other lights begin to dim. The light of faith is unique, since it is capable of illuminating *every aspect* of human existence. A light this powerful cannot come from ourselves but from a more primordial source: in a word, it must come from God. Faith is born of an encounter with the living God who calls us and reveals his love, a love which precedes us and upon which we can lean for security and for building our lives.
>
> *Transformed by this love,* we gain fresh vision, new eyes to see; we realize that it contains a great promise of fulfillment, and that a vision of the future opens up before us. Faith, received from God as a supernatural gift, becomes a light for our way, guiding our journey through time. On the one hand*, it is a light coming from the past, the light of the foundational memory of the life of Jesus* which revealed his perfectly trustworthy love, a love capable of triumphing over death. Yet since Christ has risen and draws us beyond death, faith is also a light coming from the future and opening before us vast horizons which guide us beyond our isolated selves toward the breadth of communion. *We come to see that faith does not dwell in shadow and gloom; it is a light for our darkness.* (*Lumen Fidei*, 4, italics mine)

The second aspect is that faith is the inspiration and the medium for doing something beautiful for God with our lives in every circumstance and in every encounter with other people. Faith leads us to a deeper relationship and communion with God and with other people and the world of nature. Faith is, therefore, the key that opens the beauty of creation to us, and it is the *ratio* for the life of the church. Faith opens the door and makes possible other encounters in our lives. This is the kind of dynamics that made possible the encounter between the pope and Lizzy. Faith should foreground every human encounter with God, the other, and the world of nature. Through faith we also make sense of sin and evil, sickness, death, betrayal, and so on. Every reality in the light of faith becomes a medium for encountering God.

Third, at the core of our ecclesial life is the reality of faith. The church exists to lead people into a deeper encounter with God. Faith is the praxis which brings about the telos (the end) to which all our human actions and ecclesial priorities and practices tend. In some important verses in *Lumen Fidei* 22 Pope Francis elaborates on this dynamic of faith giving birth to church, and the church giving birth to a faith that does justice and good works.

First, those who believe come to see themselves and all things in the light of the faith which they profess: Christ is the mirror in which they find their own image fully realized. And just as Christ gathers to himself all those who believe and makes them his body, so the Christian comes to see himself or herself as a member of this body, in an essential relationship with all other believers and all God's people. However, the image of a body is much more than a social organization or a bunch of people held together by a dictator or the iron will of historical exigency. Everyone is an essential part of the church; no one is a mere cog in a great machine. Everyone counts for God and for the church. The church cannot, therefore, exclude anyone whom God counts as a child of God. This is why relationship becomes essential to our being church because of the "vital union of Christ with believers and of believers among themselves" (cf. Rom 12:4–5). Christians are "one" (cf. Gal 3:28), yet in a way which does not make them lose their individuality.

Second, the highest degree of expression of our relationship with God, with one another, and with nature is through service to one another in a spirit of love. The praxis of faith can be realized only through daily service of love to God and neighbor, especially those who are poor and on the margins. The act of service is at the same time a prophetic act because it reveals the presence of God and introduces a transforming dynamics in history. Pope Francis refers to Romano Guardini's assertion that the church "is the bearer within history of the plenary gaze of Christ on the world." The church is God's gaze on the world in history, and the church leads people within history to fix their gaze on Christ. In this mutual gaze of church, Christians, humans, nature, world, and God there is an intimate bond of love, care, and reverence specified by faith. Faith helps us see God in all things, and faith helps us to look beyond changes in history to what Parker Palmer calls "the grace of greater things." But faith does more: it opens our eyes to cast our gaze beyond the limited horizon of time into the unlimited horizon of God. It also opens our eyes to see God in the contradictions of history, especially in the brokenness of history and in the suffering of people and the planet. In a simple but profound line in *Lumen Fidei* (22) Pope Francis says that "faith opens the individual Christian toward all others."

Third, faith is not individualistic or private; it is not also one's opinion about God or things of God and the world; faith is not simply the centering of my life in God. Faith is a gift given to us out of God's own generosity.

Thus, it is also ecclesial because the Word of God is communicated to us in the community. Faith is a gift that we receive from God through the church. God gives us faith so that we can use it to bring about in history God's will for the world through the realization of our individual vocation. But above all, "Faith becomes operative in the Christian on the basis of the gift received, the love which attracts our hearts to Christ (cf. Gal 5:6), and enables us to become part of the church's great pilgrimage through history until the end of the world." Faith brings transformation for the individual, the church, and society because "for those who have been transformed in this way, a new way of seeing opens up, faith becomes light for their eyes."

This is at the core of the theological aesthetics of the church: faith becomes light for our eyes so that we see things in the light of Christ. It is a beauty that emerges in the contradictions and joys of life because faith leads us to see the hand of God in all things and the face of Christ in all things, even in the chaos of life. Using an African ontology, I will proceed to aver that every reality has vital force because every reality has the light of Christ. This light of Christ animates all things and gives them being and specifies their relationship and participation in the life of God. One can say that the life force of reality is the light of God that gives every reality existence. Seeing faith and reality in this way triggers a constant movement from *a new way of seeing* to *a new way of acting*. It offers us the surest pathway for building a healthy community of the beloved illumined by hope. Every new day we encounter reality in its fullness; we must see each day in a new light in the light of our faith. But drawing on our faith, we must also act in a new way. The church is called to be "the seeing eyes" for the world, "God's gaze upon history," in order to see ourselves as God sees us. This is the beginning of proper moral judgment on what God wants us to see and what God wants us to do in order to heal the world, bring salvation to the ends of the earth, and begin in small ways to mediate the eschatological fruits of God's kingdom. It is in this regard that Pope Francis speaks of faith as not only hearing and seeing, but of touching the wounds and pains of others like Jesus did in many encounters in the Bible. Touching Lizzy as he did was a combination of seeing the face of God in her, hearing the echo of divine presence in this little girl, and touching her in order that God will mutually touch both the pope and Lizzy in this wonderful *mysterium commercium*.

The words of Pope Francis are powerful and deep in explicating this reality:

> For the light of love is born when our hearts are touched and we open ourselves to the interior presence of the beloved, who enables us to recognize his mystery. Thus we can understand why, together with hearing and seeing, Saint John can speak of faith as touch, as he says

in his First Letter: "What we have heard, what we have seen with our eyes and touched with our hands, concerning the word of life" (1 Jn 1:1). By his taking flesh and coming among us, Jesus has touched us, and through the sacraments he continues to touch us even today; transforming our hearts, he unceasingly enables us to acknowledge and acclaim him as the Son of God. In faith, we can touch him and receive the power of his grace. Saint Augustine, commenting on the account of the woman suffering from hemorrhages who touched Jesus and was cured (cf. Lk 8:45–46), says: "To touch him with our hearts: that is what it means to believe." The crowd presses in on Jesus, but they do not reach him with the personal touch of faith, which apprehends the mystery that he is the Son who reveals the Father. Only when we are configured to Jesus do we receive the eyes needed to see him.

In *Laudato Si'*, Pope Francis develops a whole section (nos. 63–100) under the title "Light of Faith." Here he shows how faith is a light that leads us to understand the intrinsic relationship between all created realities. Faith also gives the foundation for and orders Christian stewardship of the earth through an ecological ethics. This begins with the appreciation of beauty in all things. Indeed, *Laudato Si'* explicitly states that seeing beauty in all things, especially the smallest things, is eminently Christological because that is what the Son of God did:

> The Lord was able to invite others to be attentive to the beauty that there is in the world because he himself was in constant touch with nature, lending it an attention full of fondness and wonder. As he made his way throughout the land, he often stopped to contemplate the beauty sown by his Father, and invited his disciples to perceive a divine message in things: "Lift up your eyes, and see how the fields are already white for harvest" (Jn 4:35). "The kingdom of God is like a grain of mustard seed which a man took and sowed in his field; it is the smallest of all seeds, but once it has grown, it is the greatest of plants" (Mt 13:31–32). (*LS*, 97)

Faith leads us to discover in the light of Christ the beauty in the world of nature, and the way of beauty through grace, and to bear witness to beauty in our daily choices and encounters with nature, humans, world, and God.

The church is reflected as in a mirror through stories of encounters like the one between Pope Francis and Lizzy and our own personal stories and encounters with people, nature, and God. The church can be called the site for the continuing stories of the acts of the new apostles of Christ. The saving, teaching, liberating, and healing ministry of Christ is continued today in the church through the stories of the words and deeds of communities and people gathered in every part of the world in the name of Christ. These stories are mirrors in which the church's identity and mission are reflected to the world. Furthermore, these stories are the footprints of God in history. In this kind of church, the daily stories of the people of God—their joys and sorrows, hopes and fears, their sins and failings, pain and brokenness, their life and death, all that relate to their existence—are embraced as the new revelation of the presence of God and the way to beauty. They offer new dimensions for seeing the footprints of God in history and new pathways to how and where God is present among God's people.

When it struck me as a revelation that Pope Francis's approach to ministry and service in the church is like a light that shines out from within the heart of the church and the heart of the world, I immediately thought of Jesus' words to his disciples, "You are the light of the world" (Mt 5:14), the celebration of the Easter Vigil, and the theme of light that fills our liturgies. I also think of the image of Jesus Christ as the light of the world (Jn 8:12) and how he has sent us into the world to be the light in such a way that anytime we shine the light of love or mercy to others we make Christ present. I think of the theme of the Second African Synod, which used the image of light to capture the mission of the church in Africa at the service of reconciliation, justice, and peace and its connection to the image of the church as family of God chosen by the First African Synod members in 1994. I also remember the beautiful World Youth Day I attended in Canada in 2002 where the theme of "salt and light" captured the spiritual, cultural, and social imagination of close to half a million young people from all parts of the world. Indeed, the title for the Dogmatic Constitution of the Second Vatican Council on the church was *Lumen Gentium*, light to the nations. It is an image which has not been developed in the discussion on post–Vatican II ecclesiology, communion ecclesiology, or the people of God ecclesiology. This missing link in post–Vatican II ecclesiology has now been filled by Pope Francis. He has retrieved aspects of the identity and mission of the church that have been features of the church since the time of the Lord.

The image of the church as light is a central motif in biblical, patristic, and pastoral preaching. It is so constant that it seems to me an appropriate key for unlocking what Pope Francis is doing in the church today. But it is much more nuanced and extensive in its content beyond Pope Francis and goes back to the time of Jesus and the early church; it was also a powerful image found in the earliest reflections of the fathers on the church. What Pope Francis has accomplished has been described in many ways, but I locate him within a richer and deeper ecclesiological tradition. The papacy of Francis is a summons to all members of the church to celebrate this dynamic and diverse identity of the church and to embrace the mission anew in our changing and uncertain times. He is calling us to a new way of illumining the city of God and to a humble openness to God so that the light of Christ can illumine the beautiful way for the world in our earthly journey through a new force of love and mercy, which is a light to the nations. Pope Francis, unlike his two predecessors, is not a renowned theologian. It is not surprising that he has not given the church and the world high-sounding theological and scholastic teaching on aspects of the life of the church or doctrine. What we have seen are powerful words and some daily symbolic acts and practices, like his meeting with Lizzy, that help us name the theology that we see at work in this papacy's portrait of the identity and mission of the church. However, the foundation of all these is faith.

In what follows in this chapter, I wish to develop what I have termed illuminative ecclesiology—a way of being church that I identify in Pope Francis's pastoral ministry and papacy. I point out five moments of this ecclesiology and how they fit into the renewal of Catholic ecclesiology in the twentieth and twenty-first centuries by discussing the ecclesiology of two important influences on Pope Francis: Hans Urs von Balthasar and Yves Congar. I then conclude the chapter with a section on the implications of this new ecclesiology for world Christianity and especially for those who are poor and waiting at the doors of our churches, the borders of our nations, and the gates of our homes, like poor Lazarus in search of mercy and love.

WHO IS THE CHURCH?

Illuminative ecclesiology is an identifier of who the church is through what the church does and where the church is found. It is the answer to the question: What form of witnessing and proclamation can I experience in every instance of the life of Christians and in my encounters with the other in churches which points to Christ and shows the face of the world to God and the face of God to the world? The church has a representative function. It does not exist for itself. It mediates to the world the gifts and graces of the Lord. Pope Francis calls it the church of tenderness, which not only mediates the tender love of God to people but also changes the hearts of people to become tender to one another and to creation. In his famous TED talk, he describes this tenderness in detail:

> It is the love that comes close and becomes real. It is a movement that starts from our heart and reaches the eyes, the ears and the hands. Tenderness means to use our eyes to see the other, our ears to hear the other, to listen to the children, the poor, those who are afraid of the future. To listen also to the silent cry of our common home, of our

sick and polluted earth. Tenderness means to use our hands and our hearts to comfort the other, to take care of those in need.[3]

The church's identity and mission of tenderness is accomplished through proclaiming and living the whole gospel when it presents the whole of Christ to the world as the Good News, which is capable of meeting the present hunger of humanity for unconditional love and for saving and healing grace. At the same time, the church brings the whole of humanity and creation before God. That means that the wounds of many men and women and the groaning of creation must be present in all the four marks of the church—holiness, catholicity, apostolicity, and unity.

Witnessing to Christ in the church is not simply a matter of presentation of doctrines or laws or celebration of rituals, although these are important because they give form and structure to the church and provide sound grounding to the central affirmations of our faith. However, as Bruno Forte points out, "Christ is not a mere doctrine to let himself be manipulated according to our tastes and plans; rather, he is a person, alive with new life, who comes to us and calls us to follow him."[4] What the church does should flow from union with Christ. This is because the church, as Saint Cyprian wrote, is illumined by the ray of Christ that shines in every aspect of the church and from there to every part of the world.[5] Immersed in history, the church is an incomplete subject, an incomplete light, and an unfinished work bearing the wounds of humanity and nourished by the graces of God and the guidance of the Holy Spirit.

How can the practices and priorities of the Lord be mediated through the identity and mission of the church? How can the fate and future of humanity be embodied in the life of the church and Christians today? How can the eschatological fruits of God's kingdom be harvested in the church so that the church can contribute to human history and move in the direction of God's dream and plan for the world? How can the church heal the divisions in the world? My contention in this chapter is that illuminative ecclesiology, reflected in the ministry of Pope Francis, offers an answer to

---

[3]Pope Francis, TED Talk, April 25, 2017, www.ted.com.

[4]Bruno Forte, *To Follow You, Light of Life: Spiritual Exercises Preached before John Paul II at the Vatican*, trans. David Glenday (Grand Rapids, MI: William B. Eerdmans, 2005).

[5]Cyprian writes, "You cannot separate a ray of light from the sun, because its unity does not allow division. You can break a branch from a tree, but when broken, it will not be able to bud. Cut a stream off from its source and it dries up. It is the same with the Church. Filled with the light of the Lord, it shines its rays over the whole world, yet everywhere it is one and the same light that shines, and the body is not divided. The Church's fruitfulness spreads branches over the whole world. It sends forth her rivers, freely flowing, yet the source is one, and she is one mother, plentiful in fruitfulness. We are born from her womb, nourished by her milk, given life by her spirit." St. Cyprian, *The Unity of the Church*, introduction by Stephen Tomkins, edited and prepared for the web by Dan Graves: www.christianhistoryinstitute.org.

these questions and an approach to being church that is capable of meeting the concerns and aspirations of a wounded world.

My proposal is that the poor constitute the form of the church. The church's poverty or poor-first mission and ministry of mercy are the forms that the church must assume today if it is to reflect its true identity as an instrument of God's love and mercy in the world. The splendor of Christ shines out in the hidden beauty of the poor. The glory of the Lord's majesty is hidden in the darkness that surrounds the poor and in the hidden wounds of many people today as they search for mercy and healing. No debate, laws, or structures should be upheld in the church if they do not center on how the healing balms of mercy can be applied to the wounds of people in the world today, especially those on the margins. Salvation is that transformative grace that the Lord ministers to a wounded world through a poor and merciful church. This is the only way through which the church and Christians can help meet each other at the deepest points of our human fragility and inner hunger where all human beings are most in need of divine intimacy and transcendence. In this dynamic salvation and liberation become events in history.

A picture, they say, is worth a thousand words, and in Pope Francis we have seen the power of images and pictures. Pope Francis is not a showman, but his simple acts of service, the places he has visited, and the people he associates with have painted a portrait of the church that has had a far-reaching impact. His words and actions have given the church new categories and images that capture the cultural and spiritual imagination of many—the church as a field hospital, the church of wounds, the church of the poor, the church of mercy, and the church with open doors, the revolution of tenderness through the church, and so on (*EG*, 47–49). Each image answers the question: What form of witnessing and proclamation can I experience in every instance of the life of Christians and in my encounters with the other in churches which points to Christ and shows the face of the world to God and the face of God to the world?

So one can say, for example, that the witness of a church of mercy or a church of the poor in the witnessing and proclamation of the gospel of the Lord in the church will show the face of God to the world and the face of humanity to God. The same could be said of other images listed above. In addition, these images are interchangeable: for example, the church is a field hospital because it has within it people who bear deep wounds and who are left on the sidelines of history; the church has wounds because it is poor and in need of mercy; people in the church-in-the-world need mercy because they bear wounds; and the church should have an open door because millions of people who are wounded and poor are knocking at many locked doors, and the church's door must be open to them to bring them home into the very heart of the God of love and mercy. The revolution of tenderness happens when the church is poor, merciful, and open to everyone, especially those who are wounded in the battle of life.

These images are keys to understanding how Pope Francis retrieves and appropriates Vatican II's ecclesiology. They are significant as portraits of the central affirmation and practices foundational to the theological aesthetics of *illuminative ecclesiology*. The church is the dynamic instrument, which shines the light of God's continuing act of love and mercy in history especially in the life and reality of the poor of the Lord and the poor in the Lord.

Pope Francis is not introducing a new ecclesiology. Like a prophet, he is calling the church to recover a central dimension of its mission as salt and light. The church's identity and mission as a poor and merciful church have always nourished the spirituality and the pastoral and social mission of Christian communities. However, the form of the church as light has sometimes been neglected in the divisive cultural and ideological battles in the church and the unholy struggles for power and positions by its leaders at some points in history.

This desire to return to the sources in order to renew the church and meet the challenges and opportunities of the changing times was central to the theological ferments of *ressourcement* and *aggiornamento,* two pulsating theological, spiritual, pastoral, and cultural currents among many at work in Vatican II. In a sense, Pope Francis is canalizing in his ministry different ecclesiological streams and countercurrents that began to emerge before and after Vatican II and which had already begun to set the outline of a paradigm shift in the priorities and practices of the church in the twentieth and twenty-first centuries. Illuminative ecclesiology is a restatement of a central feature of the church from its origins and identifies an irreducible form of being church already proposed by Vatican II. It offers a theological aesthetics for translating and judging the adequacy of any model of the church.[6]

Illuminative ecclesiology refers to practices and Christian witnessing in the church, which lead to what Hans Urs von Balthasar calls "a satisfactory ecclesiology." This is a way of being church that is able to adequately account for "the inmost essence of the church" and how this form is manifested in history while being faithful to and modeled after its Trinitarian origin and destiny. How can the church's way of being church in the world be witnessed to by all the people of God in the life of a church, which is "transparent

---

[6]When I write of the models of the church I am referring to the six models popularized in the important book of Avery Dulles—the church as institution, the church as mystical communion, the church as sacrament, the church as herald, the church as servant, the church as community of disciples. Avery Dulles, *Models of the Church*, exp. ed. (New York: Image Books, 2002).

enough to convey her inner radiance"?[7] What form of witnessing can I see in every instance of the life of Christians in their churches which points to Christ and shows the face of the world to God and the face of God to the world? How does this form of life become concrete in the churches and in the lives of people as an evangelical witness to the gospel message?

These images can be summarized in the two recurring themes in the message and ministry of Pope Francis—a poor and merciful church. Both terms capture the *identity and mission* of the church in many ways. The image of the church of the poor specifies the identity of the church as originating from God and subsisting in God. It also reflects the identity of a humble church that holds on to nothing other than the gifts and graces of God. It is the portrait of a church that is the home for all. It also points to where the church is as the site that offers agency to the poor for the reversal of history so that history can conform to God's will of human and cosmic flourishing, especially for those who are weak and on the sidelines.

The image of the church as merciful captures the mission of the church to heal a broken world ravaged by injustice, falsehood, selfishness, pride, and sin. It is the portrait of a church that sees its vocation and the vocations of its members as healers of wounds and menders of broken lives and societies. This church is a people called to bring salvation, liberation, peace, restoration, hope, and new life to all. The saving realities that the church receives from God are mediated through mercy as its origin, the means and end of all its activities in the church-in-the-world or the world-in-the-church. The church's identity as merciful is, therefore, self-reflective because the church is offering to the world what it is and also receiving from God what it needs. All people because of their poverty and their location—social, cultural, spiritual, personal, communal, and so on—are in need of God's mercy. Humanity is wounded, poor, vulnerable, and constantly in search of mercy and healing. The church exists from the originating merciful love of God and thus has a mission of mediating and incarnating in history the mercy of God to wounded creation so as to help bring about the fruits of God's reign.

Pope Francis offers a theological aesthetics that makes manifest essential dimensions of the church's life and being as salt and light. This theological aesthetics was becoming secondary in the fight in modern Catholicism over some of the contested issues on authority in the church, the role of women, marriage, sex and sexuality, papal primacy, the relationship between the Roman center and the local churches, and so on. This forgetfulness was drawing the church away from its mission and submerging it in a deep crisis of identity until the emergence of Pope Francis. Pope Francis shows

---

[7]See Hans Urs von Balthasar, *Explorations in Theology II: Spouse of the Word*, trans. A. V. Littledale and Alexander Dru (San Francisco: Ignatius Press, 1991), 20.

through his theological aesthetics that the church's identity and mission can be recovered fully only if the church becomes a seeing eye, showing the beautiful Christian way in the contradictions of history. This can be done if Christians and the church embrace the world and enter into the contradictions and complexities of history. It is only when churches and Christians enter into the world, while touching the brokenness and wounds of creation that they can be illumined by the love of God shining out from the heart of God's Son on the Cross. It is also in this mutuality of exchange and intimacy of contact that the church and Christians can illumine the darkness and contractions of history with the healing light and life of grace and transformation from God.

Important dimensions of faith in *Lumen Fidei* are central to understanding how illuminative ecclesiology emerges from and leads back to faith. The key here is to examine closely some of the most important themes in *Lumen Fidei* as they relate to the light of Christ in itself, the light of faith, and the light of Christ in the church, in the lives of Christians, and in the world. I can then develop how Pope Francis unpacks this in his subsequent teachings, especially in *Evangelii Gaudium* and *Amoris Laetitia*.

The first indication of the theme of light in *Lumen Fidei* (51) occurs when Pope Francis teaches that illumination comes to us through the experience of love as a gift, and is received in faith as a vocation to share the same love with our brothers and sisters, especially those who suffer: "Our life is illumined to the extent that it enters into the space opened by love, to the extent that it becomes, in other words, a path and praxis leading to the fullness of love."

Second, this illumination of faith is an offer from God to humanity and the world to enter into an ever widening circle of relationships characterized by love. These relationships become for all Christians an invitation to journey together with everyone who is out there as members of God's family into the future that God alone knows. As Pope Francis teaches further in *Lumen Fidei* (51): "The light of faith is capable of enhancing the richness of human relations, their ability to endure, to be trustworthy, to enrich our life together. Faith does not draw us away from the world or prove irrelevant to the concrete concerns of the men and women of our time."

Third, this illumination is a praxis that provides the architecture for building up human society in order to realize God's will in history. In particular, it is a light that brightens the interior life of the church; it is the ultimate foundation for the church's life and mission at the service of the common good. This light from the church shines out through every Christian who offers himself or herself in humble service to others. Thus the church becomes the instrument for doing God's will here on earth; it is also the architecture for ordering society in such a way "that [people] can journey toward a future of hope." In order for this to happen, faith enables us to appreciate the dignity and beauty of everyone and to see every human being as a blessing and that "the light of God's face shines on me through the faces of my brothers and sisters" (*LF*, 51).

These three dimensions of faith in *Lumen Fidei* touch on three aspects of the human experience essential to the proclamation and witnessing of churches and Christians in the world: (1) Our own experience of God's love and mercy is both a gift of illumination in our lives and a vocation to follow the illuminative path in bringing love and mercy to people in the world; (2) the summons is to see divine love and mercy in every instance of human and cosmic life, especially appreciating that the light of Christ shines out in the weakness and limitations of life and in the marginal worlds of so many people in our societies; (3) and the courage of faith is the logic for a praxis of hope that challenges Christians to a prophetic witnessing in the world through daily practices in order to bring out light and life where there is darkness, despair, and death.

This movement and presence of light in the human experience, and beauty in the wounds and sinfulness of humanity is accounted for in Pope Francis's other teachings. In the postsynodal apostolic exhortation *Amoris Laetitia*, one can identify the theological aesthetics of faith that specifies the identity and mission of the church as light. This document is more nuanced than initially meets the eye. Gone are the dialectical categories introduced by Pope John Paul II in *Evangelium Vitae* (33–65) between the culture of life and the culture of death. There is a broader and integrated understanding of human life not built on an anthropocentric priority but on a Trinitarian relationship of participation. Abortion (126–27, 170), birth control, population control, polygamy, pornography, sexual exploitation, child abuse, and so on (39–44, 53–57, 80–82, 135–41, 291–94) are rejected, but within the bigger context of understanding that pastoral discernment and pastoral judgment and action must be connected to people's lives (200–201). There were sections taken from *Humanae Vitae* on the use of the rhythm method (60–70, 80–81, 125, 159, 222, 250–51, 305, etc.); natural law made a comeback for grounding moral precepts and justifying the church's teachings about the nature and character of the family and gender differences for motherhood and fatherhood. However, in *Amoris Laetitia*, natural law is seen as "a source of objective inspiration for the deeply personal process of making decisions" rather than "a set of rules" imposed on the moral subject or on the church. Same-sex unions (250–51, 311–12), the annulment process (239–47, 291), and the exclusion of people from communion are still reinforced with teachings from the *Catechism of the Catholic Church* and previous popes, but there is no condemnation of people with same-sex orientation or divorced and remarried Catholics.

Integration and mercy are keys for walking with them and seeing how they can carry out God's will in their lives, in the church, and in the world.

Most significant for my purpose here is Pope Francis's constant use of the word "illumination" to refer to various aspects of the experience of the faithful and the experience of the church. In the introductory part of the document, Pope Francis wrote that the synod was "both impressive and illuminating" (4). Then in chapter 1 he reflects on the experience of the Christian family as being illumined by the natural order and states that the church must see things through the eyes of Christ because the light of Christ enlightens every person, even those in difficult situations or irregular marriages (60, 70, 72, 78). In chapters 3 and 4, he writes that the "aesthetic experience of love is expressed in that gaze which contemplates other persons as ends in themselves, even if they are infirm, elderly or physically unattractive" (128). Indeed, love opens our eyes, according to Pope Francis, so that we can see the great worth of the other. The words of consent that couples give to each other "illumine all the meaning of the signs" (214); couples and all people should allow their eyes to be opened to see God's gift in the embryo from the great moment of conception (168). Sex education should be presented in such a way that it is an illumination for living in a mature way and embracing the joy of love (280). The church and all Christians and family members must embrace the light of faith (253) in order to see the goodness in everyone, especially those who are suffering and those who are weak and experiencing distress of different kinds (296, 308). The Christian family is a source of light in every circumstance (290, 312), and we must look with contemplative eyes into the situation of people in different circumstances in marriage in order to find what gifts and resources God has given to illuminate the life of people and illumine the way for the church as a mother. *Amoris Laetitia* is an invitation to everyone to cast their gaze beyond the human, cultural, and ecclesial horizon to see the infinite horizons of God, which open up even in new, complex, and changing situations. *Amoris Laetitia* does not offer answers and definitions; it invites the church to contemplate beauty in the contradictions of life so that it can offer the world an illuminative path which leads into a hopeful future.

WHAT DOES THE CHURCH DO?

In an interview that he gave in 2016, Pope Francis spoke of what the church does, that is, the mission of the church, in the following words:

> The church does not exist to condemn people but to bring about an encounter with the visceral love of God's mercy. I often say that in

order for this to happen, it is necessary to go out: to go out from the church and the parishes, to go outside and look for people where they live, where they suffer, and where they hope. I like to use the image of a field hospital to describe this "church that goes forth"; it exists where there is combat; it is not a solid structure with all the equipment where people go to receive treatment for both small and large infirmities. It is a mobile structure that offers first aid and immediate care, so that its soldiers do not die. It's a place for urgent care, not a place to see a specialist. I hope that the Jubilee will serve to reveal the church's deeply maternal and merciful side, a church that goes forth toward those who are "wounded," who are in need of an attentive ear, understanding, forgiveness, and love.[8]

Pope Francis is aware that the church is not found in laws, structures, systems, or liturgical forms, but in the sinfulness and wounds of the world. This is why Saint Ambrose says that "the church is beautiful in the souls," because the church, as G. K. Chesterton wrote, "descends with me into the depths of myself" in order to illumine the path to new life, hope, and beauty.[9] Pope Francis thus moves away from what the church says about itself to how the light of Christ to the nations shines out through the church everywhere, especially in the margins where people are most in need of love and divine mercy. In one of his speeches, Pope Francis makes an important point on this Christological foundation, which requires further theological elaboration:

Jesus has no house, because his house is the people; it is we who are his dwelling place; his mission is to open God's doors to all, to be the presence of God's love. . . . Following Jesus means learning to come out of ourselves in order to go to meet others, to go toward the outskirts of existence, to be the first to take a step toward our brothers and sisters, especially those who are the most distant, those who are forgotten, those who are most in need of understanding, comfort, and help.[10]

The light shines in the church because the church has Jesus, and the shift from who the church is to what the church does requires some level of transformation in theology and pastoral life.

---

[8]Pope Francis, *The Name of God Is Mercy: A Conversation with Andrea Tornielli*, trans. Oonagh Stransky (New York: Random House, 2016), 52.

[9]I have relied for the development of this analogy of *ecclesia vel anima* on Raniero Cantalamessa, *Loving the Church: Scriptural Mediation for the Papal Household*, trans. Gilberto Cavazos-Gonzalez and Amanda Quantz (Cincinnati: St. Anthony Messenger Press, 2003), 65.

[10]Pope Francis, *The Church of Mercy: A Vision for the Church* (Chicago: Loyola Press, 2014), 71–72.

Pope Francis makes this transformation through a theological aesthetics that reflects the following:

(1) The church is a spiritual gift from God to which all of God's people in their different conditions and states of life are invited as children of God. Our belonging to the church is not based on rank and hierarchy. Thus membership in the church is not determined according to degrees, kinds, or types dictated by some unchanging criteria set by popes, synods, or councils. Speaking at one of his audiences, the pope was unequivocal on this ecclesiological image:

> The church is all of us: from the baby just baptized to the bishop, the pope; we are all the church and we are all equal in the eyes of God! We are all called to collaborate for the birth of new Christians in the faith, we are all called to be educators in the faith, to proclaim the Gospel. . . . We all take part in the motherhood of the church, so that the light of Christ may reach the far confines of the earth.[11]

(2) The church is not the product of ideological or cultural construction dictated by social change. The church is a gift from God where we encounter the Lord in faith and are equipped by grace to live in freedom. On this, Pope Francis says:

> For the church is herself God's great family, which brings Christ to us. Our faith is not an abstract doctrine or philosophy, but a vital and full relationship with a person: Jesus Christ, the only begotten Son of God, who became man, was put to death, rose from the dead to save us, and is now living in our midst. Where can we encounter him? We encounter him in the church, in our hierarchical Holy Mother Church. It is the church that says today: "Behold the Lamb of God"; it is the church that proclaims him; it is in the church that Jesus continues to accomplish his acts of grace, which are the sacraments.[12]

(3) The church is open to all and has an open form beyond any binding cultural or spiritual center or structure. In this light, the gift and experience of the church constantly stretches beyond the human horizon to the infinite horizon of God.

(4) Given the location of the church in space and time, and beyond time,

---

[11]Pope Francis, *L'Osservatore Romano*, weekly edition in English, September 18, 2013, 8.

[12]Pope Francis, *The Joy of Discipleship: Reflections from Pope Francis on Walking with Christ* (Chicago: Loyola Press, 2016), 79.

its identity and mission must become Incarnational. It must be embodied in the very depth of history and embedded in the very arc and wounds in the flesh of history. This means that the church's life and mission must be experientially based, historically grounded, rooted in its Trinitarian center in order to be a faithful instrument for realizing the mission of God in Christ.

(5) The church is to be found in multiple sites of encounter. However, in the light of revelation and our human experience, and the reality of our world today, the sites inhabited by the poor and those searching for mercy—which is the whole of humanity and the entire cosmos—are the loci where the church is to be found.

These five moments in Pope Francis's thought represents a paradigm shift in Catholic ecclesiology whose meaning and impact will become more evident in the future. Indeed, they point to a way of being church and living as Christians in the world today that places the heart of the church in the heart of God and which places the heart of God into the heart of the world through the humble imitation and following of the Lord in the church.

Illuminative ecclesiology proposes that the church is a mirror in two ways.[13] First, it reflects to the world in all its joys and sorrows, hopes and despair, the merciful and compassionate face of a loving and faithful God. The God who is a Trinity is revealed to the world in the person, priorities, and practices of the Lord Jesus Christ and as continued in the church through the help of the Holy Spirit. Second, the church is a mirror through which the wounded faces of the world and the diversity of human experience and history are refracted back to God in all their beauty and complexities, as both a gift to be received and a mission to be accomplished in the light of God's eternal will for human and cosmic flourishing.

I have identified five practices of illuminative ecclesiology particularly evident in the ministry of Pope Francis:

First, the pope wants an accountable church that worships God and leads God's people deeper into communion with God and one another in the celebration of the mysteries of divine love. This begins by openness to

---

[13]This image of the church and Christian life as a mirror has been interpreted historically in theological reflection on the Transfiguration of the Lord with regard to how the church and Christians image God, reflect the glory of God, and contemplate this glory. We see this in such passages as 1 Corinthians 13:12 (now we see a dim reflection as in a mirror) and 1 Corinthians 3:18 (and we with unveiled faces reflecting as in mirror the brightness of the Lord). Raniero Cantalamessa identified two ways in which this reflection takes place in the life of Christians and the church—to *contemplate as in a mirror; to reflect as in a mirror*. The church exists to make possible the encounter with the glory of the Lord similar to the transformative experience of the disciples in the presence of the Lord in the Transfiguration. It is in this profound encounter with the Lord that the glory of the Lord is reflected in the condition of God's people, especially the poor. In the same measure, the glory of the Lord is reflected in the hunger for God and the poverty of the human condition, which share a similar condition to the weakness and brokenness of the Lord in his Incarnation, Passion, and Death. See Raniero Cantalamessa, *The Mystery of the Transfiguration*, trans. Marsha Daigle-Williamson (Cincinnati: St. Anthony Messenger Press, 2008), 6.

receiving creation and everything in it as a gift. The church then welcomes all people of God and uses the many gifts and charisms of all God's people to praise God.

Second, the pope wants a church of accompaniment, which mercifully walks side by side with humanity and the entire cosmos, especially the poor, through a loving and transformative ministry in the movement toward the realization of the reign of God in history and the celebration of the eschatological fruits of God's reign.

Third, through daily action—*transformata performare*—the church helps bring human history with all its ambiguities to wholeness and in the direction of fulfillment of the reign of God.

Fourth, the pope wants the church to be a servant of love, truth, and mercy through a dialogue with history. This proceeds in a spirit of openness to diversity and catholocity. The church is called to embrace the infinity of God's love and divine horizon in order to move in the future without being enslaved by the achievements and failings of the past or the fear of the present or the future. The church is a movement of hope, an assembly of people called to joyful living and faithful hope in the transformation of history and communion of friendship among the diverse people of God. The church has a vocation to trust in God's will and inspire all to be courageous witnesses to the gospel in transforming history through respect and reverence for others and the appreciation of history, world, and cultures beyond the limited veils of any particular cultural or sociological forms.

Fifth, the pope wants the church to provide an illuminative and safe path in the often confusing movement of men and women toward human fulfillment. This is carried on through a vulnerable mission to all the wounded people of God from the church's realization of its own wounds, which are constantly being healed through the grace and mercy of God. This way, God's dream of saving, healing, teaching, and liberating the world through God's Son and aided by the Spirit can be more effectively realized in history. The church brings light to the path of men and women; the church illumines the way so that men and women can see the beauty of life beyond the pockets of darkness and the cloud of gloom that sometimes blind our perception of beauty in creation. The illuminative path is the beautiful way of the church, which shines the light of love, compassion, and mercy to all creation and humanity, so that the world can be made whole and healed from the many wounds that afflict it.

Illuminative ecclesiology refers to a poor and merciful church that witnesses and proclaims the saving message of the gospel through accountability, accompaniment, and active presence in the world by the humble practice of dialogue and vulnerable mission to all, especially those wounded in life. I develop these five practices of illuminative ecclesiology in chapters 3, 4, and 5. I use many stories from the experiences of African Christians in the African social context to show what these practices look like in concrete human and cultural settings.

Many people will say that what one sees in the mirror is only what is displayed in it. This is true. However, the mirror is not the source of illumination. No image can be reflected in the mirror in the darkness. The light, which shines through the church as in a mirror, is the light of Christ. Thus, the church and Christians are mirrors to the extent that they allow this light to illumine them from within as the foundation on which everything is built (1 Cor 3:9–13). It is also self-reflective for the church to always ask how it can serve the faces in the mirror. That Christ is the "light of the nations" and "the fullness of revelation" were central affirmations in the opening words of *Lumen Gentium* (1). The council fathers wrote that "the light of Christ . . . is reflected on the face of the Church."[14] Jean Galot argues that the council document presents Christ as the light in order to emphasize the fact that the church has received this light as a gift and bears this gift as a reflection "in order to illuminate humanity."[15] Further in *Lumen Gentium* 15, the council after admitting the challenges of divisions in the worldwide church affirms with faith the need to pray in the hope that its children will be renewed and purified so that the "sign of Christ may shine more brightly over the face of the Church."

The Christological structure of Vatican II's ecclesiology is central in explicating the foundation and source of the light that the church shines to the world as in a mirror and how the face of God is reflected in the church. This is more concrete and performative when viewed in the light of the centrality of the Eucharist and the Paschal Mystery both as a gift and a mission for the church's communion and service to the world. *Laudato Si'* explicitly identified the Eucharist as "a source of light and motivation" for human care of the environment and all creation (236). According to then Joseph Cardinal Ratzinger:

A Christologically centered ecclesiology means understanding the church in terms of sacrament. More specifically, it means a Eucharistic ecclesiology. It means the inclusion [*Einordnung*] and subordination of human sociological systems in the fundamental order [*Grundordnung*] of the *communio*, as this develops from the Eucharist. . . . In the Eucharist the church is constantly born again from the pierced heart of the Lord."[16]

---

[14]See Jean Galot, "Christ: Revealer, Founder of the Church, and Source of Ecclesial Life," in *Vatican II: Assessment and Perspectives, Twenty-Five Years After (1962–1987)*, ed. Rene Latourelle (New York: Paulist Press, 1988), 1:385.

[15]Ibid., 385–86.

[16]Joseph Ratzinger, foreword to Maximilian Heinrich Heim, *Joseph Ratzinger: Life in the Church*

The church needs to constantly examine its teachings, preaching, pastoral life, laws, and structures to see whether it blurs that mirror in which the people of God wish to see the attractive face of a merciful and compassionate God (*GS*, 19). As Ormond Rush puts it, "The acknowledgment that the face of the church is not always resplendent with the light of Christ constitutes a fundamental concern in the overall reform agenda of Vatican II: that the face of the church would faithfully mirror the genuine face of the God whom she proclaims."[17] The reality of sin within the church is the reason why Vatican II calls for ongoing conversion in the church. It is also the reason why Pope Francis constantly calls the church today to a new way of being and living so that people can have a deeper encounter with God through the sacraments and different ministries in the church, which are like "open windows through which the light of God is given to us, streams which can draw God's very life."[18]

In this regard, it is important for the church to constantly remove the deadweight that it sometimes imposes on itself and its members, which make it impossible for the light to shine through the church. It is also important for the church to think of the shattered lives in the church and in the world. These wounded people are like shattered mirrors that can no longer reflect either their face to God or see the comforting face of God. We can also think of so many people who are marginalized whose faces are not reflected in the church as in a mirror. According to Pope Francis, "The Lord wants us to belong to a church that knows how to open her arms and welcome everyone, that is not a house for the few, but a house for everyone, where all can be renewed, transformed, sanctified by his love—the strongest and the weakest, sinners, the indifferent, those who feel discouraged or lost."[19]

In his commentary on Psalms 144–47, Augustine draws an important analogy that is helpful in developing this point about humanly constructed deadweight that sets the church on a darkling plain rather than on the path of light and life. Augustine speaks of the battle between David and Goliath (1 Sm 17:1–54) and makes a distinction between the armor that both warriors put on to defend themselves and for the fight (*Enarrations on the Psalms*,

---

and Living Theology (San Francisco: Ignatius Press, 2007), 2. See also *Pope Benedict XVI's Light of the World: The Pope, the Church, and the Signs of the Times*, in which he writes that "Paul understood the church precisely not as an institution, as an organization, but as a living organism, in which all the members work with and in relation to each other, in which they are all united because of Christ. . . . If every member receives the same Christ, then we are all really gathered in this new, risen body as the locus of a new humanity." *Pope Benedict XVI's Light of the World: The Pope, the Church, and the Signs of the Times*, trans. Michael J. Miller and Adrian Walker (San Francisco: Ignatius Press, 2010), 37.

[17]Ormond Rush, "Ecclesial Conversion after Vatican II: Renewing 'the Face of the Church' to Reflect 'the Genuine Face of God,'" in *Fifty Years On: Probing the Riches of Vatican II*, ed. David G. Schultenover (Collegeville, MN: Liturgical Press, 2015), 164.

[18]Pope Francis, *Joy of Discipleship*, 81–82.

[19]Pope Francis, *Church of Mercy*, 31.

144, 1–4). Goliath, the fearsome champion, is presented in verse 4 of the text in these words:

> His height was six cubits and a span. He had a bronze helmet on his
> head and wore a coat of scale armor of bronze weighing five thousand
> shekels; on his legs he wore bronze greaves, and a bronze javelin was
> slung on his back. His spear shaft was like a weaver's rod, and its iron
> point weighed six hundred shekels. His shield bearer went ahead of him.

These protective shields were supposed to frighten the fighters of Israel, protect Goliath, and grant him victory.

David was also robed with many layers of protective shields given to him by Saul (vv. 38–40). However, these protective layers became so heavy for David that he could not walk or attempt to fight Goliath clad in them. He eventually went to war without these protective shields, and with only five stones and faith in God he eventually won victory over the heavily clad champion, Goliath. Augustine sees the victory of David as the anticipation of the victory of Christ and his church in the coming age and the futility of humanly constructed identity, stratagems, and designs for implementing God's work in history.

My concern here is not to project the triumphalism of Augustine's allegorical interpretation of the story as the image of the church. Rather, I wish to highlight the underlying lesson that Augustine proposes about deadweights. Augustine proposes that in this earthly city, God wishes to bandage the wounds of humanity so that the disjointed limbs of those who are unwell may be restored (*Enarr. on Ps.*, 147, 7). Furthermore, God has provided "certain lights in the Church comforting our night; all of whom the Apostle said, 'In the midst of a crooked and perverse generation, among whom ye shine as lights in the world, holding the Word of life'" (*Enarr. on Ps.*, 147, 8).

However, the wounds of the world cannot be bandaged and the lights provided by God in the church will not shine forth and reflect in the church and in the world if the church is bogged down by deadweight. God can grant "a sort of light of wisdom" to the church to heal the blindness of people and the world. God can grant liberty so that "the fettered are set free, and those who are dashed down are lifted up." However, this can happen only if the pride and selfishness that are the roots of sin are not ravaging the church. Indeed, the shield of Goliath could not bring him victory; whereas David removed his shield and put on the shining armor of faith, hope, and love, which brought him ultimate victory.

Herein lies an important insight which is very important in seeing the church as a mirror and how and why sometimes what people see in that mirror is not the true face of Christ or the faces of the world being transformed in the church (*Enarr. on Ps.*, 146, 8). The structures of the church, the rules of the church, and its norms and regulations in areas such as marriage, criteria and conditions for ministry in the church, and for the reception of Holy Communion may sometimes be a deadweight, and instead of protecting the church or advancing the mission of God through the church, this will hamper it and become like a shattered mirror without light and without a true reflection of the face of God and of divine love and mercy. Illuminative ecclesiology is a way of being church that frees the church of deadweight so that it can more fully and effectively carry out its mission in the world. This insight is well brought out in the theologies of Balthasar and Congar in a beautiful and compelling way.

THEOLOGICAL FOUNDATIONS OF ILLUMINATIVE ECCLESIOLOGY IN BALTHASAR AND CONGAR

Some Catholics claim that there is an absence of strong theological backing for some of the priorities and practices of Pope Francis. In this section, I wish to demonstrate how two outstanding Catholic theologians, Yves Congar and Hans Urs von Balthasar, offer a foundation for illuminative ecclesiology that one can identify in Pope Francis. Congar and Balthasar offer significant insights on the theological aesthetics of illuminative ecclesiology with regard to the key question which this ecclesiology answers: What form of witnessing can I see in every instance of the life of Christians in their churches which points to God and shows the face of the world to God and the face of God to the world?

They both propose in different ways that this fundamental question cannot be properly answered if the church loses its form. Although they did not use the term "illuminative ecclesiology," one could identify the earliest indications of what I have been describing as the way of being church which should be present in every model of church, in the total ecclesiology proposed by Congar and satisfactory ecclesiology suggested by Balthasar. They both answer in their unique ways the question as to where the church is to be found and how the presence of the church in every moment of history brings about the realization of the reign of God. Balthasar and Congar published the books that form the basis of my exposition in 1952 (*Razing the Bastion*) and 1950 (*True and False Reform*) respectively. I am not sure how much influence they had on each other when writing these two books, but both are identified as *ressourcement* theologians, Congar directly and Balthasar indirectly.[20] Both were also identified by the then Cardinal Ratzinger as important voices whose theological discoveries and new insights helped bring new perspectives and theological openness to Vatican II.[21] Their rich theological insights and productions form an essential part of the theological currents that watered the spirit and intellect of Pope Francis on the reforms of the church proposed by Vatican II early in his theological formation with the Fiorito group in Argentina.[22]

However, their theologies of the church show a commitment to the following important directions in Catholic ecclesiology that influenced discussions at the council and in the drafting of *Lumen Gentium* at Vatican II and subsequent development in Catholic ecclesiology in the twentieth and twenty-first centuries, namely: (1) an insistence that a satisfactory ecclesiology should at the same time be a total ecclesiology; (2) an insistence that the church's life and mission should be both Christological and pneumatological and that its identity and mission are not the result of theological alignment and realignment of forces or ideological and cultural claims and social construction; (3) a distinction between the relativity of the church's structural elements vis-à-vis its essential form; the first (its structures) is variable while the second (its essential form) is central to its identity. Furthermore, they argue, each in his own way, that the structures exist to give life to the form and thus have a temporal and historical standing in the bigger scheme of things; (4) a commitment to taking full consideration of the church as a historical subject, touched by cultural forces and an emphasis on the church's vocation to enter into dialogue with history and the priority of love, community, holiness, service to the poor, and prophetic witnessing in all the church's life and mission.

The Beautiful Way of the Church in Balthasar

Hans Urs von Balthasar is regarded as one of the greatest Catholic theologians of the twentieth century.[23] His greatness lies especially in the depth of his thinking and the range of themes covered in his theological and literary

---

[20]See Gabriel Flynn, "*Ressourcement*, Ecumenism, and Pneumatology: The Contribution of Yves Congar to *Nouvelle Théologie*," 219–35, and Edward T. Oakes, "Balthasar and *Ressourcement*: An Ambiguous Relationship," 278–87, both in *Ressourcement: A Movement in Twentieth-Century Catholic Theology*, ed. Gabriel Flynn and Paul D. Murray (Oxford: Oxford University Press, 2012).

[21]Ratzinger, *Salt of the Earth*, 258.

[22]Austen Ivereigh, *The Great Reformer: Francis and the Making of a Radical Pope* (New York: Henry Holt, 2014), 92–94, 197–98.

[23]See Fergus Kerr, *Twentieth-Century Catholic Theologians: From Chenu to Ratzinger* (Oxford: Blackwell, 2006); R. R. Reno, "Theology after the Revolution," *First Things*, no. 173 (May 2007): 19; also David Moss and Edward Oakes, introduction to *The Cambridge Companion to Hans Urs von Balthasar*, ed. Edward T. Oakes and David Moss (Cambridge: Cambridge University Press, 2004), 1–7.

corpus. Balthasar became one of the greatest agents for the diffusion of Catholic thought in the Western world and beyond, both before and after Vatican II. In one of his last full-length interviews, he described his life's task in the following words:

> The activity of being a writer remains and will always remain, in the working-out of my life, a secondary function, something *faute de mieux*. At its center there is a completely different interest: the task of renewing the Church through the formation of new communities which unite the radical Christian life of conformity to the evangelical counsels of Jesus with existence in the midst of the world. . . . All my activity as a writer is subordinated to this task; if authorship had to give way before the urgency of the task of which I have spoken, to me it would not seem as if anything had been lost; no, much would have been gained. This is fundamentally obvious to one who lives in service of the cause of Jesus, the cause that concretely is the Church.[24]

Balthasar saw the goal of theology, borrowing from Origen, as *anima ecclesiastica and seeing the form, which is a vocation to see beauty*. In this regard, his theological calling was like being "the finger of John pointing to the fullness of revelation in Jesus Christ, which is unfolded in the immense fullness of its reception in the history of the Church, above all in the mediation and meditation of saints."[25] Balthasar writes further on the mission of theologians: "We need individuals who devote their lives to the glory of theology, that fierce fire burning in the dark night of adoration and obedience, whose abysses it illuminates."[26] It is the Lord who illumines the heart and mind of the theologian, just as the Lord illumines the heart of the church. The church is the light of the world because it is illumined by the Light of the Word (Jn 8:12; Mt 5:14).

What form of witnessing can I see in every instance of the life of Christians in their churches which points to God and shows the face of the world to God and the face of God to the world? The answer for Balthasar is not simply in the transformation of ecclesiastical structures. It is not simply a return to the sources of faith, an all too common concern in both pre– and post–Vatican II debates. It is a recovery of beauty, the form of the church.

---

[24]Hans Urs von Balthasar, "Another Ten Years—1975," in *The Analogy of Beauty: The Theology of Hans Urs von Balthasar*, ed. John Riches (Edinburgh: T. & T. Clark, 1986), 223.

[25]"Spirit and Fire: An Interview with Hans Urs von Balthasar," *Communio International Catholic Review* 22, no. 3 (Fall 2005): 574.

[26]Hans Urs von Balthasar, *Word and Redemption: Essays in Theology 2* (New York: Herder and Herder, 1964), 22. This quotation is also published in Hans Urs von Balthasar, *Explorations in Theology 1: The Word Made Flesh,* trans. A. V. Littledale with Alexander Dru (San Francisco: Ignatius Press, 1989), 160.

This means a humble surrender and immersion into that form in openness to how this form reveals itself as a ray that spreads throughout all that the church does and in its members and in the world. Balthasar proposes that the church can existentially become one single testimony to Christ because it is already gifted from its origin by the Lord and with the help of the Holy Spirit to bear witness to the Lord. Witnessing to its form—the Lord Jesus—is grounded on its foundation and objective constitution. Balthasar argues that people will not convert to Christ simply because of a magisterium, sacraments, a structure, a clergy, canon law, apostolic nunciatures, beautiful basilicas, gigantic ecclesiastical machinery, or simply by being enclosed in monasteries. The church's heart, he states, has been exposed to the world, and it must encounter the world daily and bring together the shattered mirrors of its past and present historical conditioning through a recovery of its true form.[27]

There is a departure or forgetfulness of this form in the history of the church. This is what in Balthasar's thinking is at the root of all and any crisis in the church because

> most of the Church's representatives remained immersed in their own tradition, vigorously restoring it once again at the end of the century, unconcerned with the expanded field of view. . . . The Church's sidelines—position and self-preoccupation have aroused a feeling of discomfort; indeed, this ancient Church which, out of its vast storehouse of the wisdom born of old age, continues to teach and admonish, evokes in the young a sense of unreality.[28]

People are searching for a church and a theology of church that describes the Christian life from the point of view of service and particularly of "sharing both in the shining and radiating" and in being consumed in the fire of divine love and love of neighbor. People want a church that calls them to plunge into the demands of the gospel and that invites them to model their lives after the example of Christ rather than "clinging tightly to structures of thought."[29]

Christ as the center of history is the existential center for the church, the Christian, and the world. Jesus can share the goodness, beauty, truth and love of God with the church and with people because his gospel can penetrate all cultures and all human hearts by opening windows "on the transcendental,

---

[27]Hans Urs von Balthasar, *Razing the Bastions: On the Church in This Age* (San Francisco: Ignatius Press, 1993), 99–102.

[28]Ibid., 18.

[29]Ibid., 69.

joining together webs of human sensibility so that people can apprehend the transcendental in their full reality."[30] Christ is the form of the church. This is not a Christomonism that reduces the church to an extension of Christ that often denies the space between created reality and God. It also rejects any form of ecclesial transcendentalism that suppresses the human and historical in such a way that it becomes less visible and active in the shaping of the historical conditioning of the church as a pilgrim. It is an affirmation of the origin of the church, its destiny, the theological aesthetics of its priorities and practices. It also highlights the church's relative and representative function in bringing about the reign of God in such a way that God sees and loves in the church and its members what God sees and loves in God's Son.

In *A Theology of History*, Balthasar points out that Jesus Christ is the concrete form through which the universal love of God is made manifest in the church. "The church, then, must be conceived of as having her center not within herself, as an external, worldly organization, but outside herself in Christ who engenders her."[31] It is through obedience and surrender to Christ through exigencies of history that the church can be faithful, credible, and effective in history. This requires the imitation of Christ by the church and its members. However, the disciples of the Lord cannot choose and drop this or that aspect of the life of the church, but must embrace the whole Christ. However, it is the Holy Spirit that will guide the church in embracing the life of Christ and thus becoming radiant to the world. The Holy Spirit disposes of "the infinite wealth in the life of Christ that it can blossom out in the variousness of history, and that at the same time history, thus made subject to this norm, shall be able to discover the fullness within itself."[32]

Christoph Schonborn's commentary on Balthasar's *Razing the Bastions* captures the essential message of this book that is central to the theological aesthetics of illuminative ecclesiology. He argues as follows: the form of the revelation of the love of God is in the wounded and broken Lord on the Cross—this is the path of renunciation that the Lord has chosen in order to show the face of God to the world. This renunciation was already present at the beginning of his earthly ministry, when the Lord rejected the devil's temptation. The power of God is revealed in poverty and vulnerability, thus the Crucified Lord

> does not need to disclose its power in order to convince. It is suffi-
> ciently full of light in order to be clear; it bears its evidential character

---

[30] Aidan Nichols, *A Key to Balthasar: Hans Urs von Balthasar on Beauty, Goodness and Truth* (Grand Rapids, MI: Baker Academic, 2011), 20.

[31] Hans Urs von Balthasar, *Explorations in Theology II: Spouse of the Word* (San Francisco: Ignatius Press, 1991), 34.

[32] Hans Urs von Balthasar, *A Theology of History* (San Francisco: Ignatius Press, 1994), 102.

in itself. This is why the Church needs no bastions in order to be the "city set on a hill." Her form of existence is most intelligible when it is like his [Christ's] form of existence.[33]

On the centrality of Christ for the church, Balthasar writes as follows:

Christ, by contrast, is the form because he is the content. This holds absolutely, for he is the only Son of the Father, and whatever he establishes and institutes has meaning only through him, is dependent only on him and is kept vital only by him. If for a single moment we were to look away from him and attempt to consider and understand the church as an autonomous form, the church would not have the slightest plausibility.[34]

A church that does not remain in the Lord and that does not reflect the priorities and practices of the Lord, in the theology of Balthasar, is a church that lacks plausibility as a religious institution. It will also lack power for influencing cultures from within and will lose all credibility and all moral authority and spiritual power.

According to Balthasar, the form of the church is a light in the world; "for this reason the church fathers often compared the church's light with the light of the moon, borrowed from the sun and showing its relativity most clearly in all its phases. The plausibility of Christianity stands and falls with Christ's, something which has in essence always been acknowledged."[35] In the Creed, we profess that Jesus is "light from light"; already this reminds us that the church or Christians are not the source of the light that we are called to shine to the world. As we read in the prologue of Saint John's Gospel, "the Word (Jesus Christ) is the true light that enlightens all people"; "he is a light that shines in the darkness"; "he is that life which gives light to all people" and the light that darkness cannot overcome. Later in John 8:12, Jesus will call himself "the light of the world," and then this quality which he attributes to himself he directly attributes to the church in Matthew's Gospel: "You are the light of the world" (Mt 5:14).

The church and Christians have no light other than the light of Christ; we are called children of the light (Eph 5:5; Phil 2:15; 1 Thes 5:5) because of the life of God that we have received through Christ, and the church and Christians are called to always and everywhere reflect the attitude,

---

[33]Christoph Schonborn, foreword to Hans Urs von Balthasar, *Razing the Bastions: On the Church in This Age*, trans. Brian McNeil (San Francisco: Communio Books, Ignatius Press, 1993), 15.

[34]Hans Urs von Balthasar, *The Glory of the Lord: A Theological Aesthetics: Seeing the Form*, trans. Erasmo Leiva-Merikakis (San Francisco: Ignatius Press, 1982), 1:463.

[35]Ibid.

mind, and example of the Lord in all we do or say in order to be his light in the world. In this regard, what is important according to Balthasar is "the discernment of what is Christian" in every moment of Christian life; "for the Christian there is no 'neutral' form of existence, which is not affected or illuminated by the mystery of absolute love, and whose fortuitous and doubtful nature is not justified or made meaningful by it. . . . Why? Because God became flesh."[36]

People will embrace the church not because of its self-attribution and claims, or the beauty of its liturgies and ordered ranks, but rather when people encounter a Catholic who communicates the Christian message and the face of Christ by the quality of his or her Christian witness as a light in the world. It is only when the lives of Christians—the "inner form" of the church—are attractive and illuminative will people come to see the church as a living testimony to the imitation of Christ rather than simply a structure, system, institution, or social reality with divine claims. Any discussion of Balthasar's ecclesiology will start with Christology, on one hand, and the integrity of theology, contemplation, and spirituality, on the other. Balthasar, as Adrian Walker shows clearly, distinguishes himself from most other contemporary theologians of the Catholic tradition by the radical consistency of his commitment to starting theology from, and letting it be normed by, the uniquely Christian revelation of God's Trinitarian love in Christ. The form of Christ is the light of love that shines from the Cross and that shone in the lives of so many touched by Christ in the course of his earthly ministry, especially the poor, the marginalized, the rejected of society, and those who are crying for God's mercy and healing.

According to Adrian Walker, Balthasar's starting point of theology as "love alone" is not an antiphilosophical theological positivism. This "love alone" is a light in the world that draws attention not to itself but to Christ, the Source of this light. It is a light in the church that is meant for the world because it has apostolic, redemptive, and missionary significance.[37] On the contrary, Walker argues that Balthasar's project in the *Trilogy* is to maintain Christological love as the first principle of theology while developing a philosophy with a truly metaphysical range, whose intrinsic openness to that love secures the connection between the uniqueness of Jesus Christ and universal human reason in its quest for first principles. This Christological first love should be foundational for the church's identity and mission.[38] In other words, "love alone" should be the Christian call to duty; it should

---

[36]Hans Urs von Balthasar, *The Moment of Christian Witness*, trans. Richard Beckley (San Francisco: Ignatius Press, 1994), 30.

[37]Balthasar, *Explorations in Theology II: Spouse of the Word,* 35.

[38]Adrian J. Walker, "Love Alone: Hans Urs von Balthasar as a Master of Theological Renewal," *Communio International Catholic Review* 22, no. 3 (Fall 2005): 520–21.

be the battle cry of Christian mission; and the song on the lips of every Christian, and the narrative of anyone who encounters the church.[39]

Razing the Bastions offers a fourfold structure—departure, descent, endurance, contact—which is helpful in understanding how "love alone" can be a light that shines from the church and guides the movement that the church at every phase of its history is called to make. First, there is a departure, which represents a twofold movement of the church away from its true form, the Lord Jesus. The second departure is the church's movement away from the world. This forgetfulness of the form of the church—its coming from the Lord, and its commitment to the world—tends to lead the church away from its mission and identity. In both instances, the church constructs what Balthasar calls *bastions*, which may hold it back from posing the questions that former generations never posed because the historical conditions and situations were different.[40] Balthasar's proposal is that the Lord through the Holy Spirit continues to "illuminate new depths of revelation from century to century" in the church. This depends, as he argues, "on the awareness that we have of our Christianity,"[41] especially of the calling of the church to bear witness to Christ. The church can do this by being open to the effervescence of the Spirit as it immerses itself in history, interpreting and responding to the signs of the times and understanding "how to move and to make use of herself and her own structures, like living limbs, in a new and different way."[42]

Ultimately, Balthasar offers some of the foundations of theological aesthetics of illuminative ecclesiology found in the teaching and ministry of Pope Francis. As I read through the teachings of Pope Francis, I could see immediately the finger of Balthasar in various places—the choice of title for Pope Francis's first encyclical (*Light of Faith*) is a title of a chapter in *The Glory of the Lord*; the structure of his second encyclical *The Joy of the Gospel*, follows the same structure as *The Glory of the Lord*: there is first a focus on the centrality of God in Christ—the form; a discussion of the gift of the church, and then the application of the gospel values to history and cultural contexts. There is also in Pope Francis an insistence that the form of the church has been lost; there is a forgetfulness of its identity, which has affected the mission. In a series of instructions in 2013 on the four marks of the church, Pope Francis underlines this Christological foundation of ecclesiology in discovering the identity and mission of the church when he noted that the beauty of the church is only reflected when Christ is present in its life and structure, when he said,

---

[39]Balthasar, *Moment of Christian Witness*, 27.
[40]Balthasar, *Razing the Bastions*, 31–32.
[41]Ibid., 32.
[42]Ibid., 37.

Our faith, the church that Christ willed, is not based on an idea; it is not based on a philosophy. It is based on Christ himself. And the church is like a plant that over the long centuries has grown, has developed, has borne fruit, yet her roots are planted firmly in Christ and that fundamental experience of Christ which the apostles had, chosen and sent out by Jesus, reaching all the way to us. From this little plant to our day, this is how the church has spread everywhere throughout the world.[43]

Even though Vatican II did not devote a special document on Christology, one can see that since the council, the Christological foundation of the church has been emphasized in the teaching of all the popes. It was the central theme of the first encyclical of Pope Paul VI (*Ecclesiam Suam*). At the beginning of the third millennium, building on the message of his first encyclical (*Redemptor Hominis*) and the teaching of his Bull of Indication for the Great Jubilee (*Incarnationis Mysterium*), Pope John Paul II made it clear that for the future, the church must begin afresh from Christ. He captures this message so clearly when he wrote in *Novo Millennio Ineunte*:

No, we shall not be saved by a formula but by a Person, and the assurance which he gives us: *I am with you!* It is not therefore a matter of inventing a "new program." The program already exists: it is the plan found in the Gospel and in the living Tradition, it is the same as ever. Ultimately, it has its centre in Christ himself, who is to be known, loved and imitated, so that in him we may live the life of the Trinity, and with him transform history until its fulfillment in the heavenly Jerusalem. This is a program which does not change with shifts of times and cultures, even though it takes account of time and culture for the sake of true dialogue and effective communication. This program for all times is our program for the Third Millennium. (*Novo Millennio Ineunte*, 29)

What we find in these teachings is similar to Balthasar's development of the Christological foundation of a satisfactory ecclesiology. The church's identity can only be "luminous and illuminating" if it "focuses attention on the formal object of faith" and if the church begins a conscious effort toward "dismantling old fortifications" that continue to be emphasized even in the post–Vatican II church.[44] However, this formal object has already been made manifest in the Son, who has said that he can only be found in

---

[43]Pope Francis, *Church of Mercy*, 37.
[44]Balthasar, *Explorations in Theology II: Spouse of the Word*, 40.

the least of the brethren, those who are in need of mercy. The church must be close to the illuminator who is Christ by being close to the poor who illumine the church with the splendor of Christ. This way, the church can in turn illumine the life of the poor by bringing the light of love, joy, mercy, compassion, and healing through the life of Christ which the church carries.[45] The church thus must walk with people and do "more hearing than seeing, more groping, feeling, scenting, than being immovably assured,"[46] because the one who walks is the one who is alive. The church walks even with unsteady steps in the chaos of life; it sees the footprints of God in all human realities; it shines the light of Christ to a wounded world in search of truth. However, Balthasar proposes that

> if the church is properly to be all this and do all this, one can look calmly only if the lighthouse from whose tower the beams sweep over the turbulent waters is at its base washed by these same waves; if the open intransigence, to which the church is called, is itself paid for with a hidden endurance, a genuine involvement with all the forms of human experience of world, not excluding the most alien forms, so that not only the sinners but also the saints, also the church's members . . . are able to join Christ their head in saying, the *nil humanum mihi alienum puto* [nothing human is alien to me].[47]

People come to the church to see Jesus and be touched by the hand of God; they bring their wounds and pains to God so that they can be transfigured by identifying their wounds with the bleeding side of the Lord. Balthasar insists that the life and structure of the church should always be normed by its Christological foundation in order for the church to illumine the city of God through its openness to the illumination of Christ. As Robert Imbelli writes:

> For, as the title of *Lumen Gentium* makes abundantly clear, Christ alone is the light of the world. As with Benedict, so with Francis: the ecclesiology of both is foundationally Christocentric. Indeed, in his remarkable pre-conclave address to the meetings of the cardinals, Bergoglio spoke of the *mysterium lunae*. The only mission of the Church is to be like the moon: reflecting the greater light, the light who is Christ. But, then, he invoked de Lubac to lament that when the church

---

[45]Balthasar, *Glory of the Lord*, 147–55.
[46]Balthasar, *Razing the Bastions*, 81.
[47]Ibid., 87.

becomes centered on itself, ceasing to reflect Christ, it succumbs to that spiritual worldliness that is its mortal danger.[48]

Congar: Not the Walls but the Faithful Are the Church

According to Yves Congar,

The mystery, the Father's plan, has as its center Jesus Christ, but includes also all that depends on him. Jesus, in his lordship over time, sums up in his own consciousness all those "Christian" values which his Mystical Body is called upon to live out and know through the passage of the centuries, thereby attaining its full stature. . . . We ourselves cannot try to understand the "mystery" by starting at its luminous heart; on the contrary, we can only arrive at this heart through the communion of the faithful, and chiefly through communion with the apostles, the first believers, Jesus' companions and witnesses.[49]

The centrality of Jesus Christ for the identity and mission of the church is an important theme in Congar. This has an intrinsic connection to the relationship that binds all God's people in the world church "in fellowship with God and with one another."[50] The church is the people of God, not the structures, whether physical or the hierarchy, but "the holy company of those who live in righteousness."[51] The church is like a beautiful garden cultivated, nourished, and watered by the Lord Jesus Christ through two streams, one coming from the apostolic ministry, the sacraments, and another from the personal life of the people of God who have received the gifts.[52] Those who are searching for a theological foundation for Pope Francis's constant unease with the power tussle in the Roman curia, with clericalism, and legalism in the church, and enslavement to structures and systems without openness to the surprises of the Holy Spirit need only look at Congar's thought.

Between 1945 and 1954 alone, Congar published more than 350 texts, including seven books, more than 150 theological articles, and over 100 articles in the popular press, so it will be hard to summarize his whole

---

[48]Robert P. Imbelli, "Benedict and Francis," in *Go into the Streets! The Welcoming Church of Pope Francis*, ed. Thomas P. Rausch, SJ, and Richard R. Gaillardetz (New York: Paulist Press, 2016), 17.

[49]Yves Congar, *Tradition and Traditions* (London: Burns and Oates, 1966), 268.

[50]Yves Congar, *Lay People in the Church* (Westminster, MD: Newman Press, 1956), 22.

[51]Yves Congar, *Christians Active in the World*, trans. P. J. Hepburne-Scott (New York: Herder and Herder, 1968), 29.

[52]See, for instance, Paul Lakeland, *The Liberation of the Laity: In Search of an Accountable Church* (New York: Continuum, 2003), 52.

work in a brief account of this kind.[53] My concern here is to identify three important aspects of Congar's work on the renewal of Catholic ecclesiology that could help me give a theological account of illuminative ecclesiology in Pope Francis and how this approach to being church can help the church to live true to its identity and be faithful to its mission. These three aspects are some significant features of Congar's theological proposal of a total ecclesiology, namely: the commitment to history and anthropology both for doing theology and understanding the identity and the mission of the church; the instrumental nature of ecclesial structure vis-à-vis the life of the church; and the distinctive vocation of the church and Christians to be active in a divided and wounded world.

In *A History of Theology*, Congar argues that unless one appreciated the theological roots and development of theology itself there is no way one could appreciate and respond to the theological issues that confront the church today.[54] Theologies—whether of the church or of God—are not timeless. Thus, the attempt to engage history and modernity against the "catholic catastrophism" that rejected everything in the modern world as evil or as born out of resistance to magisterial teaching was a central thrust of Congar's theology.[55] According to Congar, the first demand in doing theology is a renewal of sources, which nourishes theological thought. Through a return to the sources of scripture, the fathers and the medieval theologians, Congar establishes the bases for the major changes in the church's self-understanding at the theological level and in its pastoral ministry.[56] This return to the sources in the theology of Congar is very Christological: "Now for the Christian to return to their sources is the same thing as to be re-centered, it is always to return to Jesus Christ, the one center of Christianity. It is to reconsider the meaning of the coming, the presence and the return of Christ, for those are the three great affirmations of the gospel about him."[57]

Congar also paid attention to how cultural forces—what he calls "the human reality and terrestrial mode of the church"[58]—affect theological development. This serious engagement with culture and history was an essential character of the *nouvelle théologie*, which was opposed to the baroque theology preferred and imposed by the hierarchical church from Pope Pius IX to Pope Pius XII. Congar's approach was grounded in the

---

[53]See Rose M. Beal, *Mystery of the Church, People of God: Yves Congar's Total Ecclesiology as a Path to Vatican II* (Washington, DC: Catholic University of America Press, 2014), 51.

[54]Yves Congar, *A History of Theology*, trans. and ed. Hunter Guthrie (New York: Doubleday, 1968), 12–18.

[55]On the idea of "catastrophic eschatology" see Joseph A. Komonchak, "Modernity and the Construction of Roman Catholicism," *Cristianesimo nella Storia* 18 (1997): 360.

[56]Ibid.

[57]Congar, *Christians Active in the World*, 39.

[58]*Bulletin d'Ecclesiologie*, 552. Cited in Beal, *Mystery of the Church, People of God*, 18.

realization that when theology is unmoored from its historical mediation and Trinitarian center, it becomes a dry positive faith affirmation of revelation of the things of God, which creates a disjuncture between the rituals and doctrines and the human and cultural recipients of what is revealed.[59]

In sketching the lines of a theology of the church, Congar proposes an open-minded, receptive, and critical approach, which not only draws from the sources of faith but also embraces an adequate anthropological structure in order to give an account of the multiple layers of the identity and mission of the church as it interacts with the human and historical subjects in what constitutes what he calls "total ecclesiology."[60] Congar's commitment to history includes, among other things, a conviction that the church is a historical subject that has to develop and "make progress in the world along with the world,"[61] integrating the revealed facts, "insights from history," and human and cultural experiences;[62] fresh adaptations, new solutions, openness to new values dictated by new forces, which are no longer coming from one central cultural fortress, but "exceed the variety of types and experiences expressed in different places."[63]

Congar's commitment to developing a total ecclesiology leads him to the search for "integral ecclesiology," "an ecclesiology truly complete," and an "ecclesiological synthesis," which gives birth to "a solidly framed ecclesiology."[64] Such an ecclesiology is capable of bringing together all the dimensions of the church in a whole—structure and life, gift and task, secular and sacred, spiritual and active witnessing to the faith in the world, the hierarchy and the laity, and the Catholic Church and other churches, the Roman heartland and the margins, and communion in the church as people of God and individual freedom. Total ecclesiology concentrates not in an idealized notion of church, but on how the mystery of divine grace constitutes God's people in communion with the Trinity and in the concrete life of the church. This, he argues, is not simply a focus on the human or cultural elements dictated by historical and cultural forces, but an immersion into the supernatural mystery of the church as gift. However, the life

---

[59]Frank Fehmers, ed., *The Crucial Questions* (London: Newman Press, 1969). In this short work, the editor interviewed many leading theologians after the Second Vatican Council, including Congar, Danielou, Chenu, Rahner, Kung, Balthasar, and Schillebeeckx on the crucial issues that faced Catholic theology after the council. The quote of Congar given in the introductory part of the book is: "Difficulties of faith . . . arise from the lack of correspondence between the forms of doctrine, of cult and of ecclesiastical structures and the realities which they are meant to represent. . . . Now the whole church is in a more or less radically questioning mood" (6).

[60]Congar, *Lay People in the Church*, xxxii.

[61]Yves Congar, *True and False Reform in the Church*, trans. Paul Philibert (Collegeville, MN: Liturgical Press, 2011), 148.

[62]Ibid., 11.

[63]Ibid., 148.

[64]Beal, *Mystery of the Church, People of God*, 23.

of the church is a mystery of love and "this mystery must shine through everywhere within what is human, so that the eternal and divine structure of the church can be felt as everywhere present."[65]

The dialectic of structure and life is foundational to Congar's development of total ecclesiology. According to Timothy MacDonald, "an exaggerated emphasis on the aspect of the identity of the structure and life on the one hand, or on their non-identity on the other, seriously jeopardizes the potential that these categories possess to be foundational of ecclesiology."[66] However, Congar proposes the norming of these identities of form and structure by how they lead to Christ and make possible the flourishing of the baptismal gifts of all the people of God. According to him, "a sound theology of the laity demands a reconnecting of structure and life in order that this theology manifests the fullness of the apostolic church."[67] He sees the challenge in the church's movement away from life and human activity in its concreteness to enslavement to external forms. The institutions and structures in the church exist to give life to the church and bring about fellowship and friendship for the people of God.[68]

As a result of this, Congar argues that for many Christians "the external forms of the church have become a barrier that screens out not only the gospel and God but also the mystery of the church itself."[69] He gives a further insight into why this is the case when he noted,

> Many of our contemporaries are returning to a Christianity rooted in its sources. They stumble over the difficulties that the church poses for them, but they know that outside this church, both historically and dogmatically, they cannot find the Gospel. What turns them off is not Christianity but the Christian world which contains so many non-Christian elements within its structures, inspired by a paternalistic quest for influence—even power, a bourgeois attachment to money etc. If only we could remake the human face of the church and help it appear more like the church of Christ![70]

Congar noted that many expressions of the life of the church, which emerged in the course of history, have become so entrenched structurally that the church forgets that they are of relative value. Therefore, he proposes

---

[65]Congar, *True and False Reform*, 11.
[66]Timothy MacDonald, *The Ecclesiology of Yves Congar: Foundational Theme* (Lanham, MD: University Press of America, 1984), 14.
[67]Congar, *Lay People in the Church*, xxxiv, cited in MacDonald, *Ecclesiology of Yves Congar*, 89.
[68]See Congar, *Lay People in the Church*, 103–4.
[69]Congar, *True and False Reform*, 49.
[70]Ibid., 50.

that the church must make a distinction between what J. Folliet refers to as "organised elements of a social reality," that is, the "ecclesial realities" which are historically conditioned and the means for realizing the form and life of the church and realizing her mission. This means, for Congar, the priority of the life of the church, fellowship, and deep encounter with God in the church over its structural elements. This is because according to him: "The organization is for the sake of the organism, and 'functions' are for the sake of life, as the body is for the sake of the soul, as its expression and its instrument."[71]

Questions about where the church is or what the church does cannot be answered by pointing to the magnificence of churches, basilicas, and beautiful liturgies or through the absolutization of the church's structures. Following Congar's theology, the answer cannot be found simply by re-forming structures or through a reaffirmation of canonical and pastoral practices. Congar argues strongly on what he thinks the church needs to do: "What is in question is not just tracing an inappropriate form back to its original source but inventing new forms that go beyond the given patterns of action, based on the deep tradition of an always living church under the stewardship of the magisterium."[72]

Congar adopts the framework of the phenomenological personalism of Maurice Blondel in exploring the relation between immanence and transcendence (the *ad intra* and *ad extra* aspects of the church) in his explication of the dynamics of the structure of the church, which is a gift from God, and the life of the people of God in the church and in the world, which should flourish within this structure. According to Michael A. Conway, "Through his treatment of action, Blondel recovered—even for philosophy in the positive tradition—the subjective, the personal, and the historical, not merely as categories of reflexive thought but as living realities that always go beyond the determinations of explicit formulation."[73] Richard McBrien proposes that what Blondel achieved was the unification of philosophy and theology without sacrificing human freedom and autonomy to faith's hold on the subject. We are subjects constantly exercising our freedom through our daily choices and action within history. Human autonomy means that every free person is involved in the construction and perception of the object. But the human thrust to be and to do does not settle once and for all the quest for human fulfillment or the desire for transcendence, nor does it bring the

---

[71]Yves Congar, *Divided Christendom: A Catholic Study of the Problem of Reunion* (London: Centenary Press, 1939), 86.

[72]Congar, *True and False Reform*, 52.

[73]Michael A. Conway, "Maurice Blondel and *Ressourcement*," in *Ressourcement: A Movement for Renewal in Twentieth-Century Catholic Theology*, ed. Gabriel Flynn and Paul D. Murray (Oxford: Oxford University Press, 2012), 70.

human person to that end which he or she desires. There is, as a result, a demand for an openness of the human will to the supernatural destiny ascribed to it by the Lord Jesus Christ through his Incarnation.[74] How can this human thrust and thirst for God be enabled through the structures in the church? How can these structures help bring out the light in the world and in the heart of people? How can revelation become explicit in history? This dynamic impulse in the interaction between the acting person in history and the "revealed facts" inspired Congar to pay more attention to the movement of spirit in history and how the structures in the church enhance the agency of the Christian to be active in the world as a faithful disciple of the poor man of Galilee.

Congar discovers in the dialectic of structure and life the dynamics between the supernatural saving reality mediated through the structures of the church and the reception of these realities in the concrete lives and pastoral contexts of people who are summoned by God. The structures have a mediating and instrumental function. They do not exist as merely juridical forms frozen in time. On the contrary, they exist to form a community of the beloved called and shaped by God's love, which was revealed before Christ in figures, but fulfilled in the Incarnation and Paschal Mystery and continued as a promise in the church under the guidance of the Holy Spirit. The church is a dynamic community of love and life made up of free acting persons who are touched by the flow of history and the graces of God. God through grace is operative in the self-realization of the mission of the church, and in the witness of individuals themselves and in their active witness in the world.

As Timothy MacDonald argues, there is in Congar's theology of church a unity of identity and nonidentity between structure and life, on the one hand, and a nonidentity of both, on the other hand. An overemphasis on the former would lead to viewing the constituents of faith—for example, the deposit of faith, deposit of sacraments, and governing authority—as absolutes in themselves. When this happens, MacDonald continues, the divine is thus exaggerated without due attention to the historicity of the mediating structures. The result, he argues, will be a static church and a collapse of the eschatological realities into their mediating structures. This denies the truth of the church as the living reality between the Pentecost and the Parousia. However, if we lay undue emphasis on the historical, we lose the unifying key, which the eschatological mission of the church offers to the sometimes disjunctive and diachronic prism that the world and history present. There is the need to hold everything in balance within a totality

---

[74]See "Blondel, Maurice," in Richard P. McBrien, *Encyclopedia of Catholicism* (New York: HarperCollins, 1995), 186.

where the structures and life give form to the witnessing and proclamation in the church, which reflect the priorities and practices of Jesus Christ.[75] This total ecclesiology, which integrates both structure and life, according to Congar, will lead the church and its members to become people who "learn and receive from others and from history," just as history and the world "learn and receive" from the church and its members; there is an intimate melange of these realities, which is always "in a state of hypothesis."[76]

In *The Mystery of the Church*, Congar underlines the two moments in the body of Christ in order to explain the relationship between structure and life—the structuration and animation in realizing God's whole purpose, which is "to make the human race, created in his image, a living, spiritual temple in which he not only dwells but to which he communicates himself and in turn receives from it the worship of a wholly filial obedience."[77] Congar argues that the work of the Holy Spirit brings to realization within the Christian in succeeding ages what Christ did and established for us in a single occasion at the time of the Incarnation. There is then the objective redemption (which relates to the structures of the church) and the subjective redemption (which everyone is empowered to achieve by virtue of the merits of the redemption), which come to every Christian. The structure must be dynamic enough to make room for human freedom and the exercise of people's charism and cultural diversity so that this subjective redemption to be accomplished on the basis of individual effort is supported by the community.[78]

The mission of the church is to build up the people of God in faith (1 Thes 5:11; 2 Cor 8:1; Rom 14:19), that is, "to build Christ in men [*sic*], to increase the spread of the knowledge of his gospel, to strengthen others, to deepen their spiritual life, to help them progress in their fidelity to God, in his holy service, in obedience to his will and in strong filial love for the Absolute which is God."[79] In this regard, the church is all of us; building up the temple of God is everyone's business. But a "very inadequate notion" of the church as an institution, an ideological system, and a collection of rites have all limited the understanding of the identity and the mission of the church.[80] This is why Congar emphasizes that every Christian has the same dignity:

---

[75]See MacDonald, *Ecclesiology of Yves Congar*, 89–90, 279–84.

[76]Congar, *Christians Active in the World*, 146.

[77]Yves Congar, *The Mystery of the Temple*, trans. Reginald F. Trevett (Westminster, MD: Newman Press, 1962), ix.

[78]See Victor Dunne, *Prophecy in the Church: The Vision of Yves Congar* (New York: Peter Lang, 2000), 50–52.

[79]Congar, *Mystery of the Temple,* 171.

[80]Ibid., 171–72.

The whole body is animated and indwelled by the Holy Spirit. But the Church is an organism, that is to say, a body having different functions, where each part is animated in view of its own being and to perform its special work to the advantage of the whole. . . . The Church is an organism. All the members are living and animated, but each according to what he is and to perform what he is called to do within the body. That is the law of the Church's being and which regulates its growth.[81]

This dignity is not only for Christians because the church has both a visible and a secret aspect and includes the whole of humanity, which makes up this temple "whose stones are quarried" from its "unknown beginnings." Hence Augustine's famous words: "Many seem to be within who are in reality without and others seem to be without who are in reality within."[82]

In another work, *Power and Poverty in the Church*, Congar returns to these essential points, which more concretely could help a modern reader of present history of the church to understand some of the challenges and resistance to the reforms of Pope Francis for a poor and merciful church in some parts of the Catholic Church, namely:

1. In order to understand the mystery of the church and enter into this mystery, we must move away from seeing ecclesiastical realities (hierarchy, sacraments) as supra-temporal and atemporal. This, he argues, is why "we find it so difficult to try to imagine new forms, a new style, for these sacred realities; sometimes we even dismiss the attempt as presumptuous and idle."[83]

2. Emphasis on careerism and exaggerated clerical culture (clericalism) widen the rift between what Congar calls hierarchology and laicology. This attitude holds the church in bondage when priests, bishops, and the pope appear to be remote and removed from the people they serve, driven by what Pope Francis calls a mentality of princes. There is thus a totally different reality of service in the early church from what obtains in today's church. In the early church, unlike in our day, "The church leaders were all the more conscious of their authority in that they saw it as the vehicle of the mystery of that salvation which God wishes to accomplish in his church. They wanted to be, and know that they were, moved by the Spirit, but they also knew

---

[81] Ibid., 36.

[82] Augustine, Sermo, 354, 2, 2 (PL, 39, 1564); *Enarr. on Ps.*, 24 (25), 2 (36, 189), cited in Congar, *Mystery of the Temple*, 197.h

[83] Yves Congar, *Power and Poverty in the Church*, trans. Jennifer Nicholson (Baltimore: Helicon, 1964), 14.

that the spirit inhabits the Christian community and in the exercise of their authority they remained closely linked to the community."[84]

3. Commitment to studying and appreciating the historical development of the church allows us to find the true face of Christ in the church. "Through familiarity with historical forms we can distinguish more clearly the permanence of the essential and the variation of forms; we can locate the absolute and the relative more exactly and better remain true to the absolute while we shape the relative to the needs of the time."[85]

The final point worth noting about how Congar's theology offers a good foundation for understanding illuminative ecclesiology is what he says about the role of the church and Christians in the world. The foundation of the companionship that should govern all activities in the church is "Christian charity and human friendship."[86] Like Balthasar, Congar proposes that love is the central thing for the church and governs all relations in the church as an absolute value. This love flows from embracing in faith the existence of God as source of love and the love of God which is the ground of being of the human person. Charity should also flow from truth and be oriented to the respect and upholding of the dignity of the human person.[87] The first condition for genuine reform in the church without schism for Congar is the primacy of charity and of pastoral concerns that emerge from this love. This love as service is the source and motivation of Christian witnessing and outreach from everyone in the church to the community and the world.

Congar mentions specific dimensions of this service as witnessing, an aesthetics of pastoral service and proclamation that one can see in the words and deeds of Pope Francis. According to Congar, the person who wishes to bring reform in the church is a "'twice born' person, aware of his mission, captivated by his idea"; he is also "solitary" as many might not share his or her idea. He or she is also for the most part uncomfortable with the state of affairs and does not feel himself or herself at home in the concrete church. This is particularly true if the church is bogged down by deadweight and worn down by what Congar calls "pharisaism," that is, a situation in the church wherein religious observance becomes absolutized to the detriment of the spiritual goods of persons; legalism and bureaucratic administration are given priority over sacramental life; and living spiritual

---

[84]Ibid., 46.
[85]Ibid., 14.
[86]Congar, *Christians Active in the World*, 147.
[87]Ibid.

realities are reduced to things.[88] The reformer, therefore, is also a simpli-
fier—not because the person wants to water down the faith, but because
the person wishes that the Christian life could flourish more in freedom.
The reformer ultimately is motivated more by pastoral concern that touches
people's hearts than by a quest for order through a theological system or
metaphysical structure. The ultimate goal is holiness of life and the active
witnessing to divine love in the world. [89]

This was also central in Balthasar's theology in *Razing the Bastions*. Hans
Urs von Balthasar argues that the reform of the church is not an introduction
of a new element in the church because the central idea of the church is
love, which alone is credible. Drawing from the thoughts of Saint Ignatius
of Loyola, he proposes that *aggiornomento*, a central impulse at Vatican
II, was a movement to deepen the experience of Christians in the form of
beauty in the glory of God. Reform, according to him, involves two aspects.
The first is *"a broadening of the horizon, a translation of the Christian
message in 'language understandable by the modern world.'"* The second
aspect is the specific Christian aspect or the internal dimension of reform,
*"a purification, a deepening, a centering of its idea, which alone renders
us capable of representing its idea, radiating it, translating it believably
in the world."* Indeed, the touchstone of reform in Balthasar's proposal
for mission *"is the greatest possible radiance in the world by virtue of the
closest possible following of Christ."*[90]

In the light of the foregoing, when I think of Pope Francis as translating
a way of being church which I describe as illuminative ecclesiology, I mean
that he makes it possible for people to believe the message of the Catholic
Church and for people to see clearly the light of Christ in the church and in
the world. He achieved this by his own way of living in humility and simplicity, by his kind words and generous reaching out to people who are on
the margins and those who feel insignificant. Through his credible lifestyle
he is placing the focus of the church on what is truly important, which is a
culture of encounter with others, especially those who are poor and weak,
the reign of God and the culture of love, mercy, solidarity, and inclusion,
which defined the ministry of Jesus Christ. These are values at the heart
of Catholicism but which often are sometimes lost in the culture wars that
have characterized Catholicism since the nineteenth century.

This is why Congar warns in sentiments expressed often by Pope Francis
(about fixation with one single teaching) against the danger of "making

---

[88]Victor Dunne, *Prophecy in the Church: The Vision of Yves Congar,* 109–10. See Congar, *Lay People
in the Church*, 199.

[89]Congar, *True and False Reform*, 215–17.

[90]Hans Urs von Balthasar, *My Work in Retrospect* (San Francisco: Ignatius Press, 1993), 51.

an idol of the truth" (Pascal), which could keep a reformer or a teacher of the faith enslaved to unilateral thinking and acting.[91] Ultimately, pastoral concern

> puts us at the heart of the concrete church, making thinking and planning fruitful in terms of practical measures that can avoid the fantasies, the excesses, or the unilateralism of personal enthusiasms, as well as avoid a fixation on one single aspect or one single case. This same pastoral concern is manifest also in the realism of points of view tending toward balance or equilibrium.[92]

The invitation is for the church, in the face of human needs and pastoral concerns, to adopt measures "that spontaneously develop both an orientation toward real life with respect to common everyday needs and a sense of responsibility and of the concrete consequences for the options taken."[93] This is what I see in the pastoral priorities and practices of Pope Francis.

Total ecclesiology offers a strong foundation for illuminative church because just as total ecclesiology emphasizes that all the dimensions of the church's life should be accounted for, and there should be a balance in the church, so also illuminative ecclesiology refers to a church in which every face is reflected in the mirror. Illuminative ecclesiology is the development of practices in the life of Christian communities wherein the identity and mission are mediated as a mirror in which the face of God is reflected to the people of God *in via*, and a mirror in which the faces of all of humanity are refracted back to God, while the light of Christ remains the source of that illumination in the mirror.[94]

I have not elaborated here on the aspect of a poor and merciful church within the development of Congar's theology of the social mission of the church or the prophetic function of the church and of Christians. I have also not touched on the Marian profile of Balthasar and what it brings to understanding the identity and mission of the church in the world. This is because I am concerned here in using the theologies of Congar and Balthasar to give a theological account and foundation for the pastoral ministry of

---

[91]Congar, *True and False Reform*, 228.

[92]Ibid., 221.

[93]Ibid.

[94]The analogy of the mirror has been employed by Raniero Cantalamessa in his commentary on the Transfiguration of the Lord when he writes, "It is through contemplation that we can enter into the mystery of the Transfiguration here and now, make it ours and participate in it. The phrase that is translated as 'reflected in a mirror' can have two meanings. The first, used by the ancients, means 'to contemplate as in a mirror.' The second meaning more in use today is, 'to reflect as in a mirror.' In the first case, Christ is the mirror in which we contemplate his divine glory; in the second case, we are the mirror that, as we gaze on Christ, reflects his divine glory." See Cantalamessa, *Mystery of the Transfiguration*, 7.

Pope Francis. However, I would like to add that total ecclesiology makes possible the openness of the church to all people and the service of the people of God to all people, especially those on the margins. The liberation of the laity through the total ecclesiology of Congar makes possible the recovery of the laicity not only of individual members of the church, but of the church itself. Congar is largely responsible for the dismantling of the two-tier church structure (clergy/laity) and the undoing of clericalism, which is one of the major reforms of Pope Francis. As one of the founding members of Sant'Egidio, Andre Bartoli said in an interview with regard to Congar's influence in the church's commitment to the poor:

> Congar gave us back a sense of vocation that we didn't have. In a way, what was happening before was that the vocation was constrained in the social role. Your vocation was being in the family, was doing your work well. But Congar helped us to say no, the vocation is one, the vocation is living the gospel, is to be holy, to live your life in front of God, the vocation is to be the church! This was phenomenal, but for us, was a beginning.[95]

CHURCH, WHERE ARE YOU?

"Only when we are configured to Jesus do we receive the eyes needed to see him." When I read this phrase from Pope Francis, a powerful image, which speaks to me of illuminative ecclesiology, came to my mind from one of my charitable missions to Uganda. It was the story of a blind girl, Rita, whom I met at the Boni Consili Girls School run by the sisters of Our Lady of Good Counsel in Kyabirokwa in Uganda. Only by touching the wounds of others are we able to be touched by the illumination of the love of God, which is present in every encounter in love with the pains of others. The Sisters of Our Lady of Good Counsel in Uganda in this remote community have created a little heaven in the middle of nowhere for so many girls who have been abandoned or neglected or those who are simply searching for a sound education. In this community, these gentle sisters bring together children from rich and poor families and from different faith traditions into this community of love where they live as one family. At Boni Consili, I saw how the light of Christ could shine out from the heart of the church when we proclaim and witness to the Lord by entering into the lives of others in a humble, respectful, and compassionate way. Sister Leocardia,

---

[95]Quoted in Laurie Johnston, "To Be Holy in the World: The Influence of Yves Congar on the Spirituality and Practice of the Community of Sant'Egidio," *Catholic Identity and the Laity* 54 (2008): 68.

the principal, told me how these sisters have to go out to the remotest parts of the country to engage families and to encourage them to send their girls to Boni Consili. Every child is welcomed to the school, even those who cannot afford the school fees. As Sister Leo said, "God will provide." As one would expect, most of the students here were from poor families, and Rita was one of those poor students.

Illuminative ecclesiology is concerned not about who the church is but where the church is to be found. God continues to shine God's light in many hidden and dark alleys of life through angels who serve outside the limelight but with great distinction, humility, and courage. The sisters at Boni Consili were running a comprehensive educational program for over 600 children from the entire province. They had a primary school, high school, skills center, and special education for children with learning disabilities. How twenty sisters could coordinate this learning center with its diversity of needs and kids was so amazing to me and reflective of how much people can do when driven by faith, love, hope, and courage, which come from trusting God. The sisters also have a huge agricultural project that helps provide food for the entire student population. One of the most moving experiences for me was when we visited the section of the special needs children. The welcome song was composed and rendered by Rita, who was fourteen, and two other girls. Rita was blind and suffered traumatic abuse growing up; she was thrown out of her home when she became pregnant. She had no clue who impregnated her, but she was "happy" to be a mother. She was picked up from the streets by the sisters and brought to Boni Consili where she was covered with love by the sisters and began to flourish. Here was a very talented musician, a creative mind, and a gentle soul whose life would have been wasted if not for the love of the sisters.

At the end of my visit, I took Rita aside and asked to know her more, and she opened her heart to me and told me the story of her life. I said to her that I would like to tell the world about her story, and she gave me permission to do so. Rita's words to me were: "I was bruised and battered, but God gave me a second life through the love of my beloved nuns. Even when I was begging along the highway, I never gave up hope that somehow God is going to protect that treasure which he put in me." I asked Rita: "What is the treasure that God put in you?" She smiled, paused and then said: "Are you asking me the treasure that God put in me? It is there for everyone to see. We can see the treasure that God gave to everyone if we give them the opportunity to develop and to be themselves." It was a rare wisdom from a blind teenager! She was blind physically but I think she had a better insight than I, who could see. She saw amid her pain and sad experience that the treasure that God has put in each one of us is never diminished by hard and bad times, and that we can help each other discover this treasure through love, support, and affirmation, and by not giving up on each other.

Illuminative ecclesiology is a pointer to the truth that in the brokenness of lives like Rita, in the limitations of children like Lizzy, and in our own sense of right or wrong, there is a treasure that lies hidden in creation and in our lives which the church must help God's people to see, feel, and touch. However, the church must be an open door, must go to the peripheries and search out like the Good Shepherd did for the lost and the straying, the wounded and the bruised, the outcasts and the hurting. Pope Francis puts it so clearly:

> This is why I like saying that the position of missionary disciples is not in the center but at the periphery: They live poised towards the peripheries . . . including the peripheries of eternity, in the encounter with Jesus Christ. In the preaching of the Gospel, to speak of "existential peripheries" decentralizes things; as a rule, we are afraid to leave the center. The missionary disciple is someone "off center": the center is Jesus Christ, who calls us and sends us forth. The disciple is sent to the existential peripheries.[96]

The church is a healer of wounds because God has given it the gifts which it must share not simply by waiting in the precincts of churches but above all by going into the streets to find those who are wounded and those hungry for God. When Pope Francis writes about wounds he speaks in a direct and concrete experiential language about the human condition. To the question "Why, in your opinion, is humanity so in need of mercy?" he answers:

> Because humanity is wounded, deeply wounded. Either it does not know how to cure its wounds, or it believes that it's not possible to cure them. And it's not just a question of social ills or people wounded by poverty, social exclusion, or one of the many slaveries of the third millennium. Relativism wounds people: all things seem equal, all things appear the same. Humanity needs mercy and compassion. Pius XII, more than half a century ago, said that the tragedy of our age was that it had lost its sense of sin, the awareness of sin. Today we add further to that tragedy by considering our illness, our sins, to be incurable, things that cannot be healed or forgiven.[97]

The image of the church as a healer of wounds is already contained in grains in Vatican II's ecclesiology of the people of God. Gerard Mannion

---

[96]Address to Latin American Episcopal Conference (CELAM), July 28, 2013.
[97]Pope Francis, *Name of God Is Mercy*, 16.

rightly argues that the term "the people of God" constitutes "Vatican II's core ecclesiological concept" and offer a thematic structure for most of the documents of the council, especially *Lumen Gentium*. But particularly, he argues that Pope Francis's ecclesiology can only be understood and interpreted through how he appropriates beyond the "resistance, controversy, and compromise" surrounding this ecclesiology of "the people of God," a new way of being church—through his reform of the curia, the unshackling of episcopal collegiality, affirmation of the authority of local bishops and episcopal conferences, and so on (*EG,* 40, 111, 118).[98] But this reform agenda is with a view to giving the church a form through which its proclamation and witnessing can offer to God's people the merciful love of God and present to God the wounded faces of humanity.

Lumen Gentium presents the heart of the teaching of the council fathers on the question "Where is the church?" *Lumen Gentium* provides three answers—on the nature and degree of membership in the church (14), in what manner the church of Christ subsists in the Catholic Church (8), and the relationship between the universal church and the local churches (26).[99] Vatican II affirmed that the church is the instrument of Christ, who is the light of the nations (*LG,* 1). This section of *Lumen Gentium* has influenced subsequent debates on liberation theology, ecclesiology of communion, contextual ecclesiology, inculturated ecclesiology, ecclesiology of the people of God, church as family of God, and other models of the church. Even though *Lumen Gentium* opened the door for creativity and dynamism in developing diverse approaches to ecclesiology, the battle for the interpretation and appropriation of a satisfactory ecclesiology that celebrates the richness and diversity of the communities of faith gathered in the name of the Lord around the world has not ceased.

Lumen Gentium moved Catholic ecclesiology beyond its Tridentine transcultural and ahistorical reading and application of the four marks of the church—unity, catholicity, apostolicity, and holiness. According to Richard Gaillardetz:

> The council members recognized the reductive and atrophied state of theological reflection on the church found in the dogmatic manuals of the nineteenth and early twentieth centuries. Consequently, the council's reflections on the church took the form not of some normative systematic treatise but of a recovery of the theological breadth and depth of

---

[98]Gerard Mannion, "Re-engaging the People of God," in *Go into the Streets! The Welcoming Church of Pope Francis*, ed. Thomas P. Rausch and Richard Gaillardetz (New York: Paulist Press, 2016), 59–70.

[99]Joseph, A. Komonchak, "The Significance of Vatican II for Ecclesiology," in *The Gift of the Church: A Textbook on Ecclesiology in Honor of Patrick Granfield, OSB*, ed. Peter C. Phan (Collegeville, MN: Liturgical Press, 2000), 77–83.

the Catholic tradition with particular attention to neglected theological perspectives from the Christian heritage of the first thousand years.[100]

I propose that Pope Francis offers an approach that is capable of leading today's church to the realization of the spirit of the Second Vatican Council.

However, Pope Francis moves beyond these theological debates by placing the accent not on the question "Who is the church?" but rather on the question "Where is the church to be found?" This recapitulates the central New Testament definition of the church in Matthew 18:20 that where two or more are gathered in the name of the Lord, he remains in their midst. So the question that Pope Francis poses is: Where are our brothers and sisters? What is our locus of enunciation as theologians, Christians, pastors, and laity in the face of the complex stories of our world?

Where the church is to be found is the starting point and the point of arrival of any satisfactory ecclesiology. It touches everything in the church's mission: where the church stands in the face of oppressive and authoritarian governments; where it stands in the increasing gulf between the rich and the poor in the world and in local communities; where it stands in the battle for justice, inclusion, tolerance, and in the refugee and migration crisis, among others. This reminds me of my father's favorite saying to us about those we hang out with: "Tell me who your friend is and I will tell you who you are." The poor man of Galilee was often called a friend of prostitutes and sinners (Mt 11:19; Mk 2:13–17; Lk 6:36–50).

Lumen Gentium 8 affirmed the church's commitment to embracing "sinners in her bosom," and the church is often called the "chaste whore" to show how it is suspended between its divine origin and its immersion in history with all the sins and contradictions therein.[101] This is a gentle reprimand against those who are seeking "a pure church"; or those who are enchanted with a triumphalistic church or those embarrassed by a pope who kisses the feet of Muslim women or those who fear that receiving Jesus in Holy Communion is a contamination or sacrilege for non-Catholics or divorced and remarried Catholics.

"Who is church?" is a mystery that cannot be fully explicated through theological construction; it is a mystery to be lived in humility and thanksgiving. The attempt to fit the church into one model or another has been the greatest challenge facing the church throughout history. It has, however,

---

[100]Richard R. Gaillardetz, *Ecclesiology for a Global Church: A People Called and Sent* (Maryknoll, NY: Orbis Books, 2011), xviii.

[101]See Balthasar, *Explorations in Theology II: Spouse of the Word*, 193–288. See Jeanmarie Gribaudo, *A Holy yet Sinful Church: Three Twentieth-Century Moments in a Developing Theology* (Collegeville, MN: Liturgical Press, 2015). See also Jacques Servais, "The Confession of the Casta Meretrix," *Communion International Catholic Review* 40 (Winter 2013): 642–62.

become very pertinent in this moment of world Christianity to appreciate deeper that Catholicity means diversity of human experience and multiplicity in the response of people to the summons of the Lamb through different cultural traditions. It is only fitting that the pope who was chosen from the ends of the earth will be the pope who will lead the church to begin tentative steps toward realizing the mandate of the Lord to carry the gospel to the ends of the earth and to celebrate the diversity of faith in the unity of love in the one church from the Roman center to the margins. Answering the question, "Where is the church?" requires understanding first the changed context for evangelization in the era of world Christianity. The church's identity must now assume fully its location in the context of world Christianity.

Miroslav Volf's account of public faith is useful here in describing the texture of where the church is to be found today. Volf argues that public faith is a rich complex of changing Christian narratives, identities, and cultures, each with their partly overlapping, partly conflicting sets of beliefs and practices.[102] This requires an understanding of the changing frontiers, features, and futures of Christianity in diverse contexts of faith. World Christianity points to a greater appreciation of the diversity within both past and present Christian history. It draws attention to the new contexts of faith and practice outside of Europe and the West. It also highlights the emerging patterns, challenges, continuities and discontinuities between Christianity in the new contexts of faith in the Global South and in the Western mainline. World Christianity also brings into greater focus the new challenges facing Christianity globally in the areas of interfaith dialogue, dialogue with new epistemologies, migrant communities, religious minorities, religious persecution, and religiously inspired violence. It also challenges the churches to face with humility and courage the new and unexplored moral questions that Christianity encounters as it crosses new cultural and spiritual frontiers. It also draws the attention of Christianity to greater sensitivity and appreciation of the new narratives of faith today through an approach that Roberto Goizueta calls "borderland ecclesiology."[103]

The image of a poor and merciful church that goes out to the margins and gives an account of all of God's people in their diverse situations and needs and which cares for the earth, and accompanies God's people every day with a vulnerable mission is what I have described in this chapter as illuminative ecclesiology. This is a way of capturing theologically how the Lord's mandate that the church should be salt and light to the world looks

---

[102]Cf. Miroslav Volf, *A Public Faith: How Followers of Christ Should Serve the Common Good* (Grand Rapids, MI: Brazos Press, 2011), 85.

[103]Roberto Goizueta, "Corpus Verum: Toward a Borderland Ecclesiology," in *Building Bridges, Doing Justice: Constructing a Latino/a Ecumenical Theology*, ed. Orlando O. Espín (Maryknoll, NY: Orbis Books, 2009), 143–66.

like in the daily priorities and practices of the Christian communities. I have shown how Pope Francis models this illuminative ecclesiology through his papal ministry. The next chapter develops the theological, biblical, and historical foundations of this way of being church in order to locate Pope Francis within the bigger portrait of an identity and mission of the church that preceded him and that will definitely outlive him.

2

The Poor Church of the Poor

Biblical, Historical, and Theological Foundations

Returning to Rome in mid-April after a one-day visit with refugees in Greece, Pope Francis told reporters traveling with him that the situation of the refugees, what they experienced getting to Greece and how they are living in the refugee camp "makes you weep."

Going to the back of the plane where the media were seated, the pope carried some of the drawings the refugee children had given him. He explained the trauma the children had experienced and showed one picture where the child had drawn the sun crying.

"If the sun is able to cry, we should be able to shed at least one tear," he said. "A tear would do us good."

In meetings with priests, Pope Francis repeatedly asks if they are able to weep when pleading to God in prayer to help their parishioners. He told priests of the Diocese of Rome in 2014 that the old Missal had a prayer that "began like this: 'Lord, who commanded Moses to strike the rock so that water might gush forth, strike the stone of my heart so that tears . . .'—the prayer went more or less like this. It was very beautiful."

"Do you weep?" he asked the priests. "Or in this priesthood have we lost our tears?"

"You see, sometimes in our lives, the glasses we need to see Jesus are tears," he said at a morning Mass early in his papacy. "All of us in our lives have gone through moments of joy, pain, sadness—we've all experienced these things."

"In the darkest moments, did we cry?" he asked his small congregation, which included Vatican police and firefighters.

"Have we received that gift of tears that prepares our eyes to see the Lord?"
—Cindy Wooden, "Theology of Tears: For Pope, Weeping Helps One See Jesus"

As part of the Holy Year of Mercy (December 8, 2015–November 20, 2016), the pope scheduled a May 5 prayer vigil "to dry the tears" of those who are weeping, inviting parents who have lost a child, victims of war and torture, the seriously ill, the desperate, those enslaved by addiction, and everyone else in need of consolation.

Sometimes, he has said, tears are the only true response to the question of why the innocent suffer.

In January 2015, the pope listened to a fourteen-year-old boy in Manila describe life on the streets as a struggle to find food, to fight the temptation of sniffing glue, and to avoid adults looking for the young to exploit and abuse.

A twelve-year-old girl, Glyzelle Palomar, rescued from the streets by the same foundation that helped the boy, covered her face with her hands as she wept in front of the pope. But she managed to ask him, "Why did God let this happen to us?"[1]

"Why did God let this happen to us?" The cry and question of Glyzelle is one that we hear every day in our world. If you are like me, I have shed some tears in the face of the personal tragedies of my life and when confronted with the devastating effects of war, poverty, natural disasters, and epidemics which I have seen in my pastoral and humanitarian work in many countries of Africa.

One thinks of many stories in our news these days and the painful images of refugees drowning in the Mediterranean in the thousands, hundreds of people dying from terrorism in many countries; millions of people dying from preventable and treatable diseases like HIV/AIDS, malaria, cholera, high blood pressure, heart diseases, diabetes, Ebola, and so on; millions of people starving in many parts of the world; and millions of others lacking the basic necessities of life. One thinks of the vulnerable women and children who are exploited and abused even in our religious institutions and millions of others who are living in situations of modern-day slavery; workers who are exploited; and many of our children and young people in our cities and suburbs who are victims of violence, drugs and gang.

We live in a world where the structures of sin and injustice and structural violence continue to reinforce the destruction of many lives and the impoverishment of a greater portion of humanity. How can the church be

---

[1] Cindy Wooden, "Theology of Tears: For Pope, Weeping Helps One See Jesus," Catholic News Service, May 5, 2016, www.catholicnews.com.

an agent in the reversal of the shameful conditions of so many people in our world who are on the margins and who are forgotten because of their place of birth, the color of their skin, their religion, gender, or sex? What kind of church will embrace concrete daily practices as an option for the poor in order to break the unacceptable cycle of intergenerational poverty, which holds many people and families in bondage? How can the "culture of encounter" proposed by Pope Francis become a praxis and priority in our churches in order that the church can touch and be touched by the painful condition of the poor? How can the church dry the tears in the eyes of many people around the world who are crying by night and day for God to intervene in their terrible and painful conditions?

Writing in his apostolic exhortation *Evangelii Gaudium*, Pope Francis made this appeal:

> I want a church which is poor and for the poor. They have much to teach us. Not only do they share in the *sensus fidei*, but in their difficulties they know the suffering of Christ. We need to let ourselves be evangelized by them. The new evangelization is an invitation to acknowledge the saving power at work in their lives and to put them at the center of the church's pilgrim way. (*EG*, no. 198)

The term "the church of the poor," referring to the identity and mission of the church, was first used in modern times by Pope John XXIII (*Acta Apostolicae Sedis*, 682). However, it is a term that has always been central to the church's self-understanding, mission, and pastoral priorities from its earliest history.[2] The Church shines brightest when it becomes a light not unto itself, but to the world, by illumining the darkness, shame, injustice, and disorder caused by the scandal of poverty and sin, all of which defeat God's purposes for creation, crush the human spirit, and insult the dignity of the children of God.

Pope Francis's poor-first teaching is an invitation to all Christians to return to the true evangelical path that has guided authentic Christian living and witnessing through the ages. This return will definitely give credibility to the church. It will also bring about the authentic living out of the true identity of the church as a humble instrument in God's hand by leading the people of God on a journey toward "all that is honorable, just, pure, lovely, gracious, excellent and worthy of praise" (Phil 4:8–9). This is the journey

---

[2]See, for instance, the collected studies on the evolution of the understanding of the church's identity and mission to the poor from New Testament times to contemporary times in Geoffrey Dunn, David Luckensmeyer, and Lawrence Cross, eds., *Prayer and Spirituality in the Early Church: Poverty and Riches*, vol. 5 (Strathfield, Australia: St. Pauls Publications, 2009).

of divinization. That is the vocation and mission of all Christians and the church to become more conformed to Christ by having the mind of Christ and living like Christ in the way we treat our neighbors and creation. This image of a poor church is central to illuminative ecclesiology because it brings about a form of the church which shows the face of a caring, merciful, and compassionate God who enters into the social condition of the poor in order to transform their condition from within. It also becomes a form of the church and the face that the church presents to God. This is because by being a poor church, the church embodies in its priorities and practices the faces and conditions of a wounded and suffering humanity ravaged by poverty and suffering, and draws attention to the mission of churches and Christians to the least of the brethren of Christ.

The vocation of a poor church demands among others: (1) a robust and in-depth social analysis of the social context and analysis of power dynamics in particular contexts, especially within the church itself; (2) a clear theological understanding of the social conditions of the people through an immersion in their social locations; (3) a harvesting of the riches of the social gospel and application of the best practices from multiple Christian and nonfaith contexts for addressing the unacceptable social conditions through direct involvement in social ministry and poverty-eradication programs; and (4) sociocultural discernment of the foundations and vocational nature of this *identity of the church as being poor and existing for the poor in its identity and mission*. It also requires (5) a clear articulation of the principles and daily practices that must draw naturally from this identity of the church, for Christians, and all God's people in order to bring about social transformation. This is the import of Pope Francis's speech to the Food and Agriculture Organization when he spoke of the need to *analyze (see), understand (judge), and engage (act)* with the social conditions of poor people in these words:

> There is need to move beyond indifference and a tendency to look the other way, and urgently to attend to immediate needs, confident that the fruits of today's work will mature in the future. We cannot devise programs which are bureaucratic and antiseptic, which do not work today. Every proposal must involve everyone. To move forward constructively and fruitfully in the different functions and responsibilities involves the ability to analyze, understand, and engage, leaving behind the temptations of power, wealth or self-interest and instead serving the human family, especially the needy and those suffering from hunger and malnutrition.

In order to do this kind of analysis, it is necessary to trace the foundation of "the church of the poor" in illuminative ecclesiology. In this chapter I show how the Trinitarian image of illuminative ecclesiology in Vatican II offers a strong foundation and model for the practices of illuminative ecclesiology that I develop in the rest of the book. I further demonstrate that Pope Francis's poor-first approach has even deeper roots in both biblical theology and in the preaching of the early church. I have chosen the Letter of James and the homilies of John Chrysostom as two sources to show the poor-first identity and mission of the church in the biblical traditions and the priorities and practices of the early church.

THE MESSAGE OF VATICAN II

> We shall not meet the truest and deepest demands of our times, we shall not answer the hope of unity shared by all Christians, if we do no more than make the preaching of the Gospel to the poor one of the many themes of the Council. In fact, it is not *a* theme; it is in some measure *the* theme of our Council. If, as has often been repeated here, it is true to say that the aim of this Council is to bring the Church into closer conformity with the truth of the Gospel and to fit better to meet the problems of our day, we can say that the central theme of this Council is the Church precisely in so far as it is the Church of the poor. (Cardinal Lercaro, Archbishop of Bologna, *Documentation Catholique*, March 3, 1963, col. 321, n. 2).[3]

Pope Francis's call for a church of the poor is an invitation to recover the sacramental and Trinitarian center of illuminative ecclesiology proposed by Vatican II (*LG* 1, 4, 5, 9, 48, 59; *SC* 5, 26; *GS* 42, 45; *AG* 1, 5). This requires embracing the mission and identity of the church as the humble servant of the poor of the Lord through a form of the church that shows the Trinitarian face as love and which initiates in history an eschatological journey toward the realization of abundant life for all God's people, especially those who suffer.

In addition to Yves Congar's total ecclesiology, described in chapter 1, another aspect of the church's self-understanding that was rediscovered at the Second Vatican Council was the Trinitarian origin of the church. A consequence of this retrieval is a richer appreciation of both the historicity and the eschatological nature of the church. An important dimension of this Trinitarian image was the appropriation of an ecclesiology of vulnerable mission in Catholicism. The church understands itself as a learning church,

---

[3]Cited in Yves Congar, *Power and Poverty in the Church*, trans. Jennifer Nicholson (Baltimore: Helicon Press, 1964), 149.

open to being touched profoundly by "the world" especially through the stories and experiences of brokenness among the poor of the Lord in our churches, communities, and in the world. This openness to serving all creation and all human beings, especially those who suffer, is clearly stated in the words of *Gaudium et Spes*:

> The joy and the hope, the grief and the anguish of the men of this age, especially of those who are poor or in any way afflicted, these are the joy and hope, the grief and anguish of the followers of Christ. Nothing that is genuinely human fails to raise an echo in their hearts. For theirs is a community composed of men. United in Christ, they are led by the Holy Spirit in their journey to the Kingdom of their Father and they have welcomed the news of salvation which is meant for every man. That is why this community realizes that it is truly linked with mankind and its history by the *deepest of bonds*. (*GS*, 1)

This "deepest of bonds" referred to by *Gaudium et Spes* is enacted and made possible through the Trinitarian origin that gives a unique identity and mission to the church. Vatican II, harking back to New Testament times, makes a clear theological judgment that the church is brought into being from the unity of the Father, the Son, and the Holy Spirit. This creates a bond of unity that includes humanity, God, and the entire cosmos that God has made (*LG*, 4). According to Anne Hunt, "The rediscovery of her Trinitarian origins opened up new avenues and vistas, an expanded horizon and mind-set for the council's understanding of the church, both *ad intra* in regard to its life and mission and *ad extra* in regard to its dialogical outreach to others."[4]

The Trinitarian origin of the church is essential to understanding the theological link between the identity of the church as a vulnerable church in the service of vulnerable mission to the world and its service to the poor which it embraces as the consequence of its Trinitarian origin and identity. It also offers a structure for the form and praxis of illuminative ecclesiology.

TRINITARIAN STRUCTURE OF ILLUMINATIVE ECCLESIOLOGY

Illuminative ecclesiology has a Trinitarian structure following the teaching of Vatican II. The church exists to communicate God; it has an instrumental character as servant of the Lord. Divine communication is central

---

[4]Anne Hunt, "The Trinitarian Depths of Vatican II," *Theological Studies* 74 (2013): 3.

to the mission of the church, and it happens in the diversity of peoples and cultures through a "communion rooted in the initiating action of the Trinity, in the Eucharist and in anthropology."[5] In *Evangelii Gaudium* 92, Pope Francis writes of "a mystical fraternity, a contemplative fraternity," which makes us capable of seeing the "sacred grandeur of our neighbor and of finding God in all things." However, the source of this grandeur is not the human person or the church or the world but rather the truth of God's love, which at core shines forth in beauty as the saving love of God made manifest in Christ (*EG* 36).

The church is led by the Holy Spirit to see this grandeur in everything, but especially in the least of the brethren and in suffering creation. It is the Holy Spirit who brings to the church the spirit of "humility, meekness, magnanimity, and love." Through this gift the church and all God's people are able to discover the true treasure of the church in the Trinity so that it can find the true road to its mission and for unity of identity in the diversity of mission.[6] There is then asserted in this teaching of Pope Francis something deeper than a metaphysical principle about the order of truth or the identity of the church or of *sacra doctrina* as truth revealed by God through some self-evident metaphysical principles.

The first truth in the Trinitarian life is love. This love is made manifest in history—in the chaos and wounds of life, in the hunger and joy of searching for God, in the search for meaning, and so on—as they are encountered directly through the life and witnessing of the churches and Christians. The Lord Jesus is the prior Word of love spoken to creation and present in creation; he is the first truth, which is intuitively grasped in every experience in our encounter with the other, especially those on the margins and those wounded in life.

The core of the theological aesthetics of illuminative ecclesiology is the love of God, which is encountered as first love and internal Word of life in every instance of encounter with the other, especially in the experience of human brokenness. The Lord is present in every human and cosmic reality. This is an incomparable incarnational moment. The Lord has promised to be present in the church and in history, especially in the life and reality of the least of the brethren. The answer then to the question "Where is the church?" is always to be found in the portrait of the everyday experiences of humanity and the world as touched by the hand of a loving and merciful God through the instrumentality of the church and its members. The love of God the Father is revealed to all Christians and the church in the midst

---

[5]Bruno Forte, *The Church: Icon of the Trinity: A Brief Study*, trans. Robert Paolucci (Boston: St. Paul Books and Media, 1991), 74.

[6]Pope Francis, *The Church of Mercy: A Vision for the Church* (Chicago: Loyola Press, 2014), 28–29.

of the wounds of people and in all realities through the mediating love of the Son, who is present in all the complexities of life.

This Trinitarian structure grounds the theological aesthetics elaborated through the distinction that Pope Francis makes between two kinds of logic of thought and of faith: the "logic of the scholars of the law and the logic of God." The logic of the scholars of the law proceeds from preconceived and rigid notions of truth, purity, and so on, whereas the logic of God proceeds from mercy and love in order to transfigure evil into good through God's Son by his entering into contact with sin.[7]

One can identify this theological aesthetics in Pope Francis's focus on the concreteness and experience of the church's being-with God as a way of being-in-the-world through "making contact" with sin or "the culture of encounter" with people. The point of encounter with the divine principle of love—Jesus Christ—which is the starting point of illuminative ecclesiology—is contact with beauty in the brokenness of sin and the wounds of people. This is a contradiction and a source of pain and anguish for those who want a pure church without stain and blot. Such a church is an eschatological promise beyond history. In contrast, the church of the present has been sent on a mission to heal the wounds of the world and is generated through the wounds of the Cross.

The first truth for Christians, according to Pope Francis, is not a nameless being or truth, but a truth that has a wounded face, Jesus Christ. This Incarnate love—the light of the world—is prior to and is the foundation and source of all being and all things that the church teaches, professes, and lives. This Incarnate love, as Aquinas states, is an interior beauty as well as an interior grace (*EG*, 37), which gives beauty to creation and specifies the path of beauty for the church. It is present in every instance of joy and pain of suffering humanity and the entire cosmos. Its presence in creation and in all of God's people becomes the primary identifier of where God is present and the sites of God's work in history of which the church is a servant. Christian life is a vocation to embrace the "way of beauty" (*EG*, 167) even in the contradictions and complexities of life. The church is called to walk the "way of beauty" with humanity; this is an invitation to live in the truth by touching "the human heart and enabling the truth and goodness of the Risen Christ to radiate within it" (*EG*, 167).

In illuminative ecclesiology, the subjective condition for believing and acting shows forth the splendor of truth in the encounter with the reality of people's lives. Personal witnessing and accounts of faith point to where

---

[7]Pope Francis, *The Name of God Is Mercy: A Conversation with Andrea Tornielli*, trans. Oonagh Stransky (New York: Random House, 2016), 66.

God's grace, love, and blessing are at work. Furthermore, personal and local stories of God's great deeds in the lives of the people are embraced as the "way of beauty" where the people of God are to be found. People's faith and life are not judged only through some idealized notion of ecclesial life, right faith, and right conduct, but rather the church is searching for how to bandage their wounds and help them get up and walk again. In this way, the ecclesiological method corresponds with the living faith of the people, while the love of God incarnate in history stretches human beings to live beyond their limitations and sinfulness through the liberating, healing, and transforming grace that comes from God through the crucified and risen Lord.

This unifies both the ecclesiology from above and that from below because the illumination of the human and cosmic reality by God happens through the nearness and participation of the church in the complexities of people's daily lives. It also emerges from their daily pains and wounds as revelations whose intelligibility can only be asserted through deep encounter with the mystery of God. This kind of experience of being present in the lives of people, sometimes with empty hands, is presented clearly by Mother Teresa in one of her letters:

> Every Sunday I visit the poor in Calcutta's slum. I cannot help them, because I do not have anything, but I go to give them joy. Last time about twenty little ones were eagerly expecting their "ma." When they saw me, they ran to meet me, even skipping on one foot. I entered. In that "para"—that is how a group of houses is called here—twelve families were living. Every family has only one room, two meters long and a meter and a half wide. The door is so narrow that I hardly could enter, and the ceiling is so low that I could not stand upright. . . . Now I do not wonder that my poor little ones love their school so much and that so many of them suffer from tuberculosis. The poor mother did not utter even a word of complaint about her poverty. It was very painful for me, but at the same time, I was very happy when I saw that they are happy because I visited them. Finally, the mother said to me: "Oh, Ma, come again! Your smile brought sun into this house."[8]

What is important here is that witnessing to God's presence and manifesting God's presence in the wounds of others is not something that merely occurs within the sacramental action of the church alone but in every

---

[8]Brian Kolodiejchuk, ed., *Mother Teresa: Come Be My Light: The Private Writings of the "Saint of Calcutta"* (New York: Doubleday, 2007), 27.

instance of genuine Christian encounter. Christian praxis in illuminative ecclesiology is not to be understood only as doing; it is being present with the other, because when a Christian is wholly present in the pains of another, the Lord Jesus is totally present. Therefore, it is not simply a matter of our performance and action, but it is also the Christian presence of faith, love, hope, and mercy. The church, therefore, is not simply what happens in the church, what is decided in synods, or what is enshrined in canon law; the experience of the church is concrete where people's wounds are open and festering, waiting for healing. It is in these realities that the church is found, and it is in the darkness, which surrounds life, that the illuminative church is most vivid, relevant, and authentic.

The church then should be attracted to all reality, especially the wounds of the many, because the church is drawn by the Holy Spirit to see God in these moments. The church becomes attractive to the people of God, especially those who are far from God, when through closeness to the least of the brethren, it shines forth with the glory of God, whose beauty and radiance is so brightly mediated through the poor of the Lord. It is in doing this that the church becomes an ever widening open space for God's action and revelation in the world. [9]

TRINITARIAN ORIGIN
OF ILLUMINATIVE ECCLESIOLOGY

The inner life of the church has as its source the Mystery of the Trinity. It gives form to illuminative ecclesiology; what shines from the heart of the church is the creating, saving, and sanctifying love of God. God bends down to creation and is totally available to creation. At the same time, God still remains a mystery that cannot be contained in a single vessel. The humility of God is reflected in this movement into history; the emptying of the majesty and glory of God in the divine processions in history for the good of humanity and the entire creation. God as unconditioned love and absolute love that cannot be surpassed makes this love wholly and fully available to creation in the diversity of human and cosmic histories. God does this in a dynamic way through a divine humility that holds nothing to itself and rather gives everything to us out of total love for us in order to bring goodness and beauty to creation and the entire cosmos. Our lives and our world are filled with the beauty, goodness, and love of God despite the brokenness and darkness that we find around us. It is this mysterious love

---

[9] Pope Francis, *Name of God Is Mercy*, 7–8, 34.

of God, which is stronger than death and sin, which speaks to humanity and creation from the heart of God. God's love for creation and humanity brings the assurance of hope that creation is not destined to death and destruction, but to love, salvation, and redemption. This is the mystery beyond all telling, the Good News that gives the church its life, identity, character, and mission.

This Trinitarian identity is a mystery. In this regard, Hunt argues: "Given an understanding of the mystery as primordial and intrinsic to the church's very being, she is then recognized as ever in process, on her pilgrim way, developing and maturing, always incomplete and short of her goal and never fully possessing or understanding her own nature and mission."[10] This aspect of mystery also points to the self-identity of the church as a gift beyond simple human and political manipulation or sociological calculations. Rather, the church is a pilgrim, journeying within history and touched by the conditions and complexities of history, especially the groaning of the poor of the world in their search for fulfillment and abundant life. In the words of *Lumen Gentium* (8), "The church 'like a pilgrim in a foreign land, presses forward amid the persecutions of the world and the consolations of God,' announcing the Cross and Death of the Lord until he comes (cf. 1 Cor 11:26)."

There are three important dimensions of the Trinitarian origin of the church that specify the identity and mission of illuminative ecclesiology:

The first dimension is what Saint Pope John Paul II highlighted in his teaching on Mary about the inner and external life of the church. The church is not simply a spiritual ahistorical community. The church is profoundly sociological in nature even though its identity cannot be understood and interpreted solely in terms of sociology. The church being embedded in history has an external character because as *Lumen Gentium* (9) teaches, the church is "destined to extend to all regions of the earth and so to enter into history," but at the same time it transcends all limits of space and time while carrying out its mission in space and time.

The interior character of the church's pilgrimage is a second dimension of its identity. The church remains in history as salt and light, but the source of its strength and the origin of its light is the interior grace, love, and truth that comes from "the power of the Risen Lord" (*LG*, 8), "the power of God's grace" (*LG*, 9), and by the renewing comfort and presence of the Holy Spirit (*parakletos*, Jn 14:26; 15:26: 16:7), the interior mistress and teacher of the church in its mission from the center to the margins.

The third dimension is the properly Marian image of the church as source. Mary is the model of how to journey with God through her total availability

---

[10]Hunt, "Trinitarian Depths of Vatican II," 8.

to God's grace, and unstinting gift of herself to God and her wholehearted gift of her Son to the world. Mary becomes a mirror and model for the church in its pilgrimage of faith because she shows how the mighty works of God (Acts 2:11; Lk 1:49) can be done in history through weak vessels in the ordinariness of daily life.[11] She points to the fruitfulness of humility in receiving the gift of God in both the coming into history of God in Christ, and the humble reception of the Word in history in Mary. In the interior renewal of the church through its return to its Trinitarian origin, and in its external vocation to the world in reaching to the margins, the church is called to a pilgrimage of faith, which can only bring about the fruits of salvation through a redemptive economy of grace born of humility.[12]

How is the image of Mary the mirror of the church?[13] Hans Urs von Balthasar offers some helpful theological insight too rich to be presented in a short exposition of this kind. I wish to indicate some important aspects of what he calls the Marian profile in order to show how these provide a fundamental structure historically of a church that is called to listen to the Lord so as to respond to the mission it has been given for the world.

Fundamentally, Balthasar points out that authentic Marian theology does not in any way undermine the image of Christ. On the contrary, he notes in *Elucidations*—following Saint Bernard—that the person of Mary becomes questionable when her person is isolated within the context of a theology of salvation such that it sets Mariology in competition with the saving function of the Son of God. What Balthasar emphasizes is that the Marian profile casts a light on the personal in the theological principle of church as Marian. This emphasizes the concretization of the true spirit of Mary—or, rather, that the true spirit of Mary should be allowed to illumine the inner recesses of the life of the church because it is through its internal

---

[11]Pope John Paul II, *Redemptoris Mater*, 25–29. Mary is "the mirror of the church," "the primacy of the church," "the budding church," "the virgin made church" (St. Francis of Assisi). See Raniero Cantalamessa, *Loving the Church: Scriptural Meditations for the Papal Household*, trans. Gilberto Cavazos-Gonzalez and Amanda Quantz (Cincinnati: St. Anthony Messenger Press, 2003), 58.

[12]See John Paul, *Redemptoris Mater*, 24.

[13]The task of interpreting Balthasar's Mariology is very challenging because he uses a wide range of tropes in an apparently interchangeable and unscientific manner. For instance, Mary is "archetype" of the church; it is the *Real Symbol*; it mediates Christ-form; and it is a model. Balthasar also conflates the Marian principle with the wider and very convoluted question of Mary's role per se, vis-à-vis Mary's role and symbol as a representative of a gender. Since our task here is not a Marian hermeneutics in Balthasar in its personal, theological, feminist, Christological, and ecclesiological dimensions, I shall not go into details on this. My concern is to see how the Marian principle in its general understanding is consistent with Balthasar's general theological system and how this is foundational in conceiving and reimaging the church as a listening church that is totally and wholly available in radical freedom and response to Christ as he reveals the Triune God. See Lucy Gardner, "Balthasar and the Figure of Mary," in *The Cambridge Companion to Hans Urs von Balthasar*, ed. Edward T. Oakes and David Moss (Cambridge: Cambridge University Press, 2004), 64–78.

life as a church open to God and to all realities that it can shine forth the light of Christ to the whole world.

Mary's spirit is the spirit of the handmaid—of service, of inconspicuousness, the spirit that lives only to pass on what it has received, which lives only for the other. No one demands personal privileges more than the mother of Christ; yet she can rejoice in such only insofar as they are shared by all her children in the church.[14] Balthasar argues further:

> Without the Marian principle in the Church, Christianity can edge imperceptibly toward becoming inhuman. Without the Marian principle, the Church becomes functionalistic, soulless—a hectic enterprise without any point of rest, estranged from its true nature by the planners. And because, in this mainly-masculine world, all that we have is one ideology replacing another, everything becomes polemical, critical, bitter, humorless, and ultimately boring. People run away from such a Church in droves.[15]

Seen in this light of Mary or what Balthasar calls a Marian principle in the church, the understanding of the church as mystery in the Trinity summons the church to a self-emptying humility and recognition of its insufficiency.[16] This should lead it to the realization of its weakness and the constant need of grace, conversion, and renewal of its structures, theologies, systems, teaching, pastoral priorities, and plans. This disposition equips the church and its members with the inner grace and sensitivity to the weaknesses and vulnerabilities of its members who are in need of solidarity, healing, and transformative grace to transcend the limitations imposed on them either by sin or social injustice or any other factors.

Being grounded in the mystery of the Trinity, which is the source of love and holiness, also gives the church a deeply spiritual identity. It also reveals that the church is not simply given to us as a finished project. The church is an open crack always in need of healing and completion. The church bears the marks and carries within it the brokenness of our wounded humanity. It also has received the blessed summons from God to discover in the pains and sufferings of those on the margins the voice of God who calls us again and again in mystery. Seen in this light, the church is the custodian of a gift that it has received as a servant of the Word and a steward of the

---

[14]Hans Urs von Balthasar, *Elucidations* (London: SPCK, 1975), 71.

[15]Ibid., 72.

[16]Brendan Leahy asserts that "principle" or "profile" is not defined by Balthasar; when he uses these terms, he wants to refer to the fundamental dimensions of the very nature of the church. Brendan Leahy, *The Marian Profile: In the Ecclesiology of Hans Urs von Balthasar* (New York: New City Press, 2000), 9.

graces that it has received through weak and imperfect structures, human beings, and systems. Its identity, therefore, is not simply the result of some consensus or ideological shenanigans by theologians or clerics or laity. Its mission and vocation are not some abstracted notions of power or authority constructed by dogmatists or woven in absolute terms to conform to any particular cultural system or ideology.

Furthermore, the identity of the church is not to be worked out through seminars, workshops, or contextualized formulas to reflect the specific cultural innovations dictated by social change. Rather, the identity of the church is a dynamic, organic, and experiential reality dictated by the intimations and intuitions of the Holy Spirit. It is the Holy Spirit who leads the church and Christians in the right path to the truth, which alone reveals to us the mind of God and the purpose of creation. The Holy Spirit also brings to light for the church, Christians, and the world the concreteness of divine revelation and salvation in history. It also helps the faithful embrace with courage the promise of the Lord for fulfillment of all things through the hope for the realization of the reign of God in our lives and in our times. The church is called to be the mediation of daily practices that conform to the divine purposes dictated by faith such that through human cooperation to divine purposes in total trust and abandonment to God's will, it can bring people to God and God to people. It is also important to note that although the church must respond to the signs of the times and discern these signs in the light of its mission, its identity is not to be understood or constructed through an unmediated cultural knowledge, cultural behaviors, or cultural artifacts. Faith also mediates these cultural forms to bring about some familiar traits in every ecclesial form across cultural and historical boundaries.

What this means is that the church is not simply some abstracted notion of community or some transcendental form outside history. Christians experience and identify the presence of God and God's work in history in the stories of faith and life in their communities of faith when people gather some gifts and money to support another Christian or a practitioner of African Traditional Religion who has been visited with tragedy. If we pay attention to the faith-in-action in our Christian communities on multiple levels and places, we can see clearly a Trinitarian narrative (creating, saving, healing, and transformational love, which is stronger than death) of who we are as Christians and as a church. Authentically lived Christian life always points back to its source: the Trinity.

The true identity of the church in the light of the teaching of Vatican II can be found only through a return to its Trinitarian center in a spirit of humility and obedience. It is through this return to its true identity that the church and its members can become more attentive to and discern the signs of the times. It is in this way that the church will constantly reform itself by placing its gaze on the love of God, revealed in Christ and renewed in the Holy Spirit. The reform of the church is always an invitation to become more like God in the Trinity by conforming to this original love, light, life, and grace, and reflecting and receiving fully the gifts of the Holy Spirit. This way, it can become a suitable instrument for the mediation of the healing, restorative and transformative grace of God to all. In a special way, this humility makes the church open to being taught and led by the new events of meaning mediated especially through the poor.

TRINITARIAN ORIGIN AND MISSION OF THE POOR CHURCH TO THE POOR

The Trinitarian origin characterizes the mission of the church in history, especially to the poor and the marginalized. Pope Francis brings out this dimension in *Evangelii Gaudium* 89 when he writes:

Today, our challenge is not so much atheism as the need to respond adequately to many people's thirst for God, lest they try to satisfy it with alienating solutions or with a disembodied Jesus who demands nothing of us with regard to others. Unless these people find in the Church a spirituality which can offer healing and liberation, and fill them with life and peace, while at the same time summoning them to fraternal communion and missionary fruitfulness, they will end up by being taken in by solutions, which neither make life truly human nor give glory to God.

The church is called to embrace the "precepts of charity, humility, and self-denial" in proclaiming and establishing among all peoples the kingdom of Christ, and of God as the seed and beginning of the kingdom (*LG*, 5). Being *in the world* means that the mission of the church is defined by how it is touched and shaped profoundly by the joys and sorrows of the people of God and the groaning of creation in their search for abundant life (*GS*, 2). This heals the ecclesial dualism between the church and the world, the sacred and the profane and new forms of theological tribalism that create unhelpful polarization and division in the things which should hold God's people together. Rather, this ecclesiology proposes that the inner dynamism of the church is reflected in its missionary outreach, which flows from its inner identity. This overcomes the theological abstractions on the church, which often isolate the church from its mission of entering into the concrete life situations of people. This inner life, which is the result of the mission of God, is also the foundation of the church's external mission, which reflects diversities of expressions and manifestations through a unity of faith that abhors uniformity or conformity but the celebration of unity in diversity.

TRINITARIAN ORIGIN AS AN INVITATION TO BUILD RELATIONSHIPS

The Trinitarian origin of illuminative ecclesiology is the source of the "culture of encounter," relationship, participation, and friendship. Bruno Forte argues that the central character, nature, and identity of the Trinity is communion and an openness and intention to be a communion of participation in history for all of God's people:

> As the communion of Persons in the Trinity is related to the Father, the eternal source of love, so the communion of the people on earth is related constitutively to God the Father, Lord of heaven and earth. This means that the community is a communion of different *springs of love*, which must be related among themselves in order to become together a single wellspring of life and love.[17]

The Kingdom of God that Christ preached is to be realized through sharing together every good thing around us that God wishes to offer humanity and creation through Christ in the Holy Spirit. This is more so in situations of suffering, neglect, alienation, and pain, which afflict many of God's people. Vatican II proposes a church that sees itself as a unity in diversity, a church that is not closed in on itself but is open to embracing the world, especially those people who are on the margins. This church is presented by Pope Francis through his words and deeds as a church that self-identifies not with the strong and mighty but with all of creation, especially the weak in their hunger for communion with God.

Trinitarian communion is the union of love, friendship, community, solidarity, and divinity in the three Divine Persons and the participation of humanity and the entire creation in this community of love.

> Charity is love received and given. It is "grace" [*charis*]. Its source is the wellspring of the Father's love for the Son, in the Holy Spirit. Love comes down to us from the Son. It is creative love, through which we have our being; it is redemptive love, through which we are re-created. Love is revealed and made present by Christ (cf. Jn 13:1) and "poured into our hearts through the Holy Spirit" (Rom 5:5).

---

[17]Forte, *Church: Icon of the Trinity*, 191.

As recipients of God's love, men and women are subjects of charity, and thus they are called to make themselves instruments of grace, so as to pour forth God's charity and weave networks of charity. (Pope Benedict XVI, *Caritas in Veritate*, 5)

This union is the origin of all things. One can theologically conclude from the foregoing that creation and everything in it are the fruits of the creative love of God the Father, the saving love of Jesus Christ, and the sanctifying love of the Holy Spirit. Love is, therefore, to be seen by all Christians and all men and women of goodwill as our origin and destiny. Thus, the proper locus, means, and end of all Christian vocation and the identity and mission of the church ad intra and ad extra is a loving relationship, expanding the horizon of love and relationship in the world, making people friends of God and friends of one another all built around the Holy Trinity. This is why charity is the basis of the church's social teaching and has its pulsating heart in the Trinity (*CV*, 2).

Human relationship is, therefore, to be based on this divine model of mutual relationship, intrinsic openness to the other, communion and shared existence, solidarity, different but related operations, autonomy, and diversity. A good relationship respects, reverences, and upholds each individual, while allowing their mutual involvement in each other's lives and appreciating their unique personal stories as reflections of the image of God that everyone carries deep within his or her very being. Miroslav Volf captures this very well when he writes:

When I speak about human imaging of the Trinity, I mean that human beings receive themselves as created in the image of the Trinity by the power of the Spirit. Their imaging of the Trinity is the gift of God's movement out of the circumference of the Trinitarian life to create human beings and, after they have sinned, to restore them by dwelling within them and taking them into the perfect communion of love, which God is. . . . Because God has made us to reflect God's own triune being, our human tasks are not first of all to do as God does—and certainly not to make ourselves as God is—but to let ourselves be indwelled by God and to celebrate and proclaim what God has done, is doing and will do.[18]

This mission of embracing humanity and the entire creation as a community of relations and a communion of friends of God, friends of one another,

---

[18]Miroslav Volf, "Being as God Is: Trinity and Generosity," in *God's Life in Trinity*, ed. Miroslav Volf and Michael Welker (Minneapolis: Fortress Press, 2006), 6–7.

and friends of the earth is a grace and a vocation. It means that the church is open to relations with the "other" and learns from the world. It is also in this light open to being actively in dialogue with the world in order to hear the new evangelical summons that God echoes from the heart of the world and from the cries of creation and tears of the little twelve-year-old Filipina girl. This immediately rejects any form of Christian discipleship that is carried on with a deeply embedded bias and prejudice against other people because of their color, ethnic identity, sex, sexuality, religion, Christian denominations, social, economic, or spiritual status, or background. This is a familiar case in many of our Christian communities and has wounded the church in many parts of the world and works against the building of God's kingdom where everyone is a firstborn child (Heb 12:22–24). A church that is faithful to its Trinitarian communion of friendship and participation cannot settle for any kind of stereotypes, discrimination, clannishness, ethnocentrism, sexism, racism, or nepotism within its ranks or perpetuated by its officials, nor will such a church be silent in the face of structures of sin, injustice, and any system or policies and programs that make it impossible for God's people to have abundant life. True Trinitarian communion in the church is the foundation of illuminative ecclesiology.

TRINITARIAN ORIGIN OF THE CHURCH AS A SUMMONS TO ILLUMINATIVE ECCLESIOLOGY

The Trinity is the foundation for illuminative ecclesiology. Illuminative ecclesiology simply means a church that is faithful to its inner Trinitarian life and faithful to its mission to the world through re-presenting in history the priorities and practices of its founder, Jesus Christ, in such a way that the faces of humanity are presented to God, and the loving face of God is seen in the churches and by all God's people as in a mirror. It refers to a church that harmonizes its divine origins with its earthly life and that sees in its Trinitarian origin something deeper and richer than what is merely human and cultural. Illuminative ecclesiology is the clear rejection of the separation of spirituality from life, laity from clergy, nature from grace, private devotion from active witnessing in the world. It also rejects the gulf often present when the pains and tragedies in the lives of many people are not seen as part and parcel of the inbreaking of God's Word and the living out of God's command of love in the church.

Illuminative ecclesiology proposes a higher accent on "the people of God" as the identity of all who are summoned by God's love to become children of God. This Trinitarian communion is both a model and a mission. The union within the inner life of the Trinity is a perfect relation of persons in the diversity and unity of missions. It is also in itself the source for the restoration and renewal of creation. Such a mode of being and acting should model the church's communion and social mission. The church's social mission to the poor is, therefore, to be based on this Trinitarian model of mutual relationship, openness to the other, communion, shared existence, solidarity, respect, autonomy, and diversity.

Seen in this light, I aver that the crisis in the church today is not primarily an ecclesiological crisis, but a Trinitarian crisis. If the church is suffering from an identity crisis and a crisis of mission, it is because the face of God is not fully reflected in the church, and the form of Christ is not embodied fully in our priorities and practices in the church. The church cannot solve the human riddle today if it does not embrace the complexities reflected in the drama of history and the struggle for meaning of what it means to be human. The way the church self-identifies and acts toward its members and to the world is only an external indication of how the church sees the human person and God's creative and saving works in the life of men and women today and in the world. If many people are excluded and neglected in our churches, it seems to me to be the result of a crisis beyond an unhealthy ecclesial attitude which is far removed from the attitude of the poor man of Galilee. This reveals a fundamental rupture of the church's self-understanding and living out of its Trinitarian identity. This proposition will answer most of our questions about some of the main problems and challenges of the church today (the place of women, clerical sexual abuse, the tension between Rome and the margins, the questions about the use and abuse of power and authority in the church, the place of the laity in the church, the conditions of divorced and separated Catholics, the criteria for entering into priestly and religious lives).

This Trinitarian crisis occurs when the church departs from its true identity, which is the mediation of divine love, and is lost in protecting or preserving ecclesial hierarchies and privileges, which, Pope Francis points out, arise from a certain "spiritual worldliness" (*EG*, 95). When this happens in the church, there is a gradual loss of the evangelical poverty, humility, and spirituality required for meeting the challenges of spreading the good news to the poor. Instead of a vulnerable and humble disposition, negative ecclesial attitudes emerge, and positions, offices, and structures in the church and even the poor of the Lord become instruments to be manipulated. This most often may affect the church's ability to be a credible and effective witness of the Trinitarian life to the world, while the mission of God of healing the world and bringing the ambiguities of human history to conform to God's plan of love is often marginalized. Gradually, the image of God and the living out of love can become nuanced, distorted, or absent in some of our practices and priorities. When this happens in the church and afflicts Christians who embrace this kind of negative ecclesiology, then many in the church will actually be bowing to idols and giving their allegiance to realities that are removed from the Christian Trinity. The recovery of this Trinitarian bond will help our churches re-image God in our identity and mission.

Illuminative ecclesiology also heightens the sense of union with Christ, through a culture of encounter and through union with one another and with all that God has made. This is especially directed to those who are on the margins who cannot fulfill the purpose of their lives because they have been robbed by poverty, separated from the church, or wounded by sin and thus lack the freedom to apply themselves to their world in a wholesome manner. Union with Christ is the purpose of our creation; it is often described as divinization. Union with Christ is about becoming like God and attaining fulfillment by attuning our wills and desires to God's will. When we are united with Christ, we are led at the same time to be united with all humanity and creation. In this way we can identify with all those who suffer. Indeed, the Christian is reminded that one is diminished when one sins against God or one's neighbor, for example through injustice. Indeed any abuse of the humanity of my brother, sister, or neighbor through poverty or the wounding of the earth through human violence affects the harmony of earth. The church is called to help bring about this harmony by creating transformational communities of faith united in acts of love, mercy, and kindness. Ilia Delio shows that union with God requires some spiritual and practical exercises and commitments to virtuous acts for our own good and that of our neighbors:

> We are to be divinized not by making ourselves royal, self-centered kings and queens but by becoming the presence of the Suffering Servant, the compassionate Christ so as to divinize the world. We are to be the sacrament of God's humble love in the world and we are called to bear witness to this love by our lives. Evolution toward Christ requires bonds of compassionate love and we are called to make those bonds of love in the world visible and tangible.[19]

Illuminative ecclesiology is the most valid approach through which the church and Christians can live out fully and faithfully a life of redemption from sin for individuals and for groups and the whole earth. This is because it offers the most helpful approach to creating a new earth and a new heaven through the spiritual path of "theosis," grounded in our humility before God.

---

[19]Ilia Delio, *The Humility of God: A Franciscan Perspective* (Cincinnati: Franciscan Media, 2005), 164.

It also brings about the realization in faith of the path to integral salvation and the coming of God's kingdom in history in our journey to God's house. As Kenneth Paul Wesche points out, in both Latin and Greek "salvation" always refers to healing and redemption; it is also abundant life in Christ. Healing implies removal of all things that destroy life and the restoration of wholeness to individuals, groups, and creation. Healing is the liberation of creatures and creation from sin and evil, and any negative realities that make it impossible for us to enjoy abundant life in Christ.

Poverty, especially negative material poverty, is not a natural condition nor is it destiny; hence it is a situation always in need of healing and redemption. Even though the church is not a social agency or an NGO whose primary mission is poverty eradication, it is part of its mission. The church is the sacrament of God's salvation in history. Because of this identity, the church has a mission of mediating to the world all that Christ has offered to humanity and the whole earth for the integral salvation of this earth and everything in it. The rejection of the values of this kingdom of God embodied in Christ and the rejection of the values and virtues of illuminative ecclesiology are often the cause of poverty and human suffering on earth. The church is thus called to become an effective instrument for divinization open to all of God's people. This can be achieved through many ways, one of which is through healing the earth and ridding God's people of all occurrences of evil, selfishness, pride, greed, injustice, hatred, intolerance, discrimination, and violence. These rob God's people of joy and diminish the realization of God's will for human and cosmic flourishing. Divinization and bringing all things together are the goals of illuminative ecclesiology. The interior spiritual disposition that we are united with God and should be united with one another will inspire actions and practices of faith for the realization of the goal of life, which is a path toward the conquest of self-love, which, as Augustine writes, is what creates the chaos and disorder in the city of man.[20]

Being a Christian who is embraced in the loving arms of God and belonging to a church characterized by the Trinitarian life proposed by *Lumen Gentium* means the following from theological and spiritual perspectives: (1) we are immersed in the mystery of God in faith; (2) we are united as the community of the beloved in sharing in the life of God and participating in the joys and sorrows of one another; (3) the whole of our human and cosmic reality belong in this logic of grace within the rhythm of

---

[20]This analysis of theosis draws heavily from two essays: Kenneth Paul Wesche, "Eastern Orthodox Spirituality: Union with God in Theosis," *Theology Today* 56, no. 1 (April 1999): 29–43; Vladmir Kharlamov, "Theosis in Patristic Thought," *Theology Today* 65, no. 2 (July 2008): 158–68.

divine action; (4) our whole reality and actions, our mission and vocation, our lives and structures (personal, group, and ecclesial) are united in the mystery of God's love; (5) and the church and Christians are open in this light to being part of God's salvific plan for all humans and all creation by cooperating with God's love and grace in working toward the realization of the reign of God. This requires abiding in divine love through listening to and keeping the Word of truth and walking humbly every day with God through acts of justice, charity, compassion, mercy, peace, and righteousness.

Being a Christian requires that we see our unity with God as an invitation to center our lives on Christ and to bring to God every day the groans of creation and our brothers and sisters in the stories of their daily lives. This amazing sense of mutuality in our relationship with God, which the ancient spiritual fathers and mothers termed *mysterium commercium*, that is, a mysterious commerce or exchange, is a theosis in God: the faith-filled Christian, trusting in God's providence comes before God with the good and bad events of life, and allows God to become part of that story; and God, the loving and compassionate Father, receives that story in its beauty and ugliness and transforms it into a new story for the restoration of the Christian and the world.

DIVINIZATION AS THE VOCATION
OF THE CHURCH, CHRISTIANS, AND THE WORLD

Divinization requires holding all things together; avoiding the spiritual dualism that sees the things of this earth and concerns for the redemption of the earth and liberation of human suffering as merely secular concerns while glorifying the spiritual mission of the church beyond the realm of the concrete and the present. Ilia Delio's insight on this is illuminating and helpful:

To be divinized means to have the grace of Christ within you, to lay down your life for your neighbor and to wash the feet of the poor. To be divinized is to be like Christ, unafraid to go to the margins and touch the sick, the wounded, the sinners and all those shunned by society. To be divinized is ultimately to live in the spirit of martyrdom, willing to offer up one's life for the sake of the gospel. It is no wonder that we never desire to be divinized because it is easier to follow fleeting earthly images than to risk one's life for a person we really don't know or love someone who cannot repay us in return. Yet divinization is what lies at the base of our deepest desires. We want to be "like God" only we are unsure of what God we want to be like: the God of Jesus

Christ, the god of culture, the god of progress or the god of our own self-centered egos.[21]

We can find the true path for divinization through a total picture approach which sees every story in the world as part of the unfolding of the story of God's great deeds in history.

Sometimes the stories are those of pain, brokenness, and despair, but in this mysterious exchange with God, God takes upon Godself our human brokenness, pain, and despair, and in exchange grants us wholeness, comfort, and hope. At other times our stories might be that of confusion, doubt, and uncertainty as we find in the case of Thomas on the Second Sunday after the Resurrection (Jn 20:24–29). God embraces us in the shadows and clouds that flood our minds, and through the wonderful exchange grants us the certainty of faith and clarity of vision. The Good News for us as Christians is that the stories of our lives, our joys and sorrows, our hopes and dreams, are not outside the compass of God's grace, love, and divine providence. Illuminative ecclesiology also holds that the stories of humanity and creation are central to the mission of the church and are sources of divine revelation for the church and Christians.

One of the saddest aspects of our modern life is the seeming sense of normalcy in many lives, when there are many people who are dying silently, emotionally, spiritually, and physically. There are many who live lives of silent despair characterized by unfulfillment, fear, anxieties, and worries. There are many whose past is such a dead weight to their present lives and who are so overwhelmed about uncertainties of the future that their present life is unpleasant and unexciting. In many instances, the root of our pain and despair goes back to our sad experiences in our childhood, schools, parishes, workplaces, and families. Illuminative ecclesiology is also about a church that is concerned with both the inner and external lives of people. Jesus invites the church, following his example, to be concerned with everything that happens in the life of every child of God. Thus, there are many Christians whom the church should help to open their wounds to the Lord so that the Lord can bring healing and restoration.

There are so many in our communities and societies who are poor, isolated, abandoned, sick, wounded, and rejected. Many are crying silently. One can think of the conditions of so many barren women in Africa, so many childless couples, those who are haunted by day by ancestral curses and hounded at night by fears of being punished by angry ancestors. One thinks of so many jobless young people in our communities, those who would rather get infected with HIV/AIDS as the only way to flee from starvation and get

---

[21]Delio, *Humility of God*, 149.

access to basic health care. We think of the millions of street children in our cities and highways, the displaced refugees, the thousands of migrants who are dying in the seas and the deserts in their search for a better life, the struggling orphans, and the many slum dwellers who have no hope of decent accommodations or better jobs in the near future. The *theosis* of God means that the agony, fears, and hopes of the least of the brethren are the agonies of Christ, and should be at the center of the mission and priorities of a church that understands itself in the light of the ecclesiology of the Second Vatican Council.

A renewed Catholic ecclesiology grounded in a Trinitarian image and a communion of friendship could become a strong cultural and spiritual influence in the church's search for a praxis for realizing its preferential option for the poor (*EG*, 198–201). This is especially needed today as the church is called even more than ever to walk and work with the poor in finding answers to the challenges of poverty, diseases, abuse of the rights of the powerless and those on the margins, migration and human dislocation, ethnic and religious conflicts, radical Islamic fundamentalism, religious intolerance, all forms of discriminations against minorities, wars, political and economic problems, and how to mitigate the effects of climate change and natural disasters. *Lumen Gentium* teaches that the church sees itself as called to follow the path of Jesus in bringing hope to all by re-presenting Christ anew to people of our times, especially those who are poor for whom Jesus made himself poor through his kenosis. In a particularly illuminating teaching on the mission of the church the council fathers write: "The Church encompasses with love all those afflicted by human infirmity and recognizes in those who are poor and who suffer the image of its poor and suffering founder. It does all it can to relieve their need and in them it strives to serve Christ" (*LG*, 8).

Finally, the Trinitarian origin of the church described in *Lumen Gentium* offers a theological hermeneutics for appropriating an integral Christian anthropology that illumines a new understanding of human dignity, human identity, intersubjective relations, and the goal of human communities, especially the social and spiritual conditions of those who suffer. When people are denied the capacity to apply themselves to their environment because of poverty, diseases, and the absence of the basic necessities of life, there is a rupture in the human and cosmic ecology, which wounds the heart of God and communion in the church. When human security[22] is

---

[22]By "human security" I refer to the definition of the United Nations Development Program in its most recent definition of this new concept in 2003 as "the liberation of human beings from those intense, extensive, prolonged, and comprehensive threats to which their lives and freedom are vulnerable." Cited in Clark B. Lombardi and James K. Wellman Jr., "Introduction: Religion and Human Security: An Understanding," in *Religion and Human Security: A Global Perspective*, ed. James K. Wellman Jr.

undermined by institutional and global systems and processes that sustain the scandalous and iniquitous economic order that has placed the majority of the world's population in perpetual servitude and heart-wrenching suffering, it is a rebellion of the world against the relational God. This is the God who is concerned with everything that concerns us. Catholic ecclesiology would see anything that degrades the dignity of any person as a wound in the very heart of the church and in the heart of Trinitarian communion. The church's social mission to the poor is, therefore, to be based on this divine model of mutual relationship, openness to the other, communion and shared existence, solidarity, autonomy, and diversity, which uphold each individual, while allowing their mutual involvement in each other's lives. How these can be realized is taken up in chapter 3.

THE CHURCH IS A HARBOR FOR THE POOR

Biblical Theological Understanding

The church of the poor is an image that has deep roots in the Christian scriptures' presentation of poverty as an unacceptable sinful condition. The community of faith is presented in scripture as having an essential identity and mission of replicating in history God's solicitude and offer of integral salvation and justice for the poor of the Lord.

According to Raniero Cantalamessa, in the Christian scriptures, one can identify many references to material poverty and spiritual poverty, both of which can be both negative and positive. *Negative material poverty* is poverty as a social condition that is crushing many people in the world. This is a dehumanizing condition that must be combated. *Positive material poverty* is the attitude of detachment from wealth, an attitude that liberates and raises people to a new level of existence despite their wealth. This does not imply the absence of material resources or insufficiency of adequate resources to meet present or future needs. There is also *negative spiritual poverty*, which is the absence of spiritual wealth and of authentic human and spiritual values; negative spiritual poverty is the condition of those who make an idol of their material wealth, the adequacy of their own ordained ends and pursuits; as a result they become slaves to the inventions of their own hands. This is the kind of poverty that we often do not hear about in the discussion of poverty because most of the issues of poverty are based on the discussion of material wealth and the calculus of capital. A fourth kind of poverty is *positive spiritual poverty* or *poverty of spirit*, which consists

---

and Clark B. Lombardi (New York: Oxford University Press, 2012), 7.

of humility and trust in God; those who are poor in spirit and who anchor their lives and fortunes in God have spiritual wealth.[23]

The church of the poor in this book refers to the church that embraces positive material poverty and positive spiritual poverty (its inner life and identity). I am also referring to a church that is called through its external activities and mission to be actively involved in the eradication of *negative material poverty*. Part of this mission is to transform individuals and society to overcome the *negative spiritual poverty* that breeds injustice, greed, selfishness, and the sinful living conditions of many poverty-stricken people around the world. The church of the poor is one that mirrors the kingdom of God and anticipates its eschatological fulfillment in its concerted effort to orient its actions and inner life to the will of God revealed in Christ. This is the fundamental teaching of the Christian scripture about the identity, mission, and life of Christians and the church. Barnabas M. Ahern captures this so well when he argues that the burdens of material poverty can crush the soul's aspirations and torture the mind with dark, hidden cravings to be satisfied at any price. However, he argues that it is only

> when the poor see in their misery an external sign of their complete dependence on God, only when the rich are free of clutching possessiveness, only when all people hold their hearts open to God and their hands widespread to their neighbors, can they become the *anawim* Yahweh spoke of in the scriptures. The eyes of such people are constantly turned to the Lord and their ears are always alert to the cry of the needy.[24]

The different words used to describe the poor (*anaw, ani, ebyon, rash, dal, ptochos, tapeinos*) in the Christian scriptures reflect diverse conditions brought on the unfortunate members of society through negative material poverty (mendicancy, sicknesses, starvation, homelessness, inability to earn a living, despair, discouragement, lack of family stability, being underprivileged, lacking the basic necessities of life, and having no voice); material poverty is thus presented especially in the Old Testament as an existential evil.[25] The poor cry out to God for deliverance through the community (Dt 15:11; Sir 4:1–6), and because the poor are suffering and are crushed by the unjust and the all powerful who follow the ways and

---

[23]See Raniero Cantalamessa, *Poverty*, trans. Charles Sérignat (New York: Alba House, 1997), xi; see also J. F. Kavanaugh, *Faces of Poverty, Faces of Christ* (Maryknoll, NY: Orbis Books, 1991).

[24]Barnabas M. Ahern, foreword to Albert Gelin, *The Poor of Yahweh*, trans. Kathryn Sullivan (Collegeville, MN: Liturgical Press, 1964), 8.

[25]See Albert Gelin, *The Poor of Yahweh*, trans. Kathryn Sullivan (Collegeville, MN: Liturgical Press, 1964), 15–26.

whims of the world outside of the compass of God's ethical prescriptive (Am 4:1; Is 10:1–2; Ps 81:3–4; Jb 34:28; Prv 19:1: 28:6; 19:22), the poor are often identified as the righteous (*tzaddik*).

The poor one (*ebyon*) is by definition assumed to be righteous and to suffer economically for his or her refusal to pursue money-making at any cost. The Old Testament describes God as siding with the poor over the wealthy and powerful. Like the *tzaddik*, the *ebyon* enjoys special divine protection in this world and a promise of reward in the world to come. Both suffer the same fate because of the absence of justice in the world. Rabbi Jill Jacobs argues that the Old Testament's insistence on God being on the side of the poor is because when injustice is rampant and when many people resort to accumulating wealth at the expense of meeting human needs, both the *ebyon* and the *tzaddik* suffer, and the righteous will most likely become an *ebyon*.[26]

The theme of poverty in the Bible is intrinsically connected to the context of oppression and suffering, something that is still true today. Elsa Tamez argues that the Bible clearly identifies who is poor, the causes of poverty, the condition of the poor, and the mechanism of poverty at various levels of society. God's revelation is made manifest in the context of the suffering and poverty of God's people.[27] The Old Testament traditions do not reject wealth, or tar all rich people with the brush of injustice. A rabbinic tradition has it that God once said to Job, "Would you prefer poverty or suffering?" and that Job replied: "Master of the universe—I will take all the sufferings of the world as long as I don't become poor, for if I go to the marketplace and don't have any money to buy food, what will I eat?" So poverty is presented in biblical and rabbinic teaching as worse than all the other sufferings in the world. In many instances poverty is presented as a curse and prosperity as a blessing for those who fear the Lord.[28]

In Old Testament times, the poor person is less one who is indigent and more one who is oppressed. It is a social idea. This is why later, when the poor began to spiritualize their condition, their ideal will not become detachment from the goods of this world but rather a voluntary and loving submission to the will of God.[29] The spiritualization of poverty as positive spiritual poverty in the Old Testament away from the understanding of poverty as

---

[26] Jill Jacobs, *There Shall be No Needy: Pursuing Social Justice through Jewish Law and Tradition* (Woodstock, VT: Jewish Lights Publishing, 2009), 50–51.

[27] Elsa Tamez, "Poverty, the Poor, and the Option for the Poor: A Biblical Perspective," in *The Option for the Poor in Christian Theology*, ed. Daniel Groody (Notre Dame, IN: University of Notre Dame Press, 2007), 33.

[28] Jacobs, *There Shall be No Needy*, 57.

[29] Michael D. Guinan, ed., *Gospel Poverty: Essays in Biblical Theology* (Chicago: Franciscan Herald Press, 1977), 6. Leslie J. Hoppe argues that poverty was seen in the Deuteronomic tradition as the result of the violation of the law of God and hence there is no positive value to poverty in this tradition; see Leslie J. Hoppe, *Being Poor: A Biblical Study* (Wilmington, DE: Michael Glazier, 1987), 31.

a socioeconomic idea was a later development in the self-understanding of the people of Israel, especially in postexilic times. It was easier for a people in exile to fully grasp the importance of positive spiritual poverty and solidarity with those suffering and to develop a sense of closeness to God and to one another (especially evident in the prophetic oracles of Zephaniah, Ezekiel, Jeremiah, and Second Isaiah). Such a community appreciated the relative and instrumental role of wealth, and the need to embrace *tzedakah* (the practice of charity) and social justice and to walk humbly with God.[30] This self-consciousness and a way of living before God and the world were made manifest in the life, words, and deeds of Jesus, which I will refer to in the next section. In the words of Michael D. Guinan:

> Until he came, poverty, in any meaning of the term, was considered an evil: we must fight against it by communal assistance; we ask God unceasingly to deliver us from it; at best, we can consider it as a test to educate us (Ps 16:13–14); we always hope to be saved from it, and this salvation was conceived only in terms of this world with its temporal values.[31]

I have chosen biblical and historical sources for illuminating the social consciousness of the early church, namely the Letter of Saint James and the writings of John Chrysostom. I wish to briefly highlight how these sources help shed light on the image of the church of the poor which is being revived in the church of Pope Francis.

The Message of the Letter of James

The Letter of James focuses on the theological aesthetics and praxis of a poor church. This praxis is a key aspect of illuminative ecclesiology. As I pointed out in chapter 1, Pope Francis has not offered the church high-sounding systematic theological tracts like his predecessors, Benedict XVI and John Paul II. What he has proposed is how the church can be the "seeing eyes" in a world of poverty and pain in search of mercy. In addition, through his emphasis on the "culture of encounter" modeled after the practices and priorities of Christ, we are offered "a grounded theory" of immersion in the complex human condition of today.

As Elsa Tamez proposes, one of the reasons for the seeming neglect of the Letter of James is that rather than develop a theological treatise

---

[30]See Michael D. Guinan, *Gospel Poverty: Witness to the Risen Christ* (New York: Paulist Press, 1981), 34–45.

[31]Guinan, *Gospel Poverty: Essays in Biblical Theology* (1977), 15–16.

similar to Paul's letters on "the reasonableness of faith," the Letter of James concentrates on the concrete "practices of faith." Tamez writes, "A letter like that of James which focuses its attention on the daily practice of Christian life, is easily marginalized, while the 'theological' letters of Paul are highly esteemed."[32] However, for Tamez a closer study of the Letter of James shows that it offers three angles for Christian engagement with the social context—the angle of oppression-suffering, the angle of hope, and the angle of praxis.[33]

The Letter of James captures the essential dimensions of the church of the poor in the following ways: (1) the letter illustrates that the theme of poverty and the social critique of the unequal power relations that sustain the dominant social system and the judicial system in any social context were central to the preaching and praxis of the early Christian communities;[34] (2) it shows that the diatribe against the oppression of the poor and the protreptic for the radical commitment to social justice were always proposed by the Christian community as a pathway to creating a world that mirrors the will of God; (3) the unambiguous call for a church of the poor and for the poor in the Letter of James offers a strong justification for why God's preferential option for the poor should become a praxis for the church (Jas 2:5)—those who are poor according to the world are the ones God chose to be rich in faith and to be the heirs to the kingdom which God promised to those who love God; (4) the letter begins to indicate in small ways the early church's commitment to building a new and alternative community of the beloved where the will of God is done because everyone has access to the good things of life. There is always an unresolved tension in every authentic Christian community that commits itself to the values of the gospel that the Lord Jesus proclaimed. This is particularly in terms of the relationships with wealth, power, and privilege that are often acquired and maintained through unethical practices that harm the weak and the vulnerable. The Christian community is challenged in the Letter of James to become countercultural with regard to false and sinful ethical practices that promote inequality, poverty, and injustice.

There are four passages—1:9–11, 27; 2:1–7, 14–17; 4:13–17; 5:1–6—in the Letter of Saint James that help us understand how the early Christian

---

[32]Elsa Tamez, *The Scandalous Message of James: Faith without Works Is Dead*, trans. John Eagleson (New York: Crossroad, 2002), 4. The same line of argument was proposed by Luke Timothy Johnson, "The Social World of James: Literary Analysis and Historical Reconstruction," in *The Social World of the First Christians: Essays in Honor of Wayne A. Meeks*, ed. L. Michael White and O. Larry Yarbrough (Minneapolis: Fortress Press, 1995), 192.

[33]Tamez, *Scandalous Message of James*, 11.

[34]On James's critique of the "dominant social system and the judicial system" see Steven J. Friesen, "Injustice or God's Will? Early Christian Explanations of Poverty," in *Wealth and Poverty in Early Church and Society*, ed. Susan R. Holman (Grand Rapids, MI: Baker Academic, 2008), 24.

communities viewed wealth and poverty. They are also some of the most powerful evangelical summons from the heart of the gospel, which challenge faith communities to an alternate pathway for establishing a just society based on the values, practices, and priorities of the Lord Jesus Christ. These four passages reflect the four key dimensions of the letter on poverty— critique of social injustice; condemnation of the unequal relations of power between the rich and the poor and the rejection as sinful and unacceptable of the painful conditions of the poor; the vocation of the church to be a poor church for the poor; and the presentation of the ideal of the Christian community as an alternative community of hope and an instrument for bringing about a just and peaceful world. In such a community, the poor and marginalized are given a voice, while their interests, well-being, and integration are central to the mission, identity, and daily practices of the church and its members. These four dimensions, I propose, should be central to the life and ministry of the church in all places and times, and they are found in many aspects of the teaching and ministries of the church from earliest times.

The Vocation of the Church to Be a Poor Church for the Poor

I have often wondered why the Letter of James is neglected in the discussion in our churches, especially in Africa, about poverty, the kind of church we want, authority in the church, and the place of women. Many preachers will happily quote texts about tithing, submission of women to their husbands, and obedience to church authorities, but rarely is the Letter of James employed as a critique of corruption in our churches and societies or an inspiration to a spirituality of detachment and a commitment to social justice and option for the poor.

Patrick J. Hartin has argued that the Letter of James is significant because it can be situated "within the context of the thought world of Judaism and early Christianity." Of all the New Testament writings, this letter "appears to lie closest to Jesus' spirit and message."[35] Even though this letter has not been well received at various times in the churches, especially after the Reformation, it has an enduring significance. It is particularly used in this chapter to illuminate the central message of Pope Francis and to show how the message of a poor church has been essential to the self-identity of the church from its earliest beginnings.

The letter emphasizes a faith that does justice through works of mercy (Jas 2:13). Wesley Hiram Wachob draws parallels between Aristotle's explication

---

[35]Patrick J. Hartin, *James*, vol. 14 of the Sacra Pagina Series, ed. Daniel J. Harrington (Collegeville, MN: Liturgical Press, 2003), ix, 1. I acknowledge the research of Hartin, on whose useful commentary I have relied in this section.

of pathos as an aspect of rhetoric and James's appeal to mercy.[36] In both, the sight of undeserved evil arouses pity[37] and suffering can be mitigated when one views the other as a friend.

The Christian community is called to be a merciful community and a community touched by the sorrow and pain of the poor. The Christian community must embrace a sense of vulnerability and powerlessness in the face of a complex constellation of social, economic, racial, ideological, and cultural factors, all of which create the iniquitous social context of global poverty and the intergenerational cycle of poverty and pain. The vocation of the church to be poor and for the poor is clearly stated in James (2:5–9) when he writes:

> Listen, my dear brothers and sisters: Has not God chosen those who are poor in the eyes of the world to be rich in faith and to inherit the kingdom he promised those who love him? But you have dishonored the poor. Is it not the rich who are exploiting you? Are they not the ones who are dragging you into court? Are they not the ones who are blaspheming the noble name of him to whom you belong? If you really keep the royal law found in Scripture, "Love your neighbor as yourself," you are doing right. But if you show favoritism, you sin and are convicted by the law as lawbreakers.

Here we see some essential points on the vocation of the church of the poor for the poor. In the first place, as we noted in the analysis of the Trinitarian origin of the church, the church has no identity of its own other than that which it received from God. James makes an important claim that God has chosen the poor. This preferential option of God for the poor is a fortiori the vocation of the church, which is God's instrument in history for bringing about divine purposes. Hartin shows that the whole of scripture is filled with this idea of God's election as essential to understanding human identity and history:

> God is portrayed as the champion of the poor. For James, as for the prophets, God is the God of social justice. In defining religion James says, "Religion that is pure and undefiled before God (who is) also father is this: to care for orphans and widows in their affliction, and to keep oneself unstained from the world" (1:27). Just as the prophets called their hearers to a religion that embraced social justice, so

---

[36] Wesley Hiram Wachob, *The Voice of Jesus in the Social Rhetoric of James* (Cambridge: Cambridge University Press, 2005), 178.

[37] Ibid.

James does likewise. The motivating vision behind his conception of religion is the way God acts toward us. God is the champion of the poor, and those who imitate God act in like manner. This way of life must embrace a concern for the poor (5:1–6), the avoidance of every form of discrimination (2:1–7), concern for those who are ill (5:13–18), and the bringing back of a brother or sister who wanders from the truth (5:19–20).[38]

The choice of the poor by God is so decisive because the poor do not have any helper other than God. Thus the painful and sometimes tragic fate of the poor is sealed permanently if the Christian community acting in history in the name of God does not come to their aid when every other social or institutional structure fails them.[39] The choice of the poor by God, just like other instances of divine election, may not make sense to us (the scriptures are filled with examples of such choices by God: Dt 4:37; Jn 15:16; 1 Cor 1:27–28; 1 Pt 2:9; Eph 1:4). However, God always chooses the weak, the poor, the humble, and the foolish because they are the ones who truly long for God and are open to God because they trust God totally to restore their agency. In a sense, in choosing the weak, God is working hard in preserving the beauty that God has put in them, which their social location and context will potentially destroy, which would defeat the divine purposes.

Furthermore, in choosing the weak and the poor, God is continuing the great reversal that we find in the Magnificat and which is common in biblical writings—the poor become rich; the weak become strong; the sick gain their health; the dead are raised again to new life; the foolish are given wisdom; the humble are elevated; and the proud are brought down to earth. "The poor rejoice in their status within the community because they are the object of God's special love and care. The whole biblical tradition has stressed God's special choice of the poor. At the same time the poor hope for the eschatological reversal of fortunes at the end-time."[40]

However, this reversal is not simply a chiliastic reality to be waited for with patient endurance by the poor; this reversal is also embodied and incarnational in present time as a mission to be accomplished by the church and all those who long for the reign of God to come on earth as it is in heaven. In the same way, the Christian community is called to become part of and the instrument for this reversal in both its identity and in its mission. The church does this with confidence that being a poor church for the poor is actually the gateway to being rich in the Lord, that being on the side of the

---

[38]Hartin, *James*, 33.
[39]Ibid., 119.
[40]Ibid., 70.

poor and in the dumps of history is the pathway to being at the center of history. However, if the church is on the side of the rich and the powerful, and if the church becomes a hostage to rich patrons, the great reversal will happen, which will topple the church and actually effectively marginalize it and make it irrelevant to the direction of history in the trajectory of God. This is why the church must become the voice of the voiceless and a prophetic church constantly reading the signs of the times and offering the illumination to brighten the dark world of social sins and injustice that hold God's people captive to failed systems and structures of injustice and evil.

Critique of Social Injustice

Hartin writes so powerfully about the significance of James for today's church:

> The Letter of James provides a message that remains a challenge to everyone who reads it: the challenge to put faith into action. The focus on social issues transcends time and place. Although it was written to communities in the second half of the first century CE, many of the issues this letter raises are as relevant today as they were then. The concern to avoid every form of discrimination resonates with us in the twenty-first century. The letter's concern for the poor and the obligation of the Christian community to champion their cause is one that faces Christians today in a world where divisions between rich and poor nations are becoming increasingly more acute. James gives a voice to the poor and challenges every Christian community to re-evaluate its approach to those in need.[41]

James heavily criticizes the structures of injustice in society. He condemns the patron-client relationship between the rich and the poor as well as the discrimination and marginalization that the poor suffer. This evil social condition rears its ugly head in the church when deference is given to the rich and powerful and when social rank and status are established in the church. Social stratification when it happens in the church works against the dignity and equality of every human person before God (Jas 2:1–4). James addresses his letter to the twelve tribes of the Dispersion (Jas 1:1). This already locates the concerns of the letter to a globalizing Christianity even in the time of the early church. As the church goes out beyond Jerusalem to "the ends of the earth," it had to deal with questions of identity, exile, transitions, and the suffering, marginalization, and poverty of most Christians. The social condition of suffering was not only felt by poor Christians but

---

[41]Ibid., 5.

also by their neighbors who were often living on the fringes of the elitist Greco-Roman world of the first few centuries in the history of the church. As Luke Timothy Johnson noted:

> James is not simply a compendium of wisdom themes or a free-floating piece of parenesis, but a vivid exhortation that emerges from and addresses real human beings in specific social settings. Everything in the letter and everything lacking from the letter help confirm the impression that this social world was that shared by a leader of the Jerusalem church and Jewish messianists of the Diaspora during the first decades of the Christian movement.[42]

James also inveighed against the unethical practices of land ownership and excessive materialism that are forms of idolatry that Christians must not only avoid but also must denounce as unacceptable for creating a just and peaceful society. Discrimination in society, the abuse of the rights of the poor, the reinforcement of structures of injustice, and the honor-for-the-rich and shame-for-the-poor template framed into the social construction of daily life in society are seen as rooted in an evil desire that rejects God and that could lead to murders and deaths (Jas 4:1–4).

James 5:1–5 contains some of the most strident New Testament critiques of wealth and the social injustice and chaos that emerge in society by the unethical pursuit and possession of wealth, the neglect of the poor and the needy in society, and the failure to show mercy to the poor through charity. However, many commentators argue that James did not offer a strong critique of wealth and that it does not have a well-developed theology of social justice and theological anthropology. Some others also present the book as an unsystematic collection of prophetic diatribes and protreptic discourses on ethics with no coherently argued teaching either against wealth, neglect of the poor, or social injustice. But deeper intertextual reading of these texts show that the message of James is to be located within the wider context of Old Testament and New Testament biblical traditions of prophetic critique of the social context, which are valid and relevant for our times, not because they are an unbroken thematic discourse, but because of the radical acerbity of the message and its link to the message, parables, and ministry of Jesus Christ. Even though James mentions the Lord Jesus only two times in the whole letter, what he offers is a portrait of how an early Christian community looked at the disorder in the world. The letter also shows how a limited worldview could lead society into embracing spiritual or ethical paths that would lead them farther away from God and from the promotion,

---

[42]Johnson, "Social World of James," 196–97.

preservation, and protection of the common good from which all should draw equally. He also shows the destructive effects of poverty on people.

The prophetic tradition that rejects any social context opposed to God is present in James. The letter is prophetic because it condemns any social condition that sustains the iniquitous cycle of poverty and suffering for many and promotes abundance and wasteful materialistic choices for a few at the thin top layer of society. It shows how the future can be constructed through the commitment of the church and Christians to social justice. It also offers a model for the church of the poor today in the following ways:

1. *The church of the poor must be a site for discernment of what is going on in history.* Faith should inspire the church and its members to interpret through their daily activities how cultural factors and social realities in a particular society harm the realization of the common good and cosmic and human flourishing, especially for the poor. When James writes (2:15) of a brother or sister who is going naked and lacking food, he recapitulates in one sentence the various iterations of the conditions of the poor person in the biblical tradition. It is a classical critique of the social context. As Hartin notes, in this simple expression one sees first the gender sensitivity of the writer. He wants to make it clear that suffering and poverty ravage all humanity, both male and female. Second, he notes that people who are poorly clad are people who are desperately in need of help because they lack the basic necessities of life (Jb 22:6; Tb 4:16; Is 20:2–3; 58:7). Hartin points to two other instances where this same meaning is implied to portray the wretchedness of poverty and to appeal to the deepest compassion and stimulate action in the Christian community: Matthew 25:36: "I was naked and you gave me clothing." Revelation 3:17–18 present nakedness along with pitiable condition, blindness, shame, wretchedness, and lack of daily food as deplorable human conditions that are unacceptable to God. Thus being able to name the chaos in society which breeds poverty and how this is opposed to the will of God must be seen as essential to understanding the mission of the church. If this social critique and rejection of structures of injustice were true in the time of James, they are even more urgent in our times. This is because there is a concerted effort to blur or remove that line of distinction between the trajectory of history as dictated by failed and limited human construction of social order, and a gospel driven attempt to reconstruct a world history tainted by sin and injustice which is creating a cycle of unrest, angst, and war.[43]

Hartin argues that Bruce J. Malina's research points to a very important realization among scholars of the Letter of James that one cannot understand the Letter of James (2:1–13) and his critique of discrimination without

---

[43]Hartin, *James*, 150.

seeing how contexts of honor, shame, and patronage play out in traditional Greco-Roman and Jewish cultures.[44] In many cases, the honor code is not only maintained by the rich over the poor, but also by the poor who "honor" the rich and are beholden to them for their livelihood. These relationships contrast with the theological anthropology that everyone should be accepted as a child of God and that all have dignity. The Christian anthropology thus demands respect for all people, especially the poor and the vulnerable who are the ones who need God's love most if they are to realize in their lives God's purposes for human beings and creation. In this regard, Hartin argues:

> It is chiefly in the area of wealth and poverty that one sees a distinct reversal of values. While the wider society proclaimed wealth to be valuable and deserving of honor, and poverty the path to shamelessness and degradation, Jesus, James, Paul and all reversed this condition. In the community of the followers of Jesus, honor came from faith in God (see James 1:9–11) rather than wealth and status in society. Christians receive their honor from being part of God's own people.[45]

2. *The church of the poor for the poor must be an alternative community of hope and inclusion.* James warns against all kinds of favoritism and discrimination (2:1–13). The people who suffer most from any exclusionary practices in any society and even in religious groups like the church are the poor, minorities, the sick, and marginal groups as a result of gender, race, ethnic group, sex, sexuality, color, and so on. James's critique of societies who "make distinctions between classes of people" was as valid then as it is today in determining how particular churches embody the traits and ministry of the poor man of Galilee. The letter rejects what it calls using "two different standards in your mind" in judging people. The use of double standards could be seen in the light of this letter as opposed to building relationships that reflect the priorities and practices of the Lord Jesus Christ.

3. *The church of the poor for the poor can only become an alternative site of hope against the prevailing ethical and spiritual practices of the world that are opposed to God if it translates faith into action.* In this regard, the church and Christians must move from mere pity for the suffering of the poor and the downtrodden to daily practices for lifting them up from poverty and helping them stand on their feet (Jas 2:14–23). Writing on the translation of faith into action, Tamez argues, "In situations of oppression like that experienced by the communities of the Epistle of James, hope . . .

---

[44]Ibid., 97. See also Bruce J. Malina, *The New Testament World: Insights from Cultural Anthropology*, rev. ed. (Louisville, KY: John Knox, 1983).

[45]Hartin, *James*, 144.

is fundamental. Without it life would be nearly impossible. Nonetheless, hope is not sufficient; there is also a need for praxis, deeds. . . . For James, it seems, Christians are recognized not by their being but by their doing; by their fruits they are known."[46] The church and Christians should embody daily acts of faith that reflect compassion, mercy, patience, peacefulness, love, and kindness.

4. *The church of the poor for the poor must embrace a different approach to wealth and its use.* James introduces a theology of the poor that is unique in the whole of the New Testament in both its understanding of the mission of the Christian community and its interpretation of the place of wealth in the Christian community in the light of the eschaton.[47] The church of the poor is not presented in James as an impoverished church; rather it is a church that is waiting upon its kind and compassionate Lord (5:7–11) to intervene in history in present times and at the end time. There is an element of urgency and expectancy in James for the Christian community, but that expectancy is not passivity but daily actions driven by faith in reversing history. The critique of wealth in James is not a rejection of wealth in toto because the writer also shows a keen sense of the need for charity from the rich to the poor. Ostensibly, wealth is among the many good and perfect things that come from God above (Jas 1:16-18).

What it seems the letter is pointing out is how wealth is acquired and how it is used. Wealth should not be pursued through unethical means and through structures that pauperize the masses of God's people and exploit them through cheating the laborers, by paying them low wages or denying them payment in many cases and by denying them social benefits in such a way that they are crying to God (Jas 5:4). Wealth should not be considered as an end; hence the warning in James 4:13–17 for those who spend all their time planning about how to make money or building this or that estate or pursuing this or that line of business that God should be the center of all things and that God's will should come first.

There is an echo here—a life of comfort and luxury, eating to your heart's content—of the parable of the rich fool (Lk 12:13–21) who said to his soul, "Soul, you have plenty of grain laid up for many years. Take life easy; eat, drink and be merry." This mind-set is one of selfishness and pride (Jas 4:16–17). It fails to recognize God and the fleetingness of time and wealth. As James says (1:10), "Riches last no longer than the flowers in the grass; the scorching sun comes up, and the grass withers, the flower falls; what looked so beautiful now disappears. It is the same with the rich man: his business goes on; he himself perishes." In another verse (4:6)

---

[46]Tamez, 42.
[47]See Hartin, *James*, 239.

James strongly states that "God opposes the proud and he gives generously. Give in to God and resist the devil." It is clear that James sees wealth as good only if it comes from God—if it is acquired through ethical means and if it is placed at the service of others, especially those who are poor and underprivileged.[48]

The Christian community is a place of inclusion and equality without ranks and status; it is a harbor for the poor where they feel safe and protected from the oppressive structures of sin erected by the rich and the powerful which batter them by day and haunt them by night. The Christian community is also a site of friends of God and friends of one another who work in the Spirit to fight the "enemies" of God in the world. These "enemies of God" are found in the structures of injustice and the unequal power dynamics that are sustained through the systems of oppression that nail the people of God to the Cross of suffering and pain. Authentic Christian religion in such a Christian community is a religion that shows concern for the poor, and those who seek friendship with God in the church must act like God and be the champion of the poor.[49]

The option for the poor proposed by James is not an exclusionary choice by God for only the poor within the church. It is an appeal for the church to embrace an option for all the poor of the Lord—those within the church and those outside the church. It is a call to become one with the poor no matter their creed, color, sex, sexuality, or nationality. While James did not fully elaborate the sites where the poor are located, it offers sufficient evidence and teaching for us to have insight into such questions as to what it means to be poor, who the poor were in the early church, what the fundamental Christian attitude should be toward both the condition of the poor and the structures that sustain poverty and human suffering. Ultimately, what the Letter of James offers is a validation of my primary claim that Pope Francis and modern Catholicism's renewed consciousness about the poor in the world is not a new message. It is rather a renewal of a central teaching of the church, which needs to be retrieved and appropriated to meet the challenging and frightening reality of persistent poverty ravaging whole populations all over the world.

The Examples of the Early Church

Do not overlook the poor and let not his tattered rags incite you to contempt, but let them rather move you to pity your fellow creatures. For he is also a man, a creature of God, clothed in flesh like yourself,

---

[48]See ibid., 234–236; Tamez, *Scandalous Message of James*, 51.
[49]Hartin, *James*, 239.

and perchance in his spiritual virtue mirroring the common creator more than you do. Nature has not made him indigent in this way, but it is the tyranny of his neighbors that has reduced either him or his parents to indigence, while our lack of pity and compassion has maintained or even aggravated his poverty.[50]

This quote by Photius, a ninth-century patriarch, summarizes the attitude of Christians and the church to the poor in both the pre-Constantinian and the post-Constantinian periods. There were different approaches to accompanying the poor like the micro-credit and new community, *basileias,* of Saint Basil or the reform of the social mission of the church in John Chrysostom's Antioch. However, the basic theology of a poor church for the poor and a commitment to walking with the poor and addressing the causes of poverty from the roots have been common in Christian history. The self-understanding of the earliest Christian communities as a poor church for the poor is indisputable. Even though the formation of the rule of faith concentrated more on creedal formulas at the councils, being a church of the poor and being a church that is open to the poor was an unwritten rule of faith for the Christian community. It is one central aspect of the belief and practice (as attested to in the *Didache* and *Apostolic Tradition of Hippolytus*) of the church that was not included in the Creed mainly because it was so evident in the Christian community as its most distinguishing mark. The creedal formulas needed to be harmonized because the rationalistic mind of Greco-Roman cultures needed such clarity amid false teachings.[51] However, charity was the way of life of the early Christian community and was the practice until the time of Constantine in the fourth century, when the secular practices and systems of the Roman Empire began to change the dynamic structures and outreach of the church and Christians to the poor.

Many studies have shown that there were different forms of charitable assistance in both Greco-Roman and Jewish societies that shaped the Western Christian traditions of charitable outreach to the poor.[52] However, Christianity brought something radical in the approach to charity because

---

[50]Photius, *Hom* 2.4, quoted in Demetrios J. Constantelos, "The Hellenic Background and Nature of Patristic Philanthropy in the Early Byzantine Era," in *Wealth and Poverty in Early Church and Society*, ed. Susan R. Holman (Grand Rapids, MI: Baker Academic, 2008), 206.

[51]See, for instance, the discussion on the rule of faith by Everett Ferguson, *The Rule of Faith: A Guide* (Eugene, OR: Cascade Books, 2015).

[52]See, for instance, Gildas Hamel, *Poverty and Charity in Roman Palestine: The First Three Centuries CE* (Berkeley: University of California Press, 1990); Bruce W. Winter, *Seek the Welfare of the City: Christian Benefactors and Citizens* (Grand Rapids, MI: W. B. Eerdmans, 1994). See also Helen Rhee, *Loving the Poor, Saving the Rich: Wealth, Poverty, and Early Christian Formation* (Grand Rapids, MI: Baker Academic, 2012); L. Michael White and O. Larry Yarbrough, *The Social World of the First Christians: Essays in Honor of Wayne A. Meeks* (Minneapolis: Fortress Press, 1995).

of what subsequently was understood as Christian humanism and Christian universalism. This was the belief that every human being is made in the image and likeness of God and that the poor person particularly stands in the place of the Lord Jesus. Thus charity was a foundational virtue for being in the kingdom of God.[53]

In addition, Christianity brought with it a new understanding of the instrumental nature of the secular city, material wealth, and all earthly goods. These were presented as relative and useful for our common life here on earth as a preparation for the fullness of life in the kingdom. The Christian seeks the good of the earthly city with an eye on the heavenly kingdom, and works within the structures and systems of the earthly city to the extent that they promote daily practices that bring about the eschatological fruits of God's kingdom. Christianity brought what Paul Veyne calls "a new ethic of religiosity" to charitable giving, which led to the emergence of new forms of reaching out to the poor and those suffering—old people's homes, hospitals, orphanages, etc.—which were unknown in the pagan world.[54] What emerged was what the Christian apologist Aristides wrote about the life of the early Christian communities:

> Kindliness is their nature. There is no falsehood among them. They love one another. They do not neglect widows. Orphans they rescue from those who are cruel to them. Every one of them who has anything gives ungrudgingly to the one who has nothing. If they see a travelling stranger they bring him under their roof. They rejoice over him as a real brother, for they do not call one another brothers after the flesh, but they know they are brothers in the spirit and in God. If one of them sees that one of their poor must leave this world, he provides his burial as well as he can. And if they hear that one of them is imprisoned or oppressed by their opponents for the sake of their Christ's name, all of them take care of all needs. If possible they set him free. If anyone among them is poor or comes into want while they themselves have nothing to spare, they fast two or three days for him. In this way they can supply the poor man with the food he needs.[55]

Those practices of the early church are different ways of appropriating the pattern already established in the first century as reported in Acts 4:32–35:

---

[53]See Raniero Cantalamessa, *Navigating the New Evangelization*, trans. Bret Thomas (Boston: Pauline Books and Media, 2013), 2–9.

[54]Cited in Bruce W. Longenecker, *Remember the Poor: Paul, Poverty and the Greco-Roman World* (Grand Rapids, Michigan: William B. Eerdmans, 2010), 61.

[55]Quoted in Longenecker, *Remember the Poor*, 61–62.

All the believers were one in heart and mind. No one claimed that any of their possessions was their own, but they shared everything they had. With great power the apostles continued to testify to the resurrection of the Lord Jesus. And God's grace was so powerfully at work in them all that there were no needy persons among them. For from time to time those who owned land or houses sold them, brought the money from the sales and put it at the apostles' feet, and it was distributed to anyone who had need.

Christian charity was not restricted to Christians alone, but to all those who needed help. Tertullian testified to this when he wrote of the tradition among Christians to put away every month some money in their treasure chest, "to support and bury poor people, to supply the wants of boys and girls destitute of means and parents, and of old persons confined now to the house; such too, as have suffered shipwreck."[56] Such was the outreach of the early church to all the poor in the cities that Emperor Julian (332–63), who was opposed to the Christian faith, could not hide his admiration for Christian charity. Longenecker commenting on this writes: "Noting the way in which the poor were 'neglected and overlooked' by pagan sectors and the way that Christians (and Jews) 'devoted themselves to benevolence,' Julian also took note of the way that 'the impious Galileans (i.e., Christians) support not only their poor, but ours as well,' not least since 'everyone can see that our people lack aid from us' (Ep. 22–430D)."[57]

However, as Peter Brown has demonstrated, the emergence of Constantine, the "cheerful giver," ultimately changed the way collections and benefactions were made both for the upkeep of the church and the care of the poor. Constantine became, as Brown noted, "a towering exemplar of old-fashioned euergetism,"[58] building gigantic churches, and dwarfing the other rich patrons and charitable members of the Christian community in the scale of his outreach to the church and by extension to the poor. However, in exempting the churches from taxes and in making huge provisions for the clergy, and in upholding the *annona civica* system which provided food and supplies to citizens, especially the poor, for free or at reduced price, the care of the poor that had been common among Christians gradually became state-based and began to lose its evangelical edge. It became something similar to modern forms of aid—controlled, structured, pursued for some end that is not often the best interest of the poor, and selective in its nature and

---

[56]Tertullian, Apol. 39, cited in Longenecker, *Remember the Poor*, 61.

[57]Longenecker, *Remember the Poor*, 62.

[58]Peter Brown, *Poverty and Leadership in the Later Roman Empire* (Hanover, NH: University Press of New England, 2002), 27. "Euergetism" is an aristocratic practice of doing good deeds.

distribution. However, Brown argues that despite the changes in the Roman society of the fourth and fifth centuries during the time of Constantine and post-Constantine, the common understanding was that the church received offerings because it looked after the poor. In that regard, the traditional care for the poor by the Christian communities for its members came to be regarded over time as a public service that the church performed in return for the public privileges it received.

Indeed the changes in society forced the church to reinvent its charitable work. As Brown noted: "The rise to prominence of Christian forms of care for the poor registered this new situation," and while maintaining some of its ancient roots, it was also creating a new approach that would define the future of Christian charity. The bishops, clergy, and laypeople became agents of change in bringing succor to the poor. As Brown writes: "To put it bluntly, in a sense, it was the Christian bishops who invented the poor. They rose to leadership in late Roman society by bringing the poor into ever sharper focus. They presented their actions as a response to the needs of an entire category of persons (the poor) on whose behalf they claimed to speak."[59] Those who are uncomfortable with Pope Francis's poor-first pastoral program and message may need to be reminded that from the earliest times of the church's history, when the position of bishops emerged, "love of the poor" and "care of the poor" were seen as the central mission of the episcopacy. So important was this role that in Cappadocia, rural bishops were appointed for the new communities in far-flung territories outside the cities where they were involved in charitable outreach—feeding the hungry, caring for the sick and taking care of the poor.[60] "The notion 'care of the poor' helped define the place of the Christian church in Roman society. It acted as a discreet control on the clergy. They were to know their place—closer to the poor than to the top of society. Thus, in 326 a law of Constantine ruled that rich townsmen might not join the clergy. The emperors did not want the town councils to be drained by 'lateral promotions' of wealthy members into the new hierarchy of the Christian church, as bishops and clergymen 'for the wealthy must be there to support the obligations of the secular world, while the poor are maintained by the wealth of the church.'"[61]

The point is that no matter how favorable or unfavorable the political and social contexts, Christian groups everywhere have always believed that the poor stand in the place of Christ, and that being engaged in concrete actions in liberating them from their pain and suffering is a way of identifying with

---

[59]Ibid., 8.

[60]See Susan R. Holman, *The Hungry are Dying: Beggars and Bishops in Roman Cappadocia* (New York: Oxford University Press, 2001).

[61]Brown, *Poverty and Leadership in the Later Roman Empire*. 31.

Christ. The church from its origins has always been identified as a church of the poor and for the poor; everything it has and all that it is are oriented toward the poor. The church has no other identity than the poor and cannot exist without the poor. Conversely, the poor cannot exist or survive without the church, and they will die if the church ignores this central mission of being a church of the poor and for the poor. The church shines brightest when it becomes a light not unto itself, but illumining the darkness, shame, injustice, and disorder brought about by the scandal of poverty and sin.

By way of conclusion of this section I highlight briefly two aspects of the teaching on the church of the poor in the first centuries of the church through the lens of Saint John Chrysostom in two homilies, *Homily 50 on the Gospel of Matthew* and *Homilies on Almsgivings*. Chrysostom's powerful homilies will help answer two questions of concern to the development of the foundation of Pope Francis's poor-first policy, namely, Who are the poor? and How is the identity of the church tied to that of the poor?

1. *Who are the poor?* The poor person is the Lord, as John Chrysostom wrote: "Through our help to the hungry, strangers, the sick and prisoners, we become God's friends. If we do good, we make God our friend. He voluntarily becomes our debtor."[62] This is the central teaching of the early church, drawing from the Lord's teaching on the last judgment in Matthew 24. John Chrysostom brings this out so clearly in his homily 50 on Matthew 14:22–23 when he reflected on how the Lord came to the apostles walking on the sea. The Lord calms the sea and then continues with his disciples to Genneseret, where many people came to Jesus and touched the hem of his garment and were healed (Mt 14:34–36). John Chrysostom draws some important conclusions from this. First, touching Jesus today will involve two things: touching him in the Eucharist and touching him in the poor. Second, the one whose body we touch in the Eucharist is the one who suffers in the poor, and in touching the poor and reaching out to them we touch Jesus. On touching Jesus in the Eucharist, John writes:

> For indeed his body is set before us now, not his garment only, but even His body; not for us to touch it only, but also to eat and be filled. Let us now then draw near with faith, every one that hath an infirmity. For if they that touched the hem of his garment drew from him so much virtue, how much more they that possess him entire?[63]

Chrysostom then goes on to enumerate several sins that should not be associated with those who touch and are touched by the Lord in the Eucha-

---

[62]Hom. Heb. 25.1 (PG 63:174).
[63]John Chrysostom, *Homilies on Matthew* 50, 3.

rist—violence, enmity, clinging to wealth, attachment to material wealth in such a way that it "lavishes the soul." Other conditions that he considered unacceptable for those who touch the Lord include people who betray the Lord like Judas or those who deny the Lord like Peter, and those who exploit the poor by stripping widows, orphans, and the vulnerable of their livelihood. It is not the altar and the churches, according to John Chrysostom, which should be beautified with gold. On the contrary, the beauty that the Lord desires is when people adorn themselves with the beauty of the mysteries of salvation represented in the gift of the sacrifice of the bread. On this John preached with so much force on the ecclesiological significance of detachment from material things in order to help the poor:

> Let not this therefore be your aim, to offer golden vessels only, but to do so from honest earnings likewise. For these are of the sort that is more precious even than gold, these that are without injuriousness. For the church is not a gold foundry nor a workshop for silver, but an assembly of angels. Wherefore it is souls which we require, since in fact God accepts these for the souls' sake.[64]

Chrysostom then proceeds in the concluding part of this homily to make a direct connection between the poor and Christ. He begins by asking the question, "Do you wish to honor Christ's body?" He responds by saying that then one should not neglect the Lord when he is cold, naked, and needy, for "he that said 'this is my body,' and by his word confirmed the fact, this same said, 'ye saw me an hungered, and fed me not,' and 'inasmuch as you did it not to one of the least of these, ye did it not to me.'"[65] He exhorts the people in Antioch that the best honor Christ desires of them is to honor him in the poor, "give him the honor which he commanded by spending your wealth on poor people. Since God hath no need at all of golden vessels, but of golden souls."[66] He concludes his homily by warning that the severe judgment of hell is threatened for those who refuse to show mercy and reach out to brothers and sisters who are in distress, but that no one ever gets punished for not decorating the altar with gold and silver.[67] He admonishes Christians to think of the Lord and see him in the poor when he writes:

> For what is the profit, when his table indeed is full of golden cups, but he perishes with hunger? First fill him, being hungry before decking his

---

[64] Ibid., 4.
[65] Ibid.
[66] Ibid.
[67] Ibid., 5.

table. Dost thou make him a cup of gold, while thou givest him not a cup of cold water? And what is the profit? Dost thou furnish his table with cloths bespangled with gold, while to himself thou affordest not even the necessary covering? And what good comes of it? For tell me, should you see one at a loss for necessary food, and omit appeasing his hunger, while you first overlaid his table with silver; would he indeed thank thee, and not rather be indignant? What, again, if seeing one wrapped in rags, and stiff with cold, thou shouldest neglect giving him a garment, and build columns, saying, "thou wert doing it to his honor," would he not say that thou wert mocking, and account it an insult, and that the most extreme?[68]

2. *The identity of the church as being poor for the poor.* "How long will you not cease from introducing poor men and beggars into your sermons, prophesying disaster to us and our own future impoverishment, so as to make beggars of us all." This was the question which the rich in Antioch posed to John Chrysostom concerning his constant preaching on poverty and the need for the church and Christians to support the poor.[69] Whenever the gospel of the poor is preached, it always poses a challenge to the established structures of power and privilege in society. Whereas my goal here is not to discuss the church's own relationship with wealth and the wealthy in the time of John Chrysostom, I am more concerned here in demonstrating my primary argument that Pope Francis's call for a poor church is not a new message. Rather, it is an invitation for contemporary Catholicism to return to its origins and walk away from accommodating its life and identity in the pursuit of wealth, secular power, and privileges, to the neglect of the poor, who are the treasures of the church. For John Chrysostom, the church was a harbor for the poor.[70] He was led to this understanding of the identity of the church through the writings of Saint Paul. Bruce W. Longenecker, contrary to some other scholars, argues strongly for a distinctive Pauline exposition of a theology of poverty and the mission of Christians and the church in poverty eradication. Care for the poor, he argues, was central to the message of the gospel that Paul proclaimed:

---

[68]Ibid., 4.

[69]See citation and commentary in Rudolf Brandle, "This Sweetest Passage: Matthew 25:31–56 and Assistance to the Poor in the Homilies of John Chrysostom," in *Wealth and Poverty in Early Church and Society*, ed. Susan R. Holman (Grand Rapids, MI: Baker Academic, 2008), 128.

[70]On the identity of the church as a harbor for the poor in John Chrysostom's teaching and pastoral program see Eric Costanzo, *Harbor for the Poor: A Missiological Analysis of Almsgiving in the View and Practice of John Chrysostom* (Eugene, OR: Wipf and Stock, 2013).

For Paul, economic assistance of the poor was not sufficient in and of itself, nor was it exhaustive of the good news of Jesus; but neither was it supplemental or peripheral to the good news. Instead, falling within the essentials of the good news, care for the poor was thought by Paul to be a necessary hallmark of the corporate life of Jesus-followers who lived in conformity with the good news of the early Jesus-movement.[71]

John Chrysostom saw in the examples of the Pauline church an ideal of "a 'loving' community made up of benevolent and generous householders. . . . Social distinctions between rich and poor, between slaves and masters were accepted, but they were to be softened by generous giving and by gentle dealing."[72]

John Chrysostom saw the church in many ways: it is the body of Christ in the suffering body of the poor, it is a place for social work, and a home for outreach to the poor and the needy (he had a hostel for strangers and four dining halls in it for feeding the poor). In his teaching, the Christian home is the domestic church, but it is also a house church with a little treasury for keeping the "holy collection" that he proposed following the example of Saint Paul for almsgiving on a weekly basis.[73] In order to illuminate Chrysostom's teaching on the poor and the church, let me refer to three important points from his homily on almsgiving (homily 10) that can help guide the church today. This homily was delivered when John Chrysostom passed through the marketplace during the winter and saw so many poor people and beggars lying helpless and homeless on the streets.[74]

The first is the *connection between helping the poor and mercy.* The church of the poor can only serve the poor by being merciful. In this regard, Brandle writes:

Central to John is the performance of *eleemosyne*, a word from which the English word "alms" developed. However, *eleemosyne* includes far more for John than alms. For him it is a behavior of loving openness to fellow humans and can be expressed in varying acts of compassion. It may include the kind word just as much as material

---

[71]Longenecker, *Remember the Poor,* 1.

[72]Brown, *Poverty and Leadership in the Later Roman Empire,* 19.

[73]Brandle, "This Sweetest Passage," 131. John Chrysostom on this said: "On each day of the Lord, let everyone lay aside in his house the Master's money; and let the deed become a law and immovable custom. And then we will require no other recommendation or counsel. For discourse and advice do not have the power to achieve these things as much as the habit that is established firmly with time. If we ratify this—to lay aside something toward the succor of the poor on every Day of the Lord—we will not transgress this law, even if innumerable needs fall upon us" (Homily 10, 12).

[74]*St. John Chrysostom on Repentance and Almsgiving,* trans. Gus George Christo (Washington, DC: Catholic University of America Press, 1998).

help. *Eleemosyne* is a power that leads God to people and people to God. John calls on people to love *eleemosyne*. For if she once knows us, he says, the Lord will also know us; if she denies us, the Lord will also deny us and say: "I never knew you." John, who was living as an ascetic, valued *eleemosyne* more highly than any form of abstinence. For through mercy and compassion, not through asceticism, we can become like God.[75]

In opening his homily, John Chrysostom makes the constant appeal to mercy (*eleemosyne*): "We must always make sermons on almsgiving, because we, too, have much need of this *mercy* issuing from the Master who created us, but especially during the present season when the frost is severe."[76] Elsewhere in the homily (10, 4, 19) he preached that Christians must show an earnestness and readiness to be merciful toward those who are in need as a way of becoming worthy of God's grace. Further in the homily (10, 5, 22), he speaks of God as having "*a principle of mercy*," which God gives to humanity (Christians), and he challenges the church and Christians to show "*great mercy*" to all, in imitation of God, through benevolence in "words, money, and deeds."

John Chrysostom was very strong against those who discriminate against the poor and the needy and those who judge the poor, strangers, migrants, and homeless people as lazy and criminals. In the homily (10, 6, 25) he enjoins that mercy is an unmerited good that Christians must show to everyone. He preaches as follows:

Therefore, of what pardon and defense would we be worthy, when our ancestors appear to support with their own money even those who are settled far away, and run to help them, while we drive away even those from another place who flee to us for refuge, and we demand exact audits and that sort of thing, although we are responsible for myriads of evils? And if God should examine minutely each of our issues as we investigate about the poor, we would not bring to pass for ourselves one single pardon or mercy.[77]

The second is *that helping the poor is the responsibility of every member of the church; it is not an optional thing; rather it is a way of life for the*

---

[75]Brandle, "This Sweetest Passage," 131. *Eleemosyne* also has the meaning of "being concerned about people in their need, mercy, sympathetic, compassionate." See Frederick William Danker, ed., *A Greek–English Lexicon of the New Testament and Other Early Christian Literature*, 3rd ed. (Chicago: University of Chicago Press, 2000), 316.

[76]John Chrysostom, Homily 10, 1.

[77]Ibid., 6, 25.

church and all Christians. The vocation of helping others is central to what it means to follow Jesus. In his homily on Lazarus and the Rich Man, John Chrysostom writes with clarity:

> Therefore let us use our goods sparingly, as belonging to others, so that they may become our own. How shall we use them sparingly, as belonging to others? When we do not spend them beyond our needs, and do not spend them for our needs only, but give equal shares into the hands of the poor. . . . You must do this. For you have obtained more than others have, and you have received it, not to spend it for yourself, but to become a good steward for others as well.[78]

John in the homily admonishes even the poor to contribute to the common purse meant to help those who are suffering: "I do not say this only to the rich," he says, "but also to the poor; not only to the free but also to slaves; not only to men but also to women. Let no one remain unaccomplished in this ministration. Let no one refrain from sharing in the gain; rather, let everyone contribute."[79] One sees here in this insistence a rejection of a dependent almsgiving or charity, but an approach to empowering the poor to believe in themselves and trust that God can lift them up. However, viewed in this light, John Chrysostom sees the poor as having some assets that they can bring to the church as treasures.

The third and final point which is of interest is that *money, almsgiving, and helping the poor is a way of life for the church, a path toward mercy and salvation.* Thus, money meant for the poor is called "sacred money" (homily 10, 4, 15) because the poor stand in the place of Christ; so what is given to the poor becomes holy because it is given to Christ. Giving to the poor is the best insurance for storing up treasures in heaven:

> Let everyone's house become a church that will have sacred money stored up within it. For the forfeited banks that are unassailable on earth are symbol of these treasuries in heaven. Wherever money is stored up for the poor, that place is inaccessible to the demons and the money that is collected together for almsgiving fortifies Christian homes more than a shield, spear, weapons, physical power, and multitudes of soldiers.[80]

---

[78]John Chrysostom, *On Wealth and Poverty*, trans. Catherine P. Roth (New York: St. Vladimir's Seminary Press, 1984), 50.

[79]John Chrysostom, Homily 10, 13.

[80]Ibid., 4, 15.

The philanthropy of God is presented in the final section of this homily (10, 6, 26) as a model for all Christians. Salvation is a gift from God and the manifestation of God's philanthropy toward humans. Charity is *imitatio Dei*. As a result, just as God freely gives to humans so also humans should freely give to the poor without judging them. Rather, Christians are called to "correct the poverty" by making sure that the hungry are fed, the naked are clothed, the homeless are given shelter, strangers and migrants are welcomed, and the orphans and widows are given the help they need. But "correcting the poverty," as John Chrysostom proposes, will require also changing the structures that promote poverty and the selfish and sinful hearts that hoard the goods of the earth in the hands of a few. As Susan R. Holman writes with regard to the practices proposed for reaching out to the poor here:

> Both rich and poor also take on the face of divine. The rich do this by imitating God's mercy and justice, God's model of patronage. The poor do this by their basic needs for food and water, thereby imaging Christ. Service to the poor is treated as a liturgy; in other words, it is just as important for true worship as is going to church.[81]

There are limitations obviously in what John Chrysostom is presenting about how to interpret poverty and the approaches and paradigms that churches and Christians can embrace—for example, he fails to condemn the institution of slavery and instead calls for mercy and better treatment of slaves; he does not offer sufficient critique of state policies that perpetuate poverty and the economic practices of the rich patrons of the church. There is also a view of salvation that narrows Christian ethics and Christian life to almsgiving without admitting the other forms of spirituality and morality that add together in creating an integrated Christian witnessing. However, what John Chrysostom offers is a strong exemplary picture of the centrality of charity to the poor, social justice, mercy, and compassion in the church of his times. This model obviously can be seen at work in the teaching and practices of Pope Francis, and his papacy can rightly be framed in these concluding words of John Chrysostom's homily 10:

> For in truth, if we are going to examine lives, we will never have mercy upon any human being, rather hindered by this inopportune meddlesomeness, we will remain fruitless and destitute of all help,

---

[81]Susan R. Holman, *God Knows There's Need: Christian Responses to Poverty* (Oxford: Oxford University Press, 2009), 69.

and we shall submit ourselves to great toil to no purpose and in vain. For this reason, I now beg you truly: banish far from us this ill-timed curiosity, and give to all who have need, and do this abundantly, so that we may obtain much mercy and the philanthropy of God on that day.[82]

---

[82]John Chrysostom, Homily 10, 6, 26

3

The Praxis of Illuminative Ecclesiology

Accountability, the Art of Accompaniment, and a Vulnerable Mission

Making the gospel message an ideology. This is a temptation which has been present in the church from the beginning: the attempt to interpret the gospel apart from the gospel itself and apart from the church. An example: *Aparecida*, at one particular moment, felt this temptation. It employed, and rightly so, the method of "see, judge and act" (cf. no. 19). The temptation, though, was to opt for a way of "seeing" which was completely "antiseptic," detached and unengaged, which is impossible. The way we "see" is always affected by the way we direct our gaze. There is no such thing as an "antiseptic" hermeneutics. The question was, rather: How are we going to look at reality in order to see it?
—Pope Francis, Speech to CELAM, July 28, 2013

There are four moments of illuminative ecclesiology that I have identified in the message and ministry of Pope Francis and in the history of the church, namely: accountability, the art of accompaniment, a vulnerable mission, and dialogue with the poor and the world. In this chapter, I develop these key moments, drawing from biblical theology, Catholic social ethics, and social analysis illumined through some of the writings of Pope Francis and his approaches to pastoral ministry. I conclude the chapter by showing how the church can transform the social context through these moments. I use stories from the African social context to show how this praxis brings healing to the wounds of God's people and transformation and salvation.

It is important to note at this preliminary stage in the development of this praxis that Illuminative ecclesiology is not a theological system or a model of the church to be replicated by rote in every context. Rather, it is a way of being church in multiple sites of pain, in diversity of expressions, and multiple dimensions, which should reflect all aspects of the church's life, teaching, liturgy, social mission, structures, and pastoral practices in such a way that it shows God's face to the world and reflects the faces of humanity and the cosmos to God as in a mirror. In this regard, it is also a paradigm of mission for the world church.[1] Illuminative ecclesiology is grounded in a "culture of encounter" by an affirmation that faith makes of the concreteness of God's presence and the resplendent seed of God's love and presence in every human and cosmic reality. In this chapter I show that the praxis of illuminative ecclesiology begins with daily encounters in our churches through which God in Christ becomes concrete in the church and in the world. In this regard, daily witnessing of Christians and the form of all ecclesial structures and pastoral and social ministries should be so designed that they always reflect the priorities and practices of the Lord Jesus in his attitude to the world and humanity. This way of being church is identifiable in the words and deeds of Pope Francis.

Pope Francis affirms that the church mediates, in its identity and mission, God's ceaseless invitation to all to enter into the boundless love and mercy of God. God's heart is permanently open to all without conditions and without any prior qualifications. This is how Pope Francis presents this message in one of his speeches: "The Lord wants us to belong to a church that knows how to open her arms and welcome everyone, that is not a house for the few, but a house for everyone, where all can be renewed, transformed, sanctified by his love—the strongest and the weak, sinners, the indifferent, those who feel discouraged or lost."[2]

The light of Christ shines through the reality of sin, pain, suffering, and brokenness in history. This is why the mission of the church and Christians can be grounded in Christ only if it is lived with hope in the midst of brokenness, suffering, and pain. This is the dynamic through which it can receive the light of Christ and give the same light to the world. In this way, it can lead God's people deeper into the mysteries of God by showing the presence of God even in the darkest shadows or deepest valleys of history and the most painful wounds of God's people. The mission of the church then in this light is to be an open door and a mediation of diverse points of light. It exists to call God's people to embrace daily practices of hope, mercy, love,

---

[1] I have proposed in a previous work that the illuminative ecclesiology of Pope Francis offers the church in Africa and in the world a Triple A pastoral method—accountability, accompaniment, and action. See Stan Chu Ilo, "The Church of Pope Francis: An Ecclesiology of Accountability, Accompaniment, and Action," in *The Church We Want: African Catholics Look to Vatican III*, ed. Agbonkhianmeghe E. Orobator (Maryknoll, NY: Orbis Books, 2016), 23–30.

[2] Pope Francis, *The Church of Mercy: A Vision for the Church* (Chicago: Loyola Press, 2014), 31.

and fidelity, and stewardship of oneself and others in the concrete realization in history of God's will of abundant life for humans and the entire cosmos.

This mission is to be achieved, as I pointed out in chapter 1, through the response of faith in the church. It is then the summons to the people of God to daily commitments and choices that meet the ultimate moral demand of discipleship and authentic witnessing to the values of the gospel. These daily practices are inspired by the desire—in the hearts of all and in the very heart of the church—to see God in every human and cosmic reality.

The church, seen in this light, is the site for encountering God in the dumps of history. Human and cosmic reality are then seen through the light of faith as radiating or concealing the beauty or the inner Word of love and truth vis-à-vis their ordination to the eschatological fruits of God's kingdom in history. Illuminative ecclesiology offers multiple images of a church—in all its members and in the world—led by the Holy Spirit as the "seeing eyes," discerning the presence of God in history. This way, the church becomes an instrument for opening the eyes of the world to see and witness in history and creation God's transformative grace in Christ. This is how the gospel can become a source of hope, especially in the brokenness of the world, the limitations of humanity, and the cry of those on the margins and those who are carrying some festering existential wounds. It is only by being present with people in their wounds and in places where they are hurting or suffering that the church can bring about, by God's grace, in the words of Balthasar, "the greatest possible radiance in the world by virtue of the closest possible following of Christ."[3]

A CULTURE OF ENCOUNTER:
AN ACCOUNTABLE CHURCH

When we speak about an accountable church, it has often been projected in terms of clerical sexual abuse and the need to hold the church accountable for the failings of the church's leadership.[4] The biblical foundation of accountability is much more nuanced and richer in meaning than this. The most important biblical insight for me is the preface to the gospel of Luke (1:1–4). It begins this way, "Seeing that others have undertaken to draw up an *account* of the events that have taken place among us, exactly as these were handed down to us by those who from the outset were eyewitnesses and ministers of the word, I in my turn, after carefully going over the whole

---

[3]Hans Urs von Balthasar, *My Work in Retrospect*, trans. Brian McNeil (San Francisco: Ignatius Press, 1993), 51.

[4]Paul Lakeland, *The Liberation of the Laity: In Search of an Accountable Church* (New York: Continuum, 2003), 257–85.

story from the beginning, have decided to write an ordered *account* for you." There are three important insights from this preface to the Gospel of Luke that I have employed in this section to explicate what I mean by an accountable church.

First, the account or narrative (*diegesis*) written about in the preface is of "events that have taken place among us"—*pragmata peplerophoremena*. Luke concentrates his narrative on the efficacy of Christ's actions and presence as witnessed to in the community. Therefore, the events in the lives of the Christians and the community—great and small, good or bad—are embraced, interpreted, and judged in their connection with Christ. What the Lord does is the event; and what happens in people's lives relates to the Lord. The divine identity and the authority displayed through the action of the Lord make such a compelling story that the world can see and believe it through how it is taking flesh in the community as "event." The story of what is going on in the community, what God is doing, has an evidential character. This evidential character has healing, liberating, saving, and teaching effects witnessed to in the church and seen in the world.

Luke is concerned about what is going on in the community and how the Christian community is immersed in what is going on in their communities. He is also interested in telling the story of how the daily pathos and struggles of the people are central to how the community of faith sees the presence and action of Christ in the community, from local communities to the universal community or the globe. Luke's use of "account," or "narrative," refers to all that has taken place—the great and small, the good and the bad, life and death, sin and righteousness—nothing is left out. To tell the story of "all that has taken place" the narrator must be present in the story and is actually telling his own story of a life that he is living with his brothers and sisters. As he noted, he "examined everything carefully" in order to make sure that no aspect of "what happens" or "what happened" in the community is excluded in his story.

Furthermore, the account is ordered. This is not because of its logical or chronological coherence, but rather in terms of the whole story coming together because the Lord is present in the story to make all things whole. The shattered lives of people and the complex challenges facing the early Christian community are presented as having an ordered destiny because Christ is present to bring all things together so that the story will be a complete one with a beginning, a complex middle, and an ordered end. It is a continuum which is integrated by the participation of all in the life of all and by the presence of Christ through the church in bringing order in the disorder and chaos that sin, poverty, suffering, and pain inflict on wounded hearts and on a wounded world. The summons to Theophilus that the account is being put together for him in order that he might believe is an assurance that God is present in history. Therefore, every aspect of the human condition is within the compass of God's love and mercy. The stories of life lived in faith will come together—everything works together for those who trust God (Rom 8:28). The emphasis on what the Lord does in the community is not about a past reality but actually a dynamic and active event that Luke wishes to pass on to all the lovers of God who receive the Good News. The divine offer of salvation in Christ is for all peoples and all could see this divine action in the man Jesus.

Second, narrating the stories of what is taking place in the community and in the life of people will require that one should *be an eyewitness* (*autoptes*, Acts 1:2) and be present with the people in order to give what the writer of the First Letter of Peter (3:15–16) calls an *apologia* (confession or an answer) of the hope in the Christian community.

Third, in order to give an answer to the world of Christian hope, the eyewitness must follow closely (*parakoloutheo*, Acts 1:3) and participate fully in the lives of individuals and the community of faith. The account is not something that can be told from a distance. One has to tell the story as an insider; it is a grounded account because the writer is in touch with the phenomena being described. It is an account that one tells from a first person perspective as a witness to what one is describing. We find that the writer is giving testimony to what he is living; what he saw and heard and what he believes (see 1 Jn 1:3; Acts 4:20–21, 1:21). The account is about how the community of Jesus is present in the chaos of the lives of people and in this way is continuing what Jesus did—healing, teaching, liberating, and saving a wounded world.[5]

It is in the light of this analysis of the preface of Luke's Gospel that I wish to use the term "an accountable church" to designate (1) *a church that is an eyewitness to what is going on in the lives of the people* in particular communities and in the lives of all of God's people in every part of the world; (2) *a church that takes an interest in what is going on in the lives of people and in finding how people can be healed, saved, liberated, taught, and affirmed* to appreciate that they are loved unconditionally by God and gifted by God to play a full part in the work of God in the world; (3) *a church that by being present and participating in the life of people in a particular and personal way is able to be a mirror for shining the merciful and loving face of God to the people and for reflecting the faces of everyone to God*; (4) *a church that lives in such a way that the stories that come out of its communities are able to move all men and women who love God to learn and receive the message of the Gospel as good news* because the church and

---

[5]I have been helped in this section by Max Zerwick and Mary Grosvenor, *A Grammatical Analysis of the Greek New Testament* (Rome: Editrice Pontificio Istituto Biblico, 1996), 168.

its members have first lived and witnessed to it for themselves. Pope Francis points to this in his catechesis on the church's holiness when he describes the church as the point of contact for all people in their search for God:

> Throughout history, some have been tempted to say that the church is the church of only the pure and the perfectly consistent, and it expels all the rest. This is not true! This is heresy! The church, which is holy, does not reject sinners; she does not reject us all; she does not reject us because she calls everyone, welcomes them, is open even to those furthest from her; she calls everyone to allow themselves to be enfolded by the mercy, the tenderness, and the forgiveness of the Father, who offers everyone the possibility of meeting him, of journeying together toward sanctity.[6]

In the light of these four aspects of an accountable church, we can see that the vocation of the church is among others to render praise to God for the gifts of creation and of all lives by embracing them as unqualified good. As a result, central to the mission of the church is to render account to God for all these gifts, especially the gift of the least of the brethren who are close to the heart of God. The beauty of God is reflected in creation. "The revelation that God is the creator, the origin and the ground and destiny of all creation, is the ultimate basis for our affirming the truth (knowability) and goodness (lovability) and beauty (delightfulness) of all things. All things can be loved and enjoyed because they are created."[7] The beauty of God is not lost in creation in the face of evil, suffering, poverty, sin, and pain. Therefore, to give an account as an ecclesial practice is about how the church discerns in the midst of the stories found in the contradictions and shadows of life both in particular and universal contexts how and where God is present.

In order to be an instrument for bringing light, especially in the pains and sufferings of many people who are on the margins, an accountable church immerses itself in history. It is a church that seeks to encounter each person—even the worst sinners and the lost souls in human eyes—as a unique instance of God's beauty. The church remains present to people in pain. In this kind of church, no one is lost. Rather, like the Good Shepherd, the accountable church must take stock of all of God's children and go out in search of the lost, the forgotten, and the scattered children of God. It is this attitude, which Pope Francis has lived, which fascinates the world. He has encouraged all Christians to go out and not remain shut up in parishes and communities, rectories and chanceries, convents and monasteries, especially

---

[6]Pope Francis, *Church of Mercy*, 31.
[7]John Navone, *Toward a Theology of Beauty* (Collegeville, MN: Liturgical Press, 1996), 1.

in the prevailing culture of neglect where "there is no place for the elderly or for the unwanted child; there is no time for the poor person in the street."[8]

Accountability unites us to God who is the source of all things and for whom all reality and all persons count, no matter their situation or condition. There is a certain unique particularity to the union of all creation to God in how this is manifested and incarnated in the lives of individuals. The church is invited to see beauty in creation and to render to God a fitting praise by working hard in identifying instances in creation and in life where suffering and pain, injustice and structures of sin make it impossible for the beauty of God to shine out in creation. The accountable church is thus a church that cares for all creation—a church that has a merciful heart open to all people. It is also a church where people are embraced as beautiful unto God, not because of their present condition but because of their intrinsic and priceless value because they have been created in the image and likeness of God. An accountable church is one that sees salvation and liberation as possible for all people, especially those who are losing their way and those who are far away from God, truth, beauty, holiness, and love. An accountable church is one in which no one is lost.

There are many biblical images that can guide the church in becoming accountable: 1 Peter 3:15 on Saint Peter's call to Christians to always be ready to give an account or answer (*apologia*) for the hope which they have embraced; the parable of the steward (Lk 16:2); the parable of the talent (Mt 25:14–30); the parable of the sower (Mt 13:1–23); the parable of the lost sheep (Lk 15:1–7); and the Good Shepherd analogy (Jn 10). In these passages, there are many moments that stand out in helping to guide pastoral action and methods in the ministry of an illuminative church.

Accountability in scripture begins with recognizing that we have received all these gifts in earthen vessels (2 Cor 4:7). Stewardship of these treasures requires affirming constantly their source and the model that we have received from the Good Lord on how to live faithfully and fully the reality of these gifts. It is the Lord who is the owner of the vineyard; the Lord is in charge; the Lord is the one whose *logos* is our being and whose *logos* is our mission and our ultimate destiny. We are servants in the vineyard, not masters of the vineyard (Lk 16:2, 17:10; Rom 1:1–4). How have we used the gifts and charism that the Lord has given us in the church and in the world?

A bishop once said to me that "the Catholic church is one institution that perhaps has the greatest abundance of gifts, but has not learned how to harvest them. There is something to be learned from Jesus who had a very small group of followers, but did not keep them like a hen under his wings, but gave them wings to fly."

---

[8]Pope Francis, *Church of Mercy*, 60.

When I was appointed the pastor of Saint Thérèse Parish, Courtice, Ontario, Canada, in 2010, the first thing I did was to conduct a parish survey and opportunity scan. I asked the parishioners to answer questions relating to what they wanted to see happen in the parish, the kind of homilies they would like to hear at Mass, and the type of ministries we should adopt. A senior priest friend of mine and spiritual counselor was so disturbed about this step that he called me to ask: "Are you going to run this parish like a Protestant church?" My reply to the priest was that I find it unacceptable that I should come to a parish, which had existed for twenty-nine years before my arrival, with more than four thousand families, and four Catholic schools and roll out pastoral plans and programs without the input of all parishioners who have equal or even more stake in the parish than I had. He was not supportive of my initiative. However, this was one of those few moments when I went on my own without his guidance. The response of the parishioners was quite positive, and we had close to five hundred respondents.

As I pored through the feedback, three thoughts came to me, which challenged me to rethink what I had learned about the structure of governance and pastoral administration in our parishes, dioceses, and at the Vatican. They are also relevant for developing a pastoral theology of accountability in the church.

The first, I learned that the lay members of the church are a rich treasure for the church, which has been neglected. In my home in Eastern Nigeria, the Catholic Church is called *"uka fada"*, meaning "the priest's church" (literally), but properly "the church owned and run by priests." In many parts of Africa, the priest runs the parish finances and controls the offertory collection; he nominates those who will serve on the parish council and the parish finance council (where there is one). The priest makes most decisions in the parish. He is the one who alone determines the nature and structure of parish life with little input from the people. His authority is often unquestioned; criticizing or disagreeing with a priest is still considered a serious sin for which one should go to confession before receiving Holy Communion. There might be different situations in some African parishes, especially in the cities, but the church in Africa is still pyramidal and clerical.

I thought that this was only a pastoral challenge in Africa until my experience in parishes in Italy, France, Canada, and the United States taught me otherwise. Catholic parishes and dioceses just like the Vatican still revolve around the clergy, a situation that lends itself to an unhealthy clericalism and lack of transparency, accountability, and growth in the church. The only places I have witnessed great input in the pastoral life of the church and active participation in leadership on the part of the laity were in Austria, Germany, and Switzerland. As Jon Nilson observed:

When Congar wrote [*Lay People in the Church*] in the fifties the question of the laity seemed almost an exotic interest, even to many lay people. Thirty years later, with the issue barely advanced beyond Congar's treatment, the laity, though critical to the future of the Church, remains peripheral to its theological self-understanding and to its decision-making. Early in the next century the Church will flourish or wither depending not only on how vigorously laity have come to understand and take up their responsibilities as Christians, but on how prudently Vatican officials understand and exercise theirs. If we are now walking in the dark, it's because someone keeps diminishing the light.[9]

As Aurelie Hagstrom argues, the emergence of the laity in the church since the Second Vatican Council has become an ecclesiological, pastoral, and juridical issue. Although *Lumen Gentium* and *Apostolicam Actuositatem* do not speak of lay ministry per se, postconciliar texts including *Ministeria Quaedam*, *Evangelii Nuntiandi*, *Codex Iuris Canonici* (1983), *Christifideles Laici*, and *Redemptoris Missio* have called the laity to diverse ministries in the church.[10] *The Catechism of the Catholic Church* has also clearly taught on the role of the laity.[11] The interdicasterial document *Priests and Laity*, addressing the need for the full participation of all members of Christ's faithful in the church's mission, was more concerned about drawing clear lines of competence between the laity and the clergy than in developing a pastoral theology of the laity.[12] A lot has been written about the theology of the laity, but not much has been done in terms of developing a praxis for integrating the laity fully into the structures of authority, governance, and ministries in the church beyond tokens that are given to them based on the pastoral or theological predilection of a pastor of a parish or a bishop in the diocese.

The second lesson, which I learned from being a parish priest, was that my priestly formation was inadequate in meeting the leadership challenges of running a modern parish. Therefore, in order to be a good pastor I needed to rely on the treasure and wealth of competence in the parish. The question I could not answer was: If the laity are better equipped than I am in many of the matters brought to me—marriage and family life, health and well being, human resources management, financial accounting and procedure, preaching on certain topics on the gospel text (which I observed in my weekly bible study), for example—then why can't they exercise that function

---

[9]Quoted in Jon Nilson, "The Laity," in *The Gift of the Church*, ed. Peter C. Phan (Collegeville, MN: Liturgical Press, 2000), 412.

[10]For a detailed study of these documents' recommendations, see Aurelie A. Hagstrom, *The Concepts of the Vocation and the Mission of the Laity* (London: Catholic Scholars Press, 1994), 166–76.

[11]*Catechism of the Catholic Church* (Nairobi: Paulines Publications Africa, 1994), 897–913.

[12]*Priests and Laity* (Nairobi: Paulines Publications-Africa, 1998), 5–9.

in a communal and liturgical setting with me as a participant rather than Fr. know-it-all, *scit omnia*?

I thought then that the inadequacy I sensed in myself was because I was an African priest who was working in North America and needed more formation in cultural proficiency. However, as the director of field education for three years at University of St. Michael's College at the University of Toronto, I reviewed the manuals and programs of priestly formation in Canada and the United States, and found the same gaping holes in formation. But this might not simply be a challenge of formation, but rather that the cultural context of priestly ministry has changed and the notion of a priest doing everything in the parish must change. How different priests meet this inadequacy is varied—some work hard at self-improvement by studying on their own about leadership; dioceses run series of ongoing formation on leadership skills and pastoral competence. However, most leadership training and formation, which I have been involved in planning as a member of the clergy personnel board, are more oriented toward compliance with certain diocesan regulations with regard to finance, clerical sexual abuse, and doctrinal orthodoxy.

What happens then is that priests in various parishes plow their own pastoral field with the oxen they have—consultation with the laity through participatory servant leadership, reactionary and defensive approaches, or dictatorial and authoritarian top-down approach,[13] or a combination of all these. There may be other approaches, but in any case, the parish still revolves around the priest because ultimately the final decision on anything that goes on in the parish will be made by the priest who is the pastor of the sheepfold. I was quite overwhelmed and sometimes vexed by the fact that parishioners and parish staff deferred to me on everything, even in things that lie within their competence and expertise. I was required to approve everything, even minutiae like when to light the candle on the altar and when to blow it out, when to decorate the altar and what color I would prefer. It dawned on me then that the institutional church has shortchanged our laity through a persistent clerical mindset. However, the future of the church cannot be constructed on this kind of outmoded structure of leadership and service that does not take into account the vast wealth, charisms, and spirituality of the lay members of Christ's faithful.

What happens in the parish is only a mini representation of what happens

---

[13]Pope Francis touches on this when he said in an interview, "This conduct comes when a person loses the sense of awe for salvation that has been granted to him. When a person feels a little more secure, he begins to appropriate faculties which are not his own, but which are the Lord's. The awe seems to fade, and this is the basis for clericalism for the conduct of people who feel pure. What then prevails is a formal adherence to rules and to mental schemes" (Pope Francis, *The Name of God Is Mercy: A Conversation with Andrea Tornielli*, trans. Oonagh Stransky [New York: Random House, 2016], 69).

in dioceses and at the Vatican. This is why many Catholics trained in this structure in which they expect the pope to give answers—yes or no—to every question facing the universal church are unable to embrace this new approach of Pope Francis, which emphasizes taking account of all perspectives and views by being a listening, dialogical, and patient church. Richard R. Gaillardetz captures this very well when he writes:

> In the Fall of 2015 Pope Francis gave one of the most significant speeches of his pontificate on the fundamental synodality of the church. He noted that the word "synod" comes from the Greek *synodos*, which could be literally rendered "traveling on a journey together." A church committed to "walking together," he insisted, must resist the neo-scholastic separation of the people of God into two separate "churches": the *ecclesia docens,* or teaching church, and the *ecclesia discerns,* or learning church. The pope claimed that, if we are to be a listening church, the commitment to synodality must be enacted at every level, at local parish and diocesan councils as well as diocesan synods and provincial gatherings.[14]

The third lesson for me was the realization that *women played a more decisive role in the parish than men and that I had to rely on women in order to get anything done in the parish.* I remember once at a parish event at which the bishop was present when I threw an innocuous joke in a vote of thanks to the Canadian Catholic Women's League. I told the audience that the reason I was particularly nice to women in the parish was that if they decided to go on strike then the parish would fold up. The bishop did not take kindly to my comments and was quite furious and had to make a corrective at the end of the ceremony by saying something like this: "It is the Eucharist that makes the church, and there can be no Eucharist without priests. Therefore, Fr. Stan is stretching it too far by saying that without women there will be no church. The indispensable person in the church is Christ who comes to us in the Eucharist and without the priests there will be no Mass. So pray to God that more of your sons could become priests so that you will not be starved of the Eucharist. You women will always remain the mothers of priests like Mary was the Mother of the Lord. You have a higher place than priests." I smiled.

However, I prayed that God should open our eyes one day in the church, and open our ears to hear anew God's answers to us about the blessings and curse of compulsory priestly celibacy in the Latin rite, the shortage of priests

---

[14]Richard R. Gaillardetz, "Doctrinal Authority in the Francis Era: Toward a Pastoral Magisterium in Today's Church," *Commonweal*, December 19, 2016, www.commonwealmagazine.org.

in the West, and the boundless gifts of women, and that the sacraments of Christian initiation give every member equal access to all other ministries in the church. Just as there is no female baptism, male confirmation, or gendered Eucharist, the continued gendering of the priestly ministry is a continuing challenge to an illuminative church that is called to be accountable for the gifts of women in the church. Illuminative church is called to be a witness to what God is doing in the community by reflecting as in a mirror the faces of all God's people to God in all its structures, life, leadership and ministries.

The failure of the church to appropriate a relevant theology of the laity and to embrace fully the gift and charism of women is being blamed for the crisis in the ministry that has rocked the church in the United States of America and for the putative ordination of some women in the United States.[15] Many reform-minded Catholics around the world hailed the "attempted ordinations" as a way of protesting against the exclusion of women in all clerical ministries in the Catholic church. However, Pope John Paul II excommunicated those women who "attempted ordination."[16]

Greater and more open dialogue is needed in our churches on how to integrate women in ministry in the Catholic church, taking into consideration the diversity and particularity of cultural and spiritual traditions in the Catholic church. The church can draw especially from the ecclesial experience of non-Western societies in Africa and Asia, for instance, where women are playing leadership roles as preachers and president of liturgical celebrations in African Pentecostalism, African Catholic Charismatic movements, and in African Independent churches.

The example of "attempted ordinations" of women only shows how far the church is from being an accountable church where every member is a firstborn child of the beloved community of God. This is why Pope Francis's new commission on women in diaconal ministry is a good first step in beginning this much-needed dialogue. Many see the difference between the laity and clergy as ontological and hence embrace a gendered ministry

---

[15]Two works stand out among many that have appeared on the crisis in the priesthood in the United States of America. In *Sacred Silence*, Donald B. Cozzens condemns the clericalism of the church, which manifests itself in an authoritarian style of ministerial leadership, a rigidly hierarchical worldview, and a virtual identification of the holiness and grace of the church with the clerical state. See Donald B. Cozzens, *Sacred Silence: Denial and the Crisis in the Church* (Collegeville, MN: Liturgical Press, 2002), 118. Although I think most of the proposals he made to address the problem are radical, I think the analysis of the problem is reflective of the lay-clergy identity crisis. The other work is by George Weigel, which argues for a recovery of the true priestly identity, by even limiting the involvement of the laity in the ministries like the Eucharist and religious instruction among others. See George Weigel, *The Courage to Be Catholic* (New York: Basic Books, 2002), 96.

[16]"Vatican Rejects Appeal by Women Priests," *Catholic News*, January 28, 2003, cathnews.acu.edu.au.

as essential to the structure of the church.[17] Pope John Paul II teaches, for instance, that the difference between the clerical and lay state is not a functional difference, but an ontological one. Thus he argues: *"We cannot increase the communion and unity in the Church by clericalizing the lay faithful or by laicising the priests."*[18] However, this conclusion cannot be sustained totally if one examines the transition from biblical times to our times in the development of ministries in the church. Have the final forms of ministries in the church been set? Is the Holy Spirit going to lead the church to further truth on how to account for the gift of women in the church? Will the same Spirit lead us even into new territories in imagining new forms of ministry in the church which will embrace women so that God's whole people and the faces of all of God's people will shine in the mirror of the church's life and structures at all levels? The challenge is always as Yves Congar pointed out the "lack of correspondence" between the structure and the realities, which they represent. There is no correspondence between a male priesthood and the gift of priesthood in terms of what God wishes to realize through the ministry of priesthood. God can use all created reality for the mediation of God's grace. God's action can never be restricted to gender or sex; otherwise, God will be restricted in divine operation by what God created. Our cultural categories and cultural norming of roles based on gender and sex must be seen as relative human appropriations in our attempt to find appropriate channels for mediation of God's grace. In this light, we need to look at ministries in the church as instruments for serving the mission of the church given to it by the Lord Jesus Christ and how other cultural narratives beyond the West can offer new experiences in the dialogue, which needs to be ongoing in our churches about how to account for the gift of womanhood in the church.

The "logic of integration" (*AL*, 299), which Pope Francis proposed in *Amoris Laetitia*, seems to me the relevant theological foundation for the praxis of accountability in the church. This logic is the principle that people should be enabled to exercise full membership in the church through full participation in the life of the world and the life of the church. It is "the key to pastoral accompaniment" (*AL*, 299) because it proceeds through a "logic of pastoral mercy" (312, 297). It is a matter of reaching out to everyone who needs help and of finding ways to eliminate exclusionary

---

[17]For a study of the development of ministries between the laity and clergy in the Catholic Church see Kenan B. Osborne, *Ministry: Lay Ministry in the Roman Catholic Church, Its History and Theology* (New York: Paulist Press, 1993); Edward P. Hahnenberg, *Ministries: A Relational Approach* (New York: Crossroad, 2003), 7–38; Edward Schillebeeckx, *Ministry, Leadership in the Community of Jesus Christ*, trans. John Bowden (New York: Crossroad, 1981), esp. 75–99.

[18]John Paul II, "The Diversity of Charisms," *The Pope Speaks*, April 22, 1994, 310.

practices which make it impossible for all of God's people to exercise their baptismal gifts. This way every member of the church is given the opportunity to participate fully in the life of the church and equal access to answer the Lord's call to service in any ministry in the church.

Accountability as presented in scriptures also speaks of the sad reality of division, exclusion, loss, and despair. In the parable of the Good Shepherd or the Lost Coin, we see the grief of the master when he takes stock of his treasures and his flock. Here one sees a link between this biblical insight and the situation of the church. I am referring to the experience of those who are inside and those who are outside; those who are accounted for because they are in the house and those who are lost; those who are saved and those who are damned, those who are on their way to the promised land and those who are lost in the desert; those who are right and those who are wrong; those who are beloved and those who are rebels; those who are poor, voiceless, and powerless and those who are rich and powerful.

The logic of integration, that is, the praxis of an accountable church challenges every local Christian community to question the existing rules and pastoral practices that have set certain criteria for inclusion in ministries and for full participation in the sacramental life of the church. The church must give account to the Lord not only of those who are in the church's good books but also those who are not with us—divorced and separated Catholics; ex-priests and nuns who are treated in some communities as outcasts; those brothers and sisters who are victims of sexual abuse, ex-convicts, drug addicts, and alcoholics. I am thinking also of Catholics who are denied communion because of their marital situation, our brothers and sisters from other denominations and from other faiths, those who have left our churches, those wounded and bruised by the way they have been treated by officials of the church in their time of need as well as those searching for their sexual or ethnic identities, our LGBTQ brothers, sisters, and fellow parishioners, and all those who are far from the home of the church as the family of God. What is important is the extent to which everyone feels a sense of belonging in our churches, how they are accepted and integrated in our parishes so that everyone sees in the Christian community nothing but the love of God, which creates a community of the beloved for all who hear the divine summons: "come follow me."

This stocktaking is the starting point of any pastoral praxis for illuminative ecclesiology, which is grounded in Vatican II and finds its origin and model in Trinitarian communion. Pope Francis by his words and deeds is calling on the church to embrace "a new horizon of God's love" in embracing a new pastoral praxis that will bring people back to the community and integrate their gifts in the church when he said,

Jesus touched the leper and brought him back to the community. He didn't sit down at a desk and study the situation; he didn't consult the experts for pros and cons. What really mattered to him was reaching stranded people and saving them, like the Good Shepherd who leaves the flock to save one lost sheep. Then, as today, this kind of logic and conduct can be shocking; it provokes angry mutterings from those who are only ever used to having things fit into their preconceived notions and ritual purity instead of letting themselves be surprised by reality, by a greater love or a higher standard.[19]

PASTORAL ACCOMPANIMENT:
HEARTS THAT FEEL AND HANDS THAT HEAL

Pope Francis writes in *Evangelii Gaudium* 169 of *the art of accompaniment* as the pastoral approach that will bring us closer to each other in solidarity, heal divisions, ethnocentrisms, and nepotism, and cure the ailments of the negative ecclesial spirit of rank segregation. This way of living will make the church a center of love, and of intersubjective connection, participation in the life of all, and communion with God, especially commitment to those who are poor and on the margins. Bruno Forte argues that the catholicity of the gospel message refers to the total ecclesiology that touches all the dimensions of the life of the Christian who is called to love and to embrace the Word and grace of God and the gift of the church. According to Forte, every local church "must be *a travelling companion* [my emphasis] of the people to whom it proclaims the Word of God, so that the gospel may be interlaced with the daily deeds of fraternity, where love becomes concrete and credible in the sharing of day-to-day life and in the choices taken on the side of the poor and the little ones of the earth."[20]

Among other practices, Pope Francis recommends that we remove our sandals before others because when we come into the presence of another—no matter how weak or vulnerable—we must remember that we are standing on holy ground. This accompaniment requires humility, listening to the other person, honest communication, conversion, openness of heart, and genuine spiritual encounters. At the heart of this *pastoral presence* is the Incarnational principle of totally identifying with the other person, especially those in need, in order to experience

---

[19]Pope Francis, *Name of God Is Mercy*, 65–66.

[20]Bruno Forte, *The Church: Icon of the Trinity: A Brief Study*, trans. Robert Paolucci (Boston: St. Paul Books and Media, 1991), 76.

what they are experiencing by a pastoral attitude of vulnerability. This is what Pope Francis highlighted in a speech to newly appointed bishops on September 19, 2013, when he taught about the art of accompaniment and the required pastoral presence. (1) He said that pastors must have the smell of the sheep because the priests and bishops are in the midst of the people like Jesus was with his disciples. (2) The art of accompaniment requires walking together in love, knowing that ministry in the church is a service or office of love (*amoris officium*), as Saint Augustine pointed out. In this light, the priests and bishops who serve the people of God are not above the people of God: "The bishop journeys with and among his flock. This means setting out with one's faithful and with all those who turn to you, sharing in their joys and hopes, their difficulties and sufferings, as brothers and as friends, but especially as fathers who can listen, understand, help, and guide."[21] (3) Pope Francis also teaches that it is only through pastoral accompaniment that the leaders in the church can discern the *sensus fidei*, *sensus fidelium*, and *consensus fidei* of the people of God.[22] (4) *Walking together* also challenges pastoral workers to *work together* in helping one another, asking and receiving forgiveness; acknowledging one's mistakes and limitations; and building flexible and open structures of accountability to one another and unity and love in the local churches. (5) The pastoral theology of accompaniment is the invitation to enter into the life of the poor, to move from providing social services, social activism, and social empowerment, to psychosocial encounters that lead to social transformation.

The art of accompaniment is a pastoral approach to ministry in which the church and its ministers as well as all Christians who have been touched by God's love are moved to make a home for all, especially the poor. Accompaniment signifies openness to others, especially those on the margins in places where they feel pain and emptiness. Thus to accompany someone is to dwell in common with that person in a relationship of mutuality and respect. It requires an openness to the other no matter how different their social status or economic or spiritual circumstances. Accompaniment also is related to the African sense of community and participation expressed in the sense of *Ubuntu*, that we all participate in each other's life and that it is by participating in other people's lives that I can actually share

---

[21] Pope Francis, *Church of Mercy*, 86. He elaborates further on this in the same speech when he says: "A pastoral presence means walking with the People of God, walking in front of them, showing them the way, showing them the path; walking in their midst, to strengthen them in unity; walking behind them, to make sure no one gets left behind, but especially, never to lose the scent of the People of God in order to find roads." See also *Evangelii Gaudium*, 31.

[22] Pope Francis, *Church of Mercy*, 76.

in the bond of life. The spirit of *Ubuntu* is a strong affirmation of the interconnectedness of all things. Ikenna Okafor sees in the Igbo concept of "nwanne" something similar to the African *Ubuntu* (I am through others) and *Ujamaa* (extended family). "Nwanne" (meaning son or daughter of my mother) goes beyond paternal and filial relationship to include a radical openness and acceptance of everyone, hence the saying "nwanne di na mba" (my brother or sister could be found abroad). The implication of this for solidarity and accompaniment is clearly developed in African theology in the thought of Okafor. Furthermore, Okafor writes that this approach to seeing others as sharing in my own life and needing my reaching out to them can furnish a new ecclesiology that focuses on tearing down the walls or barriers that separate us from each other or pitch us against another. It also helps overcome discrimination, racism, ethnocentrism, and a culture of neglect and forging the right kind of relationships, which will offer the basic ingredients for building a better world and a transformed church and society.[23]

What this African theology of relationship and participation offers the world church in development of the art of accompaniment is the commitment and inner conviction that when my brother or sister suffers, when the earth is bleeding, the African sense of community calls each person to become one with the reality of pain in order to bring healing and wholeness. Accompaniment through participation in and with others in vital union brings healing and harmony in creation because everyone is working and walking together for justice to reign on earth so that all creation, especially those who are poor and suffering, will be supported to enjoy the abundant life and peace in Christ (Jn 10:10). It requires bridging the gulf that separates people as a result of bias, sexism, racism, classism, bigotry, prejudice, discrimination, intolerance, social stratification, and division. It also requires of all especially in the church to overcome the holier-than-thou attitude of avoidance of those whom we judge to be unholy and unworthy. It requires entering into the world of the poor with respect, reverence, and compassion. As Roberto Goizueta writes:

> As a society, we are happy to help and serve the poor, as long as we don't have to walk with them where they walk, that is, as long as we can minister to them from our safe enclosures. The poor can then remain passive objects of our actions, rather than friends, *compañeros* and *compañeras* with whom we interact. As long as we can be sure

---

[23]Ikenna U. Okafor, *Toward an African Theology of Fraternal Solidarity: Ube Nwanne* (Eugene, OR: Pickwick, 2014), 166.

that we will not have to live with them, and thus have inter-personal relationships with them, we will try to help "the poor"—but, again, only from a controllable, geographical distance.[24]

Accompaniment is what Pope Francis calls the "framework and setting" that will lead the church away from "a cold bureaucratic morality" in dealing with some of the sensitive and contested issues on marriage and family life in the church and the world today (*AL*, 312). Accompaniment "sets us in the context of a pastoral discernment filled with merciful love, which is ever ready to understand, forgive, accompany, hope and above all integrate. That is the mind-set which should prevail in the church and lead us to 'open our hearts to those living on the outermost fringes of society'" (*AL*, 312).

Pope Francis proposes some practices which will make it possible for pastors "to make room for God's unconditional love" in their pastoral ministry (*AL*, 311). *Evangelii Gaudium* already showed the various steps toward developing practices for pastoral discernment and accompaniment to heal the wounds of so many in today's world. In *Amoris Laetitia* Pope Francis appropriates *Evangelii Gaudium*'s theological and ecclesiological foundation for accompaniment in developing a set of pastoral practices that neither "waters down the Gospel" nor empties the mercy of God of its unconditional quality. This can happen when the church's pastoral practices proceed from a mentality of rigorous severity, which can "put in doubt the omnipotence of God and, especially his mercy." Even though mercy does not exclude justice and truth, Francis, however, teaches that "mercy is the fullness of justice and the most radiant manifestation of God's truth" (*AL*, 311). The four practices of accompaniment proposed in *Evangelii Gaudium* are outlined in the following sections.

Seeing Others through the Eyes of Mercy and Love

The first point is that accompaniment begins with Christians and churches looking "more closely and sympathetically" at people. Looking closely at humanity does not mean an obsession with "the details of other people's lives," which as Pope Francis points out is rooted in "morbid curiosity." On the contrary, accompaniment begins with pastoral workers and ministers looking at people's lives with "the personal gaze" of the Lord Jesus. This is with the intention of making present in the lives of people the fragrance of Christ and bringing Christ closer to the people and people closer to Christ (see *EG*, 169).

---

[24]Quoted in Michael Griffin and Jennie Weis Block, eds., *In the Company of the Poor: Conversations with Dr. Paul Farmer and Fr. Gustavo Gutierrez* (Maryknoll, NY: Orbis Books, 2013), 128.

When we look at people with the gaze of Christ, something fundamentally decisive and transformational takes place: it changes our optics about who the person is and about who we are in the presence of another. The words of Pope Francis bear repeating here:

> The Church will have to initiate everyone—priests, religious and laity—into this "art of accompaniment" which teaches us to remove our sandals before the sacred ground of the other (cf. Ex 3:5). The pace of this accompaniment must be steady and reassuring, reflecting our closeness and our compassionate gaze which also heals, liberates and encourages growth in the Christian life. (*EG*, 169)

However, Pope Francis also points to another important dimension of encounter with other people. There is need for diversity of approaches to encountering people because people's conditions and situations differ, and their contexts might influence their response to God and thus challenge the church and Christians to be more creative in reaching out to people. Sometimes setting a general guideline or form for pastoral encounter with people may lead to dry and rigid pastoral ministries, which do more harm than good to Christians. It is important to understand that to accompany people is to journey closely with them in total openness to God (*EG*, 44).

Being with People: Respect, Trust, and Openness to Mutual Transformation

The second practice is about the method for accompaniment. Accompaniment is an art. This means that there is a method for being with people, walking with people and sharing in their lives with an openness to being touched by others. That method is modeled after the mystery of the Incarnation. By the mystery of the Incarnation, the Son of God entered into the chaos of our human lives, pitched a tent among us, and assumed our human conditions with all its pains and limitations in order to grant us liberation. It is similar to the African sense of hospitality or pitching a tent with another which is captured in an Igbo proverb, "May the visitor bring blessing and peace to his or her host and when the visitor leaves may he or she go with greater blessing rather than a hunchback."[25] Here sharing a home with another presupposes a prior intention to be open to the other in trust and love; it means openness to sharing in the blessing of the Lord, listening to the other, and being totally and readily available to the other in

---

[25]On African hospitality, see Gregory Ikechukwu Olikenyi, *African Hospitality: A Model for the Communication of the Gospel in the African Cultural Context* (Enugu, Nigeria: SNAP Press, 2001).

a spirit of humility, service, caring, compassion, and support. This mutual indwelling or hospitality between a minister, for instance, and a parishioner, or between a social worker and a poor person, presupposes that we are all learning and growing through each other and that every encounter in the pastoral ministry is a mutual exchange.

The art of accompaniment requires entering into other people's lives, leaving one's comfort zone, and being with other people from diverse spiritual, cultural, racial, national, and social locations; it requires meeting them as friends and as traveling companions. In a sense, the art of accompaniment is properly modeled for the church and ministers through the Trinitarian image of the indwelling of the three divine persons. Accompaniment, viewed in this light, is a relationship characterized by the same qualities that are reflected in the mutual indwelling or hospitality at the heart of Trinitarian life. The three divine persons make room for each other.[26] The three divine persons not only make a way for each other or travel with each other, but they participate in an intimate way in the life of each person of the Trinity in what traditionally has been called a sacred dance (*perichoresis*). In this sacred dance, each divine person while being a distinct *persona* shares in the life of the three divine persons and receives from each other the gift of love, which is the identity and character of their divine nature. Mutuality, trust, respect, reverence, and shared participation are some of the qualities of the inner Trinitarian life. Indwelling of the three divine persons with each other becomes a model of accompaniment because it mediates the following characteristics that are needed in pastoral ministry—mutual respect, nonjudgmental love and reverence for the other, solidarity with the other, collaboration and cooperation with each other, and participation or sharing in the life of each other.

Trust, respect, and reverence manifest themselves in the pastoral setting in a mutual relationship such that the joys and sorrows of the other become

---

[26]*Perichoresis* is the traditional Greek term used in the church to show the mutual indwelling of the three persons in the common life of the Trinity. *Perichoresis* is presented in many contemporary writings as a model for what Christians are being called to do with accompaniment as an ecclesiological practice. It is a model for the Christian mission. It is particularly in the light of the ecclesiology that I am proposing a way of being church and a way of being-with others, especially those who are weak, poor, suffering, or in any kind of cultural, material, spiritual, or personal need. In being present to another in a spirit of humility and hope, we make God present in that situation. See Janice Price's commentary on the Church of England's World Mission's panel description of a relational dimension of the Christian mission as hospitality, which is "a mutual indwelling one with another" and "our common participation in the life and mission of God" (Janice Price, *World-Shaped Mission: Reimaging Mission Today* [London: Church House, 2012], 24). See also Michael Frost, *Surprise the World: The Five Habits of Highly Missional People* (Colorado Springs: Nav Press, 2015), 43. See also Luke A. Powery on "mutual indwelling" as the basis for creating Christian communities modeled after the Trinitarian relation in which the divine persons make room for each other (Luke A. Powery, *Spirit Speech: Lament and Celebration in Preaching* [Nashville, TN: Abingdon, 2009]).

the joys and sorrows of the minister. There is an invitation to walk in the shoes of the other and to walk with the other so that he or she can assume responsibility for his or her own life and attain his or her God-ordained end. This is particularly necessary in setting the right focus and end of pastoral ministry, which is to connect people to God, themselves, the world of nature, and the world around them. It is indeed the integration of the person so as to bring wholeness to the person so that he or she feels and experiences the grace of being loved by God and being a partner with God in the sacred dance of life. As Pope Francis writes, pastoral ministry is not simply a therapy; rather it is about how to bring people closer to God, "to accompany them would be counterproductive if it becomes a sort of therapy supporting their self-absorption and ceases to be a pilgrimage with Christ to the Father" (*EG*, 170).

A New Way of Doing Pastoral Ministry

The third aspect of accompaniment in *Evangelii Gaudium* is that it is presented as a new way of doing ministry in the church following the reform of the Second Vatican Council. It also changes how one sees the person of the minister and the one who is being ministered to. Pope Francis proposes a radically different approach to ministry through the art of accompaniment. As Richard Lennan rightly argues, since Vatican II, there has been a shift in pastoral theology in the Catholic Church from the superiority of the priest over the laity to a realization of the mutuality that should exist in a pastoral situation. Ministry is a mutual encounter and a two-way street. Furthermore, ministerial service is no longer the exclusive preserve of the ordained ministers and is becoming more specialized.[27] Both the minister and the person being ministered to are in a mutual relationship of respect and reverence, and both should be changed in the process of ministry and strengthened in their individual and ecclesial journey to God. Both minister and the one being served are carrying wounds and have holes in their hearts in need of God's mercy and grace. This is why accompaniment is always a shared journey where all are touched by what is mutually seen and experienced in the journey. In *Evangelii Gaudium* 171, Pope Francis proposes some of the daily practices of pastoral accompaniment when he writes:

---

[27]Richard Lennan, "Ministry as Merciful Accompaniment," in *Go into the Streets! The Welcoming Church of Pope Francis*, ed. Thomas P. Rausch and Richard R. Gaillardetz (New York: Paulist Press, 2016), 142–44.

Today more than ever we need men and women who, on the basis of their experience of accompanying others, are familiar with processes which call for prudence, understanding, patience and docility to the Spirit, so that they can protect the sheep from wolves who would scatter the flock. We need to practice the art of listening, which is more than simply hearing. Listening, in communication, is an openness of heart, which makes possible that closeness without which genuine spiritual encounter cannot occur. Listening helps us to find the right gesture and word, which shows that we are more than simply bystanders. Only through such respectful and compassionate listening can we enter on the paths of true growth and awaken a yearning for the Christian ideal: the desire to respond fully to God's love and to bring to fruition what he has sown in our lives.

Encountering God and a New Life

The fourth practice of accompaniment is on the goal to be sought in the pastoral setting: transformation. Pope Francis explains the goal of accompaniment in this way:

One who accompanies others has to realize that each person's situation before God and their life in grace are mysteries which no one can fully know from without. The Gospel tells us to correct others and to help them to grow on the basis of a recognition of the objective evil of their actions (cf. Mt 18:15), but without making judgments about their responsibility and culpability (cf. Mt 7:1; Lk 6:37). Someone good at such accompaniment does not give in to frustrations or fears. He or she invites others to let themselves be healed, to take up their mat, embrace the cross, leave all behind and go forth ever anew to proclaim the Gospel. Our personal experience of being accompanied and assisted, and of openness to those who accompany us, will teach us to be patient and compassionate with others, and to find the right way to gain their trust, their openness and their readiness to grow. (*EG*, 172)

The beginning and end of all pastoral initiatives for accompaniment is a deep encounter in faith with God, a new experience of love, mercy, and grace, and new life in Christ through encountering the other. Accompaniment is about how we serve others by following the example of Christ and how through serving others we inspire their hearts to service to their God and neighbors. Accompaniment becomes for Pope Francis the new method for evangelization, which helps us discern in the other the wounded face of

Jesus Christ. The goal of all evangelization is achieved through a fruitful and faithful accompaniment when through our words, actions, and mercy we proclaim the Good News to others who are hungry for God and for meaning and hope. Accompaniment is the incarnational praxis of mission for the church in present time. Accompaniment goes beyond legislating unchanging manualistic moral solutions to people's problems or fixed rules for resolving moral issues. Rather, it inspires people to be present with others, walk with them in love, and search together with them for the face of Christ in their daily lives in order to find God in their daily choices. It is the most effective means for leading people to conversion and to the fullness of life.

A VULNERABLE MISSION

We Are in This Together

The accountable church that embraces the art of accompaniment carries on its pastoral praxis as a vulnerable mission. According to Pope Francis:

> Jesus, the evangelizer par excellence and the Gospel in person, identifies especially with the little ones (cf. Mt 25:40). This reminds us Christians that we are called to care *for the vulnerable of the earth* [my emphasis]. . . . It is essential to draw near to new forms of poverty and vulnerability, in which we are called to recognize the suffering Christ, even if this appears to bring us no tangible and immediate benefits. I think of the homeless, the addicted, refugees, indigenous people, the elderly who are increasingly isolated and abandoned, and many others. (*EG*, 209–10)

Pope Francis goes ahead to point out that one of the saddest experiences of vulnerability in the world today is the condition of migrants, who leave their homes and countries wandering in deserts and seas in search of a new home. These people suffer spiritual, cultural, economic, and political dislocation. A church without frontiers has a challenge to embrace the vulnerability not only of migrants but also of the unborn, the elderly, and all those who are on the margins. Also to be added here are all those condemned to a life of suffering and isolation; those left in the lower rungs of social and economic progress; those who are victims of the structures of sin and injustice as a result of the harmful effects of social reproduction; victims of modern-day slavery; victims of intergenerational poverty; and those who are alienated and who feel empty and hopeless in the midst of wealth and plenty. Pope Francis also identifies the reality of vulnerability with the whole of creation, which continues to suffer as a result of anthropogenic causes (*EG*, 215).

The experience of vulnerability is an existential one that arises in normal life when we are filled with a sense of inadequacy, dread, or insecurity.[28] It is the experience of being on the edge of a cliff, of being helpless, weak, insignificant, or empty; it is like staring death in the face and of being poor, powerless, and without help or any defense against what Teilhard de Chardin calls the passivities of diminishment. Vulnerability is the brokenness of our humanity in its state of incompletion and contingency, which shows itself so clearly in the weakest members of society.

Jeffrey Tranzillo shows in *John Paul II on the Vulnerable* that the experience of vulnerability in humanity leads to a deeper question about Christian anthropology: Who is this person who suffers or, as Pope Francis puts the question in more operational terms, "Where is your brother or sister who is enslaved? Where is the brother or sister whom you are killing each day in clandestine warehouses, in rings of prostitution, in children used for begging, in exploiting undocumented labor?" (*EG*, 211). Drawing from the writings of Pope John Paul II, Tranzillo argues that the weakest and most defenseless members of our society, the poor, the lonely, and the suffering should not be treated as nonpersons or burdens to society. While the church and society at large are challenged by the experience of human vulnerability to acts of solidarity, charity, and justice, Tranzillo argues that Pope John Paul II also sees the vulnerable as gifts in a unique way to society at large:

> So to a large extent, his [John Paul II] intellectual achievement gives formal expression to his own experience of the vulnerable, whose absolutely personal being and nature he affirms unequivocally in his philosophical and theological reflections on the human person. From this he will conclude that every vulnerable person can contribute immeasurably and indispensably to the human community in some way by the actions of which he or she is capable.[29]

I recall my 2012 visit to Reach Out Mbuya in Kampala, Uganda, at the HIV/AIDS center run by the Comboni missionaries. A man was brought in on a wheelbarrow who was very sick. He was laid down on a mat because he was too sick to sit and was too weak to feed himself. He was at the point of death. Immediately as this man was wheeled in, the volunteers there swung into action. In less than one hour, this man was cleaned, put on drip, and tested to know his viral load while his blood sample was taken to the lab. I

---

[28]See Erich Fromm, *The Art of Being*, trans. Lance Garmer (New York: Continuum, 1997), 41.

[29]Jeffrey Tranzillo, *John Paul II on the Vulnerable* (Washington, DC: Catholic University of America Press, 2013), xvi.

was quite impressed by the efficiency of the people led by Father Paulino Mondo, a very remarkable man. They had no time to start asking why this man had not been brought in earlier or why his relatives waited nearly to the point of death before seeking help. The volunteers here know that many poor families in many rural communities and even in some corners of Kampala do not have the means to provide for their sick family members. They know that there are many preachers and so-called healers who may have promised the family that spiritual healing would restore their brother. The concern was to bring back life where there is death, and to give hope where there is despair through simple but courageous acts of kindness.

Later that evening as we talked about what happened that day, I learned from Father Paolino a great lesson on vulnerability and the gift of such people like this suffering man. He said that what he sees everyday at Reach Out is a new gospel narrative about people who are searching for God in a different context. In the past, he told me, many people with HIV/AIDS came to the parish church in Mbuya asking for healing, but the Comboni priests knew that they needed holistic healing—spiritual, physical, emotional, medical, and social. Praying over them, sprinkling holy water on them and anointing them with different oils was not enough. As the number of these sick brothers and sisters kept increasing, Father Joseph Archetti decided in 2001 to begin providing counseling services for HIV/AIDS persons and began looking for ways of getting them anti-retroviral medications. This was how Reach Out was born. But what many priests, sisters, and laity who serve in Reach Out show anyone who visits is the simple lesson that both the sick brothers and sisters and the volunteers and the medical or counseling personnel are all vulnerable human beings. As one of the volunteers told me: "We are here to give them life and to help stop death, which is taking so many of our people." But there is more that happens here from what I observed later the next day when I came to see this brother who was brought in the previous day. I could see light in his eyes and hope shining through his wrinkled face. He was vulnerable in the sense that his life was in the hand of another; he was facing death and decay, but here he found hope and new life. But for the caregivers it is this kind of turnaround that happens in the life of so many who come here which gives them hope. I could see from my interaction with them that they also feel their own weakness and vulnerability when they are overwhelmed and when they come face to face with deaths here at Reach Out and begin to think of their own death. But what is so touching was the fact that at Reach Out the wounds of humanity are being touched, and people are being healed through touching the wounds of others; those with wounds are being healed by the touch of God through the loving hands of their brothers and sisters.

Developing the ecclesial praxis of vulnerable mission will demand embracing the spirit of Reach Out and many other centers of hope in many parts of Africa and in other parts of the world. If someone asks me where I found the church in Uganda, my answer will be for sure that I found it at Reach Out in its finest splendor. I visited the Martyrs Shrine in Namugongo, Uganda, and celebrated Masses in many parishes, but I never felt closer to Jesus than when I was at Reach Out. Illuminative ecclesiology must give voice to this form of witnessing to vulnerability in many sites of hope in many parts of the world. This demands a new way of conceiving the mission of the church. It requires a concrete image of seeing the identity of the church in terms of brokenness and weakness. Pope Francis speaks of the need for the church and all men and women of goodwill to embrace the vulnerable (*EG*, 209–10).

A praxis of vulnerable mission for illuminative ecclesiology refers to the life and ministry of churches and Christians who embrace the humility of God. Saint Augustine's lesson to Dioscorus on the virtue of humility as the starting point of Christian witnessing is germane here:

> My dear Dioscorus, my desire is that you submit yourself to [Christ] with all devotion and that you provide yourself with no other way to grasping and retaining the truth than the one provided by [the one] who as God saw how weak our human steps are. That way is, first, humility; second, humility; third, humility. And as often as you might ask, I would say the same. It is not that there are not other precepts, but unless humility precedes and accompanies and follows upon all our good actions . . . pride will snatch everything from our hand as we congratulate ourselves over some good deed. The other vices are certainly to be feared in the form of sins, but pride is to be feared even in our good deeds, lest our praiseworthy actions be lost through the immoderate desire of praise.[30]

The ecclesial identity of vulnerability is born out of humility. It grows out of a critical and dynamic self-consciousness of the church as poor and totally dependent on God. This is a strong identity, which places the church at the service of the poor as the place of mediation of divine love by Christians who are conscious of their created lowliness, and who through humble service before God are constantly being transformed into the image of God as servants of God and servants of the world.[31] This begins from

---

[30] St. Augustine, E. 118.3.22. Cited in Basil Studer, *The Grace of Christ and the Grace of God in Augustine of Hippo: Christocentrism or Theocentrism*, trans. Matthew J. O'Connell (Collegeville, MN: Liturgical Press, 1997), 50–51.

[31] The idea of created lowliness of Christians and by extension of the church goes back to Saint

the perspective of humility, which brings the church and Christians to their knees in the face of human suffering. In this way, the church and Christians can embrace the wounded Lord in touching the wounds of the poor with respect, reverence, and joy.

A praxis of vulnerable mission proceeds through the radical insertion (accountability) of the stories of our world into the story of the Trinity. The church exists as the continuing story of God's love to the world. The church is a mirror of divine love to all men and women. The church becomes a mirror of divine love when it incarnates the very character of the words and deeds of Christ, and embraces the priorities and practices of Christ in both its inner life and external ecclesial activities. This is particularly achieved when the church walks with the poor (accompaniment), embraces them and their conditions in all that it is and does. This vulnerable disposition of humility makes it possible for the church to embody the stories of human-ity and creation by being present and incarnate within history in order to insert the diverse narratives of our human and cosmic experience into the transformative grace of divine love. By uniting these stories to the continu-ing narrative of God's self-manifestation in history in the certainty of faith and the assurance of hope, the process of conversion toward God and to the other begins at each point in the church's mission, the eschatological fulfillment of the promises of God's kingdom.

Walter Kasper identifies the praxis of illuminative ecclesiology of Pope Francis as an immersion in the world of another: the first is "a process-oriented, dialogical style, in which the entire people of God—laity, women, religious, clergy—are all involved and in which the church becomes a listen-ing church, attentive to the many voices which make up the symphony of love and grace in the church and in the world" (*EG*, 31). This reflects the realization of the synodal tradition renewed at the Second Vatican Coun-cil.[32] Illuminative ecclesiology begins with entering into the world of the other with humility, courage, sacrifice, and risks like the Good Samaritan. Furthermore, it seeks an ongoing conversion and conversation. This de-mands both the "conversion of the papacy" and "pastoral conversion" of all the central structures of the church and hierarchy (*EG*, 32–33) in order to bring about the joy of the gospel to people in their diverse situations. It also requires different levels of dialogue because the truth of God and its

---

Thomas Aquinas. See Christopher Franks, *He Became Poor: The Poverty of Christ and Aquinas's Economic Teachings* (Cambridge, UK: William B. Eerdmans, 2009), 6–7.

[32]Walter Kasper, *Pope Francis' Revolution of Tenderness and Love: Theological and Pastoral Perspectives*, trans. William Madges (New York: Paulist Press, 2015), 51. See also a collection of essays in *Concilium: International Journal of Theology*, Reform of the Curia (London: SCM Press, 2013/5). The reform of the curia that Pope Francis is undertaking is less technical and "theological" than proposed in the essays but very effective because of the logic at play in his method.

realization in history are not given once and for all. It requires performance and dialogue at all levels and at all times.[33]

Immersion in the stories of the poor as the continuing mystery of the unveiling of God's story in the church requires searching for the presence or absence of God within the human world and in the life and activities of the church as the Christian faith engages different social contexts. It also means that the church and its members must be muddied by walking in the shadows of the dumps where many of our brothers and sisters are searching for food. This demands a deeper cultural hermeneutics on the part of the church through immersion in history using the tools of sociocultural analysis, which begins, as Dietrich Bonhoeffer once observed, through "a view from below," which is an incarnational experience of incomparable value. This viewpoint helps us see reality and the world through "the perspective of the outcast, the suspects, the maltreated, the powerless, the oppressed, the reviled—in short, from the perspective of those who suffer."[34] The church cannot hear the gospel spoken by these "icons of Christ" (St. John Chrysostom) who are the poor and vulnerable of this world if it is not walking with the poor and reflecting in its image, pastoral priorities, and practices that it is the icon of Christ because it is a poor church.

An insertion into the story of the poor will open new pathways for the church's ministry of social transformation. It will lead the church to embrace the attitude of most people who have successfully worked with the poor and vulnerable people: poor people desire to be respected and challenged; poor people want to become agents in their own liberation. The poor of the world do not want to receive handouts from the church and aid organizations. What they want is simply the removal of the many obstacles on their path because of the structures of injustice and oppression. They want justice more than charity or rather a charity that does justice. The poor wish to apply their freedom to constructing a better future for themselves. As Gustavo Gutiérrez writes: "Being an agent of one's own history is for all people an expression of freedom and dignity, the starting point and a source of authentic human development. The historically insignificant were—and still are in large part—the silent in history."[35]

The praxis of vulnerable mission is incarnational and transformative. As a pilgrim on earth, the church is called to be concerned about the condition

---

[33]I have discussed aspects of the ecclesiology of Pope Francis and the implications for the church in Africa in a previous essay. This section builds on and develops that theology further. See Ilo, "Church of Pope Francis," 27–25.

[34]Dietrich Bonhoeffer, quoted by Paul Farmer in *To Repair the World: Paul Farmer Speaks to the Next Generation*, ed. Jonathan Weigel (Berkeley: University of California Press, 2013), 183.

[35]Griffin and Block, eds., *In the Company of the Poor*, 156.

of those *in via*, especially those who are left behind in the fast-paced world of today whom I have referred to as the vulnerable, the sinners, the broken, rejected, and forgotten poor. As a pilgrim, the church does not hold onto things of this earth but uses them to serve the cause of the gospel, especially for those who are condemned to die. This disposition and way of living frees our churches and Christians to live and act as people on a pilgrimage, seekers of the face of God in the faces of men and women and the faces of creation. Indeed, the Christian journey is never finished until through the attunement of human will to divine purposes, and choices made under the intuition of the Holy Spirit, we build up the city of God where there is cosmic and human flourishing and the definitive orientation of all things toward the purposes of God. Such an ecclesiology relativizes our certainties and conclusions, and heightens our hunger for God as a never-ending quest for all that is true, lovely, worthy of praise, and joyful and draws our hearts to search for the face of God in those who are weak and vulnerable. It also moves the heart of churches to each other and to other religions and nonreligious people in the search for common ground.

The praxis of vulnerable mission *is incarnational* in nature because it models for Christians the kenosis of Christ as our source, inspiration, and ultimate destiny. This ecclesial attitude leads Christians and churches to embrace our creatureliness, and our true identity as the poor of the Lord united in our total dependence on God and on each other for the construction of a new narrative of history. It is also a praxis because it specifies the method and means for changing the social context of the people through entering into their lives and daily actions, while adopting the priorities and practices of the Lord Jesus for healing society. The incarnational and transformational aspect of the praxis of vulnerable mission requires further theological and biblical elaboration especially in showing how such an approach is inspired by the priorities and practices of the Lord.

Transformational Illumination in the Church

An authentic faith—which is never comfortable or completely personal—always involves a deep desire to change the world, to transmit values, to leave this earth somehow better than we found it. We love this magnificent planet on which God has put us, and we love the human family which dwells here, with all its tragedies and struggles, its hopes and aspirations, its strengths and weaknesses. The earth is our common home and all of us are brothers and sisters. . . . All Christians, their pastors included, are called to show concern for the building of a better world. This is essential, for the church's social thought is primarily positive: it offers proposals, it works for change and in this sense it constantly points to the hope born of the loving heart of Jesus Christ. (*EG*, 183)

According to Gustavo Gutiérrez, "The heart of Jesus' message is the proclamation of the love of God that is expressed in the proclamation of his kingdom. The kingdom is the final meaning of history; its total fulfillment takes place beyond history, and at the same time it is present from this moment on. The gospels speak to us precisely of its closeness to us today."[36]

Two inaugural proclamations of Jesus in both Mark and Luke present us with some helpful biblical theological foundations for developing practices for a vulnerable mission for an illuminative church. This will be gleaned from focusing briefly on the nature and the demands of the kingdom that Jesus came to establish on earth and which he manifested through his vulnerable mission to the poor of the Lord. In Luke 4:18–19 Jesus quotes from the book of the prophet Isaiah: "The Spirit of the Lord is upon me, because he has anointed me to bring glad tidings to the poor. He has sent me to proclaim liberty to captives and recovery of sight to the blind, to let the oppressed go free, and to proclaim a year acceptable to the Lord." The Lord goes on to conclude that this scriptural prophecy was being fulfilled as the people listened.

The central message of the Messiah is good news to the poor. The people being referred to by the Lord include all people associated with the condition of poverty: people who are starving, those who have no access to water, those who are suffering from tyranny and injustice in society, the broken-hearted, the abused, and all those who lack hope and are in distress.[37] The gospel is, therefore, an embodied reality. It takes flesh in the very social arc of the people at the deepest level of human fragility and vulnerability, which is felt most painfully by the poor and those on the margins.

The gospel, in this light, is not simply a leaven. It is much more. It assumes the concrete dynamism of a force and power that imbues and weaves the social web in a way that it practically leads the poor to a place of hope, restoration, healing, and dignified existence. It also becomes a source and means for their empowerment, and the very agency for their social construction of identity and hope and the procurement of abundant life. William Loader argues that in the Gospel of Luke, Jesus is shown not simply as a good man who preaches an empty good news, but rather the

---

[36]Ibid., 154.

[37]William Loader, "'Good News for the Poor' and Spirituality in the New Testament: A Question of Survival," in *Prayer and Spirituality in the Early Church*, vol. 5: *Poverty and Riches,* edited by Geoffrey D. Dunn, David Luckensmeyer, and Lawrence Cross (Strathfield, NSW : St Paul's Publications, 2009), 6.

proclamation and ministry of Jesus was incarnational, vulnerable, embodied, concrete, transformational, and within history enacted as the fulfillment of the promise of the kingdom of God to the people. This is true because it began with a proclamation of the Lord that "does something about poverty in the present by addressing one of its major drivers in the ancient world, sickness and disability, and as something still held out as a future hope: 'good news for the poor', affirmed also in the beatitudes and Jesus' response to John the Baptist."[38]

Jesus was able to preach the good news to the poor because he *emptied himself* (Phil 2:7) and became one with them. He has offered the church a principle of vulnerable mission because the hermeneutics of the poor within a critical hermeneutics of history that Jesus demonstrated in his words and deeds was not just an exercise or a mere mouthing of spiritual platitudes; Jesus took upon himself the poverty of the vulnerable and the brokenness of the wounded (2 Cor 8:9; 5:21; Is 53:5) in order to bring them liberation. This immediately rejects any form of Christian liberation and proclamation that does not engage in social immersion, empowerment of the poor, and concrete transformational pastoral action to reverse history. The Lord was immersed in the darkness and depths of poverty and despair. The prophet Isaiah described in detail the condition of the poor: they are blind, shackled in the chains of evil and pain, oppressed, trapped in the suffocating prison of poverty, suffering, and pain. The liberation that the Lord brings is a fulfillment of a prophetic mission.

The Old Testament prophet was a messenger who proclaimed the word of God and showed the people the implications and consequences of the message. They uttered the prophetic oracle: *Thus sayeth the Lord*. In Jesus, the message was the messenger and the messenger was the message. He embodied the irruption of God's promise and divine intention for liberation and salvation. He became the realization of the promise of liberation and the very presence of this realization in the concrete lives of people. What this message meant for many who heard Jesus was that God was entering and transforming human history for the sake of all those who have been condemned to die, that is, all the suffering people of God. It meant also that God has taken side with the poor and vulnerable. Thus all those who are on the side of God will take a radical interest in the poor, be immersed in their social condition, and rise with the poor by the power and presence of Christ to a new way of living a more abundant life freed from evils, injustice, pain, and existential fragmentation and meaninglessness.[39]

---

[38]Ibid., 12.

[39]Cf. Gustavo Gutiérrez, *On Job: God-Talk and the Suffering of the Innocent* (Maryknoll, NY: Orbis Books, 2009), 94.

Finally, based on the inaugural proclamation in Luke, we are offered another principle for a praxis of vulnerable mission: the liberation the Lord brought was critical and transformational. From the Lord's experience of the weight of evil and sin in the Incarnation, and his total identification with the suffocating yoke of poverty and marginalization of the weak and vulnerable, he confronted the very system and ideology that sustained poverty and pain. His death was the final rejection of sin and evil, and the ultimate victory over sin and injustice. Through his Cross and glorious Resurrection, the Lord brought a new manifestation of the power and transformation in vulnerability: God chose the weak to shame the strong (1 Cor 1:27). The Lukan community that read this gospel was obviously concerned with the social dimension of their Christian discipleship. It also embraced the call to a vulnerable immersion in history and a critical and transformative gospel that was rooted in the concrete and direct experience of the saving presence of the Lord in the places where the people are held in bondage by sin, evil, and injustice.

The community also demonstrated that it was involved in the process of a great reversal, which is common not only in Luke's Gospel but as we showed in chapter 2 in the lives of the communities that read the Letter of James. The presence of the gospel changes or reverses the course of history in favor of the poor, sinners, women, social outcasts, the voiceless, the people who suffer injustice, the homeless, minorities, and those on the margins of history. This is particularly so for those who are so weakened by any iniquitous social context such that they can no longer fight their own battles unless the Lord fights for them through the Christian community. This great reversal is shown for instance in Mary's Magnificat, where God lifts the lowly and brings down the mighty (Lk 1:46–55); it is the poor shepherds who had little social, economic, or political relevance who were the first to receive the Good News of joy at the birth of Christ. This shows the closeness of Christ to the lowly.[40] The social context that is accepted by the Lord is the one in which peace and equity reign (Lk 3:10–14), with justice and righteousness rolling down like a never failing stream (Am 5:24). God's reversal of the sad fortunes of the poor in an unjust social structure is shown in Luke as radical, unequivocal, prophetic, praxis-oriented, transformational, and eschatological. In this, the Lord proposes what should be the authentic mission and identity of the Christian community.

The Christian community has a mandate to reverse the course of history, especially in the present world systems in which the rich and the powerful have tilted the balance of economic, religious, and political power against

---

[40]See the introduction to Luke's Gospel in *The African New Testament and Psalms* (Nairobi: Paulines Publications Africa, 2004), 106–7.

the interest of the poor. The Christian community exists not for itself but for the world, and in a special way it exists for the poor. A church that is self-contained within its systems and that is self-satisfied with the social context that it benefits from, parallels, or reinforces the injustice within the social structure through its anti-evangelical way of living is a church that has lost its soul.

TRANSFORMATION
OF THE SOCIAL CONDITION OF PEOPLE

God is presented in the Christian scriptures as being actively involved in the history of God's people. This is particularly true of those who are poor in the Lord. According to Johann Metz:

> The history of the biblical religion is a history of the way in which a people and the individuals belonging to that people became subjects in the presence of their God. . . . Those men were called out of the anxieties and compulsion of archaic societies in order to become subjects of a new historical process. The terms of their state as subjects were dynamic—being called in danger, being called out of fear, the exodus of conversion, the raising up of their head, the imitation of their leader and so on. Religion was not an additional phenomenon. It was an active part of the process by which Israel became a subject. In the Old Testament, it was in the exodus that the people most clearly became subjects.[41]

So the question is: How is African history being transformed through the Christian faith?

What is the fundamental challenge of the gospel for the social context? In Mark 1:15 Jesus proclaims: "This is the time of fulfillment. The kingdom of God is at hand. Repent, and believe in the gospel." His Galilean ministry in all the synoptic gospels began with an offer and a challenge. In Matthew (4:12–17), the Lord began with a series of oracles from Isaiah: "The people who sit in darkness have seen a great light; on those dwelling in a land overshadowed by death, light has arisen." This has an echo to the prophecy of Simeon at the presentation of Jesus in the temple in the Gospel of Luke when he declared that Jesus will be a light of revelation to the Gentiles, and glory for Israel (Lk 2:32), re-echoing the prophecy of Isaiah 60:1–3.

---

[41]Quoted in Wilson Muoha Maina, *Historical and Social Dimensions in African Christian Theology: A Contemporary Approach* (Eugene, OR: Wipf and Stock, 2009), 81.

I will like to draw three important points among many from this proclamation on how a vulnerable mission can offer the church a praxis for
interpreting, judging, and transforming any unacceptable social condition,
especially structures of sin and structural violence against the poor. It also
shows why conversion of hearts and cultures are central to transforming
society and removing the obstacles toward realizing the divine purposes
for a particular society and context.

Any community, whether it is as small as a clan or as large as a nation
or the globe, that is not realizing the purpose or mission for its existence
should look into systems and structures in that society as well as the ethical
template on which that society is built and sustained. An honest critical
engagement with systems, structures, and dynamics of higher power and
lower power as well as an ethical critique of any society can furnish the
church with answers about how to confront the evils that ail any society. In
Africa, particularly, engaging the religious narratives and counternarratives
will be essential. God created the world to save it and transform it in the
direction of the eschatological fruits of God's kingdom, and this is what
we glean from the proclamation of the Lord in the gospel. We also glean
the terrible consequences of sin and evil, especially injustice, falsehood,
selfishness, and pride, when they ravage the hearts of people and become
the pulsating heart of a particular community.

The first point in this first proclamation is that it was made within a very
concrete historical context. The first offer of salvation is made within the
context of people's history; it was not an abstract proclamation or an empty
claim. It was a message that was drawn from their historical context and
that spoke to the social, religious, and cultural reality of the people at that
time.[42] The references to Galilee, Naphtali, Zebulun, and Capernaum invoke
the prophetic oracle of hope of Isaiah (Is 8:23–29, 1–2: cf. Is 60:1–3) after
Assyria overran Galilee in 732 BCE. However, the attack against Galilee
and the rest of the Northern Kingdom was the result of the chaos, moral
decay, and religious, economic, and political exploitation of the poor and
the weak that preceded and followed the death of Jeroboam II in 746 BCE
(2 Kgs 15).[43] Most of these acts of oppression and exploitation were carried
out in the name of God and by people in religious and political positions.

The chaos and decay in the social context of the day was the result of the
corruption and injustice in the land which the prophets Amos and Hosea
had preached against. They inveighed against the abuse of religion by
false prophets, and all kinds of false religious practices, empty rituals and

---

[42]See Daniel J. Harrington, *Sacra Pagina: The Gospel of Matthew* (Collegeville, MN: Liturgical
Press, 1991), 75.
[43]Ibid.

pretensions that mimicked the worship of the true God and debauched the ethos of justice and the good of order.[44] God's power and judgment will be made fully manifest and acknowledged by all creation when the true judge, the Messiah, comes.[45] The enactment of the judgment of God in order to bring light to the nations requires the removal of the structures of chaos and disorder that were built on sin and evil. It requires, in addition, speaking the word of truth to power, and executing judgment on the very religious and political bastions that were unjust and corrupt.

The second aspect of this inaugural offer of salvation is the dimension of time. In Luke, Mark, and Matthew, the first proclamation of Jesus is presented as an opportune time (Kairos). The content of this fulfillment is salvation and liberation from the clutches of sin and evil. The kingdom of God becomes the perfect embodiment of the Father's will for the world, which in Isaiah and the prophets was a promise and which in the liberation from Egypt was figurative; but in Christ this becomes a reality. The kingdom is presented as the reign of God or the will of God, something that Jesus presents again in the Lord's prayer: God's kingdom comes when God's will is done.

As Gutiérrez demonstrates, in the coming of Jesus in time, God's perfect will is enacted. This involves repentance from sin. It also demands standing in truth before God and rejecting all falsehood. This requires opening the door to God, whose existence is validated by the existence of the poor.[46] The poor hears God's voice because in their hopelessness and despair it is only God who comes to them as the source and origin of all things and as the ultimate liberator from bondage. God desires to transform the condition of the poor because their suffering and pain touch the heart of God and wound the Sacred Heart of Jesus. God is always waiting and desiring to break into our daily lives, especially when we are suffering and in pain, when we are victims of injustice and oppression. God is knocking at the doors of our lives because God wants to enter into relationship with us in order to save us from falling into despair and gloom (Rv 3:20).

The indifference and hardness of heart of those who are rich and comfortable highlight the need for repentance. But this observation is not simply a reprimand to the rich whose wealth and self-sufficiency may shut their hearts to the transformational grace that liberates; it is a summons to the poor as well to open themselves to God and to lay down their burdens

---

[44]See Isaiah 10:1–4; 5:25. See also Margaret Barker, "Isaiah," in *Eerdmans Commentary on the Bible*, ed. James D. G. Dunn and John W. Rogerson (Grand Rapids, MI: William B. Eerdmans, 2003), 508, 489–542.

[45]Harrington, *Sacra Pagina*, 72.

[46]Gustavo Gutiérrez, *A Theology of Liberation: History, Politics, and Salvation*, trans. Caridad Inda and John Eagleson (Maryknoll, NY: Orbis Books, 1973), 175–176.

at the feet of Jesus, while taking a new "burden" (Mt 11:30), which is the dignified agency that Pope Francis recommends. It is the freedom and the support given to the poor so that they can exercise the gift of who they are through the "toilsome good" (Aquinas) of working every day to fight their own fight and to contribute their own efforts through daily work for the reign of God. God's time of salvation will become reality in Africa as our people begin to experience divine solidarity as a way of being community, and experience conversion as a way of building the earthly city on the foundation of the Lord Jesus.[47]

It requires total trust and belief in God. If the time of salvation, as Gutiérrez proposes, is the time of God's liberation of God's people, which in Christ has also become human time, it means that the poverty and the sinful social conditions of many Africans are not part of the divine plan for the unveiling of history in Africa. This does not mean the rejection of the theology of the Cross, but rather demands locating the suffering of Africans within the salvific intention of God. Reflecting on this dimension of time and memory, Gustavo Gutiérrez writes:

> Time acquires, in this way, an urgent, salvific, and human density. Far from being an abstract category, or from being limited to a tiresome chronological succession, time becomes, thanks to memory, a space where we encounter the face of Jesus, the Son of God made flesh, and a space for encounter with others. In time are rooted two liberties, God's free self-revelation in the gratuitousness of love and the human freedom to accept this gift; the first calls forth and constitutes the second.[48]

The third aspect is that the proclamation by the Lord was a light that shines in the darkness to illumine the earthly city. This is the aspect of transformation. This light comes then as a force for repentance and becomes also the result of repentance. Here we find the main challenge of the first proclamation of Jesus in Mark and Matthew addressed to all those who wish that God's will be done on earth. It is a call that we turn our minds and hearts and life in the direction of God, so that our society will become godly, wholesome, and transformed in order to enjoy abundant life.[49]

As a result, one can see that the social context is not pregiven, value-neutral, or absolute, nor should poverty be understood as destiny. Rather, it

---

[47]Gustavo Gutiérrez, *We Drink from Our Own Wells: The Spiritual Journey of a People*, 20th anniversary edition (Maryknoll, NY: Orbis Books, 2010), 20–21.

[48]Gustavo Gutiérrez, "Prophecy and Memory," in *The Option for the Poor in Christian Theology*, ed. Daniel G. Groody (Notre Dame, IN: University of Notre Dame Press, 2007), 20.

[49]William Barclay, *Turning to God: Conversion in the New Testament* (London: Epworth Press, 1963), 25.

is a human construction tainted in many cases by sin and evil. It is, there-fore, defined by a convergence of different degrees of individual choices, social forces, and cultural currents. The social context is never value-neutral because it is always driven by some worldviews or ideologies or power dynamics, which are embodied in cultural knowledge, cultural artifacts, and cultural behavior. Therefore, the social context is always governed by the interest of the dominant individuals and groups who control the economic, political, religious, and cultural systems. This is why African theology must constantly be immersed in history to question the prevailing countervalues that inform the social context in Africa where many people are not realizing their God-given potential. In many African communities today families, clans and communities spend so much time, money, and ritual burying their dead because of the high mortality rate across the rank and file. Rather than confronting the causes of so many sudden deaths in the continent and adopting preventative measures and changing the structures that produce so much suffering, it seems that fulfilling the burial rites have assumed a life of its own for many African communities.

The will of God for every society is that all should embrace the truth and life embodied in the person of Christ. This embrace is the leaven for the earth, the light for the world, and the hope for the future. Any society can be judged to the extent to which the life of Christ reigns in it. Christ is the embodiment of divine love. We can reread the human social context in the light of this basic inclination toward love and justice in the basic structure of divine love in Christ.[50] The true conversion that Jesus calls forth springs from the revelation of the Incarnate love of God on the Cross.

We are called to a change of attitude, a change in the way we see ourselves, others, and society. This turn from darkness to light requires a movement of both the intellect and the will. There is a shift in the center of value, joy, and meaning. It is a new discovery that in Christ the apparently unconquerable power of sin and evil that holds personal and group lives in bondage can be overcome. It shows the possibility of change and reversal in the lives of individuals and societies, which are dealing with dysfunctional values that undermine the good life.[51] Such a reversal can happen only through a vulnerable church that feels the weight of the sin and suffering of the poor in its very veins and which becomes an instrument for integral healing for the poor and for social transformation.

The people walked in darkness in the time of Isaiah and were consigned to long years in exile because their society was no longer tenable. The people

---

[50]Bruno Forte, *He Loved Them to the End: Theological Meditations on Love and Eucharist*, trans. Robert D. Paolucci (Boston: St. Paul's Book and Media, 1993), 56.

[51]Cf. Barclay, *Turning to God*, 29–32.

were homeless in every sense of the word because they lost personal and group identity, having lost the God who gave them meaning and direction. In the same way, a sick social context like the one we find in Africa in the midst of so much human suffering and so many tragedies leaves the members of society in exile. The people in the time of Isaiah were in chaos and disorder because they broke the commandments of God, rejected the life-affirming covenantal love of God, and worshipped all kinds of idols. Darkness becomes a metaphor for lives that are lived outside the moral and spiritual compass of God. In a sense, the dark cloud of poverty, disease, despair, and pain that overcomes many Africans today is the result of the absence of true religion and social justice. The hope which many African Christians embrace should become a principle of light to reverse the course of history in Africa. What is the fate of the poor in Africa today, especially millions who flock to our churches almost every day in their search for abundant life?

All the poor who came to Jesus found in him a friend, a helper, and support as he healed them of their diseases, restored their sense of dignity devastated by poverty, took away their shame and their sins, and gave them a new identity, a new image, and a new hope. Selfless love, vulnerable mission, unconditional acceptance, concrete acts of kindness, practical acts of compassion, sensitivity, and understanding of the painful condition of the poor were habitual attitudes of Jesus. He looked upon the publicans, sinners, prostitutes, criminals, immigrants, foreigners, lepers, widows, homeless and nameless children, the sick, the suffering, the possessed, among others, with eyes of mercy and even pronounced a blessing on them and all those who place their trust in God and not on the things they have: "Blessed are the poor in spirit, for theirs is the kingdom of God" (Mt 5:3).[52] Giving to the poor, reaching out to the needy, and being there for all those on the margins of society and those who are far from God were essential to the mission of Christ. They should also be central to the church's mission of proclaiming the kingdom of God and witnessing to the coming of the kingdom in history. This is a mission both for the universal church and the local churches and all Christians.

Jesus' care for the poor is shown in the scriptures to be the necessary consequence of the irruption of God's kingdom. It was not a long-distance, arm-chair ministry, but a total immersion in the very depth of sin, evil, poverty, and brokenness in order to bring healing, salvation, justice, right order, and transformation for humanity and the entire world. This attitude of Jesus has been described in many ways in the Pauline corpus: self-emptying

---

[52]See Stan Chu Ilo, *The Church and Development in Africa: Aid and Development from the Perspective of Catholic Social Ethics* (Nairobi: Paulines Publications Africa, 2013), 200–201.

for the sake of humanity (Phil 2:7); he became poor (2 Cor 8:9); he became sin (2 Cor 5:21) so that we can become the righteous of God.

Salvation was both a spiritual and a material gift from God since the whole person is to be saved and restored to the full human dignity fitting for a child of God. In the ministry of Jesus, his healing miracles and his outreach to the poor were central to the realization of the messianic reign of God. The liberation from the net of sin and evil, as well as from the clutches of poverty and suffering caused by injustice, was central to the proclamation and ministry of the Lord. The kingdom of God and the submission of all things to the lordship of Christ demanded the toppling of sinful structures and unjust and unacceptable conditions. This is why the Lord did not stop at simply providing food for the hungry and healing the sick. He also was concerned with empowering the poor so that they can take control of their lives. He did not preach or practice a dependent charity, but a liberating charity that freed the people, on one hand, and gave them the impetus to transcend and change their condition, on the other. It was a charity that was concerned with doing justice and confronting the root cause of poverty—the sinful hearts and sinful conditions and structures of his times.

Here we find the quality and distinctive character of God's kingdom being made manifest in Christ's words and deeds. The liberation from poverty is rooted in the transformation of human hearts and human institutions so that there will emerge a new reality characterized by just and fair social conditions. The charitable outreach to the poor is not a dependent chain, but a liberative ministry that empowers people to transcend their personal limitations to pursue their missions in life. The Lord reached out to the poor to remove the obstacles that held them down so that they can live fully as children of God and participate in building up and protecting the common good. He also liberated them so that they can become disciples who work in bringing the world to conform to God's plan. The words and examples of the Lord should be the foundation for a praxis of vulnerable mission.

The church in Africa must read our present history from the side of the poor, in the light of the unequal relations and increasing income inequality that are ravaging the lives of the poor. This means that the church in Africa must pitch its tent with the poor, not in presidential palaces and royal chambers. The refugee camps of Dadaab, Kenya; the thousands of prisons in many African countries where the poor and the disinherited continue to suffer injustice and dehumanizing treatments; the killing fields of the Congo, Darfur, and South Sudan; the battle grounds of Northeastern Nigeria, and the repression in some other African countries are all places where the gospel of social and political engagement should be present and active. As millions of Africans suffer from untimely deaths because of AIDS, malaria, other diseases, and poverty, there is a greater sense of urgency for the churches to show that Africans are living in the acceptable time of the Lord. Jesus embodied the irruption of God's promise and divine intention for liberation and salvation. He became the realization of the promise of liberation and the very presence of this realization in the lives of people.

Illuminative ecclesiology answers the question, What form of witnessing in the proclamation and witnessing of Christians and churches reveals to people the compassionate face of God and reflects as in mirror to God the many faces of humanity in their joys and sorrows? In other words, what form should the church assume through its priorities and practices which will make people believe that the light of Christ shines in its life?

In this chapter, I have shown that illuminative ecclesiology presents the praxis of accountability, the art of accompaniment, and a vulnerable mission as form through which the church establishes a culture of encounter with a wounded world and brings about in small ways the transformation of the world. I have also showed how these approaches to praxis can be located in the priorities and practices of Jesus Christ. In sum, the church's engagement with the social context involves (1) the search for the eschatological fruits of God's kingdom within history. How is God speaking to the church through the voices and silence of the poor? (2) self-critical examination of conscience for Christians and churches with regard to how they are contributing to the darkness of sin, evil, pain, poverty, or suffering by extinguishing the light of Christ and by compromising the identity and mission of the church in the social context; (3) an uncompromising proclamation of the prophetic word of repentance as the first step in bringing the kingdom of God near to all; and (4) a message of hope that God is near to those who suffer and those who do God's will. This message will demand a rejection of anything that is opposed to the values and virtues of social ethics, a recovery of a social conscience for all, and a search for the presence within history of the tools for changing the sad social context; and (5) a transformative praxis that privileges the people's agency in social reconstruction by identifying their assets and valorizing the inner enrichment of their group and personal history. Describing how this is happening in Africa through the impact of Pope Francis and how it can happen in other parts of the world is a humble task that I will take up in the next chapter.

4

Illuminative Ecclesiology
and the Church's Social Mission in Africa

I once read a distressing news story on the webpage of Radio France International. The title was "Sierra-Leone: Crowd Digs Up Damaged Chicken from Garbage Dump."[1] According to the news, on the weekend of July 24, 2016, thousands of poor people in the biggest slums in Freetown, Sierra Leone, fought with police officers who tried to prevent them from unearthing buried chicken in a garbage dump. The meat, according to the report, was imported from Brazil. However, upon tests by the Ministry of Health, it was determined that the meat was no longer good for human consumption. The ministry officials, therefore, ordered that the meat be disposed and buried.

However, for thousands of poor people in Freetown, this was unthinkable. The meat should not be wasted! So the following day, with shovels and diggers in hand, thousands of people went to the dumping ground where the chickens were buried to unearth and take the meat home for consumption. The police had to use tear gas to disperse the crowd who refused to leave the garbage dump area. Some of the people who already retrieved some of the meat were happy to run home with some meat to "enjoy" themselves. The authorities, the report indicated, were worried about an outbreak of disease in the area because not only was the chicken meat unhealthy for consumption but also because the ground where it was buried was a dumping ground for industrial wastes as well as contaminated food and garbage. The report noted that many pressure groups in Sierra Leone called for an inquiry into how such meat considered unfit for consumption was imported into the country. They were also calling for the arrest of the businessman who was responsible for importing the meat.

I don't know how this situation was resolved. What distresses me is the suffering and desperation that could drive my African brothers and sisters

---

[1]"Sierra-Leone: Crowd Digs Up Damaged Chicken from Garbage Dump," Radio France International, July 24, 2016, www.rfi.fr/afrique.

to search for meat in the stinking refuse dumps of Freetown. There are many people in our continent who are at the margins or the precipice of life. Millions of Africans are falling into the bottomless abyss of poverty and pain. This is not simply to play into the stereotype of painting Africa and African reality in negative light. There are many bright lights in our continent as I will show in this chapter. However, we cannot engage in any social mission in the continent without properly diagnosing the true situation that our people face. As Pope Francis wrote on the miracle of Jesus, when Jesus saw a leper (Mk 1:40–45), "Jesus does not remain indifferent; he feels compassion; he lets himself be involved and wounded by pain, by illness, by the poverty he encounters. He does not back away. . . . He didn't sit down at a desk and study the situation, he didn't consult the experts for pros and cons. What really mattered to him was reaching stranded people and saving them like the Good Shepherd who leaves the flock to save one lost sheep."[2] In the face of suffering, we cannot remain indifferent nor can our theologies be valid in Africa if the stories of our people do not inform our theological methods.

These kinds of stories are not unique to Africa. I have read of similar terrible conditions and heard of gut-wrenching tales of poverty from my colleagues from many parts of the world. Whose heart will not be torn apart by stories from the favelas in Rio de Janeiro, the horrible conditions of many Filipinos in Manila's Payatas dump site in Quezon City and the shameful conditions of many African Americans in Chicago, or the painful living conditions of many Afro-Carribeans in the Jane and Finch area in Toronto and in many Western cities, or the wretchedness of people's lives in Aleppo, Syria, or in the Gaza Strip? The suffering and poverty in the world is so pervasive that the 2011 Cape Town Commitment (article 7, c) of the Lausanne Movement confessed that God's will to uphold the cause of the oppressed, to defend the rights of the widows and orphans, to protect the stranger and homeless, and give food to the hungry and liberty to those in captivity is far from being realized in today's world. Part of why God's justice and redemption has not become reality for many poor people in the world is because Christians have been too weak and complacent in fighting for the poor to bring about the justice of God to the poor. In *Evangelii Gaudium*, Pope Francis was unequivocal that the church in the face of so much human suffering should not be a comfortable or complicit church. Rather, the church should be "bruised, hurting and dirty because it has been out on the street" (49), because "the evangelizers must have the smell of the sheep," supporting and standing by the poor and weak and all God's people (24).

---

[2]Pope Francis, *The Name of God Is Mercy: A Conversation with Andrea Tornielli*, trans. Oonagh Stransky (New York: Random House, 2016), 64–65.

In this light, my goal here is not about stating how Africans are like or unlike others in the way our people are being nailed to the Cross of suffering and pain or to reinforce the narratives of Afro-pessimism. Rather, what I wish to do in this chapter is to show through the analysis of the social condition of Africa that the praxis of illuminative ecclesiology is sorely needed in the ferment of Christian expansion in Africa. I will do this by identifying *the poor in Africa* who like Lazarus are crying out at our gates for mercy because their wounds are festering in conditions of increasing hardship. I propose some pathways for dialogue in our search for how best to live the social mission of the church and what principles can be drawn from the teaching of Pope Francis in developing a hermeneutics of multiplicity needed for dialogue in the church. I will demonstrate why a dialogue with the poor is needed in the church today, especially in Africa.

Stories like the Freetown crowd digging up buried contaminated chicken are the phenomenological foundation of my theological reflection. Another related but different experience that also challenged me as an African in search of God's hand in our history took place in 2013. I was crossing the Busia border from Uganda to Kenya by bus. Everyone in the bus had to cross the border by foot, while the customs and police officers did their normal security check of the bus and the baggage of the passengers. This will normally take an hour or more. As we waited for our bus to be cleared, having passed through immigration, I was quite hungry and decided to buy some bananas and cashew nuts. I bought a bunch of bananas and started to eat and was suddenly surrounded by about eight small boys whose ages I will put to be under twelve.

These boys were begging for alms from passersby. They approached me begging that I share my bananas with them because they had not eaten all day. These were street boys who have taken this open space of the border and the hazards of this place as their home. It was 2 p.m. I then bought the entire bunch of bananas at the table and shared with them. I wished them well and then boarded the bus to continue my journey. I had one banana left, that I ate inside the bus and then threw the peel away through the window. Much to my pain, these young boys ran after the banana peel to scrape whatever remained there worth eating!

This was a scene that will always remain with me as a point of reference and a source of sorrow. However, it also challenges me to shape my theological writings in such a way that they are informed, inspired, and touched by these stories. It also posed a challenge to me to do something about so many in Africa who might be in situations similar to the ones the boys were in.

When I shared the bananas with the boys, they thanked me saying that they knew God would bring them some help that day. The question for me then as well as now is: What is this experience of God that these young boys expressed to me in their condition? How could this God have sent me to share bananas with them when they should be living in well-functioning societies with food, education, a good home, and all that makes life beautiful, fulfilling, and joyful? How can the theology I write emerge from the dumps of history, from the experience of poverty and powerlessness of many poor Africans, and be a source of light and hope? What theological method can account for the stories of these boys and the society in which they are growing up, that has robbed them of their childhood and a future while giving them a wretched existence in their present life? How can I articulate the Christian religion in Africa in such a way that it offers hope to Africans? How can the theology that I write provide agency for the self and group transcendence for the poor, and praxis of transformation for these young boys and many like them who are growing up in Africa today? How can one see in the stories of these children the narrative of God's revelation of the realization of the reign of God in the church's mission to the men and women, young and old, who are living in poverty and those on the margins in Africa?

The images of the Freetown slum and the young street children at the Busia border and similar stories in our continent are the portraits that should foreground our social mission in Africa. There are millions of our people who are suffering and dying, and the gospel message cannot simply be an empty proclamation to them; it must be a concrete force felt in the Christian community as a transformational praxis for the people. Pope Francis reminded the church in the Year of Mercy (2016):

> How many are the wounds borne by the flesh of those who have no voice because their cry is muffled and drowned out by the indifference of the rich. . . . Let us not fall into humiliating indifference or a monotonous routine that prevents us from discovering what is new! Let us ward off destructive cynicism! Let us open our eyes and see the misery of the world, the wounds of our brothers and sisters who are denied their dignity, and let us recognize that we are compelled to heed their cry for help! May we reach out to them. . . . May their cry become our own, and together may we break down the barriers of indifference that too often reign supreme and mask our hypocrisy and egoism.[3]

African theologians and church leaders need not look to Freetown, we need to look around us to see the poverty that surrounds us—in our immediate or extended families, clans, communities, neighborhoods,

---

[3]Pope Francis, *The Face of Mercy*, Bull of Indiction of the Extraordinary Jubilee of Mercy, *Misericordiae Vultus* (Vatican City, 2015), 15.

churches, and offices. There are so many people who are suffering, and there are many people dying in our continent because of poverty. Emmanuel Katongole describes this so well in *The Sacrifice of Africa*: "If churches and coffins represent two dominant cultural realties in Africa, they also represent the predicament of a continent suspended between hope and despair. They capture the hope and pain, the beauty and tragedy, the dreams and frustrations of a continent that is at once overwhelmingly Christian and at the same time politically, economically, and socially distressed."[4]

Our continent is filled with experiences of poverty and pain that I believe are opposed to God's will for God's people in our land. A Zimbabwean prison chaplain told me recently that when some prisoners were released in 2016 by the Mugabe government, most of the prisoners did not want to leave their jails and go back to their families. There was no hope for them outside the prison. So when you tell these prisoners that Jesus has come to set prisoners free, it will ring hollow to their ears because for them life outside the prison will be unbearable. According to this chaplain, many prisoners in Zimbabwe could get at least some meals, housing, and medical care, but outside the prison they were afraid that they would die of starvation and exposure. But this story is not only common in countries held in bondage by dictatorship in Africa. It is also a challenge for countries like Nigeria, that was said to be the largest economy in Africa in 2015.

There was a big headline in 2013 in Owerri in Eastern Nigeria about a prisoner who was acquitted and released from jail. Rather than rejoice at the judgment of the court, the poor man broke down in tears before the judge and said that he would like to go back to prison. According to the man, he would rather stay in jail where he could get some meals and housing rather than be released. In a moving speech, he said, "I have no place to go or anybody to go to. I have no job or business. I want to go back to prison where I can at least be sure to eat something everyday."[5]

I remember again the desperation that a partner in one of our projects in East Africa shared with me (to protect the person's privacy, I cannot name the country or the person). However, this local agent at one of our sites told me that there are some of the women in the group who because of their total lack of any means of livelihood or access to any health care services are choosing to become HIV positive.

I wondered why one would expose herself to this terrible sickness knowing that it means that the person will live on medication for the rest

---

[4]Emmanuel Katongole, *The Sacrifice of Africa: A Political Theology for Africa* (Grand Rapids, MI: William B. Eerdmans, 2011), 31.

[5]"Man Refuses to Leave Prison after Being Released in Owerri," Nairaland Forum, August 5, 2013, www.nairaland.com.

of her life and will be susceptible to other unpredictable health problems. The agent told me that a few of these women believe that since having HIV gives one access to some of the basic health care intervention available and a daily food ration, it was okay to get the disease. In a few cases, the number of HIV positive people is inflated to get access to food and medication, and some people who were not HIV positive are presented as being positive to get extra help from the government and NGOs. This was one of the most distressing stories I have heard in the field. But the questions this situation presents to me are clear: What kind of gospel can you preach to people in this kind of situation? How can my theological writing give an account of this kind of condition and where is God in all these situations? Is God hearing the cries of these women? And how will God intervene in their history to bring about the promise of a new and better day?

All the women's groups with whom I have worked in five African countries always begin every meeting with prayer and songs of praise and thanksgiving to God. I remember a prayer said by a woman at one of our partnering organizations, the Crisis Center for Carers (Triple C) in Mombasa, Kenya. This prayer was said at the beginning of the Harambe (group work) outreach to members who were sick. This center cares for women who are living positively with HIV. In addition, the center's affiliated lawyers defend the rights of women in any kind of cultural or marital bondage. This lady, who founded her own Pentecostal church, prayed as follows:

> Lord Jesus, you said you will have the poor with you.
> We are the poor and you are with us in our poverty.
> You are poor and so we claim you as our own in our poverty.
> You will make us rich because you became poor to make us rich
> in Jesus' name [the group says "Amen"].
> We are the women who follow you.
> We are widows but we are mothers.
> We give life, but death surrounds us in this land.
> We are suffering and many of our members are dying.
> We do not have money, but we have hope.
> We do not have cars, *tuk tuk* [tricycle] or *boda boda* [motor bike]
> but you have given us legs.
> Send help to us from heaven; send angels from heaven to watch us.
> When we are sick heal us; when we are naked send us long skirts
> from heaven.
> When we are despairing, fight the evil spirit of hopelessness; when
> we are alone be our group leader.
> Send your Holy Spirit to us.
> Send miracles on our way so that today we go out to bring hope to

all our members and any strangers we meet today [here they mention the names of members to be visited and conclude with blessing]. . . .

When one looks closely at this prayer, one can see immediately that there is a theology behind it. There is echoed here the "blessedness" of Luke 6:20 that the kingdom belongs to the poor because they are closest to God. The poor are so close to God because God's Son sees and loves in them what he sees and loves in himself in his utter powerlessness and vulnerability on the Cross. Echoed here is also the hope that lies beyond the valleys of pain but that emerges through their daily practices. What was particularly interesting was how this preacher-woman translates the words of the Lord, "the poor you always have with you" to mean that Jesus is the poor one who will always be with the poor. Jesus was not simply saying that poverty is commonplace and should be accepted as the inevitable consequence of our social compact. Rather, Jesus has made himself poor in the least of the brethren and remains present in history in those veiled faces. Thus, by identifying with the poor, Jesus transforms their condition. "The poor are always with us" can be translated as "the Lord is always with us in the faces of the poor."

However, what struck me most was that this prayer was a call to arms rather than an expression of a wish or a shopping list for God. It was a prayer for action, that moves from being the poor of the Lord to being poor in the Lord. But another thing that struck me and that always makes an appearance in my own personal prayer for the poor is not so much what God will do for the poor, but what God can do for the poor through us and what God can do for the poor through the agency of the poor. As one woman leader quoted to us in our meeting, "We are not asking for money; we are only asking that the obstacles on our way be removed."

The sentiment expressed by this woman leader is similar to the position well articulated in the important document prepared by the Commission on World Mission and Evangelism (CWME) of the World Council of Churches (WCC), *Together Towards Life: Mission and Evangelism in Changing Landscapes* (2012). In Articles 40 and 41, the document emphasizes the importance of beginning all social missions from the social location of the people because "the aim of mission is not simply to move people from the margins to the centers of power but to confront those who remain at the center by keeping people on the margins. Instead churches are called to *transform* power structures" (40). This resonates with the perspective and insight of the woman leader about the removal of obstacles rather than Band-Aid solutions. It reflects the call and urgency of how the agency of the people emerges in the midst of suffering. As *Together Towards Life* highlights clearly, our social mission has "often been directed at people on the margins of societies"; we have treated the poor as if "they are recipients and not as active agents" in their own history" (articles 41–42). This manner of treating those on the margins as passive recipients "has too often been complicit with oppressive and life-denying systems. It has generally aligned with the privileges of the center and largely failed to challenge economic, social, cultural, and political systems that have marginalized some people. Mission from the center is motivated by an attitude of paternalism and a superiority complex" (41).

In writing this chapter, I constantly thought of a prayer that still evokes strong feelings in me. It is a line from a prayer said by an elderly man in my town at one of my Masses a few months after my priestly ordination in 1998. I remember this man saying to God during the prayer of the faithful, "God, our nights are too long and our days are too dark. *Anyi ji eze ekpe ekwere*—we are using our teeth to literally knit our yarns into fabrics of existence." How will God respond to the prayers of this man? How will the God who hears the cry of the poor respond to such prayers, that come straight from the bleeding hearts and wounded hands of our people who are hanging on the Cross? Thinking about the answers to these questions always brings to mind the import of the favorite saying of Saint Mother Teresa of Calcutta, "Christ has no body now on earth but yours; no hands but yours; no feet but yours. Yours are the eyes through which the compassion of Christ must look out on the world. Yours are the feet with which He is to go about doing good. Yours are the hands with which He is to bless His people."

The church and Christians are the hands, heads, and hearts through which God will change the world around us. This is what the church's social mission seeks to stimulate in the Christian community. The social mission of the church is not simply a top-down approach to helping people; it is about making the Christian community come alive as a witness to the integral salvation that God has won for us in Christ. It is about giving agency to the people, recognizing the gifts of everyone, and removing the obstacles in people's paths. This way, people, especially the poor, are equipped to take ownership of their lives and to assume responsibility through their daily commitments to bringing about the reign of God in history. This is the import of Pope Francis's speech to the UN General Assembly on September 25, 2015:

> To enable these real men and women to escape from extreme poverty, we must allow them *to be dignified agents of their own destiny* [my emphasis]. Integral human development and the full exercise of human dignity cannot be imposed. They must be built up and allowed to unfold for each individual, for every family, in communion with others, and in a right relationship with all those areas in that human social life develops—friends, communities, towns and cities, schools, businesses and unions, provinces, nations, etc.

I have seen significant transformation in the lives of women, for example, through the heroic support and collaboration of the women at Triple C as they volunteer to reach out to others. We all can recount our own experiences in many more ways than one where we have heard the summons of God inside of us to work to improve the quality of life of others, to bring light where there is darkness. These women, like many Africans today, are looking up to God for a better future. But how will that future emerge in the midst of their brokenness, and what role should the poor and merciful church play in the light of the teaching of Pope Francis on the revolution of tenderness? How can our revolution of tenderness be translated from charitable and social ministries that address people's needs to being a praxis that builds on the assets of people and gives them agency to rebuild their future through their own hands? This forms the context of what follows in the rest of this chapter. The church's social mission is a vocation that it carries out through its members, its ecclesial structures, in dialogue with the poor, and in collaboration with the state, religious groups, and men and women of goodwill. However, the church's social mission must begin with its way of being—the life of our churches. Indeed, the choices that I make, my way of life, and the method and content of my writings as a priest and theologian from a continent where the stories from the slums of Freetown are still commonplace cannot remain the same.

THE POOR OF THE LORD AND THE POOR
IN THE LORD IN AFRICA

The Church has realized that the need to heed this plea is itself born of the liberating action of grace within each of us, and thus it is not a question of a mission reserved only to a few: "The Church, guided by the Gospel of mercy and by love for mankind, hears the cry for justice and intends to respond to it with all her might." In this context we can understand Jesus' command to his disciples: "You yourselves give them something to eat!" (Mk 6:37): it means working to eliminate the structural causes of poverty and to promote the integral development of the poor, as well as small daily acts of solidarity in meeting the real needs which we encounter. The word "solidarity" is a little worn and at times poorly understood, but it refers to something more than a few sporadic acts of generosity. It presumes the creation of a new mind-set which thinks in terms of community and the priority of the life of all over the appropriation of goods by a few. (*EG*, 188)

Mama Ann began a novena tonight. She is doing what they call in this part of Africa "midnight prayer" for the next nine days. This simply means the same prayer ritual started at midnight for nine days. She wakes up at midnight, lights a candle, and offers prayers and petitions to God for her special intention. She has a heavy burden in her life: her daughter has not been able to conceive in more than five years of marriage. Mama Ann is doing this novena for healing for her daughter's infertility in order to save her daughter's crumbling marriage. Her son-in-law is already "sleeping around" with other women and threatening to take a second wife. He claims that even though he is Catholic, being a true African man requires that he should take a second wife because he needs to have some male children who can continue his line after him. Mama Ann's daughter has endometriosis, and the doctors have told her that she can never conceive because the fertilized eggs cannot implant in the uterus. However, Mama Ann believes that nothing is impossible for God and is trusting God to "break the yoke" imposed on her daughter by some evil persons or the devil.

In another case, Mama Tess is a widow who lost her husband to AIDS and is the chairwoman of a women's support group on the outskirts of Mbale in Eastern Uganda some five kilometers from the pristine Mount Elgon. These women have organized themselves to support each other by pulling their resources together to promote agricultural production for each woman through loans. Mama Tess has also been receiving the ARV drugs from an agency run by the local church. However, for the last six months she has been distressed by the side effects of the drugs, which were giving her terrible pains in her ears and affecting her hearing. She therefore decided to stop the medication and rely on faith healing, trusting that ultimately God is the best doctor.

Bishop Eduardo Hiiboro, a man I have come to know and admire from Southern Sudan, shared with me the challenges he faced when he had to run a seminary for Southern Sudanese aspirants to the priesthood in the Democratic Republic of Congo because his country was at war. It was for him a path to trusting God and depending totally on God, as he literally had to take each day as a gift. According to him, he struggled to provide for the distressed and displaced seminarians, and find teachers to teach the courses in this makeshift formation house. In the midst of this terrible disaster, they prayed daily, offering daily Masses to God for divine intervention in their homeland and to help them find means of livelihood for the seminarians and his remaining staff members.

Another story that I like to share is that of Bishop Taban of Sudan who established an inclusive community in Southern Sudan to help heal the wounds of division and be a model of a truly ideal Christian community. He rightly gave the community the name Kuron Holy Trinity Peace Village, a unique experience at reversing history, and creating a zone of peace, prosperity, and community where people despite their ethnic, religious, class, and sexual identities are treated as firstborn children of God. He tells anyone who cares that he depends totally on God for daily provision and that reversing the course of history in Africa demands practical action, sacrifice, and selfless leadership. When he conceived of the idea of building a safe haven where everyone from any racial, religious, and ethnic background would find love and support, he did not know how things would unfold. However, he depended totally on God and put everything in God's hands. In one illuminating reflection, Bishop Taban talks about his approach this way:

> When it came to the evangelisation methodology, our policy was not to focus too much on material things, so as to foster a spirit of self-sufficiency and also to put more stress on our spiritual mission, avoiding the temptation of unconsciously "attracting" people to the church merely because of material development or handouts. We decided to start in a very simple way, making small steps according to the pace and the possibilities of the people.[6]

These four scenarios offer a good narrative starting point to make a distinction between two important categories that I am proposing here in any context but especially applied to an analysis of the African social context, the *poor of the Lord,* and *the poor in the Lord*. All four cases mentioned here are examples of *being the poor of the Lord*, but not all four cases reflect what I have termed *being poor in the Lord*. This distinction could help to understand the link between poverty and liberation in Christ, and human cooperation in the realization of the purposes of God. The distinction is also made as a way of offering some helpful theological and spiritual distinctions for understanding both the healing ministry of Jesus and the search for abundant life in today's Africa through new Christian religious movements. Rather than simply condemning "healing priests," "sangoma priests," African Pentecostals, and charismatics, one needs clear theological foundations to guide pastoral discernment, pastoral action, and spiritual judgment. I propose that Mama Ann and Mama Tess could be said to be the *poor of the Lord* because they totally surrendered their lives to God. However, in abandoning everything into the hands of God, refusing, for instance, to take medication or to seek medical intervention, they were not cooperating with God in bringing about God's purposes for their lives.

Kate Bowler, a professor at Duke University in the United States, in early

---

[6]Alberto J. Eisman, *Peace Deserves a Chance: Bishop Paride Taban, a Sudanese Shepherd* (Nairobi: Paulines Books Africa, 2011), 175.

2016 received the sad news that she had terminal cancer. I want to draw from her moving article in a *New York Times* op-ed outlining why she thought that some versions of the gospel of healing and God of the gaps display an insufficient understanding of the interaction of divine intervention in human history and the place of faith and human agency in realizing the purposes of God. She first points to the origin of this kind of worldview that God will do everything when it comes to our human condition:

> The modern prosperity gospel can be directly traced to the turn-of-the-century theology of a pastor named E. W. Kenyon, whose evangelical spin on New Thought taught Christians to believe that their minds were powerful incubators of good or ill. Christians, Kenyon advised, must avoid words and ideas that create sickness and poverty; instead, they should repeat: "God is in me. God's ability is mine. God's strength is mine. God's health is mine. His success is mine. I am a winner. I am a conqueror."

This mind-set then translates into a certain spiritual practice that refuses to accept suffering but at the same time refuses to assume the paradigmatic praxis of faith through daily actions to bring human experience in conformity to God's will of consummation of all things in Christ. She writes further about her encounter in her pain with a fellow Christian who held strongly to the God of impossibilities who believes that sickness and death for her at the young age of thirty-five is not a sign of God's blessing:

> "I am blessed." . . . The prosperity gospel holds to this illusion of control until the very end. If a believer gets sick and dies, shame compounds the grief. Those who are loved and lost are just that—those who have lost the test of faith. In my work, I have heard countless stories of refusing to acknowledge that the end had finally come. An emaciated man was pushed about a megachurch in a wheelchair as churchgoers declared that he was already healed. A woman danced around her sister's deathbed shouting to horrified family members that the body can yet live. There is no graceful death, no *ars moriendi*, in the prosperity gospel. There are only jarring disappointments after fevered attempts to deny its inevitability. The prosperity gospel has taken a religion based on the contemplation of a dying man and stripped it of its call to surrender all. Perhaps worse, it has replaced Christian faith with the most painful forms of certainty.[7]

---

[7]Kate Bowler, "Death, the Prosperity Gospel, and Me," *New York Times*, February 13, 2016, www.nytimes.com.

Mama Ann and Mama Tess each wanted a miraculous intervention in their lives that is obviously possible for any believer, but did not see the realization of this miracle as embodying the exercise and wholesome use of their human freedom. *The poor of the Lord refers to all those who totally depend on God, and surrender their lives and future to God.* It is indeed our Christian vocation to abandon our lives into the hands of our loving and merciful God. This is particularly so because all our lives and all that we have and are we have received from God. Being the poor of the Lord is an existential act grounded in faith and trust in divine providence; it is the existential openness of all believers to being led by God, and belonging to God. It does not simply refer to material poverty and the hope of the poor that God hears their cry and will rescue them in God's own time. It is, in other words, the way of being in the world as Christians who realize that our lives and our futures are not simply the result of our own carefully conceived and executed plans and programs. Rather, we are held in care by an all-loving God, who is interested in everything that concerns us and is actively working in us and with us to bring about the realization of the divine purposes for our lives.

Being poor in this sense is, therefore, to be understood as an existential disposition rooted in humility. This requires stepping outside of ourselves and abandoning our pretenses, fears, defenses, and ambitions while at the same time attuning our human desires to the divine purposes for our lives. Here, being the poor of the Lord transcends material or spiritual deprivation. This is because there are many who are materially poor but lack the virtue of humility or self-contentment, torn apart by the cravings for wealth, and obsessed with schemes and stratagems for how to break the cycle of poverty. There are also others who may be wealthy in material things but are so spiritually deprived and isolated that they lack inner peace and happiness. Being the poor of the Lord is thus to be understood as a state of total dependence on God whether we sense our own lack of material means to meet our immediate ends or our lack of spiritual depth to respond to our vocation in life.

Whatever the spiritual state of any Christian (or non-Christian for that matter), there is fundamental to our living in the world a need to find a center for our lives. Finding this center is understood in the Christian ontology of grace as embracing the truth based on faith that our lives are hidden in Christ, who is the author and finisher of our lives (Col 3:3). Being the poor of the Lord has in this sense a relationship to the brokenness, humility, and powerlessness of Christ. Thus in every cry of women like Mama Ann, in the emptiness and brokenness of many mothers and wives like Mama Tess, in the dislocation of many exiles who are far from their homes, the immigrants, the war-torn nations of Africa, and in many hotspots of the world—in all these lies the bleeding heart of Christ. The Lord Jesus Christ, who Christians believe is the center of all things, cries and is wounded in the brokenness of the least of the brethren. We can say in the light of the foregoing that all of humanity stands in a sense of poverty to the Lord, and the poor of the Lord in Africa, for instance, refers to all Africans in their creaturely dependence on God.

Being poor in the Lord is also to be understood in terms of the existential condition of social injustice and brokenness in our society and how God can intervene in our long nights and dark days to pull us from the depth and restore us to wholesomeness of life. There is so much suffering in our continent; there is also so much enthusiasm, joy, and passion for life and survival. So we must enter into the stories of brokenness and pain in our world today especially in Africa. We must ask the question: Why? Why are we using God to fill the gaping holes that we have created in Africa through global structures of injustice and exploitation, wrong choices, dictatorships, corruption, abuse of religious and political authority, and the exploitation of the poor? Why do we use our cultural traditions as a nice excuse to uphold patriarchal traditions and customs that effectively marginalize and defeat the flowering of the creativity and ingenuity of African women? Why do we fail to become self-critical of our locus of enunciation, and the unequal power relations that are at the root of the structural injustice and sins that continue to perpetuate poverty in Africa? Why are our actions as Christians and leaders in the church sometimes delegitimizing the prophetic voices of churches and people of faith because of unequal power relations and exploitation of the weak and the marginalized and voiceless through some of our policies and practices? How can we preach the message of God's love as a church to poor people in our continent and give hope to the despairing in the context of today's Africa?

Thus, we must accept that the poor of the Lord are also in most cases the millions of our people, family members, neighbors, and parishioners who have been made poor by some of our preaching and practices in our churches. These include all those who have been reduced to nothing; rendered voiceless and powerless because of the silence of the church in the face of misrule, injustice, and structures of sin in our cultures, societies, and in our churches. The poor of the Lord in Africa include those who have been misled through our preaching to believe in divine intervention without being challenged and supported to embrace a spiritual praxis to become agents who can bring about God's plan in their lives.

The greatest effect of poverty in Africa, which unfortunately can be silently worsened through some versions of African Christianity, is the weakening of the people's capacity to act in freedom to change their lives. People whose agency has been so weakened by poverty and suffering are sometimes misled by some versions of Christianity in Africa. It is that false Christian narrative that promises the people an irruption of power and prosperity and false hope without enabling their human agency through a praxis of faith that is counterhegemonic and counter-ba'al. Indeed, God does not work in a vacuum. As a result, preachers of the good news must not forget that an essential component of preaching should be the transformation of the individual from a hearer of God's Word to a doer of God's word. This requires that we not only preach the message of hope or provide social services, but that we accompany the poor daily in order to lead them to identify their gifts, equip them to use these gifts, and to embrace practices that embody the divine purposes in concrete personal and group history. This requires some hard choices and hard work on the part of the church by embracing another way of being poor, that is, *being poor in the Lord* as a natural progression from being *the poor of the Lord*.

Being poor in the Lord is a spirituality of both contemplation and action; of hearing and doing, of knowing and acting, and of translating what is received in faith to practices driven by hope that can help to reverse the course of history for the procurement of abundant life for God's people. Being poor in the Lord is the actualization in history of God's plan of abundant life for everyone and creation through authentic exercise of human freedom of all the poor of the Lord who are being liberated from the structures of sin and social injustice through daily practices that create a new narrative of hope and transformation. When Jesus said that the kingdom of God belongs to little ones such as these, it was not a promise of a future of prosperity and a problem-free existence. Jesus was not saying that God will miraculously intervene in their lives while they are sleeping, or that God will bring them down from the Cross by a sudden heavenly force: someone has to remove the nails, someone has to stop the crucifixion, someone has to pull down the bastions of injustice. . . . The message here is clear: the wounded and the crucified, the poor and abandoned have hope because they have made a choice for God as the center of their lives. As a result, they acknowledge the centrality of grace and affirm through faith their willingness to cooperate with God in bringing about God's will for the reversal of the unacceptable course of history. This is the fundamental juncture for an authentic spirituality of contemplation and action required in embracing the poverty in the Lord.

What is problematic for Mama Ann and Mama Tess is that although they wanted God to intervene in their lives, they were so weakened by their suffering and misled by a false belief to conclude that God will bring about what they desire without their human freedom, agency, and active cooperation. God does work in our lives in many ways beyond human comprehension, and God does intervene in our lives without our knowing when and how. I believe in miracles, and God continues to work many great miracles in our lives and histories. Again, like the mustard seed, God's action in our lives does happen sometimes without our explicit action, but God does not act in our lives without our implicit openness and cooperation. This is why I contend in this book that being the poor *of* the Lord is our existential condition and vocation as Christians. However, being poor *in* the Lord is an action we must take in order to subsist in God by cooperating with God in bringing about the divine purposes in concrete personal or group history through our active daily choices.

In this light, the challenge of social transformation should begin with how the gospel is presented and enacted as a means to empower African Christians to become the agents of their own liberation and empowerment through the transformation of attitudes, cultural assumptions, and cultural practices. Some false religious practices lead many Christians into projecting hope as achievement, and presenting wishes and prayer intentions as if they are the end product of our action rather than a starting point for our work with God. Transformation in Africa will not occur through human and spiritual agency simply because our preachers, prophets, and politicians are wrapping themselves in the cloak of religious narratives and promising better days. It will happen through daily actions, choices, and a praxis that leads to small victories in the direction of the fulfillment of the eschatological fruits of God's kingdom.

Being the poor *of* the Lord is related to being the poor *in* the Lord. The first is a choice to allow God to use me, to enable my freedom, to illumine my heart, and empower my will to believe in the possibility of liberation from any unacceptable social sin or sinful situation. The second, being poor *in* the Lord, is a call to action; the Christian battle cry for practices for transformation: my sense of material, spiritual, or existential poverty inheres in God as my source and destiny. It also grounds my vocational identity and energizes me to action and hopeful daily choices that I gain through my faith in God that my life here on earth is not simply a valley of tears, but that sometime it is necessary to go through the bitter valley so that I can come to the mountaintop of redemption.

Since I inhere in God in my poverty, God accompanies me in my journey toward transformation, and God is sharing in my poverty and is suffering with me on the Cross. At the same time, God is also equipping me by grace to meet the challenges of my poverty with God's grace through my daily commitments and positive actions and attitudes born of faith. God mediates such redemptive acts in my favor through the agency of so many people and agents committed to justice, especially through the church, that is always an alternative community of hope and light in societies where structural injustice has put the people of God in a revolving cycle of poverty and suffering.

Above all, God uses the human agency through my daily choices in order to bring transformation in my life and in society. Being poor in the Lord is then to be seen in this light as a spirituality of cooperation, collaboration, and partnership with God and the church through the art of accompaniment and vulnerable mission.

Poverty, especially material poverty, the kind that ravages life, denies freedom to people, and limits their unrestricted desire to love themselves, to love God, and enjoy all that God has made is opposed to the message of the gospel. It is also the direct consequence of sin and human failure to use the gifts and resources of God in an equitable manner. It is particularly painful in many contexts in Africa where there is absolute poverty and total absence of the means needed to meet urgent and pressing needs. The church in Africa must, therefore, give an account of poverty in Africa and through the art of accompaniment and vulnerable mission become a poor and merciful church by being with God's people in their places of pain and suffering. This will require courage, honesty, humility, hard work, and hope anchored in local processes for reversing history. However, because it is also at the root of our humanity that we are intrinsically limited, being the poor *of* the Lord no matter how we conceive it will always require recognizing God as central to our lives, and being poor *in* God as a way of self-transcending through God.

This leads me to consider the fundamental truth that I draw from Christian spirituality. This truth, I propose, should be central to Christian proclamation and praxis everywhere, not only in Africa: God does not change people's condition or take control of their lives without using the agency of the people. God's relationship with humanity and the entire cosmos is a dynamic interaction and partnership. It is not simply passivity on our part. God does provide food for God's own while they slumber (Ps 127:2), but God does not cultivate the land for them. Rather, God will make the earth yield its fruit for those who farm (Ps 67:6). Therefore, when Mama Ann is doing her novenas for her daughter's healing from infertility, she failed to seek every medical intervention necessary. When Mama Tess refused to take her ARV medications to fight AIDS, she put the Lord to the test. In both cases, God does wish to intervene, but God can only do this through the instrumental mediation of human and natural realities within the created world. This a critical point in the development of my thinking on strengthening the agency of the poor, especially in my continent of Africa; this topic requires further socioethical elaboration.

Mama Ann's daughter lives in a rural Ugandan community and has no access to modern health facilities or fertility treatment centers. Even if she went to Kampala, the capital of Uganda, the best she could get at the general hospital would be painkillers to help her with her pains as there was no fertility treatment in the Kampala general hospital (when I was there in 2012). The question then is, how can Mama Ann's novena help her daughter since the help she needs cannot be found in her country? Is it God who should be asked to intervene here when the society in which Mama Ann lives has failed to provide for her daughter the health care system needed to meet her health conditions? Could it be that Mama Ann's daughter needs to adopt a child or two from some orphanages in Kampala instead of hoping against hope to get a child? The challenging thing here is that the novena was recommended to Mama Ann by a "powerful priest" who had promised her that God would break the yoke of the devil and the spell cast on her daughter by some of her neighbors.

In the cases of the two bishops I mentioned, they acted in specific ways that underlie the praxis and dynamics of being the poor *of* the Lord and being poor *in* the Lord: they were suffering with the people (an accountable church); they were eyewitnesses to what they were describing (the art of accompaniment); they began to converse and build networks with people about how to seek alternative paths; they initiated steps toward creating a new situation; they began to work hard toward realizing an alternative situation. While they were doing all these, they were praying and discerning how to bring about an alternative community of hope in the midst of a very distressing and depressing national disaster (vulnerable mission). They were poor *in* the Lord (working with God), while recognizing that they are the poor *of* the Lord (trusting and depending on God, while assuming agency for the transformation of the social context). The question that is central to me in the foregoing is how can the poor become agents in their own liberation—with empty hands—in some distressing and broken conditions of seeming helplessness? How is illuminative ecclesiology reflected in the praxis of Christians and churches in Africa?

ILLUMINATIVE ECCLESIOLOGY IN AFRICA: THE EXAMPLE OF SISTER ANGÉLIQUE NAMAIKA

The heroic witness of the Congolese nun, Sister Angélique Namaika (fondly called the smile of God), the winner of the 2013 Annual Nansen Refugee Award, is a good way of illustrating the points that I am making in this section about being the poor *of* the Lord (our existential condition as people who believe in God and trust that God's hand guides our lives) and being poor *in* the Lord (as a way of working with God in bringing about a new situation that mirrors the reign of God).[8] One may say that

---

[8]"Sister Angélique: A God-Given Smile," NetforGod, January 2014, www.netforgod.tv/fr.

the visibility of the bishops and their position of influence gave them the freedom to do something with God for the good of their people. But Sister Namaika, like many ordinary African Christians, is doing something with God. She is challenging the social hierarchies that perpetuate poverty and fighting the structures of sin in society with empty hands but a strong heart, and a hopeful attitude that she can do something even when there seems to be nothing that can be done. When Sister Namaika saw in Dungu in the Oriental Province of DRC the influx of refugees, especially young men and girls who were forcibly displaced and abused by armed groups, especially the Ugandan Lord's Resistance Army (LRA), in the northeast of DRC in 2005, she went to work. She worked literally with empty hands, but with a clear vision, determination, and courage to make a change. Sister Namaika was born in poverty and grew up in poverty.[9]

According to the news release from the UNHCR, the UN refugee agency, "Many of the LRA's female victims were beaten, raped and forced to become sex slaves. Over the past decade, in and around the Orientale town of Dungu, Sister Angélique has helped some 2,000 of them to overcome trauma, counter the stigma attached to rape and rebuild their lives with newly learned trades."[10] Sister Namaika for over ten years did her visiting on foot before she got a bike. She became for many people the sister on a bike whose presence in the community became a concrete sign of God's presence. The praxis of Sister Namaika's work clearly showed the three pathways of accountability and accompaniment through a vulnerable mission.

In the first place, she was an eyewitness of what was going on in the life of the people. According to the UNHCR's press release, she was able to identify with the suffering of women, children, and the vulnerable because she herself grew up in poverty and was supported early in her life through her contact with a German nun named Sister Tone.

> But, Sister Angélique explains, the long journey that has brought her to Geneva [where she received the award] almost ended during her childhood in the village of Kembisa in Orientale province. "I was sick when I was a child and I suffered a lot. I lost a lot of weight and there was not much hope that I would survive." The young Angélique recovered and the ordeal brought her closer to her parents—the experience perhaps explains in part her strong faith and her empathy for others who have suffered.[11]

---

[9]Leo Dobbs, "Nansen Refugee Award Winner Angélique Namaika: A Profile," UNHCR, September 30, 2013, www.unhcr.org/news.

[10]Ibid.

[11]Ibid.

So her ministry to the poor was not a long-distance charity; nor was it simply gathering together the women, raped girls, and young child soldiers in order for them to fast and pray. They began every meeting with prayer, but she was also interested in how to transform their lives and what they needed most in order to weave back the shattered webs of their lives. As Sister Namaika put it, "I identified them [the child soldiers] when they were coming out of the bush after being abducted by the LRA, and directed them to structures giving emergency assistance. We then involved them in the activities of the center."[12] She first identified them (accountability—taking stock of each person); she observed them as "they were coming out of the bush"—a fitting and graphic way of painting a portrait of the suffering of the vulnerable and their movement from "the bush" with all the dangers, darkness, and peril of living in the wild and helpless to the elements; to "coming to the center" so that they can receive love, healing, light, and hope. She moved them from the periphery of the bush into the center of God's love at the compassionate home that she ran in Dungu.

Second, she accompanied the women on their journey to regain their dignity and assume agency for their lives. She also shared in the suffering of the women and children because she was displaced as a result of the war and was as vulnerable as the women and children she was helping. She describes the perilous trip on foot for over 20 kilometers with children crying, women despairing not knowing where their children and spouses were, and hunger, thirst, and hopelessness setting in. She had nothing with which to help these women apart from her hope and trust in God. However, moving from the experience of being the poor *of* the Lord (trusting in God and putting all her hope and that of the people in the hands of God), she also knew that to be poor *in* the Lord requires some action. This is why she makes this testimony, "I saw that displaced women had many difficulties; they lived through atrocities and had enormous trauma. It was important to help them. I realized that learning to write and training will help them forget the trauma, the LRA, and what they had to go through. This is what pushed me to help these women and help them become independent."[13]

Sister Namaika was able to give an account of the suffering and pain in this part of Africa and also to mediate hope because she did not only pray and trust God, but she went out to be with the people, to walk and work with them in bringing about a new situation. She thus became the instrument through which a new narrative of hope is being told and lived in Dungu for over 110,000 displaced people who hear the gospel spoken with such force by Sister Namaika. In doing this, Sister Namaika became a mirror in which

---

[12]Ibid.
[13]Ibid.

the broken and displaced people in Dungu saw the face of God and the face of love in this area. She also became the mirror in which the suffering and hopeful faces of many here were reflected to the world and to God. As the then UNHCR, high commissioner, and now Secretary General of the UN, António Gutterres said of Sister Namaika in an October 11, 2013, interview with *Jeune Afrique*:

> Sister Namaika works tirelessly to help women and young girls who have been rendered vulnerable by trauma, poverty, and being uprooted. The obstacles that she faced and overcame in her work make her work remarkable. She never allowed anything to stand in her way. She shows that one person alone can change the lives of families torn apart by war. She is a true hero.[14]

One of the greatest obstacles to the social mission of churches in Africa in the areas of spiritual and social transformation is the trap of devotionalism and pietism that has become a staple in our churches. This is a tendency to multiply prayers and rituals with the expectation that through such acts God's divine purposes will be realized and through them God will change the unacceptable conditions of our African societies. Prayer is central to our lives as Christians. Indeed, authentic Christian prayer offered as a union of two hearts that love each other is key to living an integral Christian spirituality. This is because it heightens our sense of affinity and unity with God and offers us an unlimited connection with God.

Devotionalism, in contrast, is a magical notion of prayer. It is rooted in a false belief that finding God's will and realizing God's plan in history is the result of ritualistic acts or payment of tithes and offerings to God. If these rituals are capable of uniting our minds with that of God, they indeed should be a path to be recommended even with greater intensity for Christians. In Africa, churches are packed every Sunday and most evenings with all kinds of spiritual activities. In many parts of Africa, almost all parishes have chapels of perpetual adoration to the Blessed Sacrament and shrines and grottoes to the Blessed Virgin Mary and many popular saints. Festivities such as Christmas, the New Year, and Easter Vigils, and Pentecostal week celebrations are legendary for their intensity, beauty, and concentrated pietistic acts and promises of divine visitation. In many of these spiritual events, there are "contracts" and "promises" of healing, divine intervention, and assurances of breakthroughs and open doors to prosperity. What one does not often hear in these spiritual gatherings is how the breakthroughs that preachers and ministers promise the people will occur through the

---

[14]*Jeune Afrique*, www.jeuneafrique.com.

cooperation of Christians, in other words, how transformation will emerge within history through the agency of these devoted worshippers. Sister Namaika was called "the smile of God" in Dungu, not because she visited the communities to say prayers for them to remove any curse placed on them or to give them nice spiritual platitudes. In *The Smile of God*, the movie made about her selfless ministry, she stated that she prayed always for God to help the women, children, and youth of Dungu. However, she was unwavering in her commitment that these abandoned people could only step into a better situation if she became an instrument for ushering in a new agency and praxis for reversal among the people. She wanted the people not to lose hope because they had agency, which could not be taken away from them, not even by the feuding politicians, the international community that ignored their plight, or the apparent brokenness of their society.

In many African churches, the assurances of divine blessing are tied to the "doing" of certain "spiritual acts" that are often not connected with conversion of hearts or the encouragement and support of the people on the margins on how to self-transcend. In most cases, the spiritual acts are often about paying tithes and monetary donations as if devotionalism plus tithes or donations to the church are the only things required to have an economic breakthrough. It seems that God's blessing is often presented as the reward for monetary donations to support, in many cases, the unsustainable lifestyles of the big men and "thick Madams" of the Big God.

Today many churches in Africa are pioneering and promoting the idea of "big men of the big God," and a cheap gospel without costly grace, which has the danger of emptying the power of the Cross of Christ. It is not surprising that many African Christians often wonder how the extravagant lifestyles of church leaders in Africa reflect the face of the simple man of Galilee who made himself poor for our sake so that we can become rich in God. How can bishops, priests, preacher men and women, ministers and founders of churches, and religious healers become poor with, for, and like the poor in Africa? How can our churches in Africa show solidarity with the poor who flock to our churches?

It is a scandal and sinful for church leaders in Africa to seek tithes from poor people who are needier than the "god" they are being asked to propitiate through gratuitous acts solely of a monetary kind. I am convinced that confronting the poverty in Africa today, and tapping into the hope that is buried in this continent and the deep faith and hard work of our people, is the path to the kind of transformation recommended by the Second African Synod. The illuminative church is a vulnerable church that not only sees and names poverty as evil, but steps into history as an instrument of God for giving agency back to the poor and working with the poor toward realizing the better future that God wills for God's people under the reign of God. It is the church of Sister Namaika that shines the light of Christ not only in the refuse dumps of Freetown, but in Dungu and Bangui. It is a church in Africa that should not be triumphant but a church of tears. As Pope Francis said in an address to clergy and religious in Nairobi, the church in Africa cannot be silent in the face of the suffering of its sons and daughters; rather it should weep, and its tears should move it to action on behalf of the poor. Pope Francis elaborates on this further:

> So never stop weeping. When priests and religious no longer weep, something is wrong. We need to weep for our infidelity, to weep for all the pain in our world, to weep for all those people who are cast aside, to weep for the elderly who are abandoned, for children who are killed, for the things we don't understand. We need to weep when people ask us: "Why?" None of us has all the answers to all those questions why.[15]

TENDERNESS AND THE SOCIAL MISSION OF THE CHURCH IN AFRICA

Pope Francis visited the Kangemi slum in Kenya where he gave a powerful message and gesture. His message touched on a praxis of illuminative ecclesiology, that is, (1) accounting for the conditions of all the members of the community, especially those on the margins; (2) experiencing with them the complexities and challenges of life through the art of accompaniment; (3) and working with them to restore their dignity and transform their lives and strengthen their agency in reversing the course of unacceptable history.

The presence of the pope in the slums was a very prophetic action. Pope Francis also captured that experiential dimension of illuminative ecclesiology in a very simple but moving speech when he said to the slum dwellers:

> Thank you very much for welcoming me to your neighborhood. . . . I feel very much at home sharing these moments with brothers and sisters who, and I am not ashamed to say this, have a special place in my life and my decisions. I am here [in the slums] because I want you to know that your joys and hopes, your troubles and your sorrows, are not indifferent to me. I realize the difficulties which you experience daily! How can I not denounce the injustices which you suffer?[16]

---

[15]Pope Francis, Speech at a meeting with clergy, men and women religious, and seminarians, Sports field of St. Mary's School, Nairobi, November 26, 2015, in *Messages of Pope Francis during His Apostolic Journey to Africa* (Nairobi: Paulines Books Africa, 2015), 15.

[16]*Messages of Pope Francis during His Apostolic Journey to Africa*, 26.

Pope Francis then spoke of the "stubborn resistance" found in people on the margins in such places as the slums and neighborhoods of Kangemi and Kibera in Nairobi. Quoting from *Laudato Si'* (149) Pope Francis noted that the language of exclusion and the injustice and insensitivity of "an opulent society, anesthetised by unbridled consumption" tends to forget that people in neighborhoods like slums have agency and wish to exercise their freedom "to weave bonds of belonging and togetherness which convert overcrowding into an experience of community in which the walls of the ego are torn down and the barriers of selfishness overcome."[17]

The agency of people living in poor neighborhoods can be identified by embracing some of the values inherent in their common experience and network in reversing the forces of structural injustice and structural violence. The emphasis on the values of the poor points to what is often forgotten in many charitable situations—the poor have assets. In that regard, an essential dimension of restoring the dignity of poor people in any situation, and in helping them to build a better society, is to identify and build on their agency. This is a point that is so central today in international development that there is a renewed emphasis even in situations of extreme humanitarian crisis to privilege the agency of the people.[18] The values found among the poor that could be harvested in strengthening their agency, according to Pope Francis, include solidarity, giving one's life for others, preferring birth to death, providing Christian burial to one's dead, finding a place for the sick in one's home, sharing bread with the hungry, and showing patience in the face of adversity. These values as, he noted, are not quoted on the stock market or subject to the speculation of market forces.[19] Pope Francis is able to identify these values embraced by the poor as an asset because such discoveries can only be made by those who accompany the poor and walk in their shoes, and it is also the path that Jesus trod. Pope Francis's words to the slum dwellers speak eloquently of the respect that is due to the poor that goes beyond the toxic charitable disposition that makes the poor feel helpless: "I congratulate you, I accompany you and I want you to know that the Lord never forgets you. The path of Jesus began on the peripheries, it goes from the poor and with the poor, toward others."[20]

One might be tempted to think that Pope Francis's speech was a kind of "consolation for the afflicted"—"you poor slum dwellers, rejoice that you have values and dignity and God loves you" or "you poor slum dwellers,

---

[17]Ibid.

[18]See, for instance, the dimensions of a people-centered humanitarian response developed by the Sphere Project and the implications for building up communities and peoples in the midst of disasters, www.spherehandbook.org.

[19]*Messages of Pope Francis during His Apostolic Journey to Africa*, 26.

[20]Ibid., 27.

pray and do your novenas until something happens in your life." But as Pope Francis writes in *Evangelii Gaudium*:

> The poor person, when loved, "is esteemed as of great value," and this is what makes the authentic option for the poor differ from any other ideology, from any attempt to exploit the poor for one's own personal or political interest. Only on the basis of this real and sincere closeness can we properly accompany the poor on their path of liberation. Only this will ensure that "in every Christian community the poor feel at home. Would not this approach be the greatest and most effective presentation of the good news of the kingdom?" Without the preferential option for the poor, "the proclamation of the Gospel, which is itself the prime form of charity, risks being misunderstood or submerged by the ocean of words which daily engulfs us in today's society of mass communications." (*EG*, 199)

His speech to slum dwellers in Nairobi contained a denunciation of the causes of poverty and its terrible consequences. The pope inveighed against "unjust distribution of land," "excessive and unfair rents for utterly unfit housing," "private developers who hoard areas of land and even attempt to appropriate playgrounds," and "lack of access to infrastructures and basic services." His words were quite strong when he made this prophetic judgment: "These signs of good living that increase daily in your midst in no way entail a disregard for the dreadful injustice of urban exclusion. These are wounds inflicted by minorities who cling to power and wealth, who selfishly squander while a growing majority is forced to flee to abandoned, filthy and run-down peripheries."[21]

Pope Francis's contention here, I believe, is more about how what he calls "new forms of colonialism" in Africa can be confronted by the church and society beyond simply preaching a prosperity gospel or reinforcing existing hierarchies and structures of social exclusion. The church must always stand with the poor through a vulnerable mission. However, it must be stated clearly that accounting for the life and condition of the people and accompanying them will go beyond "the mere proclamation of rights which are not respected in practice, to implementing concrete and systematic initiatives capable of improving the overall living situation, and planning new urban developments of good quality for housing future generations."[22] Social transformation for people who dwell in the slums and for all poor people, according to Pope Francis, is essential to the mission of

---

[21]Ibid.
[22]Ibid., 28.

the church. The church, Pope Francis proposes, should "accompany them in their struggles." The goal of any pastoral praxis or social mission in this regard for African slum dwellers particularly will be on how to build a new society where the sacred right of all people, especially the poor, to the three Ls—land, lodging, and labor—are protected and promoted. Pope Francis concluded his speech with an insistence that the slum dwellers whom he called "dear neighbors," must "pray together" but they also must not stop at prayer but rather should also "work and commit" themselves to being instruments to bring about a new social situation that "they rightfully deserve on the basis of their infinite dignity."[23]

Moving from words to deed and from ecclesial claims to ecclesial witnessing in showing in concrete ecclesial life how the light of Christ shines in the world through Christians and churches is a summons to a spiritual praxis of action. The concrete human situation is the medium for the theological aesthetics of illuminative ecclesiology. Therefore, discerning the illumination of God in the world is a summons to go beyond the shadows and to seek God within the dumps of history. The basic core of the words and deeds of Pope Francis is its concreteness; it is a "grounded theory" whose performance is achieved through an immersion into mystery through "a culture of encounter." During his visit to three African countries, he chose to visit places where his message would emerge from the context of people's concrete situation—in the slums of Nairobi, for instance, to draw attention to the social dislocation and pain of urbanization and the devastating impact of the unequal distribution of wealth and exploitation of the poor; in Uganda he visited the House of Charity of Nalukolongo run by the Good Samaritan Sisters in order to challenge the church and the world to become actively involved in the concrete life conditions of people.

Pope Francis shows how illuminative ecclesiology *demonstrates* not through appeal to metaphysical categories but by a first person narrative or an eyewitness account. The church teaches not from on high but through its presence in the chaos of people's lives. In this culture of encounter, the church demonstrates the love of God not simply by proclamation but by showing the love of God in the daily lives of people and through its credible ecclesial forms, structures, and daily witnessing to the truth of the gospel. This happens when, as Pope Francis teaches, the church "enters the darkness, the night in which so many of our brothers [and sisters] live," "making contact with them," "making ourselves be wrapped up in that darkness and influenced by it."[24] This is the theological aesthetics that is mediated through encounters with wounds, pains, brokenness, sin, despair, chaos,

---

[23]Ibid.

[24]Pope Francis, *Name of God Is Mercy*, 67.

and the "smell of the sheep" in Reach Out, Mbuya-Kampala, Uganda, in the House of Charity in Nalukolongo, in the slums of Kibera, at Sister Namaika's center in Dungu, among many others.

As we can see from the foregoing, the praxis of illuminative ecclesiology begins with finding the presence of God in all things; there is beauty in all things. It is the mission of the church to discover beauty in all things with a discerning heart and a courageous will to affirm beauty, while working hard to remove the sin and evil that make it hard for the beauty of creation to shine out. Pope Francis (*EG*, 88) emphasizes that this mission is the full consequence of the Incarnation through which God identified totally with our human condition. Through the Incarnation, God turns God's merciful gaze on humanity and the cosmos. God by this singular act of immeasurable love calls the church to a revolution of tenderness. This is an invitation to contemplate love, to enter into the mystery of love through a tenderness of heart that is humbled before God like Mary (*EG*, 288). It is a summons to enter into the "pain and plea" and the infectious joy of others, which can only come through personal and intimate encounters (*EG*, 88).

Richard Rohr argues that Pope Francis through this kind of ecclesiology is rejecting a top-down approach to faith and praxis by asking the church to take seriously the mystery of the Incarnation and the way of Jesus:

> By taking the mystery of the Incarnation absolutely seriously, and gradually extending it to its logical conclusions, the seeming limitations of space and time are once and for all overcome in Francis. The Christ mystery refuses to be vague and abstract, and is always concrete and specific. When we stay with these daily apparitions, we see that everything is a revelation of the divine—from rocks to rocket ships. There are henceforth no blind spots in the divine disclosure, in our own eyes or in our rearview mirrors. Our only blindness is our own lack of fascination, humility, curiosity, awe, and willingness to be allured forward.[25]

Illuminative ecclesiology proposes then in the light of Pope Francis that the church has a double mission: first as a mirror through which the world can see and experience the merciful love of God to the world, and, second, as the mirror through which the pains and brokenness of creation are reflected back to God. It is an ecclesiology that says that "when we lovingly embrace the world, we are embracing God."[26]

---

[25]Richard Rohr, *Eager to Love: The Alternative Way of Francis of Assisi* (Cincinnati: Franciscan Media, 2014), 7.

[26]Leonardo Boff, *Francis of Rome, Francis of Assisi: A New Springtime for the Church*, trans. Dinah Livingstone (Maryknoll, NY: Orbis Books, 2014), 42.

The praxis of an illuminative church that we have developed is not some arcane truth that is to be taught and defended as one defends a fortress. Rather, it is a love to be lived through daily experiences of faith in action. It is what Pope Francis calls "a mysticism of open eyes, which becomes a mysticism of hands-on, helping hands" in the concreteness of every daily situation.[27] Here the social mission of the church is not simply an abstraction or a set of unchanging principles and rules. Contemplation is the starting point, the medium, foundation, and praxis of all theology and spiritual life. On contemplation in theology, Hans Urs von Balthasar wrote: "We need individuals who devote their lives to the glory of theology, that fierce fire burning in the dark night of adoration and obedience, whose abysses it illuminates."[28] That "fire burning" or "the heart burning within" can only result from eyes that have been purified in humility by faith or purified in tears through touching the depths of evil or the wounded body of Christ in the poor.

Pope Francis has spoken consistently about the "gift of tears." This was particularly poignant when he visited Tacloban in the Philippines and met with survivors from Typhoon Yolanda. In reflecting on this experience that moved him to tears, Pope Francis said:

> This is one of the things that is lost when we are too well-off, or when we do not really understand values, or we get accustomed to injustice and the throwaway culture. The ability to cry is a grace that we must ask for. . . . We Christians must ask for the grace of crying, especially wealthy Christians, crying for injustices, crying for sins, because crying helps me understand new realities, new dimensions.[29]

In a proper sense, Francis is proposing that the theology of the church is best done when theologians become mystics who are capable of entering into the world of others, crying with them, and are capable of seeing what God reveals in the presence of another in the tears of those wounded and what spiritual resources are given to us for meeting the spiritual and material hunger of the world.

In *Evangelii Gaudium* 24, Pope Francis points to discovering the face of Christ and touching the flesh of Christ as a praxis of evangelization that challenges the members of the church to bridge the gap or distance created by

---

[27]Walter Kasper, *The Revolution of Tenderness*, 46.

[28]Hans Urs von Balthasar, *Word and Redemption: Essays in Theology 2* (New York: Herder and Herder, 1965), 22. This quotation is also published in Hans Urs von Balthasar, *Explorations in Theology 1: The Word Made Flesh,* trans. A. V. Littledale with Alexander Dru (San Francisco: Ignatius Press, 1989), 160.

[29]"On His Flight Home, the Pope Said That the Gift of Tears, the Filipino People, the People of God, Were the Real Protagonists," *Asia News*, January 19, 2015, www.asianews.it.

cultural, social, religious, economic, and other factors. This invites everyone to become a guardian or shepherd of others. In *Evangelii Gaudium* 169 Pope Francis speaks of pastoral workers bringing the "fragrance of Christ's closeness and his personal gaze" through the "art of accompaniment" that invites everyone to remove their sandals before another. This is the way to live as Christians because in order to learn in the presence of another we need to appreciate that we stand on sacred ground in their presence. In communicating this message to the church and the world, Pope Francis often uses the term "gaze on," "openness of heart," "spiritual encounter," "the art of listening" (*EG*, 170–71), and "different forms of beauty that are valued in different cultural settings, including in unconventional modes of beauty" (*EG*, 167).

The formation of pastoral agents and social workers in the revolution of tenderness can occur through some of these concrete images that Pope Francis constantly uses in encounters with people in different sites of pain.

The first is the image of *the church as a field hospital* that brings the idea of dynamism and love in action. William Cavanaugh describes this image in many profound categories: "the church is a living subject"; "the church is not a hierarchy but all of us"; "the church is mobile, an event more than an institution." He writes further, "A field hospital is unconcerned about defending its own prerogatives, and instead goes outside of itself to respond to an emergency. As a body, it is visible, but it does not claim its own territory; its event-like character creates spaces of healing."[30]

The second is the image of *the Good Shepherd who has the smell of the sheep*, which is associated with the field hospital image. Service in the church, especially to the poor, is an act of humility, which is modeled on the example of Christ. It must begin and proceed with tenderness of heart. This highlights the instrumental nature of all service in the church, especially the service to the poor and those wounded. That is why Pope Francis associates this church with the imagery of *the church of wounds* (*EG*, 47–49). In a more explicit manner he writes:

> The church does not exist to condemn people but to bring about an encounter with the visceral love of God's mercy. I often say that in order for this to happen, it is necessary to go out: to go out from the church and the parishes, to go outside and look for people where they live, where they suffer, and where they hope. I like to use the image of a field hospital to describe this "church that goes forth"; it exists where there is combat; it is not a solid structure with all the equipment where people go to receive treatment for both small and large

---

[30]William T. Cavanaugh, *Field Hospital: The Church's Engagement with a Wounded World* (Grand Rapids, MI: W. B. Eerdmans, 2016), 3.

infirmities. It is a mobile structure that offers first aid and immediate care, so that its soldiers do not die.[31]

What is so significant in these images of church is the experiential-mystical component of illumination; the church's being is to be found in its acting; and the church's acting only makes manifest its being; there is no dichotomy between performance and identity. The concreteness of illuminative ecclesiology is its experiential base. Francis avoids the so-called "royal we" in his writings and often speaks in the first person. This does not mean that he does not wish to stand on the shoulders of what has gone before him or to locate himself in the vast ocean of the "we structure" of the people of God. Rather he embraces some form of isomorphic personal account that illumines and validates what the community believes. It is this kind of ecclesial iteration that the writer of the Letter of Saint John had in mind when beginning the account he writes: "Something which has existed since the beginning, that we have heard, and we have seen with our own eyes; that we have watched, and touched with our hands; the Word who is life—this is our subject" (1 Jn 1:1–2).

ILLUMINATIVE ECCLESIOLOGY AND SOCIAL TRANSFORMATION IN AFRICA

African social imagination is the key to the transformation of the continent, and I am convinced that the social teaching of the Catholic Church can provide both a theoretical framework for understanding the social condition of Africa and a praxis for social ministry. This will involve an analysis of the structural violence and the structural sins both locally and internationally, which continue to normalize the pauperization of God's people in many parts of the world and particularly in Africa. Every day in the continent one observes with pain how diseases and suffering make a preferential option for the poor. This has devastating consequences as HIV/AIDS, malaria, Ebola, cholera, and other preventable and treatable diseases prefer the poor who are afflicted so terribly because they cannot afford health care services. The poor and the vulnerable in Africa are the ones whose lives are being destroyed by structural violence. They are the ones who die prematurely. Writing on the devastating effects of structural violence in Africa especially with regard to public health, Annie Wilkinson and Melissa Leach argue in the case of Ebola that structural violence must be understood

---

[31]Pope Francis, *The Name of God Is Mercy*, 52.

in the context of a regional history and global economy that have cultivated inequalities. It is no coincidence that Guinea, Liberia, and Sierra Leone are three of the poorest countries in the world; their rich natural and human resources have long been extracted for elite and foreign profit—as opposed to being developed for the benefit of the majority of their populations. The result has been legacies of distrust and governments that are unable to provide basic services, health included. It is not simply that global inequalities leave some citizens and healthcare workers exposed; it is that they produce these vulnerabilities and shape the institutions of global health so that they are unable to patch over them.[32]

The church's social mission in Africa will require a vigilant and constant moral evaluation of the social question in Africa (*Solicitudo Rei Socialis*, 9) in the light of the realization of the fruits of God's kingdom in history. This will include adopting the cultural, theological, religious, moral, spiritual, economic, and cultural frameworks in Africa in conversation with best practices in Africa and from outside Africa in order to bring about gradual transformation of the African social condition.[33] Most important, agents of change and practitioners in the field of social mission must adopt a comprehensive and concrete analysis of culture in order to see the total picture of the African predicament and identify the emerging locally driven initiatives, which are procuring modest result in social transformation in many contexts of faith and life in Africa.[34]

The social mission of the church in Africa needs to be concrete, grounded in local processes rather than being driven by principles and unrealistic practices unmoored from the daily practices of the people. The social mission of the church in Africa must also be countercultural. This is a new aspect of Catholic social teaching that many people identify in Pope Francis: the idea that the option for the poor, solidarity, subsidiarity, promotion of the common good, and human dignity must sometimes involve direct conflict with the structures of power. This is because they reinforce structural violence and promote structures of sin that hold people permanently down the lower rungs of the social and economic ladder. Barrett Turner identifies this new

---

[32] Annie Wilkinson and Melissa Leach, "Briefing: Ebola—Myths, Realities, and Structural Violence," *African Affairs* 114, no. 454 (December 2014): 137.

[33] David Kaulemu, "Building Solidarity for Social Transformation through the Church's Social Teaching," in *Catholic Social Teaching in Global Perspective*, ed. Daniel McDonald (Maryknoll, NY: Orbis Books, 2010), 36.

[34] I have discussed the need for local processes and local narratives in the social mission of churches in Africa in a very systematic and extensive manner in Stan Chu Ilo, "The Enduring Significance of *Populorum Progressio*, for the Social Mission of the Church in Africa," *Journal of Moral Theology* 6, no. 1 (2017): 72–75.

movement in part 3 of *Evangelii Gaudium* where Pope Francis addresses the social dimension of evangelization and develops four new principles for Catholic social teaching in the search for peace and good order: "time is greater than space" (222–25); "unity prevails over conflict" (226–30); "realities are more important than ideas" (231–33); "the whole is greater than the parts" (234–37).[35] This means that the social mission of the church acts on sets of principles that emerge from the actual realities and narratives of people, which must also be embodied in those narratives as models and praxis for bringing about a new reality.

The principles and praxis of reversal must be used to construct a more abundant life in Africa. This means that particular attention must be given to local processes in terms of what Africans can do for themselves using their own resources—material and spiritual. The social mission of the church in Africa should be constructed outside of a dependent and mendicant approach evidenced by the search for aid and incessant cries in Western churches for help by African bishops, priests, nuns, and religious. The future of African development and the church's social mission in Africa will be built on new forms of being church, which will be informed by the context and agency of Africans by people like Sister Namaika. Sadly, understanding this context, strengthening this agency, and harvesting the assets of Africa are complex.

In a previous work, I dealt with the three false images of Africa in the narratives of many non-Africans.[36] Some of these false images are rooted in racism and bias, which historically goes back to the legacy of slavery, colonialism, apartheid, and Western missionary work in Africa. The false images of Africa and discrimination against people of African descent persist even within the Catholic Church. Africa continues to suffer from what Pope Francis calls "paternal welfarism" or what Robert D. Luton called "toxic charity."[37]

Pope Francis insisted in his first audience after his trip to Africa (Wednesday, December 2, 2015) that he saw Africa as a land of hope and strength. He has been a strong advocate of a proper hermeneutics of the poor and of history in order to understand the bigger picture of people who live in poverty and to show the true face and praxis of liberation. In a speech to participants of the World Meeting of Popular Movements organized by the Pontifical Council on Justice and Peace and the Pontifical Council of Social Sciences, he said:

---

[35]Barrett Turner, "*Pacis Progressio*: How Francis's Four New Principles Develop Catholic Social Teaching into Catholic Social Praxis," *Journal of Moral Theology* 6, no. 1 (2017): 119–24.

[36]Stan Chu Ilo, *The Face of Africa: Looking Beyond the Shadows* (Ibadan, Nigeria: Spectrum Books, 2008), 50–68.

[37]Robert D. Lupton, *Toxic Clarity: How Churches and Charities Hurt Those They Help (And How to Reverse It)* (New York: HarperCollins, 2011).

The poor not only suffer injustice but they also struggle against it! They are not content with empty promises, excuses or alibis. Neither are they waiting with folded arms for the aid of NGOs, welfare plans or solutions that never come or, if they do come, they arrive in such a way that they go in one direction, either to anesthetize or to domesticate. This is a dangerous means. You feel that the poor will no longer wait; they want to be protagonists; they organize themselves, study, work, claim and, above all, practice that very special solidarity that exists among those who suffer, among the poor, whom our civilization seems to have forgotten, or at least really like to forget.[38]

However, in order to develop the kind of dialogue in the world church, but especially in Africa, for a mission that will be driven by the praxis of illuminative ecclesiology, it is important to understand the context and reality of Africa and the evidence for and against African poverty.

The *Lineamenta* of the Second African Synod was very direct and unequivocal in its judgment about the social condition of Africa:

In most African countries, despite recently achieved progress, the rate of literacy continues to be among the lowest in the world. In many places, the educational system is constantly deteriorating, the health system is in shambles, and social welfare is almost non-existent. With the lack of order, the weak are always the people most threatened. Likewise, in the area of demographics, one can't be silent at the imbalance between a population which is witnessing a record rate of annual growth, and resources which remain unutilized, if not being totally depleted. Africa's immense resources are in direct contrast to the misery of its poor.[39]

The quality and standard of life of many Africans today is not better than it was when Pope Paul VI wrote *Populorum Progressio* in 1967, which coincided with the independence of the majority of African nations. The 2012 Human Development Index (HDI) reveals that the twelve countries of the world at the lowest rungs of development are in Africa. In the 2015 report, thirty-four of the countries in the low-development index are in Africa. According to this report, even though the number of people living in the low HDI fell by nearly 20 million, human deprivation is still widespread and much human potential remains unused in Africa. For instance, there are

---

[38]"Pope's Address to Popular Movements," trans. Zenit staff, October 29, 2014, https://zenit.org.

[39]Lineamenta of the II Special Assembly for Africa, *The Church in Africa in Service to Reconciliation, Justice and Peace*, 15.

795 million people who suffer from chronic hunger worldwide; 11 children under five die every minute; 33 mothers die every hour; and about 37 million people live with HIV and 11 million with tuberculosis; 103 million young people between the ages of fifteen and twenty-four are illiterate, and there are 74 million young people who have no job. These statistics refer especially to Africa where two-thirds of its countries fall in the lowest rungs of the human development index.[40]

The 2015 Human Development Report, which looked at the situation of employment worldwide, emphasizes in its Overview that "people are the real wealth of nations, and human development focuses on enlarging people's choices," especially with regard to building human capabilities. The greatest asset of Africa in the third millennium has been identified as the gift of its young people:

> With 200 million people aged between 15 and 24 (the youth bracket), Africa has the youngest population in the world. The current trend indicates that this figure will double by 2045, according to the 2012 African Economic Outlook report prepared by experts from the African Development Bank (AFDB), the UN Development Program (UNDP), and the UN Economic Commission for Africa (ECA) and the industrialized countries' Organization for Economic Cooperation and Development (OECD) among others.[41]

The sad news, however, is that according to the World Bank, 60 percent of Africa's young people are jobless!

Between 1960 and 1970, youth in Africa did not constitute a social issue.[42] However, all available indices point to the neglect of the gift of the African young people by governments and churches. African young people are champions; they are so strong in their faith and commitment to God; they have big dreams. An essential dimension of the social mission of the church in Africa must be discovering ways and means to build on the assets, industry, dynamic faith commitment, and ingenuity of young people in Africa. The term *youth* designates an interface between childhood and adulthood. The United Nations defines *youth* as people between fifteen and twenty-four years of age, and they represent approximately 18 percent of the global population; that is nearly 1.2 billion people; and 21 percent of the

---

[40]UNDP, *Overview: Human Development Report 2015: Work for Human Development* (New York: United Nations Development Program, 2015), 3, 29–30.

[41]See Kingsley Ighobor, "Africa's Youth: A 'Ticking Time Bomb' or an Opportunity?" *Africa Renewal*, May 2013, www.un.org.

[42]I am grateful to Idara Otu for the research input and contribution that he made to this section of this work.

youth of the world live in Africa.[43] The large and significant population of young people in Africa compared to other parts of the world raises concerns about the capability of African nations to provide for them in terms of education, health care, employment and other social services.

Available statistics show that Africa is failing its young people. Many African youth are ill-prepared for the world of the twenty-first century. In the case of South Africa, for example, approximately 50 percent of the population is youth, according to the 2011 census, yet the rate of unemployment among the youth is about 70.9 percent. The literacy assessment of South Africa in 2011 revealed that 43 percent of South African grade 5 students have not developed the basic reading skills required for reading at an equivalent international grade 4 level.[44] Such underprivileged conditions prevalent in many African countries have led to an upsurge of youth involvement in crime, cultism, and violence. The joblessness of many young people in Africa is a potential source of violence and terrorism in the land; as the common saying goes, "Idle hands are the devil's workshop." This is similar to the demographics of church growth in Africa. African churches are filled with young people. However, the question remains as to how the continent and African Christianity can provide food for these young people, education for their young minds, and work for their strong hands.

Even though many scholars sometimes question the accuracy of these statistics, given that the calculation of development level, especially in terms of income inequality, is based on income tax reports and GNP, other indicators testify to the challenging socioeconomic conditions of Africa that have persisted for many years. Some of these indicators of a challenging social context were noted by the Second African Synod: high unemployment rate among young people in Africa, high maternal and infant mortality, poor health care, poor governance in many African countries, low life expectancy, low standard of living, deterioration in economic and social conditions, lack of capacity for mitigation and adaptation to the effects of climate change, and low levels of human security and human rights, among others. Many African countries suffer from persistent fratricidal wars, ethnic strife, and the pitiable spectacle of refugees and displaced persons.[45] Despite the decline of Africa's economy, progress is recorded in countries like Botswana, Senegal, and Ghana. However, economic growth in these countries does not translate into changes in the living conditions of citizens, especially the youth; youth

---

[43]Cf. United Nations, *United Nations Programme on Youths*, social.un.org.

[44]See Sanku Tsunke, "The University of Pretoria Releases Radical International Results on South Africa's Education System: PIRLS 2011," University of Pretoria, December 13, 2012, web.up.ac.za.

[45]Second Special Synod Assembly for Africa of the Synod of Bishops 2006, *The Church in Africa in the Service to Reconciliation, Justice and Peace.* "You are the salt of the earth. . . . You are the light of the world" (Mt 5:13–14). *Lineamenta*, no. 14–15, www.vatican.va.

unemployment in Senegal is 30 percent, and 70 percent of young people in Ghana are either self-employed or working for their families; South Africa continues to seethe with internal social convulsions as a result of growing restlessness among young black South Africans who sporadically turn their ire against black migrants.[46]

Africa's poverty is not natural; it is man-made. It is the result of a combination of many historical factors. Africa is facing the persistent effects and crisis of postcolonial statehood. This is particularly destructive because it is as if Africans were taking a prescription meant to solve other people's historical challenges. This is also true in the churches where structures of leadership and pastoral forms are adopted by African churches in the Catholic tradition sometimes without regard to context. When these unworkable structures begin to unravel, as they do most of the time in the church or in the state, Africans are usually blamed for the failure. A new theological, cultural, and social imagination is required in Africa and those sympathetic to the cause of the continent. This will mean that one has to look again at Africa through a new lens and go beyond the stereotypes and negative narratives of the African condition in order to see the wealth and greatness buried in the land of Africa and in the hearts of Africans.

However, many people have contended that the designation of Africa as a poor continent or a "dark continent" or "a suffering continent" should be questioned. It is therefore difficult and sometimes untenable to justify the designation of Africa as poor. Dayo Olopade argues strongly that African development is following a different trajectory that does not fit into the clinical development graph of the UN or the World Top Incomes Database (WTID). She contends that there is a different convergence of interests, creativity, local initiatives, significant victories, and positive stories of young people, women, and civil societies in Africa. These challenge the notion that Africa is poor, and there are signs of the changing face of Africa that do not show up in some of the analyses that inform and sustain the economic and social policies of many Western governments and international organizations like the UN, WTO, IMF. Olopade therefore argues that "when you're thinking of Africa in the context of the wars you've seen, the poverty you assume, or the government you've given up on, you're likewise missing the point."[47]

The same narrative is demonstrated by Patricia Crisafulli and Andrea Redmond, who studied Rwanda's rise from the ashes of the genocide to become the first African country to *electronify* its economy by connecting over 11 million of its citizens to the formal economy through its partnership

---

[46]*Africa Renewal*, May 2013, 10–13.

[47]Dayo Olopade, *The Bright Continent: Breaking Rules and Making Change in Modern Africa* (Boston: Houghton Mifflin Harcourt, 2014), 13–14.

with Visa. But the point here is that the rapid growth in the economy was brought about by tapping into the creativity and hard work of the people, confronting the demons of corruption and ethnocentrism, and waging an all-out war on illiteracy through education and skills development. Rwanda, despite its own peculiar political challenges, is a country in which "a new narrative is unfolding," characterized by self-determination and self-reliance.[48] However, the truth is that these are positive signs in a few African countries that have not yet been translated into durable and sustainable patterns for the whole of sub-Saharan Africa. But why has Africa remained poor despite its rich natural, cultural, spiritual, and human resources?

The analysis of poverty and the role of the church in the social mission must begin with a comprehensive understanding of the African condition, especially how Africa can be a better steward of its human, material, and spiritual resources. We cannot understand the African condition in isolation nor can one propose the pathways for social mission of the church in Africa without a correct diagnosis of the African social context. Thomas Piketty makes the following points that are so vital in analyzing the poverty of Africa and in the complex situation in many countries in the world.

The first is that the history of the distribution of wealth especially in the post–Industrial Revolution and post–World Wars world has always been deeply political. The rise of inequality, whether local or global, must be seen in the light of how economic, political, and social actors view what is just and unjust in terms of economic policies and practices.[49] In this regard, poverty, whether local or global, is the result of forces within the systems; it is about the choices of those who benefit from the convergences of factors that are manipulated to achieve specific results for a few. This was what Pope John Paul II wrote about when he offered an interior-exterior social analysis to identify the structures of sins in society and institutions that make it impossible for the poor and all God's people to have equal access to the common good (SRS, 35–40).

The second point that Piketty makes is that income inequality cannot be met locally or globally by simply redistributing income by handouts or aid from the rich to the poor in Africa, for example, or from rich countries to poor ones. The main force that will drive a more equitable world will be the diffusion of knowledge and investment in training and skills, or what has been called the "rising human capital hypothesis," which is stronger than the iron will of market forces and is a good driver of trade and economic convergence.[50]

---

[48]Patricia Crisafulli and Andrea Redmond, *Rwanda Inc.: How a Devastated Nation Became an Economic Model for the Developing World* (New York: Palgrave Macmillan, 2012), 1.

[49]Thomas Piketty, *Capital in the Twenty-First Century*, trans. Arthur Goldhammer (Cambridge, MA: Belknap Press of Harvard University Press, 2014), 20.

[50]Ibid., 22.

Piketty also points out that Kuznet's inverted-U curve, the theory that greater convergence of skills leading to a homogenizing economy and a reduction of poverty as a result of movement from rudimentary production in agriculture, for instance, to industrialization, is not an iron-clad process. The equalization mechanisms are constantly affected by specific social constructs in local and global economies that affect national income, global economy, and per capita income.[51] This happens even within industrialized and highly developed economies and topples economic equilibrium. But this is most evident at the international level, which makes global inequality a troubling reality. What happens then is that African countries are "owned by other countries" with a "recurrent and almost irrepressible social demand for expropriation." When this trend continues, as it has for some time in Africa, Western nations "own them indefinitely" while "the per capita national income of the wealthy countries remains permanently greater than that of the poor countries, which must continue to pay to foreigners a substantial share of what their citizens produce."[52]

This challenge is clearly felt when it comes to agricultural development in Africa. Calestous Juma's *The New Harvest: Agricultural Innovation in Africa* paints an objective picture of the complexity of the African predicament. Agriculture is the mainstay of Africa's economy. However, despite this gift of agrarian culture, many people in the continent are dying of hunger and malnutrition. Juma points to the statistics that indicate that "in sub-Saharan Africa, agriculture directly contributes to 34 percent of the GDP and 64 percent of employment. Growth in agriculture is at least two to four times more effective in reducing poverty than in other sectors. Growth in agriculture also stimulates productivity in other sectors such as food processing. Agricultural products also compose about 20 percent of Africa's exports."[53] Traditional African society was an agrarian society. Writing over two hundred years ago, the African ex-slave Olaudah Equiano wrote that traditional African societies before slavery and colonialism built strong economies through agriculture:

> Everyone contributes something to the common stock; and as we are unacquainted with idleness, *we have no beggars* [emphasis mine]. The benefits of such a mode of living are obvious. . . . Our agriculture is exercised in a large plain or common, some hours walk from dwellings, and all the neighbors resort thither in a body. They use no beast of

---

[51] Ibid., 58–59.

[52] Ibid., 70.

[53] Calestous Juma, *The New Harvest: Agricultural Innovation in Africa.* Oxford: Oxford University Press, 2011, 7.

husbandry; and their only instruments are hoes, axes, shovels, and beaks or pointed iron to dig with.[54]

The question must be raised, as Juma does, as to why Africa is incapable of feeding Africans and why the self-perpetuating link between hunger and Africa's weak agricultural sector has become the drama of our times in Africa since 2004, leaving one-third of Africans chronically hungry.[55]

Given this scenario, an essential dimension of the social mission of the church will be how it can help Africans to concretely hearken to the commandment of the Lord to give something to the poor to eat (Mk 6:37). Furthermore, the social mission of the church in Africa must take as primary the critique of this kind of international order, and the failed economic and political systems, weak institutions in the church and state in Africa, and Africa's failed extractive leadership at all levels. The church must find a way of leading the charge for the rejection of the African celebration of the trickle-down aid that churches and communities in Africa receive either from international organizations or church charities. The church in Africa must also stand with the poor in distancing itself from those African governments that support and reinforce this social condition through their failed economic policies and failed leadership. The church in Africa must become an alternative community of hope and an oasis for watering the vast assets of talents in Africa scattered in the desert of want, expropriation, and waste.

A CELEBRATION OF CATHOLICITY
AS BEAUTY IN DIVERSITY

The Gospel witness can be reduced in a spiritualizing way when it becomes a form of escape from history. Here the new things involved in the gift "already" received are so absolutized as to lose sight of the problems posed in the different contexts and human stories to which the Gospel is proclaimed and mediated. Catholicity here is impoverished, because it is reduced to ready-made answers, without passing through the necessary mediation of interpretation, at once both faithful and creative, required by the encounter with real cultures and persons and made possible by the action of the Holy Spirit.[56]

---

[54]Olaudah Equiano, *The Interesting Narrative of the Life of Olaudah Equiano, or Gustavus Vassa, the African* (Lexington, KY: Simon and Brown, 2012), 18.

[55]Juma, *New Harvest*, 7.

[56]Bruno Forte, *To Follow You, Light of Life: Spiritual Exercises Preached before John Paul II at the Vatican* (Grand Rapids, MI: Eerdmans, 2005), 151.

One important moment of illuminative ecclesiology is accountability, which is a praxis of paying attention to particular instances of God's action in the world in both local and global contexts. Accountability as a praxis of the illuminative church means that the church must be an eyewitness of what is going on in the lives of people, to proclaim the gospel in the uniqueness of people's situations, and to identify and bring before God the many gifts and faces of humanity. This is a Trinitarian habit that is at the core of Catholicism as an instrument for celebrating the diversity of creation and peoples in the unity of Trinitarian love.

In one of his audiences, dedicated to teaching on catholicity as a mark of the church, Pope Francis identified three ways in which the church is Catholic. First, "she is the space, the home in which the faith is proclaimed to us in its entirety, in which the salvation brought to us by Christ is offered to everyone." In this first meaning, he noted that the church's catholicity refers to how the church enables people to encounter the mercy of God, which transforms, because through the church people are enabled to encounter Jesus Christ. The church in this first meaning is also a place for encountering the Word of God and the sacraments "through which the light of God is given to us, streams from which we can draw God's very life." The church is Catholic because it is the home for all and is the mediation of God's love that creates communion in the world.[57]

The second meaning of Catholicism, according to Pope Francis, is universality, which means that the church is spread to all the four corners of the earth and reaches out to everyone and everywhere:

> The church is not a group of elite; she does not concern only the few. The church has no limits; she is present to the totality of people, to the totality of the human race. And the one church is present even in her smallest parts. Everyone can say: in my parish the Catholic Church is present, because it too is part of the universal church, since it too contains the fullness of Christ's gifts: the faith, the sacraments, the (ordained) ministry.[58]

This second meaning leads to the third and final meaning. In asserting that the church is fully present in every community and in every parish, Pope Francis was making clear that the catholicity of the church is the basis of its diversity, and that diversity is what gives harmony and beauty to the church and is a rich "source of wealth" for the church. He uses the image of a great orchestra to describe this church:

---

[57]Pope Francis, *The Church of Mercy: A Vision for the Church* (Chicago: Loyola Press, 2014), 34.
[58]Ibid.

This is a beautiful image illustrating that the church is like a great orchestra in which there is a great variety. We are not all the same, and we do not all have to be the same. We are all different, varied, each of us with our own special qualities. And this is the beauty of the church: everyone brings their own gifts, which God has given, for the sake of enriching others. And between the various components there is diversity; however it is a diversity that does not enter into conflict and opposition. It is a variety that allows the Holy Spirit to blend it into harmony.[59]

What this means is that the homogenizing tendencies and the centrist mind-set of the Roman curia over the local churches work against the beauty of this richness within the church. The illuminative church must be a mirror where the faces of all of humanity, the totality of what God has created, are reflected back to God. This affects not only the teaching of the church at the center but also its social mission; it must be governed by diversity of expressions in a unity of faith. In *Evangelii Gaudium* 40 Pope Francis points toward this: "for those who long for a monolithic body of doctrine guarded by all and leaving no room for nuance, this might appear as undesirable and leading to confusion. But in fact such variety serves to bring out and develop different facets of the inexhaustible riches of the Gospel." What is being proposed here is that the church must embrace a hermeneutics of multiplicity and an intercultural hermeneutics in order to account for the many gifts that God has given to the church in "vast numbers of peoples and nations who profess the same faith."

An intercultural hermeneutics in Pope Francis's illuminative ecclesiology is an invitation to joyfully celebrate a symphony of differences. This in an invitation to embrace the beauty of the varied faces of the people of God whose cultures and daily experiences are constantly being transformed by the Holy Spirit to become a beautiful harmony of differences. It is the admission that the church "does not have simply one cultural expression" but rather a diversity of peoples within the church (*EG,* 115–16). This is why Pope Francis emphasizes the inclusion of the voices of the historically voiceless and marginalized groups and cultures within the one Catholic family. This is because their voices help to illumine the content of the gospel and the identity and mission of the church. It is an attitude that nourishes an ecclesial openness to the surprises of the Holy Spirit and the continuing revelation of the meaning and dimensions of the traditions of the church in its earthly pilgrimage as the instrument of salvation to diverse peoples. This is the necessary consequence of cultural pluralism within the one communion of

---

[59]Ibid., 35.

faith in World Catholicism where we all learn from the experiences of joy and pains of one another.

The hermeneutic of multiplicity and inclusion is a historical exigency because the church is a historical subject. It must lead to dialogue within the church and with other non-Catholic subjects and entities. In addition, there is the need, as Pope Francis proposes, that we realize that the church's customs, precepts, and rules have deep historical roots (*EG*, 43), which may no longer be as effective today as they were in the past in conveying the beauty of the gospel. The Christian faith is not simply about rules but about the life and witness of Jesus Christ (*EG*, 42). There is the need then for proper discernment led by the Holy Spirit and openness to embracing new ways of modeling the Christian life so that it captures the cultural imagination of the modern world and addresses the spiritual and moral hunger of many who are on the margins. This is particularly important for meeting the crisis of faith and the crisis of human security in the modern world. According to Yves Congar, openness to the renewing and transforming power of the Holy Spirit to show people today new ways of meeting new challenges will require finding a new way through which we can "give truly spiritual meaning to acts that have become routine," and "adapt some of the forms of ecclesial life to the needs of new circumstances."[60] The "risk of growing old" and "becoming locked into habits, memories and institutions,"[61] according to Congar, is always present in Christianity. However, in order to maintain its spiritual impulse, the church must find a way of freeing itself from becoming enslaved to "a fixed expression."[62] According to Congar, for Erasmus the church of his time suffered greatly because, "the *pastoral* had been overshadowed or effaced *by the feudal*, the *Gospel spirit* by *the excrescences of flamboyant piety*, *faith* by *religion*, and *religion* by *practices*."[63]

The church cannot arrive at this newness of thinking and acting unless it enters into a deeper dialogue with history in order to discover in new contexts of faith and life new models for being and acting in the world. At the heart of illuminative ecclesiology is dialogue that begins with a culture of encounter (*EG*, 220). Dialogue is central to the vision of the church and society proposed by the Second Vatican Council.[64] By introducing various ecclesial channels for conversations in the church, and recognizing various practices of intercultural encounters in the world, Vatican II made possible a

---

[60]Yves Congar, *True and False Reform in the Church*, trans. Paul Philibert (Collegeville, MN: Liturgical Press, 2011), 134.

[61]Ibid., 135.

[62]Ibid.

[63]Ibid., 139.

[64]Bradford E. Hinze, *Practices of Dialogue in the Roman Catholic Church: Aims and Obstacles, Lessons and Laments* (New York: Continuum, 2006), 2–18.

new paradigm of dialogue in the Catholic Church. I am particularly interested in developing the principles and practices of dialogue, especially with the poor in Africa, in an illuminative ecclesiology. Dialogue with the poor in Africa requires a critical hermeneutics of the challenging African social context.[65]

Even though there were no strong voices on the question of poverty and the church's social mission from the African continent at Vatican II, African theologians, pastors, church leaders, and activists have taken up this fight anew within the last thirty years.[66] The two African synods spoke strongly of the need for African Christianity to give hope to Africans. The two synods accepted an option for the poor as a pastoral praxis (*Ecclesia in Africa*, 139, 113, 70, 68–69, 44, 52; *Africae Munus*, 25, 27, 29, 30, 84, 88–90). Pope Francis's call for a church of the poor in *Evangelii Gaudium* and numerous papal messages on the church's mission to the poor have given a new paradigm shift to the church today in its self-understanding and social mission. He has also given a new impetus to realizing the dream of some of the fathers of the council for a specific document dedicated to the church's mission and praxis for liberating the poor from their suffering and pain. It is important that the social mission of the church to the poor must enter into dialogue with the poor in all contexts. How can this be realized in Africa?

Dialogue with the Poor in Africa

In order to dialogue with the poor, an illuminative church must become prophetic by correctly reading the signs of the times. One of the signs of the times in Africa today is that many ordinary people outside the spotlight are reversing the course of history in Africa through their praxis of social transformation without support from governments, churches, or international organizations. These are local prophets who as the scriptures say are without honor in their churches and countries. The illuminative church in Africa should identify such success stories as well as the assets of the poor that can help strengthen their agency in the fight for social and economic space.

The prophetic tradition in Christian social thought has often been identified with individuals who through their words and actions lift the gaze of the Christian community beyond any imprisoning walls—social, doctrinal, ideological, cultural, economic, and political. In doing this, they help the community see clearly the footprints of God in their particular or communal history.

---

[65]See *Ecclesia in Africa*; *Africae Munus*, 13.

[66]I first developed these ideas in a previous essay. I have refined them further in this section of this book. See Stan Chu Ilo, "Dialogue in African Christianity: The Continuing Theological Significance of Vatican II," *Science et Spirit* 68, no. 2–3 (2016): 356–59.

From a biblical perspective, prophecy relates to the mediation, transmission, and interpretation of God's will in the words and actions of men and women. The prophet is a *legatus divinus*, the messenger of God, one who utters God's Word and whose life reflects the will of God. He or she speaks and acts on behalf of God because the words and actions of such a person communicate to God's people the will of God. A prophet is a sign in the community and like a sentinel summons God's people sometimes to follow the road less traveled, sometimes to a new spiritual or cultural imagination, and sometimes to resist the forces of decay and destruction. The whole mission of the prophet is the greater commitment and loyalty to God on the part of the people and obedience to God in order to find the face of God and receive God's blessing. The prophet makes it possible for God's people to embrace a historical trajectory that leads to the realization of the eschatological fruits of God's kingdom. He or she thus becomes a sign that people follow so that they do not fall into the pit of sin and destruction.

The prophet does not stand alone. He or she stands with God with and in the name of the community because the vocation of a prophet is tied to the fortune of the community. False prophets lead the people away from their goal and mission; true prophets are lights that lead the community to the realization and fulfillment of the goal of society. Indeed, every community has a moral and spiritual responsibility of receiving, discerning, and judging the reality of the prophetic word for the good of the community. This way, the community guards itself against false prophets and charlatans who may be angels of death in shining armor. The prophets are standard-bearers who stand on the mountaintop as sentinels of truth and bearers of light and hope. In this way, their words and deeds become signposts that illumine the dark places of human history and human societies with the truth of God, which alone can heal society and restore what is broken. Prophecy then relates to how God's revelation is received, communicated, and enacted in history. Prophecy may refer to the future but in a secondary way. It does not simply refer to a distant future, but to the immediate future and present realities to which God calls God's people.

Prophecy is not about prediction of good or ill, which will come upon God's people in the future. On the contrary, prophecy is the reading of the signs of the times in the light of God's will and Word. Furthermore, the human propensity to distort reality often presents the prophet with the challenge of constantly and critically looking at history and its ambiguities and beauty. Because the people who receive prophetic oracles and the times in which they live continue to change based on the good or bad choices of people, the prophet must continue to monitor and interpret the signs of the times that may lead to a fresh rereading of the events in the light of the Word of God.

The prophet shines forth the truth of God first by his or her lifestyle. Prophecy is made up of both word and deeds that reflect authentically the Word of God to people and the will of God. Prophecy sometimes may be a countercultural deed that points out the decay in society. It also shows the people of God the direction to attaining the values and virtues of the kingdom of God, the reign of peace, prosperity, righteousness, and good order. Illuminative ecclesiology as reflected in Pope Francis is a call for a new prophetic witnessing in the church and society. Pope Francis's emphasis on the concrete human conditions of wounds and pain through a culture of encounter is an invitation to dialogue with people, especially the poor and those on the margins. It requires, as we have shown in many parts of this book, a movement from the abstract to daily practices and calls on the church to become poor and merciful. But this can come about only if the church itself enters into dialogue with the poor. There are many ways in which this can be done in Africa:

The dialogue with the poor needed in Africa today will begin with a theology of accompaniment and immersion in the daily reality of the poor. This is a theology of vulnerable mission, humility, and immersion in the joys, sorrows, pains, chaos, and complexities of daily life in Africa. It is a theology of incarnational identification with the daily struggles of Africans as well as a pastoral praxis of listening to the cries of the poor, women, divorced and separated Christians who are denied communion in our churches, and millions of vulnerable children who are abandoned to a threadbare existence.

Dialogue with the poor can be sustained only by allowing the voices of the poor and the conditions of life and pain of many Africans today to become the new voice of God revealing to the church in Africa the data for theological and pastoral life. The Bible must be read in Africa today through the lens of the daily life of people because the Word of God grows with the reader and the reader grows with the Word as it takes flesh in the daily realities of the people. African theologians need to plow through layers of biblical narratives and commentaries today like their colleagues elsewhere, but there is even a greater need to embrace the emerging exegesis of the Bible mediated through the heroic faith witnesses of ordinary Africans in their trials and triumph. No theology will be relevant to Africa that ignores the new revelations from this text of the poor in Africa that in itself is a fifth gospel. This is so important in the development of sustainable social mission and praxis for confronting poverty in Africa and fighting for social justice to bring about good and transparent government in African politics and in the churches of Africa.

The prophetic tradition of the church has always led the church to see different ways in which God is at work in the community and among God's people. It is important that the church in Africa pays attention to grassroots actions in small Christian communities, in micro-credit unions, in the heroic witnesses of many religious, especially female religious such as Sister Rosemary Nyirumbe and Sister Namaika who are building alternative communities of hope outside the limelight. The social mission of the church in Africa will not bear sustainable fruit if it is still a top-down operation that is a hierarchical bureaucracy tightly controlled by bishops and priests. The social mission of the church will not create a strong process for reversing the harm imposed on the poor by structural violence if it is not anchored on the agency and assets of the poor themselves, who are the best equipped for constructing the structures of a new future. It is absolutely important that the social mission of the church in Africa move away from constant soliciting of aid in the West and needs-based social ministry. Social mission must begin with discovering the vitality and resilience of community-based assets and wisdom, mediated through the Christian faith.

Dialogue with the poor in Africa should go beyond mere armchair theological reflection in our libraries and studies, and beyond making magisterial and synodal statements in the comforts of conference halls in Rome and in the big cities in Africa. It will require that African theologians and church leaders enter into the chaos of the life of the poor in Africa. It requires that church leaders become muddied in the dumps with the people. In addition, it must emerge from the way in which the Word of God is proclaimed. The Word of God that is being proclaimed in Africa is both a portrait and illumination from the experience of those on the margins. The narratives of faith, love, hope, and courage reflected in the daily stories of the poor in Africa should become central to the proclamation of the gospel and in the formulation of pastoral practices in African Christianity. These narratives embody in small ways the pathway toward God's answer to the challenging social condition of God's people. This is true even when those narratives are born of lament, for as Emmanuel Katongole demonstrates, "In the midst of suffering, hope takes the form of arguing and wrestling with God. If we understand it as lament, such arguing and wrestling is not merely a sentiment, not merely a cry of pain. It is a way of mourning, of protesting to, appealing to, and engaging God—and a way of acting in the midst of ruins."[67]

To be a credible dialogue partner with the poor in Africa, the church in Africa must examine its inner life in the spirit of Vatican II and the two African synods. There is a need today in Africa for the Catholic Church to assume a form and structure that is at home with God's people. The inculturation of the gospel and of the church in Africa that was called for

---

[67]Emmanuel Katongole, *Born from Lament: The Theology and Politics of Hope in Africa* (Grand Rapids, MI: Eerdmans, 2017), xvi.

by the first African synod is far from being realized. There is the need for serious and creative theological and pastoral imagination to tap into the momentum of Christian expansion in Africa in creating a truly African ecclesial life and social mission, which is mediated through the actual faith of the people and anchored in local processes and praxis. Many years ago, shortly after Vatican II, Yves Congar bemoaned the fact that "the human vitality" in religion and the emerging theologies from the Global South have not been recognized by the church or integrated in the development of theology in the Catholic Church.[68] More than fifty years after Vatican II, this concern is still true. Even though there is strong progress in terms of theological development in Africa, there is still a great gulf between theological discussions in African Catholicism and ecclesial development in the continent.

Most African Catholic theologians are known more outside Africa than in the continent. It seems that the life of the church, its social mission, and its prophetic function are still found in largely formal and predictable pathways defined by what many African bishops still adopt as an idealized notion of church and Catholic social teaching. An accountable church in Africa must embrace the gifts of African culture, history, spirituality, social ethics, local knowledge, traditional styles of leadership, and local means of wealth creation in order to bring the faces of Africa to God. A renewed African ecclesiology will be more attentive to understanding the nature of the social and political problems in Africa, and courageously engage the internal factors that are hampering the church in Africa from being a strong agent in discovering and supporting locally driven initiatives. This can happen through listening to the poor, and moving away from a baroque theology, manualist social mission, and medieval monarchical titles and different forms of clericalism that hamper the development of the lay members of Christ's faithful, small Christian communities, local parish initiatives for social justice and poverty eradication, and grassroots evangelization of culture.

In this regard, the church in Africa must seek the reform of its structures and systems, especially identifying and rejecting those ecclesial practices that reinforce social hierarchies and unjust structures of power and privilege that exploit the poor. Also to be examined are cultural practices that are reinforced through ecclesial practices and patterns that promote patriarchy, exclusionary practices, discrimination, classism, sexism, lack of transparency, ethnocentrism, authoritarian leadership, counterevangelical lifestyles, and compromises with powers and principalities—all of which

---

[68]See Frank Fehmers, ed., *The Crucial Questions: On Problems Facing the Church Today* (New York: Newman Press, 1969), 11.

make it impossible for the reign of God to come into the lives of the poor in Africa. The extent to which the church in Africa becomes a church of the poor, a church with the poor, and a church for the poor, and a humble church will determine the relevance of the church in the continent in the coming years.

Dialogue with African Women

One area of the social mission of the church in Africa that carries so much promise is the gift of African women. The question that comes to my mind is: How can the church in Africa harvest the gifts of African women? The question of the role of women and gender equality was strongly raised in *Africae Munus* (7): "The Church has the duty to contribute to the recognition and liberation of women, following the example of Christ's own esteem for them." Paul VI's *Humanae Vitae*, while rightly highlighting the challenges facing the world by different theories and approaches to population control, was not successful in developing workable and realistic social ethical principles that could promote and protect the rights of women. The same is also true of the discussion of the dignity of women in society and family in subsequent papal documents. Beyond generalized assertions of such nebulous concepts as "upholding the dignity of women," "the genius of African women," "Africa as continent of mothers," there are no significant or sustained efforts in African Catholicism to engage in dialogue with women with a view to enriching our churches.

In relation to the lack of commitment by the Catholic Church to confronting the patriarchal thinking and systems, Peter Henriot writes,

> As several feminist scholars have pointed out, this may be the result of an emphasis on the "proper nature" and "proper role" of women— seeming to imply that women have a "nature" distinct from men's. As a result, insufficient attention is paid both to the massive contributions made by women to economic development (e.g., food production and health care) and social development (e.g., education) and to the massive obstacles they face (e.g., suffering disproportionately from poverty, illiteracy, and malnutrition).[69]

Notwithstanding the limitations in the church's documents on women's rights and the lack of courage and creativity among the male-dominated

---

[69]Peter J. Henriot, "Who Cares About Africa? Development Guidelines from the Church's Social Teaching," in *Catholic Social Thought and the New World Order: Building on One Hundred Years*, ed. Oliver F. Williams and John W. Houck (Notre Dame, IN: University of Notre Dame Press, 1993), 229.

clerical ranks in developing practices of transformation of a patriarchal church, church documents on women have proposed some helpful principles to guide action for local churches. Unfortunately, I do not see a lot of these principles being applied in many Catholic dioceses in Africa. African women are very marginal participants in the life of the church at the level of leadership despite their numerical superiority in terms of church membership and attendance.

In this light, Musimbi R. A. Kanyoro makes a very important conclusion:

> The witness of the church in Africa will not be credible unless the church takes into account the traumatic situation of the millions of women and the perilous conditions of the outcast of our societies. What meaning can faith have in churches that seek to be liberated without sharing the people's battles with the forces of oppression assaulting their dignity? . . . These questions frighten churches and communities with long-established traditions and practices of injustices to women. They threaten our institutional comfort as churches, our invested privileges, our secure situations, and they threaten the security of our judgment of what is right and what is wrong.[70]

The subjugation and marginalization of women, which is deeply rooted in various patriarchal ethos, has contributed to the violation of women's rights in Africa. I refer especially to violence against women as a way of demonstrating how the absence of respect for the rights of women in many settings in Africa continues to do so much harm to womanhood in Africa.

When one of Africa's biggest music superstars, Kofi Olumide, was caught on camera in July 2016 angrily kicking one of his female dancers at the Nairobi airport, many African women were shocked but not surprised. Violence against women in both public and private settings is commonplace in Africa. It is an open sore on the continent, and little is being done by African governments to stamp this out. Violence against women in Africa is also reflected through religious rituals not only in the psycho-emotional destruction of women, but also the often violent beating associated with "deliverance" sessions for women suspected of being witches or being possessed with evil spirits. The beating is always severe for those accused women who refuse to confess their membership in the spirit world. The international community doesn't seem to be too bothered about this. The question must be raised as to why this shameful pattern is continuing in Africa and how to break this vicious cycle.

---

[70]Musimbi R. A. Kanyoro, *Introducing Feminist Cultural Hermeneutics: An African Perspective* (Cleveland: Pilgrim Press, 2002), 80.

The 1993 United Nations Declaration on the Elimination of Violence Against Women defined violence against women as "any act of gender-based violence that results in, or is likely to result in, physical, sexual or psychological harm or suffering to women, including threats of such acts, coercion or arbitrary deprivation of liberty, whether occurring in public or in private life." In a 2005 study, the World Health Organization (WHO) observed that domestic violence is a global problem affecting millions of women. However, African women are the worst affected by violence. For example, about 51 percent of African women have been victims of violence, 11 percent suffer violence during pregnancy, 21 percent marry before the age of fifteen, and 24 percent experience female genital mutilation (FGM).[71] The WHO noted that FGM could lead to "bleeding and infection, urinary incontinence, difficulties with childbirth and even death." The organization estimates that 130 million girls have undergone the procedure globally and 2 million are at risk each year, despite international agreements banning the practice. *African Recovery* reports that violence against women in Africa includes forced marriage, dowry-related violence, marital rape, wife-beating, and sexual harassment, intimidation at work and in educational institutions, forced pregnancy, forced abortion, forced sterilization, trafficking, and forced prostitution. These practices cause trauma, injuries, the spread of HIV/AIDS, and even death to many African women.

Many people have wondered why Africa has not made significant progress in protecting women against violence despite the clear commitment made in 1995 by fifty-three African nations with the African Union's Protocol on the Rights of African Women. Beyond the lack of political will, and the unequal power relationship between men and women in a predominantly patriarchal Africa, there are other underlying causes of this problem.

First are cultural traditions. African rural communities are often held back by cultural practices that tolerate and legitimize violence against women such as wife-beating. Wife-beating is still accepted in many African countries; only twenty-one African countries have laws that prevent such practices. One of the compliments I often heard people giving to my father who was the clan head and a monarch was that he never beat up my mother. In cultures where women are considered inferior to men and women's rights are considered privileges from their husbands, wife-beating is tolerated as a necessary evil to whip an errant wife in line with her husband's wishes and orders.

Sexual violence is another aspect of the abuse of women's rights in

---

[71]See Anne Arabome, "Woman, You Are Set Free! Women and Discipleship in the Church," in Agbonkhianmeghe E. Orobator, *Reconciliation, Justice, and Peace: The Second African Synod* (Maryknoll, NY: Orbis Books, 2011), 119.

Africa that is often justified through different cultural alibis. When women activists protested against the insistence in Kwazulu Natal, South Africa, that young girls must undergo and pass virginal tests as qualification for educational scholarships, many people in the area claimed that this was an attack on their cultural tradition.

The same argument for tradition is what has sustained the "hyena" practice in some rural communities in Malawi where young girls are forced against their will to have sex with the village hyena—an older man whose role is to "open the door" of sexuality to these teenagers. Sexual violence extends to rape, which is common in many African countries with weak and ineffective laws to confront this evil. In addition, women who are victims of rape suffer social ostracism from men who avoid them and will not accept them as wives. As a result, most cases of rape are hidden wounds that women bear in order to "protect their dignity." In 2015, it was reported that young girls were given to soldiers in South Sudan as "sexual favors," which was another name for rape. Most rape cases are never reported, investigated, or tried in court except perhaps when it involves high-profile men such as the former South African president, Jacob Zuma, or UN peacekeepers in Congo and Central African Republic. In many cases of rape, women are often blamed for "seducing" the men or "exposing" themselves to attack by their looks or their way of dressing.

Religious traditions are the greatest obstacles to realizing the goal of the 1995 AU protocol. As a priest, I have been to many "healing sessions" in African churches. I have seen with horror how women are hounded, chained like animals, and severely bitten in the macabre ritual of casting out demons from them. Women are mostly the ones accused of witchcraft, sorcery, or blamed for casting spells on people. In many cases, widows are subjected to all forms of painful purity rituals after the death of their husbands. In a few cases, these widows are ostracized if they were suspected of killing their husband. This happens if these widows were found by an oracle of having been ritually married in their previous lives to a water god who killed their late husbands out of anger or jealousy.

Many African traditional, Christian, and Islamic religious groups demonize African women and frame the female body in Africa as a source of evil. Indeed, many people believe that the female body in Africa is a disability. African women are also exposed to violence because of poverty. Poverty and diseases have a preferential option for African women and children. In a continent ravaged by refugee crises, wars, conflicts, and the dislocation of whole populations, women in Africa continue to be vulnerable and susceptible to violence, exploitation, forced labor, and sexual abuse. Unfortunately, this plight of African women is below the radar globally. African nations are failing women. These violent practices are entrenched and resistant to change and pressure from African women activists and a few African women in positions of leadership.

The former UN Secretary General, Ban Ki-Moon had declared on the international day for the elimination of violence against women that violence against women and girls has no place in any society. Further, he said, impunity for the perpetrators of violence against women should no longer be tolerated. The same sentiment was echoed by the Kenyan Youth and Gender Minister Sicily Kariuki in reaction to Olumide's now infamous kick when she said, "His conduct was an insult to Kenyans and our constitution. Violence against women and girls cannot be accepted in any shape, form or manner."

The time has come for churches in Africa to pressure African nations to implement the UN CEDAW and DEVAW conventions by identifying and ending all religious and cultural customs and practices that perpetuate violence against women. African nations must educate African men to respect the dignity and rights of women. Women at all levels in Africa should be educated on their rights. I have personally been part of programs in three African countries where educating and empowering women led to changes on the part of their men. This is because beyond creating safe havens for women and legal protections, the greatest weapon in the hand of African women for combating violence from men is economic power that is the gateway to other rights.

Oppressive practices deface the dignity of African woman and are exacerbated by the consequences arising from the socioreligious, economic, and political realms. "The life of an African woman unfolds along the trajectory of vassalage: at home she serves every member of the family; in society she has limited opportunities; in the culture she is a victim of traditions."[72]

According to a survey of nine African countries by the Food and Agriculture Organization (FAO) in 1996, about 80 percent of the economically active female labor force is employed in agriculture. Food production is the major activity of rural women, and their responsibilities and labor inputs often exceed those of men in most areas in Africa. Women also provide much of the labor for men's cultivation of export crops from which they derive little benefit. Women are responsible for 70 percent of food production, 50 percent of domestic food storage, 100 percent of food processing, 50 percent of animal husbandry, and 60 percent of agricultural marketing.[73] These statistics have not changed for more than two decades. Rather, the income inequality between men and women continues to

---

[72]Ibid., 120.

[73]Takyiwaa Manuh, "Women in Africa's Development," *Africa Recovery*, no. 11 (April 1998): 4.

widen, as noted in *Worlds Apart*, a 2017 publication of the United Nations Population Fund (UNFPA). About 50 percent of women in Africa are married by the age of eighteen, and one in every three women in Africa lives in a polygamous marriage. The fertility rate for women in Africa is about 5.7 children per woman. In my work with the Canadian Samaritans for Africa in over twelve women's asset-based projects in four African countries, I have seen how the conditions of women can change with solidarity, wealth creation, and participatory practices. African women do not need handouts; they need to have the patriarchal obstacles removed by the church and state, especially through the abrogation of cultural norms and practices that prevent them from entrepreneurial activities like owning land and maintaining a bank account without a male co-signer.

What practices for the development of the assets of African women and protection of their rights can the illuminative church bring about in Africa? I propose especially that pastors of churches, pastoral agents, and counselors should embrace the following practices:

Listen to women who bring their pains and sorrows to you without being quick to judge, blame, and condemn them. I have heard some colleagues talk down to women or pass harsh judgments like "what is it that you are doing that makes your husband to beat you?" Or when a woman brings a case of adultery against her husband, some pastors will say, "Why don't you prepare him good food and good wine so that he doesn't go looking for them outside especially in the home of another woman?" These kinds of judgments make a woman a double victim. Religious leaders must learn to enter into the mess, chaos, brokenness and pain of many African women and accompany them with mercy, compassion, and hope.

Use the language of love and affirmation in embracing women's stories of pain. Religious leaders should use appropriate language of communication, which is respectful of women and preserves their dignity and privacy in helping those who come to them with their daily stories and struggles. Sometimes simply citing passages from the Bible or appealing to "for better or for worse" do not get to the root of the problem and will not help or heal. Also spiritualizing the situation by calling domestic violence "a time of temptation" for the woman and calling for more prayers may actually be a way of enabling the man's unacceptable behavior. Men's violence against women in Africa—domestic violence, sexual violence, verbal violence, sexual harassment, rape—reflect immaturity, irresponsibility, and some personality problems on the part of some men and a patriarchal mind-set that needs to be addressed culturally, legally, and also pastorally in a more comprehensive way. Priests and other pastoral workers and counselors in Africa, therefore, must speak from the heart and show how religious texts can heal the pain and darkness of the woman who is suffering;

Strengthening the agency of women even when they are broken and suffering. The whole goal of pastoral intervention is to give the woman hope and agency to fight her own fight and to walk away when necessary from an abusive and destructive marriage or relationship. Justice also demands that healing of both victim and victimizer requires appropriate measures to hold the victimizer accountable under the law. Sometimes the appeal to the Christian proposition that marriage is "for better and for worse" in order to remain in a bad and abusive marriage creates double victimhood for women. Pastors should not be too quick to fix marital problems especially where violence is present. Sometimes it might be necessary to journey with the woman and then the man rather than read the riot act to them or rush into fixing the problem; sometimes it might require helping the woman get legal services to press charges against a man and secure the rights of the woman should a divorce become inevitable.

Given the rate of violence against women in Africa, I think that there should be a legal aid group in most churches to provide legal and counseling support for women. A lot of our pastors have limited professional training or skills to adequately address domestic violence. In that regard, I propose that churches may need to engage the services of social workers and work in a more coordinated way with other agencies in this fight to secure the dignity and rights of African women against violence. In addition, leadership in churches is male-dominated, so some religious leaders are biased against women and may even be complicit in covering up sexual abuse against women through a culture of secrecy, which still exists around some of these crimes against women. In this kind of situation, the women who come to them become double victims. I propose that establishing a committee of experts, populated by women and those who understand the context and structure of oppression against women even in religious groups might be a good starting point.[74]

In this chapter I have shown how an illuminative ecclesiology can offer a form for the praxis of the social mission of the church in Africa. I proposed that it is important to make a distinction between those who are the poor *of* the Lord (all of the people of God in their dependent relations to God), and the poor *in* the Lord (all of the people of God who cooperate daily with God in assuming agency for their lives through daily choices that lead to human and social fulfillment). Even though we developed a strong theological, biblical, and pastoral analysis of poverty in the economy of salvation and in the practices of the church for integral human development, this chapter presents a portrait of poverty from African sociocultural and

---

[74]See my interview with the Carter Center, Atlanta, forumonwomenblog.cartercenter.org.

economic perspectives. The "culture of encounter" that is the starting point of illuminative ecclesiology must be a decisive framework for beginning the dialogue with the poor in Africa.

There is a certain *anonymity of the poor* in Africa and in most societies that is antithetical to human dignity, integral, and sustainable social transformation, and the emergence of a just society. This anonymity fosters a *culture of neglect* and a *culture of enforced silence* that is often imposed on the poor: no one asks the poor what they want because all of us social and pastoral workers know what is best for them; no one wants to pay attention to the poor or enter into deeper encounter with them to identify their agency and assets because we presume we know how they can be helped. The anonymity of the poor—which makes the poor voiceless and invisible—in the social mission in Africa is perhaps the main reason for failed aids and interventionist measures in Africa. It is also the main reason for the double victimhood of the poor in most cases: they are victims of structural violence and victims of charitable and social missions structured in foreign lands and in collaboration with local agents without their input. Pope Francis's message during his visit to Kenya especially on the importance of giving voice to the poor should be taken seriously by all those interested in becoming partners in development in Africa.

My contention is that the poor can collaborate among themselves to create networks of new life and alternative sites of hope. These new sites and networks of hope are present in Africa in small Christian communities, parishes, village self-help groups, and micro-credit food security co-operatives of women. Some of these groups may sometimes come in direct conflict with political and ecclesiastical ways of doings things; they may sometimes not produce results that are reported in "success stories" of African and Western charities. However, they are summons to the church in Africa to different levels of dialogue with the poor, and with women in Africa. By paying attention to these local processes, one can see in them the footprints of God as the anchor points for the strengthening of the social mission of the churches and nonfaith entities in Africa whose ships are often tossed here and thereby changing priorities and practices of interventionism and aid in Africa.

5

Illuminative Ecclesiology and the Ministry of Mercy for a Wounded World

Central African Republic (CAR) was the last country Pope Francis visited in Africa in November 2015. CAR is rich in material and human resources. Unfortunately, it has been plagued since independence by a failed leadership. It was the creation of France, which brought together many distinct ethnic nations under a single government. As a result, CAR, like many other African countries, struggles with the challenge of forging a coherent national identity. This is because most of the ethnic groups who inhabit this country were migrants from neighboring countries like Cameroon, Congo, Chad, and Sudan. The diverse people in CAR have most often been identified by religion: Christian and Islamic. This has become a source of tension, especially when the politicians use these identities to divide the people. Thousands of people have lost their lives in CAR because of the division and enmity between Christians and Muslims.

According to a report on the BBC website, Seleka rebels—a brutal alliance of northern groups and foreign Muslim fighters from Chad and Darfur, Sudan—invaded huge swathes of the countryside around Boboua, a small village about 120 kilometers from Bangui, the capital of CAR. Muslim Mayor Dewa Adamou had worked hard to forge an alliance of peace between Muslims and Christians in his community, insisting that they were all brothers and sisters and that no one should be discriminated against or eliminated based on their faith. He appealed to Muslim rebels not to harm any Christians in his community, and due in large part to these efforts, Boboua was spared. One night, a group of Christian militiamen entered Boboua, claiming that it was Mayor Adamou's Muslim brothers who killed so many Christians, and that he, like every other Muslim, was an enemy of Christians and deserved to die. These so-called Christians broke into the mayor's house, killing him and his son. Interestingly, it was a Catholic priest who came to bury Mayor Adamou because as he said, we are all brothers—Muslims, Christians, and practitioners of African Traditional Religion.[1]

While this tragedy was occurring in Boboua, in another shantytown called Boali, Father Xavier Fagba, a Catholic priest, was busy protecting over 600 Muslims in his church against those he termed "blood-thirsty Christians." These Christians regarded Muslims as their enemies and took revenge on them for their brothers and sisters who they claimed were killed by Muslim fighters when they were in control of the country. It is obvious that if anyone wanted to be a good Muslim or Christian, he or she would not be looking up to such people who do these despicable things in the name of God. As Pope Francis said in a speech to Christian ecumenical leaders and theologians in Bangui:

> For too long, your people have experienced troubles and violence, resulting in great suffering. This makes the proclamation of the Gospel all the more necessary and urgent. For it is Christ's own flesh which suffers in his dearest sons and daughters: the poorest of his people, the infirm, the elderly, the abandoned, children without parents or left to themselves without guidance and education. There are also those who have been scarred in soul or body by hatred and violence, those whom war has deprived of everything: work, home and loved ones.[2]

These stories are not peculiar to Africa. Many of the bloody wars and conflicts in our world today are unfortunately supported and legitimized through religious narratives and false constructions of identity. There is a strong argument made by Steven Pinker that the world is becoming less violent and more peaceful because the crisis, wars, and violence of the modern period pale in significance when compared to past human history. He argues strongly that our present history has become better compared to the past because "people in past generations were appalled by violence in their time and worked to reduce it, and so we should work to reduce the violence that remains in our time."[3] Those who may not agree with his reasoning and evidence that the world is a less violent and more peaceful place today than in the past cannot fault his argument that "across time and space, the more peaceable societies tend to be richer, healthier, better educated, better governed, more respectful of their women, and more likely

---

[1] See Andrew Harding, "Obituary for a Village Mayor," BBC News, February 16, 2014, www.bbc.com.

[2] *Messages of Pope Francis during His Apostolic Journey to Africa* (Nairobi: Paulines Publications Africa, 2015), 64.

[3] Steven Pinker, *The Better Angels of Our Nature: Why Violence Has Declined* (New York: Penguin Books, 2011), xxvi.

to engage in trade."[4] There is also an inverse to this claim by Pinker, that just as peace and stability help people work together to bring about prosperity, the absence of justice and the presence of structural violence lead to unrest, wars, and failed societies and nations. History shows that the emergence of inclusive societies was a slow process from centralization and domination by one person, group, or society over others, whether locally or globally. Most conflicts in the world and in societies must be seen as the rupture of structures of sin present in the world today and among nations. These are often the result of internal incoherence in societies, because unjust societies can never give birth to a peaceful and secure world.

Pope Paul VI was so prescient in 1972 in his World Day of Peace address when he gave that famous address titled "If you want peace, work for justice." In this address, he argues that world peace must be anchored in justice, human rights, respect of individual autonomy, and the rights of people everywhere to pursue their own development and their own goals, free from domination by others. He rejected all forms of tyranny and abuse of rights of people, especially their religious liberty. This statement, whose foundation in Catholic theological ethics had already been established through Pope John XXIII's *Pacem in Terris* and the synodal document *Justice in the World*, was a clarion call from the church that poverty and human suffering are the result of injustice in the world and sources of conflict and disorder. According to Pope Paul VI:

> Peace is not treachery (cf. Job 15:21). Peace is not a lie made into a system (cf. Jer 6:14). Much less is it pitiless totalitarian tyranny. Nor is it, in any way, violence: though at least violence does not dare to appropriate to itself the noble name of Peace. It is difficult, but essential, to form a genuine idea of Peace. It is difficult for one who closes his eyes to his innate intuition of it, which tells him that Peace is something very human. This is the right way to come to the genuine discovery of Peace: if we look for its true source, we find that it is rooted in a sincere feeling for man. A Peace that is not the result of true respect for man is not true Peace. And what do we call this sincere feeling for man? We call it Justice. But is not Justice also an immobile goddess? Yes, it is so in the expressions of it which we call rights and duties, and which we arrange in our illustrious codes, that is, in laws and pacts which produce that stability of social, cultural and economic relationships which cannot be infringed. It is order, it is Peace.[5]

---

[4]Ibid., xxiii.

[5]Pope Paul VI, "If You Want Peace, Work for Justice," World Day of Peace, January 1, 1972, w2.vatican.va.

There is also a different kind of war, which leaves secret and festering wounds in the minds and hearts of many people. The battles for power and position in corporations, universities, organizations, and in governments are often carried out through destructive corporate habits, exploitation of workers, manipulation, and personal vendetta. "Spiritual leprosy," as Pope Francis has called it, can ravage the church with favoritism, a culture of secrecy and lack of transparency, gossip, sycophancy, corruption, negative and destructive criticism, envy, lust, and greed, among others.

The war could be pastoral, when the pastor fails to listen to his or her people or when people are rejected or condemned without being listened to or given a welcoming heart where they can bring their wounds to God. There is also the war going on in families. In my experience as a priest, who has worked in three continents, it seems to me that the wars in the families are omnipresent—ruptures in relationship, rivalry, broken families, wounded and hurting separated or divorced partners. The breakdown in family life often creates deep wounds in children and permanent scars in the memories of former spouses. In many families, the fight for inheritance is a big source of conflict and breakdown of families. There is also the ego which is often present in our unredeemed selves, which becomes a wedge to authentic and deep human encounters.

The people who suffer from all these wars are usually the poor and the most vulnerable. Pope Francis calls on the church

> to heal these wounds, to assuage them with the oil of consolation, to bind them with mercy and cure them with solidarity and vigilant care. Let us not fall into humiliating indifference or a monotonous routine that prevents us from discovering what is new! . . . Let us open our eyes and see the misery of the world, the wounds of our brothers and sisters who are denied their dignity, and let us recognize that we are compelled to heed their cry for help.[6]

Pope Francis has used the image of field hospital to capture this mission of the church, whose biblical foundation is the parable of the Good Samaritan. This parable brings together in a vivid way all the features of illuminative ecclesiology with regard to the praxis of mercy.

The parable of the Good Samaritan is a good paradigm for seeing the wounds of the world and of individuals, especially of people who look up to the church as their home. It seems to me a good representation of all the aspects of illuminative ecclesiology: (1) accountability, which begins

---

[6] Pope Francis, *The Face of Mercy, Bull of Indiction of the Extraordinary Jubilee of Mercy, Misericordiae Vultus* (Nairobi: Paulines Publication-Africa, 2015), 15.

with a culture of encounter when we step into the chaos of other people's lives through which we see the face of God and show the face of people to God; (2) the art of accompaniment, through which the church journeys with people in their daily joys and sorrows and participates in their lives and welcomes them despite their wounded state to share in the life of the church; (3) the praxis of vulnerable mission, through which the church identifies itself with the poverty and wounds of the world and people as essential to its own identity as a poor church in need of God's mercy and brings tenderness and compassionate healing to the wounded; (4) a spirituality of transformation, which brings people to a new experience of love and mercy through their encounter with the church in the church's proclamation and witnessing to the gospel through its priorities and practices. The mission of the illuminative church is to bring people to that visceral experience of the transforming power and presence of God's grace and love, and to bring people's wounds and daily situations into close encounter with the mysteries of God's love and mercy as a gift.

The parable of the Good Samaritan is an invitation addressed to the church to always be a church of mercy and compassion, a church touched through and through by human suffering and touched by the sins and brokenness in the world and called to be a source of healing in the world. The Good Samaritan paradigm is also an invitation to heal the world of the many wounds inflicted on people by poverty, injustice, sin, evil, betrayal, hatred, and violence, among others. As Henri Nouwen put it so strongly, a Christian community is "a healing community not because wounds are cured and pains are alleviated, but because wounds and pains become openings or occasions for a new vision. Mutual confession then becomes a mutual deepening of hope, and sharing weakness becomes a reminder to one and all of the coming strength."[7] The Good Samaritan stepped into the messiness of the life of the fallen and wounded traveler. He took the risk involved not minding the "diseased state" of this wounded man or questioning the man's moral or spiritual state. He could have passed by this man like the others or he could have justified his not wanting to get involved by blaming the wounded man for his lack of good judgment in traveling on a lonely and insecure road without any company. He was moved by compassion and pity by the question, which has been popularized by Martin Luther King Jr.: *What will happen to him if I did nothing to help him,* rather than *What will happen to me if I did something to help him?*

The culture of encounter with the wounds of this man began a series of

---

[7]Henry Nouwen, "The Wounded Healer," in *Images of Pastoral Care: Classic Readings*, ed. Robert C. Dykstra (St. Louis, MO: Chalice Press, 2005), 83.

other steps for the Samaritan and the beaten, battered, and bruised man—accompanying the wounded man to the inn (art of accompaniment), gently bandaging his wounds, tenderly placing him on his donkey (vulnerable mission), making him as comfortable as possible; bringing him into the inn where he received care and healing (transformation); and following up with him, while paying the bills for his treatment. In this way, he makes this stranger a member of his family and takes upon himself the pain and anguish of this man. The culture of encounter of the illuminative church is a summons to step into the wounds of the other; to accept people for who they are and see in their sinful or joyful state a beautiful road through which we can see the face of God and show the face of God to others.

The question posed to Jesus by the scribe, which Jesus answered with the parable of the Good Samaritan was: "Who is my neighbor?" Like the people in Jesus' time, we are suffering today because there is a growing distance among nations, races, ethnic groups, social classes, and religions. In the time of Jesus, the word "neighbor" referred mainly to people from one's nation and religion. One can show charity to people outside one's nation and religion, but it is not an obligation or duty to do so. Love of one's neighbor was often interpreted in the time of Jesus as applying primarily to one's own people. In addition, in those days normally those who will live around you will most likely be people from your race, nation and religion. Africa offers a very good example of the meaning of neighbor. The question "who is my neighbor?" in African spirituality and the notion of community are inclusive. Neighborhood in Africa is an open space in which all humans and all reality freely associate. Participation and closeness to each other are what it means to be a neighbor; it is not simply spatial proximity but a relational proximity. This is grounded on the conviction in Africa that all people have a common ancestry, coming as we all do from the eternal womb of God. Being a neighbor is to be a source of life to another and a linkage for further interconnected bonds and ties with other people and other realities. It is in the bond of interconnection that abundant life is found with its associated values of health, wealth, and hope. It is a radical orientation of all to community.

What Christianity offers is an ideal of a universal family; every human being is not simply my neighbor but my family member, my friend, and fellow pilgrim. We are all children of one God; we live in a shared world; and we all have a common destiny. Christianity says that we are all in this together, and that the pain and anguish of anyone in any part of the world should also be my own grief and anguish.

This is a challenge to the world today. The beauty of human diversity has become a burden too heavy for many people to bear, and many people are hiding in their own small worlds of race, nation, and religion in the false search for security and peace. It seems that we do not want each other anymore and are often afraid of who is coming into our neighborhood, who is coming into our nation, and who is coming into our lives. Our individual, ethnic, racial, religious, and gender identities have become our small prisons where we are hiding from the rest, rather than a palace where we all can celebrate each other's gifts as dignified members of the divine royal household. There is in our churches a false sense of Christianity or Catholicism as a fortress for the strong and the worthy, while those who are weak and considered sinful are marginalized or are invisible or totally anonymous. We want to pass by the sites of wounds and pains in the world like the two individuals who walked away by the other side when they saw a wounded and dying man on the highway from Jericho to Jerusalem.

How can the illuminative church be a healer of wounds through the healing balm of forgiveness? Pope Francis provides a fitting answer in *Evangelii Gaudium* 270 when he teaches as follows:

> Sometimes we are tempted to be that kind of Christian who keeps the Lord's wounds at arm's length. Yet Jesus wants us to touch human misery, to touch the suffering flesh of others. He hopes that we will stop looking for those personal or communal niches, which shelter us from the maelstrom of human misfortune and instead enter into the reality of other people's lives and know the power of tenderness. Whenever we do so, our lives become wonderfully complicated and we experience intensely what it is to be a people, to be part of a people.

The parable of the Good Samaritan is a challenge to the church today, especially at a time in world history when people are displaying signs of brokenness and a crisis of the heart. As Pope Francis writes in *Evangelii Gaudium* 67, the sin of the modern world is individualism, which harms the development of deeper relationships through the culture of encounter. Jeanne Stevenson Moessner points out that the parable of the Good Samaritan could be read as a paradigm of interconnection through love of God, self, and neighbor. This, she argues, is particularly a model worth embracing because of what she perceives as a lack of connection between people in the pastoral life and by extension in modern society. This is at the heart of what Henri Nouwen calls the wounds in our modern world—alienation, isolation, separation, loneliness, and brokenness. As he put it, "We live in a society in which loneliness has become one of the most painful human wounds. The growing competition and rivalry which pervade our lives from birth have created in us an acute awareness of our isolation. This awareness has in turn left many with a heightened anxiety and an intense search for the experience of unity and community."[8]

Like the Samaritan who was immediately connected to the devastating condition of the man who was dying on the roadside, Moessner sees pastoral ministry as a form of interconnection at the healing site of the inn. The inn functions as a metaphor for a site of healing and hope. It is the place and space for healing, comfort, and love that the church is called to offer to all those who are wounded in life.[9] The inn also becomes, to borrow Carrie Doehring's characterization of co-creating meanings through entering into each other's stories, "a trustworthy space for exploring new meanings" through "a compassionate and respectful care relationship." The inn paradigm is also a way of presenting the church as a site where in entering into each other's story, we "lament with each other" by touching each other's wounds in a "relational and communal" manner.[10]

In the face of violence, hatred, and prejudice, which poison many minds, hearts, and hands, the light, which shines from the beauty of Christian witness and proclamation, should not be kept in the prison of a self-satisfied and self-contained church. Like the bruised and wounded man on the road from Jerusalem to Jericho, there are so many poor and marginalized people in our communities and in many parts of the world who are crying out for help. The road from Jerusalem to Jericho in our times has become the streets of Nairobi, Ougadogou, Maiduguri, Bangui, which continue to be sites of violence and bloodletting; it is the lonely path of El Paso, where many migrants are trying to cross over to the United States. The wounded and bruised of our world include, among others, African and Syrian migrants who are drowning in the Mediterranean, those Africans who are fleeing from war and lawlessness in Libya and Mali, who are dying in the Sahara Desert, and thousands who are killed in violence in South Sudan, in the killing fields of Somalia and in the fighting in many parts of Africa today as a result of border disputes, terrorism, political crises, failed leadership, or economic and communal disputes.

Illuminative ecclesiology is grounded on the theological aesthetics built on a culture of encounter that, for example, could happen through touching the wounds of others. God is found in the wounds of the world. The wounds of many people in life are the sacred spots where the beauty of God can be found. The theological aesthetics of illuminative ecclesiology emerges

---

[8]Ibid., 77.

[9]Jeanne Stevenson Moessner, "The Self-Differentiated Samaritan," in *Images of Pastoral Care: Classic Readings*, ed. Robert C. Dykstra (St. Louis, MO: Chalice Press, 2005), 64–67.

[10]Carrie Doehring, *The Practice of Pastoral Care: A Postmodern Approach* (Louisville, KY: Westminster John Knox Press, 2015), xiv–xv.

from seeing the beauty in the challenging reality of daily life beyond the crisis and pain. There is a deeper revelation and more intimate connection between reality in its ambiguity and the concreteness of God's love which is embodied in daily existence. This is why theologians are challenged to be feeling people who are in touch with reality. The kind of marginal theology required of theologians today, in many parts of the world, is a theology of wounds. Theologies and pastoral ministries should be nourished by tears that theologians shed with their brothers and sisters in their places of pain and isolation.

The foregoing biblical theological reflection serves to highlight what most people experience in their lives, communities, and the world. Our world is wounded and in dire need of mercy. Identifying the wounds of humanity have occupied the minds of many people, especially psychologists who burrow into the vast recesses of the human mind to bring to the surface painful memories buried in the psyche and how they weigh on people's daily lives. However, it was Carl Jung who in *Fundamental Questions of Psychotherapy* first drew attention to the truth that the psychoanalyst must heal himself or herself first before thinking of healing others. According to him, "For only what he can put right in himself can he hope to put right in the patient. This, and nothing else, is the meaning of the Greek myth of the wounded physician."[11]

Viewed in this light of a Jungian axiom, the church cannot be a healer of wounds if it has not dealt with the wounds within the church and the wounds that the church has inflicted on people through priorities and practices that excluded people or reinforced and institutionalized forms of racism and intolerance against minorities and victims of clerical sexual abuse. This is why the question posed by Pope Francis at the beginning of the Year of Mercy remains valid for understanding the church's ministry of mercy. It is also important in guiding a theological reflection on how the church can be a healing inn, where the Good Samaritan brings the wounded for healing and restoration:

> We cannot escape the Lord's words to us, and they will serve as the criteria upon which we will be judged: whether we have fed the hungry and given drink to the thirsty, welcomed the stranger and clothed the naked, or spent time with the sick and those in prison (cf. Mt 25:31–45). Moreover, we will be asked if we have helped others to escape the doubt that causes them to fall into despair and which is often a source

---

[11]Cited in Kathryn C. Larisey, "The Wounded Healer: A Jungian Perspective," *Newsletter of the C. G. Jung Society of Atlanta* (Fall 2012): 13.

of loneliness; if we have helped to overcome the ignorance in which millions of people live, especially children deprived of the necessary means to free them from the bonds of poverty.[12]

"Your defects are the ways that glory gets manifested. Whoever sees clearly what is diseased in himself begins to gallop on the way. There is nothing worse than thinking you are well enough."[13] This quote from the poet Rumi is a starting point for looking deeply at the church to discover whether it sees the internal wounds in the church and how it is addressing the wounds in its internal life. Most of the time "helping institutions" wish to have a perfect image, and the things or people who do not fit into this image are often on the sidelines or invisible. When the clerical sexual abuse scandal erupted in the United States in 2000 and eventually spread to many parts of the Western world, many people were shocked by the secrecy and cover-ups in the church. The concern of most bishops was to protect the image of the church rather than the dignity and lives of so many children who were being abused. In a different way, this could be seen in the way in which LGBTQ Christians are treated for the most part. It is easy to say that we are an inclusive church as long as it doesn't involve visible and concrete signs of inclusivity that might challenge us to make some changes in our churches. How has the church identified itself with people who are on the streets of life and those whom society wants to be invisible because they are considered sinners, misfits, and unworthy?

The idea of wounds in the church was first used by Pope Innocent IV (1243–54) in his opening homily at the First Council of Lyons (1245). In this homily, given after the recitation of the prayer to the Holy Spirit, Pope Innocent denounced the emperor of the Holy Roman Empire, Frederick II, for "disregarding papal authority by 'despising the keys of the church.'" Pope Innocent, in addition, spoke of the other wounds in the church, in addition to the persecution of the church by the emperor, to include the poor morals of the clergy and laity, the invasion of the Holy Land by the Saracens, the Great Schism, and the cruelty of the Tatars in Hungary.[14] Historians such as Gerald O'Collins, Mario Farrugia, Christopher Belitto, and others interpret the wounds of the church at this point in history to include the exile of the pope in Avignon and the strife over antipopes, the persecution of the Jews and heretics, deterioration of relations with Muslims, the Crusades,

---

[12]Pope Francis, *The Face of Mercy.*

[13]Cited in Larisey, "Wounded Healer," 14.

[14]Christopher M. Belitto, *The General Councils: A History of the Twenty-One Church Councils from Nicaea to Vatican II* (New York: Paulist Press, 2002), 58. See also Fordham University online source book on the Tatars: sourcebooks.fordham.edu.

and preaching by Innocent IV and successive popes on indulgences and remission of sins, which were to be granted after death to all Catholic patrons who left money in their will for the Crusades.[15]

However, the wounds in the church were also seen at some point in history as the wounds and pains of the poor, especially in the devotion to the Sacred Heart, which grew from the thirteenth century to the sixteenth. As Robert Maloney observes, "It was only in the eleventh and twelfth centuries that we find the first clear indications of devotion to the heart of Jesus. The wound in Jesus' side began to be seen as symbolizing a wound of love in his heart."[16] However, beginning in the late sixteenth century and during the seventeenth century in the spiritual revival in France, which gave birth to such spiritualities as the Devotion to the Sacred Heart, people began to look at the sufferings and pains of the world from the five wounds in the body of Christ on the Cross. There was a movement to associate the heart of love of the Lord Jesus to the calling addressed to all the people of God to incarnate love in their daily lives as a way of healing the world of suffering and pain. This is because to heal the wounds of a suffering brother or sister is to be associated with the wounded heart of love of the Son of God.

Many Christians at this time began to identify the suffering of the poor with the wounds of Jesus on the Cross. There was a grassroots movement of reform in the church in sixteenth- and seventeenth-century France, which at the core recognized "the eminent dignity of the poor in the church."[17] According to Edward Udovic, the spirituality which was growing at that time was built on the conviction that no spiritual or moral conquest could be achieved without a correlative spirituality of charity to meet the seething population who were sweltering under the heat of poverty because, "The sad material and physical plight of the abandoned poor weighed heavily and personally on the collective conscience of the forces of the Catholic renewal in France. The thought of thousands of men, women, and children abandoned to the hopelessness of poverty was also more than the spiritually minded could bear."[18]

The spirituality of this period focused on experience, expression, and the explanation of the human condition with an identification with the love of God, which demanded action on the part of Christians to embrace charity. This attitude of paying attention to the wounds of the poor and the conditions

---

[15]Gerald O'Collins and Mario Farrugia, *Catholicism: The Story of Catholic Christianity* (Oxford: Oxford University Press, 2003), 73.

[16]Robert P. Maloney, "The Heart of Jesus in the Spirituality of Vincent de Paul and Louise de Marillac," *Vincentian Heritage Journal* 32, no. 1 (2014): article 8, 4.

[17]Edward R. Udovic, "Seventh-Century France," in *Vincent de Paul and Louise de Marillac: Rules, Conferences, and Writings*, ed. Francis Ryan and John E. Rybolt (New York: Paulist Press, 1995), 10.

[18]Ibid.

of the poor and the marginalized were championed by saints such as Vincent de Paul, Jean-Jacques Olier, and Louise de Marillac, among many others.[19]

The spiritual tradition of seeing the suffering of the poor as additional pain inflicted on the wounded and bleeding Sacred Heart has remained very solid in the church today. It is a particularly powerful symbol and motivation in Africa today where devotion to the Sacred Heart is very popular and has influenced the spirituality of mercy, reconciliation, and outreach to the poor. An inspirational example of how this spirituality is shaping the ministry of mercy and social mission of the church is the moving witness of the work of Sister Rosemary Nyirumbe, a sister of the Sacred Heart.[20] The association of the wounds in the world with the Sacred Heart of Jesus in Africa is also strengthened with the image of the Good Samaritan. These images help us develop the kind of praxis that should shape the ministry of mercy for the illuminative church. This is because it reveals the face of a church that leads from the heart, a church that is a wounded healer. As Henri Nouwen describes it,

> Nobody escapes being wounded. We all are wounded people, whether physically, emotionally, mentally, or spiritually. The main question is not "How can we hide our wounds?" so we don't have to be embarrassed, but "How can we put our woundedness in the service of others?" When our wounds cease to be a source of shame, and become a source of healing, we have become wounded healers.[21]

In what follows in this chapter, I outline what Pope Francis means by the church of mercy. I propose that the church of mercy is a wounded healer and that the church of wounds is the form of a merciful church in need of God's mercy, on one hand, and which shares the mercy of God, on the other hand. The illuminative church brings the wounds of its inner life and the wounds of all of God's people before God. It is also born from the wounds of the Lord. This is how it is able to show the healing grace of the Lord to a wounded world, through its deep encounter with both the wounds of the Lord and the wounds of the world, like the Good Samaritan. I will show that this image of the church is central to the identity and mission of the church from her origin. Using the African social context as a case study, I will show

---

[19]Michael J. Buckley, "Seventeenth-Century French Spirituality: Three Figures," in *Christian Spirituality: Post-Reformation and Modern*, ed. Louis Dupré and Don E. Saliers (New York: Crossroad, 1989), 31–32.

[20]See the account of this ministry given by Emmanuel Katongole, *Born of Lament: The Theology and Politics of Hope in Africa* (Grand Rapids, MI: Eerdmans, 2017), 136–43.

[21]Nouwen, "Wounded Healer."

how this way of being church can help meet some of the challenges that Africa is facing in the area of justice, peace, and reconciliation, and what a church of mercy will look like in Africa.

MERCY AS A LIGHT IN THE CHURCH AND IN THE WORLD

In *Misericordiae Vultus (MV)*, the Bull of Indiction of the Extraordinary Jubilee of Mercy (2015), Pope Francis writes of the four aspects of the Trinitarian origin of mercy:

> We need to contemplate the mystery of mercy. It is a wellspring of joy, serenity, and peace. Our salvation depends on it. Mercy: the word reveals the very mystery of the Most Holy Trinity. Mercy: the ultimate and supreme act by which God comes to meet us. Mercy: the fundamental law that dwells in the heart of every person who looks sincerely into the eyes of his brothers and sisters on the path of life. Mercy: the bridge that connects God and man, opening our hearts to a hope of being loved forever despite our sinfulness. (*MV*, 2)

The Christian God is revealed in history as mercy beyond measure. God's mercy is the source and origin of all things. Mercy has been identified by many saints and fathers of the church as God's supreme attribute because God gives mercy without requiring it of God's creatures. Mercy is an inner movement from the heart of God to creation purely arising from God's generosity and God's compassion, pity, and pain at how sin and evil ravage creation.[22] Mercy is the consequence of God's unconditional love for humanity. God displays the supremacy of this attribute when God forgives sins in order to heal the wounds and brokenness of creation. As Congar rightly argues, "God pays the cost of his justice, *and his payment is mercy.* But the renunciation implied by the complete forgiveness of mercy in no way diminishes God's reign. On the contrary, it displays its supremacy with greater splendor, because forgiveness is a more regal attribute than justice."[23] Ultimately, mercy is God's way of dealing with humanity in history. At the end of all things, it is mercy that will bring us home to the Father's house. The God whom Jesus Christ revealed in history is the God who is rich in

---

[22]Cf. Yves Congar, *The Revelation of God*, trans. A. Manson and L. C. Sheppard (London: Darton, Longman and Todd, 1968), 51.

[23]Ibid., 62.

mercy. This is a God who created the world in mercy, saves the world in mercy, and ultimately will transform, heal, and bring the world to restoration and ultimate consummation through divine mercy.

In his encyclical on mercy, *Dives in Misericordia (DM)* (1980), Pope John Paul II teaches that the mercy of God that Christ revealed in the Incarnation is addressed to all, but especially to the poor and those on the margins:

> It is very significant that the people in question are especially the poor, those without means of subsistence, those deprived of their freedom, the blind who cannot see the beauty of creation, those living with broken hearts, or suffering from social injustice, and finally sinners. It is especially for these last that the Messiah becomes a particularly clear sign of God who is love, a sign of the Father. In this visible sign the people of our own time, just like the people then, can see the Father. (*DM*, 3)

The people of our times can come to embrace the message of the gospel only if the church in its teaching, life, and advocacy and in the examples of its members shows the face of God who reveals divine love as mercy beyond measure. Mercy is the form which God's love assumes when it comes in contact with our human condition; the illuminative church must take the form of mercy if it is to reveal the face of God to humanity and the wounded faces of the world to God. What is the form of this mercy?

God's mercy has been revealed to us in history in the scriptures. It is a deep reality that is a gift that all those who believe experience in their encounter with God. Pope John Paul II teaches that mercy is a rich concept. Mercy can be seen in the nature and action of God in history and in the way of life of God's chosen people. Mercy is an invitation to all those who have received this gift to model in their lives and attitudes to one another and the rest of humanity and the earth the same merciful way of relationship with which God has blessed them. However, mercy, as Pope John Paul II points out, does not pertain only

> to the notion of God, but it is something that characterizes the life of the whole people of Israel and each of its sons and daughters: mercy is the content of intimacy with their Lord, the content of their dialogue with Him. Under precisely this aspect, mercy is presented in the individual books of the Old Testament with a great richness of expression. It may be difficult to find in these books a purely theoretical answer to the question of what mercy is in itself. Nevertheless, the terminology that is used is in itself able to tell us much about this subject. (*DM*, 4)

Being a church of the poor presupposes living as a church of mercy. This is because it is through the experience of poverty whether in its negative or positive aspects that the church and its members affirm their openness to receiving mercy and mediating mercy to all.

William Mounce's dictionary is a good source for the biblical meanings of mercy, which John Paul extrapolates in *Dives in Misericordia*. The first Old Testament word for mercy is *hesed*, which is "one of the richest, most insightful terms in the Old Testament."[24] *Dives in Misericordia* develops this rich insight in a helpful manner (no. 52). I think it is fittingly helpful to draw fully from this rich interpretation as a way of illuminating the proposals that I offer here with regard to the meaning of mercy and how God mediates mercy in history to those who are poor. It is also important in doing this to show how mercy relates to the central affirmation of our faith and identity as a church. It is also helpful because it shows that Pope Francis's call for a church of mercy, like his advocacy for a church of the poor, is in continuity with the teachings of the church from its origins. He is only calling us to wake up from slumber because sometimes the church and its members forget the calling and mission of the church and through its laws, teaching, and practices make it difficult to see clearly the merciful face of God.

According to John Paul II, the books of the Old Testament use two expressions in particular in rendering the word, mercy—*hesed* and *rahamim*—each having a different semantic nuance. *Hesed* indicates a profound attitude of goodness.

> When this is established between two individuals, they do not just wish each other well; they are also faithful to each other by virtue of an interior commitment, and therefore also by virtue of a faithfulness to themselves. Since *hesed* also means "grace" or "love," this occurs precisely on the basis of this fidelity. The fact that the commitment in question has not only a moral character but almost a juridical one makes no difference. When in the Old Testament the word *hesed* is used of the Lord, this always occurs in connection with the covenant that God established with Israel. This covenant was, on God's part, a gift and a grace for Israel. Nevertheless, since, in harmony with the covenant entered into, God had made a commitment to respect it, *hesed* also acquired in a certain sense a legal content. The juridical commitment on God's part ceased to oblige whenever Israel broke the covenant and did not respect its conditions. But precisely at this

---

[24]William D. Mounce, ed., *Mounce's Complete Expository Dictionary of Old and New Testament Words* (Grand Rapids, MI: Zondervan, 2006), 447.

point, *hesed*, in ceasing to be a juridical obligation, revealed its deeper aspect: it showed itself as what it was at the beginning, that is, as love that gives, love more powerful than betrayal, grace stronger than sin. (*DM*, note 52)

Mercy viewed in this light, Pope John Paul II continues, emerges as God's own faithfulness to God's nature as often reflected in the "frequent recurrence together of the two terms *hesed we'emet* (grace and fidelity), which could be considered a case of hendiadys (cf. e.g. Ex 34:6; 2 Sm 2:6, 15:20; Ps 25[24]:10, 40[39]:11–12, 85[84]:11, 138[137]:2; Mi 7:20): 'It is not for your sake, O house of Israel, that I am about to act, but for the sake of my holy name' (Ez 36:22)." God acts with mercy not because Israel has claim to God's love "on the basis of (legal) justice," but it can hope for mercy and put its trust in God acting with mercy toward it because "the God of the covenant is really 'responsible for his love.' God's mercy is necessarily tied to God's covenantal love and brings with it forgiveness, healing, grace which restores a relationship which is broken thus re-establishing the covenant and bringing about a renewed relationship."

Pope John Paul also writes of the second word that reflects the meaning of mercy in the Old Testament, *rahamim*:

While *hesed* highlights the marks of fidelity to self and of "responsibility for one's own love" (which are in a certain sense masculine characteristics), *rahamim*, in its very root, denotes the love of a mother (*rehem*: mother's womb). From the deep and original bond—indeed the unity—that links a mother to her child there springs a particular relationship to the child, a particular love. Of this love one can say that it is completely gratuitous, not merited, and that in this aspect it constitutes an interior necessity: an exigency of the heart. It is, as it were, a "feminine" variation of the masculine fidelity to self expressed by *hesed*. Against this psychological background, *rahamim* generates a whole range of feelings, including goodness and tenderness, patience and understanding, that is, readiness to forgive.

The Old Testament attributes to the Lord precisely these characteristics when it uses the term *rahamim* in speaking of Him. We read in Isaiah: "Can a woman forget her suckling child, that she should have no compassion on the son of her womb? Even these may forget, yet I will not forget you" (Is 49:15). This love, faithful and invincible thanks to the mysterious power of motherhood, is expressed in the Old Testament texts in various ways: as salvation from dangers, especially from enemies; also as forgiveness of sins—of individuals and also of the whole of Israel; and finally in readiness to fulfill the (eschatological) promise and hope, in spite of human infidelity, as we read in Hosea: "I will heal their faithlessness, I will love them freely" (Hos 14:5).

In the terminology of the Old Testament we also find other expressions, referring in different ways to the same basic content. But the two terms mentioned above deserve special attention. They clearly show their original anthropomorphic aspect: in describing God's mercy, the biblical authors use terms that correspond to the consciousness and experience of their contemporaries. (*DM*, note 52)

The New Testament uses the words *elew* (to have mercy, feel sorry for, have pity) especially in referring to God's mercy and undeserving kindness and forgiveness to those who do not deserve it) and *'ilaskoma* (to atone, have mercy on, to make atonement for, propitiate) and refers in the New Testament to the atoning work of Christ.[25] There are four different areas from Mounce's commentary on the New Testament terms for mercy where people either receive or are called to give mercy or where mercy is used to describe the form of God's acting toward creation:[26] (1) The New Testament shows that the ultimate model of mercy that God showed to the world and that continues in history to the end of time is the suffering and death of Jesus in order to save sinners (Rom 11:30–31; 1 Tm 1:13, 16; 1 Pt 2:10); (2) Jesus shows mercy to those who are hurting—the sinners, the rejected, the poor, marginalized people, those who are misunderstood (Lk 18:13; Rom 12:8; Mt 9:27, 20:30; Mk 10:47–48); (3) Mercy is the vocation of all those who belong to God; it should be central to the ministry of the church. All Christians who identify as children of God are shaped by the mercy they have received from God; (4) Mercy as compassion, kindness, and concern for those in need is presented in the New Testament as an attribute of God in Godself and in God's attitude to God's people. In many New Testament passages God is spoken of as *being rich in mercy* (Eph 2:4; Rom 9:8); God has *a great mercy*, and Zechariah celebrates *the tender mercy of God*, while Mary sings of *God's mercy which is without end* because it extends from age to age (Lk 1:50, 58, 78). The mercy of God is a wisdom from above and bears great fruit in creation (cf. Jas 3:17).[27]

Some of the fruits that God's mercy produces is shown in many New Testament passages, according to Mounce: Paul in writing to Titus reminds him that our salvation is not by works but according to God's mercy (Ti 3:5); Peter reminds his audience that our new birth in Christ is as a result of

---

[25]Mounce, *Mounce's Complete Expository Dictionary*, 447–48.

[26]I have relied on Mounce's commentary for what follows on the idea of mercy in the New Testament.

[27]Mounce, *Mounce's Complete Expository Dictionary*, 448.

the great mercy of God (1 Pt 1:3); and Jude writes that the mercy of God in Christ for us leads us to eternal life (Jude 21). God's mercy is so important for us that the writer of the Letter to the Hebrews admonishes believers to always draw near to God in order to "receive mercy and find grace to help in time of need."[28]

Finally, the believers are called to show compassion and mercy to one another in the same manner that God shows compassion and mercy to them. There is no change in terminology between the term for mercy used of God and the invitation to be merciful addressed to believers. Mercy is the prerogative of God and is essential to God's nature, but God shares this with humanity and invites people to exercise the same divine quality with others. Thus in being merciful we are sharing in divine nature and a Christian is no closer to God than when he or she shows mercy, forgiveness, compassion, and love. Mounce is illuminating in this aspect:

> Since God is merciful, he in turn desires his followers to show mercy in their relationship with others. God desired eleoς more than sacrifice (Mt 9:13). The best example in the New Testament of mercy on a human level is seen in the reaction of the Good Samaritan to the one who fell into the hands of robbers on his way to Jericho (Lk 10:30–37). "The one who had mercy on him" bandaged his wounds, took him on his donkey to an innkeeper, and paid for his care. Jesus' admonition was, "Go and do likewise" (v. 37). Here the image of the Good Samaritan is presented as the model for healing wounds through mercy. The outstanding negative example is the servant who was forgiven a great debt he owed, but then refused to forgive a small debt owed to him. His master's response was, "Should not you have had mercy . . . on your fellow servant as I had mercy on you?" (Mt 18:33).[29]

In the light of these, it is obvious that mercy is the means and goal of all Christian acts of believing, acting, and living with and for others. A Christian is closest to God when he or she forgives another person, because in forgiving we exercise the prerogatives of God in bringing healing and new creation where once there was death and decay, brokenness and darkness. However, forgiveness is not simple; it is a process of healing both for the one offended and the one who committed the offense. True forgiveness and healing takes time, conversion, patience, prayer, energy, and sacrifice. It is costly to let go of the pain and sense of injustice and regret, which often afflict the soul of a wounded and bruised heart, but it pays at the end of the day.

---

[28]Ibid.
[29]Ibid.

MERCIFUL FACES OF AN ILLUMINATIVE CHURCH

Some aspects of mercy need to be emphasized in the church today. The first is what Jon Sobrino refers to as attention to individuals who are not just carrying wounds and burdens of life, but those who are crucified on the cross in their daily life like Christ. Being merciful to these people "means to do everything we possibly can to bring them down from the cross. This means working for justice—which is the name love acquires when it comes to entire majorities of people unjustly oppressed."[30]

The second is about how we interiorize the suffering of the other person, how we react in the face of evil and the activity and choices we make as our response to the presence of suffering, pain, injustice, and human alienation in what Jon Sobrino calls "making someone else's pain our very own and allowing that pain to move us to respond. We are to be moved simply by the fact that someone in need has been placed along our way."[31]

The third is the specifically biblical teaching on mercy that Pope John Paul II underlines as the full consequence of the Incarnation of love for believers and for the mission of the church. He teaches that mercy is "the mode and sphere in which love manifests itself." It is more so because the Incarnate love and the daily practices of Christians who follow Jesus Christ should be characterized by love, which is most credible when it embraces suffering, fights against injustice and poverty, and embraces the whole of our human condition in all its fragility, both moral and physical. Mercy is not only the divine quality par excellence, it is the only contact of intimacy with God and the community. It is also the means of union with others in their daily joys and sorrows.[32]

The principle of mercy that Sobrino proposes as a specific kind of love should become a practice in the church in such a way that it shapes and molds the entire life, mission, and fate of the church.[33] It should become the principle of a theology that touches hearts, changes minds, and inspires a praxis of healing because it emerges from the wounded and compassionate heart of the church, the world, and the wounded and bleeding hearts of many people. There are so many people in Africa and in the world who are bruised and beaten down by suffering often reinforced through religious ideals, claims, and practices that do not mediate mercy and healing to the

---

[30]Jon Sobrino, *The Principle of Mercy: Taking the Crucified People from the Cross* (Maryknoll, NY: Orbis Books, 1994), 10.

[31]Ibid.

[32]John Paul II, *Dives in Misericordia on the Mercy of God* (Nairobi: St. Paul Publications-Africa, 1981), 12.

[33]Sobrino, *Principle of Mercy*, 14.

whole person. So what will a merciful church look like in the world? I will focus on the African experience in engaging this rich identity and mission of an illuminative church.

Mercy is a common attribute of an illuminative church because in this kind of ecclesiology the church and its members are invited to enter into the mystery of human reality and pain with a "seeing eye" with the goal of reaching the depths of the pain and brokenness of life. Church ministers are servants of mercy and not dispensers of punishment and condemnation. The theology of mercy in Africa must begin as Pope Francis proposes in the Bull with first contemplating the mercy of God as it is revealed in the Trinitarian structure of God, who created us in love, saves us in mercy, and sanctifies us in mercy. God grants us mercy and love even before we seek it. When we reflect on the image of the prodigal son, we see a double movement. This takes place between the father who was waiting for his Son to come home and the wounded and sorrowful heart of a son who from the distance was looking for the merciful face of his father.

The theology of mercy must draw from the life of the church, the traditions, scriptures, and the daily context of God's people in the conditions of suffering and pain. In Africa particularly, the theology of mercy must also be grounded in sound cultural practices on forgiveness, restorative justice, and integral reconciliation. The understanding of reconciliation in many African traditions is a holistic restoration of both human and cosmic reality in a bond of life and friendship. This is the kind of reconciliation that was most successful in South Africa, Rwanda, and Togo. Togo's case was especially interesting because the government and people decided to bring together traditional, Christian, and Islamic rituals and practices in healing the nation and reconnecting the broken strings that held society. This approach to mercy places a strong emphasis on healing the whole community as way of healing both victims and perpetrators of violence. Closure when there are serious crimes like rape and murder is not achieved simply by incarceration or death for the criminal, but through a multilayered process of healing, restoration, forgiveness, and mercy, which must touch the whole community. The theology of mercy, constructed along these lines, will be by its very nature a theology of hope for integration into the body of Christ and for the restoration of lost fortune or loss of friendship with God or with others and the entire cosmic life. In this regard, we can say that a theology of mercy is by its very nature a theology of friendship.

As a theology of hope, a theology of mercy gives people a reason to believe in God and to believe in the church as a healing inn where the Good Samaritan brings the wounded to receive care and to be saved from death with a new life. A theology of mercy must show the merciful face of God to people in a way that gives them hope and confidence to face the future because they realize in faith that their sins are not curses. God is not out to get them, nor is God seeking to punish and destroy them because of ancestral ties and bondages with the past. The fear of ancestral curse in Africa sometimes fills people with deep anxiety and dread, which cripples their hope of a future with God. Unfortunately, in many parts of Africa, it seems that church leaders are often propagating a gospel of fear. In contrast, the illuminative church preaches a saving and healing gospel, which invites people to enter into the mystery of the boundless love and mercy of God. A theology of mercy is grounded in the prophetic words of Baruch (5:5–9), which make intelligible to God's people the unfailing promise of God that in Christ their time of mourning is over. It is a gospel that shows people through concrete pastoral and personal encounters with people's wounds and sins that God is near to them and actively healing and helping them by God's ever-abiding transformative grace. God's mercy is closer to the human being than human sinfulness. This is the Good News that an illuminative church proclaims to many communities, families, churches, and nations through its witness of mercy as a wounded healer.

THE ILLUMINATIVE CHURCH AND HEALING THE WOUNDS OF WAR AND CONFLICTS

In *Evangelii Gaudium* 13 Pope Francis teaches: "Memory is a dimension of our faith which we might call 'deuteronomic,' not unlike the memory of Israel itself. . . . The joy of evangelizing always arises from grateful remembrance: it is a grace which we constantly need to implore. . . . The believer is essentially 'one who remembers.'" Healing of memory is presented as a challenge to reconciliation and the ministry of mercy. Many Africans are all too aware of the divisions in our churches and in our communities and of wounded memories, hearts, minds, bodies, and societies. These have created the kind of crisis that I noted at the beginning of the chapter about CAR. This challenge of reconciliation is one that the church in Africa must take to heart. Since the emergence of independent states in Africa in the 1960s, there has been a consistent pattern of ethnocentric violence, wars, hatred, and genocide in countries such as Nigeria, Rwanda, Burundi, Uganda, Sudan, Liberia, Sierra Leone, Democratic Republic of Congo, Central African Republic, Kenya, and Zimbabwe, among others.

According to the Norway-based Internal Displacement Monitoring Center in its *Grid 2016: Global Report on Internal Displacement*, in 2015, there were 27.8 million displacements in 127 countries caused by conflict, violence, and disasters. In Africa, more people were displaced by conflict (2.2 million) than by natural disasters (1.1 million). What this report indicates is that conflict-related displacement is growing in Africa.[34] In his July 2014 report to the 69th General Assembly of the UN, former UN Secretary-General Ban Ki-moon wrote as follows about the conflict situation in Africa: "While Africa did make significant progress in addressing and resolving its conflicts, the goal of a conflict-free Africa by 2010 was not realized, owing to persistent and new challenges. . . . These include the poor management of diversity, elections-triggered conflict, natural resource-based conflicts and youth unemployment."[35]

The causes of conflict in Africa could be located in the following areas identified by the International Committee of the Red Cross (ICRC):

> Political, ethnic, national or religious grievances and the struggle for access to critical resources remained at the source of many ongoing cycles of armed conflict, and have sparked recent outbreaks of hostilities. A number of conflict trends have become even more acute in the last few years, such as the growing complexity of armed conflicts linked to the fragmentation of armed groups and asymmetric warfare; the regionalization of conflicts; the challenges of decades-long wars; the absence of effective international conflict resolution; and the collapse of national systems. With few exceptions, almost all of the armed conflicts that have occurred in the past few years are the result of the "conflict trap": conflicts engendering conflicts, parties to armed conflict fracturing and multiplying, and new parties intervening in ongoing conflicts. Unresolved tensions that have lasted for years and decades continue to deplete resources and severely erode the social fabric and the means of resilience of affected populations.[36]

On May 27, 2013, the African Union Assembly, at its fiftieth anniversary, reaffirmed its determination to build an integrated, prosperous, and peaceful Africa that is driven and managed by its own citizens. The leaders outlined eight priorities for action toward realizing this continental vision: African identity and renaissance, the struggle against colonialism and the right to self-determination, integration, social and economic development, peace and security, democratic governance, Africa's destiny, and Africa's place in the world. African leaders stated with regard to peace and security a

---

[34]Internal Displacement Monitoring Center, *Grid 2016: Global Report on Internal Displacement*, www.internal-displacement.org.

[35]Ban-Ki Moon, UN Secretary General's Report to 69th General Assembly Session of the UN, *Causes of Conflict and Promotion of Durable Peace and Sustainable Development in Africa* (July 2014), www. un.org.

[36]ICRC, *The Power of Humanity*, Special Report of the 32nd Conference of the International Committee of the Red Cross and Red Crescent, December 8–12, 2015, Geneva, 321C/15/11, 4.5, 5.

shared determination to "end all wars in Africa by 2020" and "achieve the goal of a conflict-free Africa."[37] Whereas at the political and international level, international armed conflict (IAC) and noninternational armed conflict (NIAC) in Africa continue to be challenges in what is becoming a semipermanent humanitarian problem in many parts of Africa, a merciful church in Africa will not only be at the service of internally displaced persons (IDPs), but also should be in the forefront in creating the compassionate hearts who will toe the path of mercy and peace rather than war and violence.

Beyond these political crises is the often ignored internal turmoil in many local churches in Africa. Many African Catholics can point to many wonderful things about their dioceses or parishes. They also will admit rather sadly that there are many internal conflicts in their dioceses and parishes that are often based on ethnic and clannish considerations. In some instances, the abuse or misuse of authority by priests, bishops, religious superiors, and lay members of Christ's faithful in positions of leadership tear apart the body of Christ. In many African churches, one will observe rather painfully that those ethnic and clannish sentiments that challenge the nations of Africa have also eaten deep into the fabric of the church, making it impossible for the church to realize its rich potential. This sad reality often permeates the institutional church more than the ordinary Christians who easily mingle with faithful from other ethnic groups and have no problem chanting songs and offering prayers in ethnic languages other than their own.

In Eastern Nigeria, for more than five years (2012–17) the Catholic diocese of Ahiara had no bishop because an overwhelming majority of the clergy and laity of the diocese refused to accept the bishop nominated and consecrated for the diocese. This situation left deep pain and wounds in the heart of the people and among the hierarchy. It led to the intervention of Pope Francis in the summer of 2017 when he issued a letter threatening to suspend from the priesthood all priests who did not send him a letter of apology and a pledge of loyalty to him and the bishop chosen for the diocese. A similar situation occurred in the Northern Sierra Leonian diocese of Makeni where a bishop was also rejected. Many bishops have been murdered in Cameroon and Kenya and many other African countries because of internal politics in the church and society. Aylward Shorter in a well-documented article chronicles the incidents of ethnocentric, clannish, and racial divisions in the churches in Africa. He argues that the church in Africa is both a victim and an accomplice in ethnocentrism, clannish politics, and divisive prejudice. He gives some examples of these worrying tendencies, like the burning of the episcopal throne of a bishop in Ghana in

---

[37]African Union, "African Leaders Sign Declaration of OAU/AU 50th Anniversary," May 27, 2013, www.au.int.

the 1960s because he was appointed from another ethnic group, the killing of missionaries based on racial or ethnic differences, and the rejection of bishops and priests by people outside their ethnic groups.[38]

The African Synod of 1994 took up the issue of ethnocentric intolerance and division when it offered the church in Africa the image of family as a way of bringing people together, since as Christians we have a new birth and a new identity through our coming forth from the same inner communion and life of the Trinity. The theme was taken up again by the standing committee of the Synod of Episcopal Conferences of Africa and Madagascar (SECAM) in 1996. All these attempts, according to Shorter, were made to help African Christians see their ethnic identity as a blessing and a means of interaction with others, and not an instrument for self or group encapsulation, stereotyping others because of a particular visible identity or for competition. Conscious of the need for a theology of mercy, the Second African Synod chose reconciliation as the central theme for understanding the mission of the church in Africa in the new millennium. The final proposition of that synod states that the goal of reconciliation in Africa should be to overcome crises in churches, African countries, and societies; the restoration of the dignity of individuals, and the openness to dialogue, admission of guilt, forgiveness, restoration of justice, and conscious and courageous attempts to bring healing, lasting peace, and development in the continent (cf. Proposition 5).

I propose that the first path toward reconciliation in Africa and every other faith setting is mercy. This will begin with how we see relationship and how we view the breaches in relationship. A merciful church will be a site for an inner communion of love, acceptance, openness to dialogue, authentic freedom, commitment to truth, transparency, accountability, fairness, and respect, anchored in a common life of mutuality, repentance, reconciliation, communion, unity, sharing, and fellowship. The example of the Good Samaritan who steps down from his donkey, touches the wounds of the battered man on the roadside, places him on his donkey, and brings him to the inn is a good model of how the church in Africa can play a major part in this healing ministry. However, like the wounded healer, the church in Africa must attend to its own internal wounds. In the final section, I propose some of the steps that can be taken by the church in Africa to bring about healing in the church and society. These can be a model for other contexts of faith outside Africa.

---

[38]Aylward Shorter, "The Curse of Ethnocentrism and the Church," in *Ethnicity: Blessing or Curse,* ed. Albert de Jong (Nairobi: Paulines Publications Africa, 1999), 28–40.

MERCIFUL MINISTRY OF A MERCIFUL CHURCH
IN AFRICA: THE ILLUMINATIVE PATH

Mercy is the Good News that the church announces as its constitutive identity and mission. This news is not simply a proclamation or a claim; it is not simply the affirmation of the beauty of our liturgies, the majesty of our hierarchical structure, or the solidity of our church tradition, and the antiquity and apostolicity of our dogma. Mercy is a rule of faith and the end of all the action of the church and the content of the Good News. This Good News is the beauty of our Christian living and witnessing, that is, the authenticity and credibility of the life of the church as Christians and how the institutional church spreads the aroma of Christ. Reconciliation should be the irreducible offer that is open to every member of the church. This demands a radical inclusivity and acceptance of any person who enters the church, and openness and acceptance of those who do not belong to our visible ecclesial community or political or ethnic identity. The good news of reconciliation that African theologies should articulate is how the church offers to the people of God the gift of salvation in Christ, and how this salvation translates into concrete life experience as freedom from sin, liberation from structures of sin that imprison them, and makes possible the experience of the totality of the abundant life that Christ offers to all in his mercy.

A theology of reconciliation in the churches and societies of Africa will demand not only the proclamation of the message of reconciliation by the church in Africa, but more importantly will model the ministry of the church and the lives of Christians around the prophetic acts of the Lord Jesus Christ. The Lord's preaching was not mere words and claims; it was transformational because it was word and witness, proclamation and demonstration, or performance of exemplar acts, which had an immediate impact on the hearers and those who observed his deeds. It was a strong call for conversion of life. It was an invitation through a culture of encounter and a movement toward the other in love and respect without judging them. In the proclamation of Christ, the good news of God's kingdom became operative in the lives of all those who accepted his message. The acceptance of the message of salvation brought reconciliation, redemption, the immediate experience of physical health, wholeness, freedom, peace, and spiritual liberation to those who embraced the message.[39] It is this form of Christ that the illuminative church should aesthetically reenact in daily

---

[39]Theological and Historical Commission for the Great Jubilee of the Year 2000, *Jesus Christ, Word of the Father* (New York: Crossroad, 1997), 65.

commitments to reconciliation, justice, peace, repentance, and a new life of grace and friendship. This form of Christ is mercy, which is so beautiful when it comes directly in contact with the wounds of the people.

How can the church in Africa assume this form of mercy as a wounded healer in such a way that the crucified children of God in Africa can be brought down from the Cross? What concrete steps should be taken in developing a ministry of mercy for the church in Africa?

In order to be a church of mercy for the poor, the social and healing mission of the church in Africa must become central in every parish and diocese. The illuminative church is an invitation to enact the mission of the church not simply in providing spiritual support, but also in strengthening the civil society, creating healthy networks of peace, wealth creation, spaces for healing, support groups, and so on—all of which can help valorize the agency of Africans to safeguard basic human security and cosmic flourishing. This will require strengthening the gains made through small Christian communities. Indeed, the church in Africa is proving in many instances to be an alternative community of hope and a counternarrative of being and inclusion in many circumstances and instances where the fabric of society is weak, unworkable, and frayed. The church in Africa should be a church of the poor, a church with the poor, a church for the poor, and a church that is on the side of the poor so as to give the poor a voice. The church in Africa should also be a church of mercy with a compassionate heart to reach, touch, and heal the wounds in Africa, to wipe the tears of so many women who like Rachel are losing their children to diseases and their husbands to wars, and to bring succor and hope to people who are haunted by ancestral curses and a sad family or personal history, and those who feel alienated and rejected by the church or their communities.

An essential link to this is the search for peace. African Catholic faithful should be given the freedom and be equipped to search for paths to intercultural, interfaith, interethnic, and interdenominational dialogue at all levels without being restricted by manualistic dialogue dictated by church authorities. This way they can use local narratives and models to seek for restoration of broken relationships and weave a workable web of understanding and partnership for poverty eradication, promotion of human rights, especially for minorities, good governance, and the common good. Also to be explored are radical and integral means for healing wounded memories, bruised minds, and hurting spirits as a result of war, land disputes, family feuds, division in the churches among clergy and parishioners and between priests and bishops and in religious houses and in the presbytery, among others.

Another way of living as a merciful church in Africa is through the style of leadership in African Christianity. Pope Francis's message of a new leadership style of humility and simplicity after the example of Jesus Christ is also a paradigm shift which invites African church leaders to a new way of service and pastoral ministry. In a continent where the hierarchical structure of the Catholic Church is sometimes reinforced by African traditional patriarchal norms of power and privilege, Pope Francis's style of leadership reflected in the illuminative church offers a new model of service. This challenges African church leaders to exercise their pastoral leadership in a more participatory, transparent, and inclusive ministry where the laity and especially women participate in the decision-making process in the church. Also to be abandoned is the cult of personality and undue attachment to hierarchical power, which parallel the failed political leadership in some African countries.

Another aspect of this is the dimension of forgiveness from church leaders to those under their leadership. The call by the Second African Synod for an annual day of reconciliation in African churches must be embraced and implemented in all dioceses and parishes throughout Africa as a way of making visible and concrete signs of mercy, forgiveness, and reconciliation. How many priests and seminarians have been condemned to a life of pain, walking in the shadows because their bishops have determined that "they are not good enough" to become priests or have been kept without ministry in the priesthood for years! There are littered in many African churches the wounded souls and damaged minds and spirits of many ex-priests, ex-seminarians, ex-nuns, who have been rejected by the church and who have no other person or organization to turn to because they had committed themselves and their lives permanently to the church. They suffer either because they decided to leave the ministry or the formation house in search of a different calling or because their mistakes led them to being punished through dismissal from the clerical state or religious life.

The church in Africa must find better ways of extending merciful healing and grace to those who are found to have erred and who can no longer be allowed to be in the ministry. There are many such brothers and sisters who are suffering in our churches, and the list is growing every day. Church leaders in Africa must act with mercy toward clerics, religious, and seminarians and not out of vengeful feeling with the intention of inflicting maximum punishment or suffering on people, sometimes without any due process. Church leaders in Africa must be open to accept criticism with joy and gratitude and not charge every disagreement to their judgment or pastoral proposal as rebellion. Indeed, the way we receive criticism and accept with large-heartedness those who do not think as we do or who do not agree with us is a measure of how mercy operates as a divine outreach to those who are hurting and those who are broken or the stranger.

It is also important to note that healing in African families must be central to the ministry of mercy. There are many families that are torn apart by division and family feuds. Parents who are alienated from each other sometimes impose a heavy toll on their children by the way they treat each other. Communities are often broken apart because the constituent family units are not bonded internally. In many cases, issues of land, inheritance, right of patrimony, accusations of witchcraft and sorcery, all create a negative atmosphere in African families and communities. The ministry of mercy must be directed to healing the family tree especially where ancient grudges and hatred continue to hamper the health of families and make it impossible for God's grace to be incarnated at the heart of the family life.

The logic of integration and the logic of mercy called for by Pope Francis in *Amoris Laetitia* (299) must be implemented as a pastoral plan in Africa. How can we integrate people into our churches without making them feel that they are the rejects of society? How can the merciful light of the Lord shine in the darkness and heal the wounds of the people? In many instances, these people abandon their faith or join other churches or simply lapse into new forms of paganism or eclectic spirituality with a high reservoir of anger toward the church and animosity to all things religious. This applies to three areas of concern:

1. Those who are living in polygamous marriages. How are they to be integrated into the church without inflicting pain on the family? The current practice is to ask the polygamous man to choose one of his wives for sacramental marriage and then live with the rest of his wives as brother and sisters. How is mercy being shown to other wives who are not chosen? What kind of message is the church sending to the children of the other wives in that marriage? If the church does not accept divorce, why does it actually promote for practical purposes a form of divorce in a marriage that was contracted properly through African cultural laws and customs? But more important, what image of womanhood is the church promoting if the ultimate decision lies with the man in these circumstances?

2. The second area where mercy is required is the painful condition of divorced and separated Catholics who have remarried. In many African societies, there is a clearly defined process and customary procedure for divorce and remarriage. The norms that govern these are different according to the family traditions of each ethnic group and have some specificity within ethnic groups according to family groups or ancestral ties. The process in most cases goes through four stages: mediation, negotiation, reconciliation, restoration. However, if repeated attempts to bring back the partners to embrace marriage fail, the two families will mutually agree to end the marriage through a formal breaking of the covenant. Once this process has come to the point of divorce, both partners are free to remarry traditionally, and there are clear customary specifications for just settlement with regard

to property, alimony, and support for children. These settlements have their limitations in many instances, but there exist some duties and responsibilities that must be upheld if a marriage ends in divorce.

There are many partners who have gone through this traditional process and have moved on with their lives and/or have gotten a divorce through the courts as well who are not allowed back into the church and are denied communion and excluded from holding any leadership position in the church. Beginning another process through the rigorous, time-consuming, and expensive annulment process in the church seems to many people to be a rejection of the African approach to healing marriages in difficulty or ending one that has been irremediably damaged. The annulment process, as Bishop Gbuji told me in a discussion, is not a positive reality. Rather it is a negative juridical process, which from an African perspective has not offered or added any new or transformative or pastoral dimension to what is already a holistic approach to resolving family disputes and failed marriages in traditional African marriage norms. The integration of the African approaches to resolving marital conflicts—mediation, negotiation, reconciliation, and restoration—and for ending marriages into the legalistic annulment process seems to me to be a prospect that needs to be explored in the development of a ministry of mercy for the church in Africa, especially in the light of the teaching of *Amoris Laetitia*.

In many dioceses in Africa, it is stated clearly that anyone who divorces for any reason whatsoever cannot hold any position in the church and cannot receive the sacraments and if they die, will not receive a church funeral. Divorce is seen then as a scandal rather than an unintended evil that happens sometimes because of the faults of the partners but in most cases as a result of the reality of sin and evil in the world, which impose limitations and imperfections on everything human. People who have experienced divorce in their marriages are already going through deep hurts and carry deep wounds and are in dire need of healing and comfort. Imposing on them punishing restrictions and laying on them a burden of guilt and shame, as is the case in some instances, is a form of practical excommunication from the church, which is opposed to the ministry of mercy. The church in Africa must find a better way of accompanying those in difficult marriage situations to help integrate them into the church and society. A ministry of mercy that accompanies people in their journey through difficult marriage situations helps them to follow the beautiful way of conversion without imposing further spiritual burdens on them or minimizing the needed spiritual discipline for full participation in the sacramental life of the church.

The same attitude of mercy should always apply to children born out of wedlock who are often denied baptism. Mercy should also be shown to parents whose children marry outside the church. Mercy should also be shown to women who have premarital pregnancies and to those who have procured abortion. There are many Africans whom I have met in the pastoral setting who are carrying heavy guilt and painful burdens for violating the church's teaching on birth control and who are having children without the material and emotional support they need to raise these children. The teaching of the church in these areas and the needed pastoral accompaniment must become essential to the ministry of mercy in the church in Africa. This requires a broader conversation in the churches and in families with a view to forming the conscience of the faithful on the teaching of the church and strengthening them to an adult faith. An adult faith is one that equips people with knowledge of the moral law and the truths of faith, and offers them the freedom to be able to make discerning choices with maturity, clarity, and hope in the grace of God and the mercy that accompanies us in our imperfect efforts to please God.

3. The condition of ex-clerics, ex-religious, and ex-seminarians. Some of the saddest Christians whom I have met in many African countries, especially in my home country, Nigeria, are ex-clerics, ex-religious, and former seminarians. The way many candidates for priestly and religious life are usually "expelled" from the seminary or withdrawn from pursuing religious or priestly life leaves much to be desired. In many cases, these ecclesial acts are carried out without mercy and compassion for these brothers and sisters. Most of these young men and women spent over two decades preparing for ordination or religious profession; in many instances they entered the minor seminary and the juniorate in pre-adolescent years and this may be the only life they have known.

Although it is true that those in charge of formation for priestly and religious life must decide the adequacy of a candidate for ministry in the church and that there are instances where people may need to be advised to choose a different vocation, a ministry of mercy demands dealing with people with tenderness, compassion, love, and mercy in helping them choose alternative pathways. When people are withdrawn from the seminary or convent without any form of dialogue or when people are asked to leave without any disclosure to them of the nature of the reports brought against them or given a chance to defend themselves, church authorities create deep wounds in the hearts of people. Such unjust and insensitive approach to withdrawing people from priestly and religious life is contrary to the ministry of mercy. Mercy calls on church leaders and those in formation to look on candidates for priestly and religious life with love and respect and to accompany them at every step on the way. Those who are deemed not suited for religious or clerical life should be accompanied with kindness, love, and solidarity, and they should be supported financially, emotionally, and spiritually in seeking other vocations in life.

The practice where people are *kicked out of the system* in a punitive and judgmental way such that they carry a heavy burden of guilt and shame for the rest of their lives and are considered by the faithful as misfits should be changed. Furthermore, the process of discernment should be between those in formation, church leaders, and the candidates themselves; it should be a dialogue rather than simply a judgment made by authorities to which the candidates have no input.

The same dialogue is called for in our chanceries, presbyteries, convents, and religious houses between bishops, senior priests, superiors, and those under their authority. The constant appeal to authority and insistence on a pyramidal structure of obedience over dialogue and the lack of transparency and honest communication in our dioceses and religious houses is creating a lot of unresolved tension and anger among those who are supposed to lead by example in showing how the church of mercy and love should live in a complex world. The time has come to put an end in African churches to all forms of favoritism, sycophancy, and the use of religious authority to dispense favors to those who fawn on church leaders while isolating and marginalizing those who would wish for a greater conversation and dialogue. Dialogue and mercy go together. Being merciful also requires that we listen to people, especially those who feel alienated or abandoned, so that one can know where people are hurting. It also requires extending the range of choices and perspectives open to the church in every decision, which has to be made for the good of the people of God and the wider society. A church of mercy in Africa can no longer be content with having so many ex-priests, ex-seminarians, and ex-nuns aimlessly wandering the streets of our cities and being treated as outcasts and people who are "cursed by God" while having the doors of our churches, rectories and chanceries slammed in their faces.

THE CHALLENGE OF SEXUAL ABUSE AMONG CLERICS AND RELIGIOUS AND THE SUFFERING OF VICTIMS

This is another area which is a big challenge to the church in Africa in its search for appropriate steps and a ministry of mercy for accompanying those who are suffering. Without belaboring the obvious, those of us who are involved in pastoral and social ministry of the church in Africa know that there are occasions of sexual exploitation and sexual abuse of women, children, and the vulnerable in our churches. There are also incidents of sexual harassment of women religious by priests and bishops. In my work with some Catholic charities in a number of African countries where education is offered to children and orphans, I have heard stories of some of the children in the orphanages being "seeds" (children) from clerics.

The protocol for protection of minors and for protecting vulnerable women, whether laywomen or religious, should be introduced and fully implemented by the church in Africa. There has to be a process and procedure of investigating cases of sexual abuse by clerics and religious, and every attempt must be made to make the work environment in our chanceries and rectories safe for women, children, and those who are poor and marginalized.

The ministry of mercy must also be extended to women who bore children from illicit and hidden relationships with priests and religious. The church must make sufficient provision to support them rather than treat them as "tempters" and impose further burdens of isolation and shame on them in addition to the pain they already bear. The Catholic church in Africa can learn from how the churches in Ireland, Germany, Austria, Switzerland, and others handle the cases of children of priests.

The same attitude of mercy applies to pre-teen pregnancies. Many times the girls are expelled from church schools rather than supported to carry their pregnancy to term in a healthy way while continuing their education. Nothing is usually done to the boys or men who impregnated these girls. The truth is that in many parts of Africa, there are more priests and religious doing heroic work for God against a few bad apples. We cannot tar all with the same brush. However, admitting the limitations in our systems and reforming the systems should be essential to an effective and credible ministry of mercy. In addition, making urgent and honest efforts to bring healing where there are wounds and hurts, and openness and accountability where there is a culture of secrecy or a "holy silence" is essential to a truly illuminative ministry of mercy. The church in Africa is called to embrace a ministry of mercy, especially in the challenging circumstances of sexual abuse; it must bring light where there is darkness in the lives of both victims and perpetrators of sexual abuse, sexual exploitation, and sexual harassment in our churches and in our social ministry. The ministry of healing and mercy demands that our churches should be safe and accepting places for all, especially our vulnerable girls and women whose only hope for protection and succor is from the church.

The ministry of mercy is not only for the church leaders but indeed for the entire church, including the laity in their daily witness to the gospel in their families and workplaces. African religious and political leaders and captains of industries are being challenged by the illuminative church to hoist the banner of righteousness and moral rectitude in order to stamp out corruption in the conduct of state, church, and private businesses in the continent. Mercy calls on people in leadership to be touched by the pain and suffering of the people and thus embrace transformational ethical leadership, which places the good of the people above their selfish interest. Mercy challenges our leaders to be touched by the poverty and hopelessness of so many of our people so that they can be moved to respect the common good, to care for the weak. This way, the lay members of Christ's faithful in Africa will embrace a servant leadership that gives more to the community and society than we want to take from the people, especially through corruption and wasteful spending of the resources of the people, whether in the church or the state.

This chapter developed the praxis of illuminative ecclesiology as a ministry of mercy. It used the paradigm of the Good Samaritan and the image of "the wounded healer" to develop the practices and priorities of a ministry of mercy. It showed the outlines of a theology of mercy grounded in biblical, theological, and historical analyses. Using the experience of the church and society in Africa as its context, it showed how the practices of illuminative ecclesiology can help to heal the wounds in the lives of people and in society. Local processes and traditions of healing, reconciliation, and restorative justice are also encouraged as forms of healing and transformation that can be inculturated in the church. Pope Francis's appeal to the memory of the Uganda martyrs and the powerful witnesses of many African saints, theologians, and church leaders and laity are calls to embrace practices of mercy, which we can find in the long history of the church even in local contexts.

Conclusion

Illuminative Ecclesiology as a Mission and Embrace of the Surprises of God

The story of Stanislas Redepouzou moved so many during Pope Francis's visit to Central African Republic (CAR) in November 2015. On Christmas day of 2013, Stanislas lost his leg in a grenade blast in the city of Bangui. The grenade was planted by the Seleka Muslim militia who for over two years were fighting with the Christian militia, the anti-Baraka. This war has devastated this richly endowed country and left many people dead or homeless. It has also left deep physical, spiritual, and emotional wounds on millions of people in this richly blessed country.

Stanislas lost both parents during this attack. It was reported by the *Tablet* that when Pope Francis saw Stanislas, who was in a wheelchair, he stopped to greet him and entered into a brief but deeply personal dialogue with him. This encounter was so life-changing for Stanislas that he was reported to have said after the encounter with the pope, "I am ready to forgive those who harmed me."[1]

This book has shown that the culture of encounter is a central moment of illuminative ecclesiology. In the encounter with others, especially those who are poor and wounded, the church finds the light of Christ in the world and brings the light of Christ to the world. Pope Francis has emphasized that pastoral life begins with taking into account the diverse situations of people. This accountability, as we have shown, begins by entering into the concrete situations of people's lives and accompanying them through a vulnerable mission in the way of beauty to realizing their vocations in life.[2] All these moments work together in the transformation of individuals, churches, societies, and the world at large. All the moments and praxis of illuminative ecclesiology emerge from this radical openness and move-

---

[1] *The Tablet*, December 5, 2015, 4.
[2] See, for instance, the summary of *Amoris Laetitia* presented at the Vatican and the many references to "account," "experience," and "concrete situation" in that document.

ment from one heart to another. This is not simply a horizontal movement from the pope to a suffering brother or sister; it is a mutually grace-filled self-mediation in which people meet at a deeper level, where our human desire is radically moving toward transcendence through contact with the intimacy of divine love that is always a light in the human heart. This is the import of Pope Francis's references to the church as "a field hospital" and pastors with "the smell of a sheep": genuine Christian encounter is a mutual moment of transformation that is incarnational and aesthetical because it reveals the light of Christ in the mutual subjects of relation and opens the beautiful way of Christian life into the love and light of God in the world. Pope Francis captures this mutuality and intersubjective experience when he recalled his visits to the Palmasola prisons in Bolivia:

> I have a special relationship with people in prisons, deprived of their freedom. I have always been very attached to them, precisely because of my awareness of being a sinner. Every time I go through the gates into a prison to celebrate Mass or for a visit, I always think: Why them and not me? I should be here. I deserve to be here. Their fall could have been mine. I do not feel superior to the people who stand before me. And so I repeat and pray: Why him and not me? It might be shocking, but I derive consolation from Peter: he betrayed Jesus, and even so he was chosen.[3]

Every encounter with another person changes me and changes them. Every encounter with another, when inspired by faith, is an illuminative path to God.

In his writing on humility and pride in the growth of the Christian life, Saint Bernard of Clairvaux offers good spiritual guidance on how one can find the truth, love, mercy, and light of God through entering into a deeper encounter with others, especially those who are rejected by society and those on the margins of spiritual or temporal life. He proposes that the Christian seeks truth in three sites—in our hearts, in our neighbors, and in God as truth itself. Saint Bernard, however, teaches that Christians should first seek the truth in their neighbors before seeking truth in itself so as to appreciate why they should seek truth in itself before seeking it in themselves. The truth, which is God, is not something that is revealed simply as a private gift to the Christian. In Christ, the truth, in Christian understanding, has become a light that can be seen by everyone in the very depth of their being. The truth, which is light in the darkness, is revealed in an intersubjective manner as

---

[3]Pope Francis, *The Name of God Is Mercy: A Conversation with Andrea Tornielli*, trans. Oonagh Stransky (New York: Random House, 2016), 41–43.

part of the ordinary divine-human opportunities that emerge as gifts from God. Saint Bernard teaches as follows: "The merciful are quick to see the truth in their neighbors when they feel for them, and unite themselves with them in love so closely that they feel their good and ills as their own."

Saint Bernard's exhortation is quite profound here. The search for God begins not simply by contemplation of God in the privacy of our homes, rectories, chanceries, and other secret chambers, or even within our souls. It begins as a gift given which is beyond the human subject, but mediated through the community, in particular the community of faith and the community of those who suffer, the poor. Viewed in this light, the encounter with God and the contemplation of God begins "with hearts purified by brotherly love," which leads the Christian to the contemplation of truth in itself through being with a brother or sister and bearing their troubles.[4] What Saint Bernard is saying is that we do often contemplate God in the silence of our hearts, but the encounter with another person is always a spark that leads us into a deeper journey in which God is encountered as truth and light.

Saint Bernard proposes that Christians should enter into the pain of others and that it is through this movement that they can find God. This movement into a deep culture of encounter, is eminently incarnational, Christological, and pneumatic. According to Saint Bernard, the Lord Jesus Christ "learned mercy" by entering into our human condition. In that regard, the church should model itself after the example of the Savior by "learning mercy" through suffering with those who suffer and like the Lord bring the mercy and love of God to people. Just as the rich person may not know what the poor person suffers, and the healthy person does not know what the sick person is going through, Saint Bernard proposes that the church and Christians must "understand from your own experience" what the sick, the poor, and the wretched (as he puts it) are going through by entering into contact with people. This is the only way through which the church can learn the pain in people's lives, and how to walk with them and help them. The spirituality of learning to be with another, of being merciful to the weak, and reaching out to the poor, which emerges from the experience of our own sinfulness and poverty, is a very powerful and recurrent theme in Christianity.

However, Saint Bernard proposes that the path to this moment is humility, which moves the Christian to encounter the other with love and respect. It is then through that encounter that both subjects will come to experience the truth that is the love, life, grace, and light of Christ. The illuminative church must embrace the path of humility in order to enter fully into contact with the world. This way, it can be a healer and an inn where the Good Samaritan

---

[4]Bernard of Clairvaux, *Selected Works* (New York: Paulist Press, 1997), 106.

tenderly brings in the wounded in the battlefield of life. Indeed, everyone loves to be helped when they are wounded, sinful, weak, and down.[5]

My appeal to Saint Bernard's spiritual writing here is to show that the movements and praxis of illuminative ecclesiology are not simply inventions of Pope Francis; rather, they have been features of the life of the church from its beginning. The church today must embrace these practices more vigorously. Accountability, accompaniment, vulnerable mission, and transformative daily actions will continue to be sources of light and inspiration for the future church. They will have to be developed further, appropriated as forms of pastoral practices in our churches. How can these moments and praxis of illuminative ecclesiology be a guide for the church today and into the future?

As I thought of how to conclude this book, two ideas came to my mind about how the praxis of illuminative ecclesiology could be fully implemented in the church beyond Pope Francis. First, I reflect briefly on the patterns that are emerging in Africa, which "surprised Pope Francis" during his visit to Africa and the lessons that they offer to world Catholicism. I will point to these patterns through the ethnographic data collected in Central African Republic in December 2015 following the visit of Pope Francis to that country.

The second conclusion consists of some proposals of an unfinished agenda for Pope Francis, which ought to be continued not only by any future pope, but must be embraced by the clergy, laity, and religious in the churches everywhere today. These are presented as the continuing realization of the fruits of the Second Vatican Council. I had set this agenda in a series of syndicated and commissioned articles on Pope Francis following his election in March 2013. These essays were written for CNN, Canada Television (CTV), and for the documentary *Rome and the Margin* on Al Jazeera TV. Although Pope Francis seems to have met some of the goals on the agenda that I set in these articles and the documentary, I am convinced that meeting these challenges are keys to the future of Catholicism.

THE CHURCH SHOULD NEVER CEASE
TO BE SURPRISED BY GOD

When he said, "Africa surprised me; God always surprises me," Pope Francis summarized his lasting memory of Africa during his flight back to Rome. In one of his book-length interviews, Pope Francis spoke of the "apostolate of ears" as the starting point of a pastoral and sacramental min-

---

[5]Ibid., 108–12.

istry that touches people. This apostolate of listening and deep encounter with people puts the church in contact with "the dramas and difficulties" in people's lives.[6] People can be surprised when they allow themselves to be touched by beauty or the sense of awe even in the midst of chaos and suffering. Light always shines in every genuine encounter between people because God is present in Christ as light, grace, and love in such encounters. The crisis of our times in our churches and in the world could be said to arise from the inability of people to see beauty in themselves and in others. This is why we want to hide in our own self-constructed walls and why God has been exiled sometimes even in the life of the church. People are no longer surprised by reality and mystery because of what Pope Francis calls "the degradation of awe." As he puts it, "At times I have surprised myself by thinking that a few very rigid people would do well to slip a little, so that they could remember that they are sinners and thus meet Jesus."[7]

This is a particularly important point in realizing the praxis of illuminative ecclesiology because the *degradation of awe* arises often as a result of the attitude of pride and what Pope Francis calls "a kind of hypocrisy . . . a formal adherence to the law that hides very deep wounds," which can afflict clerics, theologians, and those in positions of authority because they make of their positions and their persons an end in themselves.[8] This inability to be surprised extinguishes the light of the Holy Spirit in both subjects of encounter:

> When a person feels a little more secure, he begins to appropriate faculties which are not his own, but which are the Lord's. The awe seems to fade, and this is the basis for clericalism or for the conduct of people who feel pure. What then prevails is a formal adherence to rules and to mental schemes. When awe wears out, we think we can do everything alone, that we are the protagonists. And if that person is a minister of God, he ends up believing that he is separate from the people, that he owns the doctrine, that he owns power, and he closes himself off from God's surprises.[9]

Pope Francis could be called the pope of surprises. The event leading up to his election, the surprising resignation of Pope Benedict XVI, was in itself one of the most earth-shattering events in modern Catholicism because he was the first pope to resign voluntarily from office since Pope Celestine in

---

[6]Pope Francis, *Name of God Is Mercy,* 17.
[7]Ibid., 70.
[8]Ibid., 68.
[9]Ibid., 69.

1294 (Pope Gregory XII was forced to resign by the Council of Constance in 1415 to end the Western Schism).[10] But beyond the surprises of the first pope emeritus in modern Catholic history, and the surprise of the unknown cardinal from Argentina, are the new narratives of God's great deeds happening through the ministry of a pope who lives on one lung, and suffers greatly as a result of sciatica. Indeed, the words of scripture are proving right in the life of Pope Francis about God lifting the lowly and bringing the mighty down: here is a man who never finished his doctoral studies in Germany and who may not fit into the traditional category of a theologian, but whose words and deeds have given birth to the healthiest, most vibrant, and open theological and pastoral conversations in Catholicism since the end of Vatican II. The impact of his theological and spiritual insights is giving birth to a new intellectual tradition in Catholicism characterized by dialogue, vibrant debates, and a courageous openness to history and cultural process in the shaping of belief and practices in the church. He has written a new chapter in the history of Catholicism.

In addition, through the surprising acts of his papacy and his unscripted outreach to the margins, he has humanized the papacy and in doing so reconnected the papacy to the church and to the world in an intimate manner. He has surprised people and the world with his direct and experiential discourses and unfiltered acts and interviews, which touch people more profoundly by their cryptic manner and their compelling images.

The pope was surprised by what he saw in Africa, but Africans too were surprised by this pope who visits the slums, kisses people, and allows himself to be kissed; a pope who rides in the same car with a Muslim Imam and who calls slum dwellers his neighbors. Pope Francis was surprised with the joy and celebratory atmosphere that he experienced in Africa, even among the poor, those "with empty stomachs," as the pope recalled in this interview. Many Africans who came in the millions to see the pope were touched by the joy, love, and tenderness with which he reached out to the people and the sites he visited where the poor and the vulnerable live. Pope Francis extolled Africa as a continent of hope and Bangui, the capital of Central African Republic, as the "spiritual capital of the world." Francis had a clear message to all: "Africa is a martyr of exploitation"; "Africa is a victim of other powers." For Pope Francis, Africa is "perhaps the world's richest continent," "Africa is a land of hope."[11]

The words of Pope Francis evoke happy memories of similar sentiments

---

[10]On the reasons for his resignation, see Benedict XVI, *Last Testament: In His Own Words*, with Peter Seewald, trans. Jacob Phillips (London: Bloomsbury Continuum, 2016), 15–26.

[11]Rome Reports, "Full Text of the Pope's Press Conference Aboard the Papal Plane," November 30, 2015, www.romereports.com.

of hope and joy expressed about Africa by popes before Francis. All of them have spoken of the beauty of Africa and the depth of African culture and spirituality and how one is touched by the way Africans celebrate life no matter the difficulties they face. Pope Paul VI in his first visit to Africa in 1969 extolled the spirituality and closeness of Africans to God and to a sense of community; he called on Africans to have "an African Christianity."[12]

The messages of hope from Pope Francis and the voices of hope about Africa from many other popes, theologians, seers, sages, African ancestors, and historians offer many African Christians the courage to embrace the mission of God in Africa with renewed optimism. This is because despite the challenging circumstances of the times, God's pleasant surprises are emerging in the new narratives of faith and belonging in a new Africa touched daily by the hand of God through Christian witnessing. These have also given rise to a new praxis of social transformation through the churches and local communities, which through their grassroots social solidarity are providing alternative sites of hope. These new moments are counterhegemonic and countercultural because they are driven by local processes and actual faith practices that are conveyor belts for bringing hope and healing to people. The challenge here is to embrace a praxis of accompaniment through concrete pastoral and theological creativity and fidelity. This emerges as an engagement with, and a response to, the actual faith of people in the wider context of the search for a valid Christian narrative for human and cosmic flourishing.

Everyone who visits Africa is usually touched like Pope Francis by the exponential growth in the number of African Christians and the large crowds of people who fill stadiums, churches, and public spaces to worship God. I have led many mission trips of American students, pastors, and professors. I have also taken people to different African countries for safaris or conferences, and the sentiments that people express about Africa surprise me: joy, appreciation for the hospitality of Africans, and the enchantment with the magical passion for life and celebration among many African peoples and ethnic nationalities. People are also surprised to see that the faith in Africa is growing and that the liturgy is filled with joy, dancing, and communal participation.

Pope Francis was also surprised, he observed, with the large crowds he saw in Africa and the exponential growth of the Christian faith in this beautiful continent. Pope Francis saw that African Catholicism is rising; that Africans take the Christian faith seriously and hold on to traditional values on family, community, and hospitality. Some people might argue that the explosion in the number of Catholics in Africa is consistent with the growth

---

[12]Ibid.

in African population and the so-called anti–population control policy of the Catholic Church in Africa; some may argue that in an environment of severe social strain in the socioeconomic and political networks, religious faith in Africa becomes a very attractive and enchanting reality, offering false hope for the oppressed and marginalized.

These arguments minimize the force and verve of the religiocultural world of Africans that forms the bedrock of their lives and the lens through which they see reality. Africans did not become deeply religious because of Christianity; Africans are deeply Christian because they are deeply religious. Christianity only offered Africans a new narrative and a new language for expressing their deep religiosity through their encounter with the person of Jesus Christ, the African Ancestor. African religiosity has an intrinsic logic in the firm belief among Africans that the whole of life is a network of connections and vital force, which works together in a spiritual chain to bring about human and cosmic flourishing. A renewed and transformed Catholicism could become a strong cultural and spiritual influence in Africa's continuing search for answers to the challenges of poverty, disease, ethnic and religious conflicts, wars, political and economic problems, radical Islamic fundamentalism, and how to mitigate the effects of climate change, and natural disasters. But above all, Africa's emerging voice in world Catholicism will act as a counterweight to the secularizing and de-Christianizing currents from the West, while proving to be once again the new homeland for Christ, where the fullness of the gospel message of love and mercy for the poor will continue to resound as a force for good. But there is a fundamental shift that needs to be made in Africa and in theological education not only in Africa but in worldwide Catholicism to help create the ground for a richer and deeper encounter with the diverse contexts of people in a changing world. It is the shift from predictable and unchanging patterns, systems, and structures, to leaving a space in our church life and structures for God to surprise us and enable us to move beyond our limited ecclesial horizon of meaning to the infinite horizon of God.

The metaphor of the surprises of God is a key for interpreting the dynamics of the culture of encounter. It is also an inspiration for enacting the praxis of illuminative ecclesiology in the local and universal contexts of church and society. The Holy Spirit, as the Lord promised, will lead the church to the fullness of all truth. This promise means that the Holy Spirit reveals to us the hidden light and beauty in reality and in history, which we often do not see clearly or which in our own prejudice, biases, and limitations we sometimes fail to recognize. I think that what Pope Francis has accomplished is to inspire in the church a missionary impetus for meeting the challenges and opportunities of today. These will require a way of being church that sees the world as filled with light and beauty even when it is surrounded by darkness and sad realities. Sin, violence, poverty, intolerance, racism, sexism, and all forms of exclusionary practices that wound the human spirit are to be engaged because these are false ends and practices that emerge from hearts that do not see clearly the beauty and light in themselves and in the world and in the other. The culture of encounter is an invitation to become open to the surprises of the Spirit. This inspires an inclusive and open "missionary impulse," which will require "the renewal of structures," and "pastoral conversion" in order to bring light to a world that is wounded and troubled by a "culture of indifference" (*EG*, 27). As Stephen Bevans proposes, "Pope Francis's call for the church to understand itself as a 'community of missionary disciples' seems to require a thorough rethinking of ecclesiology in the light of missiology."[13]

We can apply this metaphor of surprises which Pope Francis felt about Africa as an extended metaphor for what goes on in the world today and how a mission-oriented church can meet the world. Africa is a misunderstood continent. The images of Africa that many people outside Africa harbor are often negative, at least from my own personal experience—images of suffering Africa, poor Africa, conflict-ridden Africa, disease-infested Africa, violent Africa, corrupt Africa, and so on. Even in church circles, these negative images are quite predominant even with regard to the churches in Africa. The new voices and realities that are emerging in the African churches are sometimes perceived negatively as syncretistic, conservative, out of touch, and weird. Africa, like many other parts of the world, has its own problems, but Africa cannot be reduced to a single narrative.

Whenever I take people to Africa, especially first-time visitors, I notice the sense of anxiety and inner tension. This happens even with scholars and historians who have studied Africa, but who have never visited the continent before. There is a normal anxiety that comes when you are uncertain about what you will see when you visit a new place or a new continent or when we encounter a new culture. However the terror that I see in some of the people I take to Africa for the first time is a unique feeling. The good news is that at the end of the visit they always come back to Europe or North America filled with joy and surprised by the African magic. They capture "the African bug" and turn from Afro-pessimists to Afro-optimists. On one particular occasion, at the departure lounge at the airport in Lagos, almost all the American students I took to Nigeria were crying as they said goodbye to their new Nigerian friends. They told me that they never felt this kind of joy and communal participation and hospitality before. At first, there were

---

[13]Stephen Bevans, "Beyond the New Evangelization: Toward a Missionary Ecclesiology for the Twenty-First Century," in *A Church with Open Doors: Catholic Ecclesiology for the Third Millennium*, ed. Richard Gaillardetz and Edward Hahnenberg (Collegeville, MN: Liturgical Press, 2015), 12.

worries, anxiety, and even fear of going to Nigeria because of many false narratives and images they had been given about Africa and particularly about Nigeria—I remember even a doctor withdrawing from one of the trips because his wife threatened to divorce him if he went because she was certain that the man was going to die. Thus, if the man didn't love his life and his family enough, she reasoned, then it was better to end the marriage. But at the end, when those who went told their stories, the doctor and his wife decided to make the trip the next year!

What happens to the African visitor after a trip to an African country is that through a deeper culture of encounter with the world of Africans they are transformed. They become partners with Africans; they become friends and fellow travelers; and through a certain cultural immersion and mutual gift exchange a new level of meaning and transformation takes place. They realize that some of their fears and prejudices are unfounded and that Africa is more than a single story. This is exactly the kind of mission-oriented momentum which is set off when the church meets people deeply and deploys the praxis of illuminative ecclesiology. The church should be the site where transformative encounters take place, which can help bring the world together and create a space for grace, salvation, and the realization of God's dream of a world united in love.

God indeed does surprise us when we encounter other people at a deeper level. There are many people who are left outside our church doors, many people who are not allowed into our countries, many people who are treated as rejects of society and as outcasts because of their race, color, religion, sex, gender, sexuality, and spiritual condition. There are many people who are hurting in our churches and in our world. There are many people who are misunderstood, and some others whom we run away from because we think they are unworthy of our company. The world today is in dire need of the healing of relationships and rebuilding of deeper connections among peoples, cultures, nations, and religions. There is also the need to heal the polarization of society along dialectically defined ideological positions and settled prejudices and some apocalyptic versions of history, which churn out all forms of isolationist tendencies in nations. Churches and religious groups also may promote through their teachings, beliefs, and practices a totalizing and exclusionary ethos of salvation that waters the grounds for fundamentalism, intolerance, and catastrophic narratives of history and eschatology. The division in our churches over the canons of truth and the contestations over moral questions on sex, marriage, sexuality, women, celibacy, authority, and the worthy and unworthy reception of sacraments have left deep fissures in the body of the church. But God does surprise us through these divisions, and the light continues to shine through them as people genuinely seek the path of peace, good order, and the values that make for a better society and for integral salvation.

Pope Francis is challenging the church today to embrace the culture of encounter, to take account of everyone and include everyone, and to accompany everyone with a vulnerable mission so as to transform the lives of individuals and the life of the church. "An evangelizing community gets involved by word and deed in people's daily lives; it bridges distances, it is willing to abase itself if necessary, and it embraces human life, touching the suffering flesh of Christ in others. Evangelizers thus take on the 'smell of the sheep' and the sheep are willing to hear their voice" (*EG*, 24). The church's missionary transformation as *Evangelii Gaudium* presents it is not only *ad extra* (transforming the world), but also *ad intra* (transforming the church) through "a resolute process of discernment, purification and reform" (*EG*, 30). This missionary impulse in the light of the illuminative ecclesiology in Pope Francis has two dimensions, according to Richard Gaillardetz: "First, the church must be willing to encounter the world on its own turf, with humility and openness. Second, the missionary encounter must be, in the end, an encounter with Christ."[14] The creation of communities of love, joy, and mercy will require also not being afraid to encounter people or to enter into dialogue; it will require an openness to everyone as a source of light and a willingness to share the light of faith. In this regard, church ministers should go out to meet people because they cannot wait in the comfort of chanceries and rectories for those who are tired and weary from life's journey. The church, as a result, "does not wait for the wounded to knock on her doors, she looks for them on the streets, she gathers them in, she embraces them, she takes care of them, she makes them feel loved."[15]

The openness to the surprises of the Holy Spirit is the path to seeing the light in the world and in the church. It should govern the proclamation and witnessing in every aspect of the life of the church and Christians so that the people of God can see the light of God in every aspect of the ecclesial life, and the church can see the people of God—including those who are members of the church and those who are not baptized—as bearers of a light which might be hidden by their personal situations. The most important and effective way of bringing this openness about in the church is through prayer and the transformation of the language of our preaching, theologies, and teaching.

Vatican Council II first promulgated the constitution on divine worship,

---

[14]Richard R. Gaillardetz, *An Unfinished Council: Vatican II, Pope Francis, and the Renewal of Catholicism* (Collegeville, MN: Liturgical Press, 2015), 117.

[15]Pope Francis, *Name of God Is Mercy*, 6.

Sacrosanctum Concilium, because the council fathers wanted to recognize the centrality of God in the life of the church and in its activities in the world. There is a strong debate in the church today, as well as in the past, about too much centralization of power in Rome, which Pope Francis says "complicates the church's life and her missionary outreach" (*EG,* 32). However, the greatest deficit of centralization in the church is that it marginalizes Jesus Christ, whose life and salvific work gives form and life to the church through the Holy Spirit. As Louis Dupré writes, the center of the spiritual life is God, and the human person or the church can only be centers of things if they function as *copula mundi,* which always unites and points creation to the divine center because "spiritual life gains a new complexity by this greater concern with creation. Next to the turn inward to the divine center, the devout mind also moves out to the created periphery in a breathing-like rhythm of expansion and contraction."[16]

Vatican II made this important shift, and began a process of locating the heart of the church not in Rome, or the West, but where two or more are gathered in the Lord's name as the people of God. There is the need for churches both in local and global contexts to return to the source of renewal, the Holy Spirit, and place Jesus at the center again in order to be open to the surprises of God, which go beyond our plans and strategies. Our churches are often too preoccupied with debates, capital campaigns, and structural edification rather than with leading the people of God deeper into the mysteries of God's life so that they can become enraptured in the beautiful light of faith that God brings to the willing heart. In a Christological and pneumatic framework, every other thing is marginal or peripheral because they are all moving to Christ and they become central to the extent that they are connected and woven thoroughly with the life of Christ and the unction of the Holy Spirit.

The other proposal is about the language of discourse in churches. How we communicate to people can either heal or destroy. As Proverbs 15:4 says, "The soothing tongue is a tree of life, but a perverse tongue crushes the spirit." Similar sentiments are expressed in Colossians 4:6: "Let your conversations always be full of grace, seasoned with salt so that you may know how to answer everyone." The scriptures are filled with admonitions about the power of language and how much good or harm we can cause by the way we speak to people or present our message. In many business settings, "messaging" or "packaging" has become an essential part of the strategy for gaining and retaining clients. We know in recent history how the utterances of a pope or president or priest triggered off different crises

---

[16]Louis Dupré, introduction to *Christian Spirituality: Post-Reformation and Modern,* ed. Louis Dupré and Don E. Saliers (New York: Crossroad, 1989), vii.

and violence in some parts of the world. It is natural that human beings are moved by words for good or ill. One of the lasting examples of Pope Francis is how he has used simple and powerful images to pierce the stubborn hearts of a world that has grown tired sometimes of a Good News packaged in arrogant and condescending platitudes and claims.

In *Evangelii Gaudium*, Pope Francis devotes a section to preaching and communication. Even though he was writing with a specific focus on preaching, I propose that this can apply to all aspects of the life and communication of an illuminative church. He writes that language is "a kind of music which inspires encouragement, strength and enthusiasm" (*EG*, 139). He proposes further that people's hearts are profoundly touched when a discourse emerges from their context, speaks to their problems, and touches the heart of the matter for them. This is so because they feel that the preacher not only knows what to say about people's condition, but also because the preacher knows the best way to say it (*EG*, 139). Furthermore, Pope Francis recommends that the warmth of one's voice, one's facial expression, the manner of one's speaking, the joy in one's gestures, and one's genuineness through speech are all important in touching people profoundly and triggering a movement to transformation and light in their hearts and in their lives.

Pope Francis's vision of language is the communication of the fullness of revelation by people who speak from a heart filled with fire and "reverence for the truth" (*EG*, 144, 146). Language is not only the communication of truth, but it goes hand in hand with beauty and goodness, through which the church "communicates the beauty of the images used by the Lord to encourage the practice of good" (*EG*, 142). He also speaks of a communication of love that must see beyond the weaknesses and failings of people in order to bring people hope and joy (*EG*, 141; 59). All these aspects of language, according to Pope Francis, were modeled for us by the Lord Jesus:

> By his words our Lord won over the hearts of people; they came to hear him from all parts (cf. Mk 1:45); they were amazed at his teaching (cf. Mk 6:2), and they sensed that he spoke to them as one with authority (cf. Mk 1:27). By their words the apostles, whom Christ established "to be with him and to be sent out to preach" (Mk 3:14), brought all nations to the bosom of the church (cf. Mt 16:14-20). (*EG* 136)

We cannot emphasize enough how important it is that our language become an illuminative path that leads people to beauty in an illuminative church.

Most people I see who have left the practice of faith do so not because they have lost the hunger for God or because they thought less of Jesus Christ or found no meaning in what the Lord does or what the church represents. They leave the church because they do not feel connected to the church, nor do they feel that the church connects them to God and to other people as a community of love, compassion, mercy, and support.[17] They also leave the church in most cases because besides the occasional scandals in our churches, which erode the church's credibility, people sometimes find our churches cold and unfriendly, bureaucratic and too formal and rigid. I have met so many people at funerals or weddings who told me that they left the church because the church was not there for them when they were going through some difficult times in their lives or because a priest said some hurtful words to them. Many people in their sickness or when they face death in the family are hurting deeply, and the kind of language we use to speak to them can help them see the light in the church and the light in their souls.

One of the announcements that I find very troubling in my home country, Nigeria, is the one made before Holy Communion at funeral and wedding Masses where many non-Catholics are usually in attendance. The announcement is often loaded with the language of exclusion, Catholic triumphalism, and judgment when the announcer says "solemnly" that only Catholics in a state of grace may come forward for communion. This announcement harms ecumenical relationship and creates suppurating wounds in the hearts of those Catholics who are told that they should not come forward to receive Holy Communion. This is one example out of many where our communication of the beliefs and practices of the Roman Catholic Church does not speak of love and friendship or show respect and consideration for the things that hold the worldwide churches and God's people together. People are being pushed away from our churches through the languages of power, condemnation, judgmental language, aggressive language, and threatening and often cursing and abusive languages, which they hear from the pulpit or in the teaching and writings of church leaders, activists, scholars, and in some publications and sites operated by some church groups.

At the time of writing this book, a bishop in Illinois issued a decree in which among others he outlawed giving burial to any Catholic who died while living in a gay marriage. A gay friend of mine told me with a heavy heart, "Even murderers are given Christian burial, so this bishop tells me that as a gay Catholic I am worse than a murderer. I will not belong to this church." I prayed and hoped that he does not see this bishop as the face of an open and accepting church, which sees the light of Christ in his life. The decree of this bishop was filled with tasteless and condemnatory languages,

---

[17] Albert L. Winseman, *Growing an Engaged Church: How to Stop "Doing Church" and Start Being the Church Again* (New York: Gallup Press, 2007), 24–32.

reinforcing some of the sad realities of our language and attitudes to those whom we consider public sinners. James Martin noted how harmful this kind of attitude could be in his encounter with LGBTQ people. According to him, "They have shared stories with me about being insulted, slandered, excluded, rejected, and even fired" and that the attitude of most people in the church toward them sometimes lacks respect, sensitivity, and compassion.[18]

Pope Francis has made significant shifts in the use of language by moving away from the high-sounding baroque and medieval titles, attires, and appurtenances of power of the papacy. He refers to himself simply as the bishop of Rome. The pomp and pageantry that surround our liturgies, the titles we have assumed and retained of our church officials from the time of Constantine sometimes could speak the language of power rather than that of the humble man of Galilee. The question I always ask myself: Does the Church of Rome still need these outdated titles in order to be an effective instrument in God's hand in our present age?

In addition, the manner of the exercise of authority and how those in authority present themselves and carry themselves before the people can also speak the language of a hierarchy of exclusion and power rather than a hierarchy of service and love. There has to be a conscious movement in our churches to speak a new language in word and being that carries with it the force of love. As Gary Chapman noted, everyone has a love tank which is the desire in every human heart longing to be loved, accepted, and affirmed. We all want our love tanks to be filled with words and acts of love—words that affirm and encourage, words that flow from a humble and caring heart. People's love tanks are particularly low when they feel excluded, unwanted, unloved, and condemned. Chapman proposes the use of words of affirmation as a starting point for conveying to people a sense that they are loved. What he proposes for married couples seems to me very important for helping churches embrace a language of affirmation in our churches, which invites people into different levels of relationships, encounters, and other moments for an illuminative church.[19]

When the Holy Spirit came upon the early church at Pentecost, people received the gifts of tongues and spoke in various languages, and everyone understood each other. Pentecost was the first surprise of the Holy Spirit. In our day, I am convinced that we need that same Holy Spirit to inspire the churches today so that we can speak the language of love, mercy, hope, dialogue, and friendship to people, especially those who are far away from

---

[18]James Martin, *Building a Bridge: How the Catholic Church and the LGBT Community Can Enter into a Relationship of Respect, Compassion, and Sensitivity* (New York: Harper Collins, 2017), 6.

[19]Gary Chapman, *The Five Love Languages: The Secret to Love That Lasts* (Chicago: Northfield, 2010), 37–52.

God. This is the language that the world can hear in order to love and believe in God again. Language is always the illuminative path, which will lead people to the truth of God and lead a poor and merciful church to the light in the world and in the hearts of those who are wounded, weak, and often outside our church doors.

THE CHURCH IN A WORLD OF CONFLICT

In chapter 5, I addressed the challenges that the churches in Africa face with reconciliation and conflict resolution. However, these challenges are not peculiar to Africa. The world is becoming more complex, and the nature of conflicts globally has assumed the complexity of the social reality of the globe. What it means is that the church must give an account of the many people who are being killed in the world today, and accompany with love the refugees, migrants, and all God's people who are displaced by war, natural disaster, and poverty. The church must also become a stronger advocate and instrument of nonviolence and peaceful resolution of conflict. The church must also look herself in the mirror in order to remove instances in history where her teaching and practices and her way of life promotes violence and social tension. Pope Francis has been active in dousing many fires globally and in responding to all the natural and increasing humanitarian disasters in the world. The illuminative church must attend to these conflict situations and the condition of the homeless migrants and refugees. This way, it can show the face of God to people who are caught up in these conflicts and thus bring to God the wounded faces of people who are suffering because of these conflicts. Indeed, the future church must become an expert in conflict resolution especially in the era of world Christianity.[20]

Pope Francis has been active in helping to resolve conflicts and wars in the world. He was, for instance, instrumental in bringing about the diplomatic thaw between the United States and Cuba. He personally wrote a letter to the church and people of the Democratic Republic of Congo (DRC) appealing to them to walk the path of national reconciliation. He has been personally involved in encouraging the bishops' conference of DRC (CENCO) to play a direct role in mediating between the government and the opposition in finding the path to constitutional democracy and peaceful society. In 2016, Pope Francis personally reached out to the bishops of South Sudan and was actively involved in seeking paths toward national reconciliation and in providing humanitarian aid to so many people who were suffering following

---

[20]Robert J. Schreiter, *The New Catholicity: Theology between the Global and the Local* (Maryknoll, NY: Orbis Books, 2004), 52–59.

the declaration of famine in that country early in 2017. He also personally apologized in 2017 to the president of Rwanda, Paul Kagame, over the role of the church in the Rwandan genocide. According to the Vatican, during the audience with President Kagame, Pope Francis "expressed the desire that this humble recognition of the failings of that period, which unfortunately disfigured the face of the church, may contribute to a 'purification of memory' and may promote, in hope and renewed trust, a future of peace."[21]

However, the most significant impact of Pope Francis in resolving conflicts and helping to bring healing to people wounded by hatred and division in Africa was his visit to Bangui, capital of Central African Republic (CAR). His visit, words, and deeds began the definitive search for national reconciliation because people like Stanislas, whom we met at the beginning of this concluding chapter, moved beyond their hurts and pains to seek the path of peace and reconciliation together with those who had harmed them. I asked one of our local agents in Bangui to ask the people this question: What do you think about Pope Francis and what has he brought to Africa through his visit? The response people gave showed again the importance of being present in the chaos of other people's lives and how the culture of encounter inspires a movement that can bring about a new reality in the lives of people.

A twenty-six-year-old male cab driver who is a Protestant said this of Pope Francis:

> Before his visit to Bangui, we could not see eye to eye with each other especially we Christians and Muslims, and also Protestants and Catholics, but since he came and preached his message of love and reconciliation, relationships have improved. We Christians now visit the Muslim-populated areas of Bangui and the Muslims come here too. The other day, we had a friendly soccer match between Christians and Muslims.[22]

One of the women in the co-operative movement which I co-founded in Bangui, the Society for Solidarity and Hope (ESCA), spoke of the encounter which an ex-Christian militiaman recounted to her. On the last day of his visit to Central African Republic, the pope officiated at a Mass at the stadium in Bangui. This former Christian militiaman saw a Muslim who was heading toward the stadium for Mass and confronted him in these words, "This Mass is for Catholics alone; you should not come here because you

---

[21]Harriet Sherwood, "Pope Francis Asks for Forgiveness for Church's Role in Rwanda Genocide," *Guardian*, March 20, 1917, www.theguardian.com.

[22]Interview conducted January 24, 2017.

do not belong." What changed the former Christian militiaman's mind and attitude was the response from this Muslim who said, "The pope has invited all of us without any conditions—Christians and Muslims, even those who follow the religion of our ancestors. If you like you can kill me, but I am going to the stadium." The Christian fighter and the Muslim brother began to cry and embraced each other and together went to the stadium to see the pope. It was reported that at the end of this Mass as the pope drove round the stadium greeting people and waving, the people broke out into a spontaneous song saying, "It is over; the war is over."

One of the most enduring images, which many of the people interviewed spoke about, was the sight of the pope riding with the Chief Imam of Bangui in the popemobile after praying together with him in the Koudougou mosque. A sixty-five-year-old Catholic woman spoke in these words of that gesture:

> The pope brought peace to CAR. He came here even though France and all the members of the international community did not want him to come for security reasons. He has shown us by his attitude toward Muslims, the poor, and the marginalized when he was here that we are all children of one God. We are now living in peace and even though this peace is fragile, I am praying to God that the peace of Pope Francis will stay with us.[23]

These sentiments were echoed by Father Giulio Albanese, an Italian journalist and missionary of the Comboni Mission, who spoke of the two most important aspects of the pope's visit. The first was that for Pope Francis, visiting the CAR, one of the poorest countries in Africa, was a way of preaching the Good News to the poor. According to Albanese, "At the moment no one cares about Central African Republic, even our politicians don't know where Bangui is on a map. Pope Francis has given voice to the voiceless. Second, he has showed himself as the only world leader who is really trying to deal with people's problems at a global stage."[24] The outreach to the poor in Bangui was shown in a dramatic way when Pope Francis, without minding his own personal safety, visited the Our Savior Refugee camp and walked there, covering several meters on foot, which reminded me of his silent walk at the concentration camp in Auschwitz.

Accompaniment must involve walking with people, and breaking the physical distance between those who suffer and the church. This is particularly evident in many societies where the sign of the separation between the poor and the rich is the presence of gated communities and walls

---

[23] Oral interview at Bangui, December 23, 2016.
[24] *Tablet*, December 5, 2015, 5.

that protect the rich and powerful. The poor are left without any defenses; people talk about them and for them, but no one meets them in their pain. The same is true for people in situations of war. I recall the sad stories told by my father while I was growing up of over a million Igbo people who died in the war in Nigeria between 1967 and 1970. These deaths occurred because the international community did not care; no one wanted to step into the chaos of the then Eastern Nigeria or the Republic of Biafra as it was called at that time. The blockade of the enclave led to more than a million deaths. When I see the images from Syria, South Sudan, Somalia, and Libya, I recall the pain of my own childhood: the mass graves, the hordes of men and ex-soldiers who were left begging on the streets and highways with untreated PTSD and with no food or home, the refugee camps, and the endless tales of suffering and pain which all people suffered after the blockade of Biafra in my homeland. When people are suffering, one of the most painful things for them is when all they see around them are walls and barbed wire, which make them feel that no one cares and that they are alone with no escape route.

In visiting the war zones of this world, Pope Francis is showing how the church of the future must play an active role in the lives of people, especially those who are on the margins. It is by being present with people that they can see the light of Christ in the church, and through such encounters the church can see the light of Christ in the midst of human suffering. This approach of stepping into the chaos of people's lives and encountering them in their places of pain and isolation has been continued by the forty-nine-year-old Cardinal Nzapalainga, who has been called one of the three saints of Bangui. He merited this title because of his work in bringing about peace in the country and his unassuming outreach to the poor, marginalized, and suffering people in the country. When he became the first person created a cardinal in his country, he saw this recognition as Pope Francis's way of showing that the people in this remote part of Africa matter to God despite their history and economic situation. The first thing he did upon his return from Rome, after the ceremony at which he was created cardinal, was to tour the whole country meeting with warring factions, those in social ministry in churches, and ecumenical groups in order to find the path to peace, reconciliation, justice, development, and healing.

Another area where illuminative ecclesiology can offer a strong praxis for inclusion in the world is the challenge of holding in balance the tension between the indigenous and the pilgrim principle, the local and the universal church, innovation and tradition. This particularly pertains to the internal conflicts in the church. In the face of cultural pluralism and complex and contending narratives of modernity, the church must realize that it is no longer business as usual. In an era of world Christianity, the church must become more inclusive and more open to a hermeneutic of multiplicity, which I addressed in chapter 4. Many internal conflicts in the churches of the Global South, such as Africa, on issues about appointment of bishops, cultural practices, syncretism, Pentecostal and evangelical interpretations of beliefs and practices, liturgical creativity and innovation, authority, and other issues may no longer be solved through papal decrees and threats of punishment. Local churches must be given the freedom to seek local solutions to their own local issues because there are many issues emerging in African Christianity today that were not fully addressed in the canon law or the Catechism of the Catholic Church.

Pope Francis has given the church some examples of how to meet this challenge of pilgrim and indigenous principles. In meeting these often contending tendencies, Pope Francis wishes that our church should become a bright light, a listening and caring mother, who wishes to be with her children in their sites of pain and conflict in order to learn with them and pray with them in the search for the illuminative path to peace. Catholicism can help heal conflicts in its inner life and in the world not simply because of the solidity of its structures and laws or the beauty of its liturgies, but because it is playing an active part in dialogue. Such dialogues at all levels will first help people discern the horizons of differences and then work hard to bridge the gap created by divisions, historical injustices, and structural violence, which all generate poverty, conflict, and tension, as I showed in chapter 5. However, every solution begins with meeting people in a respectful and reverential manner through a culture of encounter.

At root here is the pull between the indigenous principle and the pilgrim principle, how we embrace the realities around us and how we assimilate the values and realities beyond us and from outside of us. The Christian is aware of a pilgrim principle that underlies our Christian life that our destiny and future are not tied to enslavement to an indigenous founding cultural and spiritual base. The indigenous principle at play in most issues of identity refers to natural and cultural ties to ancestry and centers of origin and birth; it is also an attachment to a pattern of response to challenges or problem-solving models that communities and societies have embraced over a long period of time. This might relate to faith, religion, social practices, marriage, or any aspect of life.

However, the pilgrim principle is the driving force for human existence and is rooted in the Christian understanding of identity and history. The pilgrim principle indicates that we are reborn in Christ to a new life that relativizes every other identity because it gives us a new sense of being; it connects us to one and all in Trinitarian communion, and we can call God father or mother and call every person our brother or sister. The pilgrim principle is also eschatological, in the sense that it moves our hearts to realize that the goal of life is not to be pursued solely through attachment to indigenous ties. It is an invitation to embrace cultural practices as instruments for realizing the purposes of God rather than being enslaved to them in such a way that we become attached to an unredeemed nativistic parochialism and its associated claims and narratives. Our identity ties are to be used as instruments for the pursuit of the greater goal of life (eternity). God uses these ties as instruments for realizing through our daily actions God's will for human and cosmic flourishing. The pilgrim principle reminds us that our true home is in God and that in a concrete sense we are constantly on the move to our Father's house. Catholicism is a strong answer to the problem of contested modernities and contending identities in the world, and an illuminative church that takes account of all things, respects the alterity of all things, and seeks to find the light of Christ in all things, has the possibility of helping to contribute to a world where everyone feels a sense of belonging, and becomes like Pope Francis said in his inaugural homily, "guardians of one another and guardians of creation."

AFRICAN CHRISTIANS LOOK TO VATICAN III

The Church We Want: African Christians Look to Vatican III is the title of a book of essays of African theologians who participated in a three-year theological dialogue and palaver facilitated by Agbonkhianmeghe Orobator. In the introduction to the volume Orobator writes: "Vatican III is best understood as a metaphor. As such, it is an attempt to generate thinking beyond the staid and familiar; to imagine with boldness, creativity, generosity, and courage issues that stretch and expand the boundaries of theological thinking in the church."[25]

According to Bradford Hinze, "It is beyond dispute that Pope Francis has initiated a new phase in the reception of Vatican II."[26] Hinze rightly observed that Pope Francis has "accentuated the importance of promoting participatory structures of decision making in the church" at all levels from the universal church to the local churches. The key to understanding this movement in Pope Francis, according to Hinze, is not only his ecclesiology of the people of God, but the dialogical character of the whole church—all the members of the church—and the dialogue with history as a way of bringing about a prophetic discipleship that bears the five marks of the church: the centrality of personal and communal discernment; dialogue

---

[25]Agbonkhianmeghe Orobator, ed., *The Church We Want: African Christians Look to Vatican III* (Maryknoll, NY: Orbis Books, 2016), xxx.

[26]Bradford E. Hinze, *Prophetic Obedience: Ecclesiology for a Dialogical Church* (Maryknoll, NY: Orbis Books, 2016), xvii.

with church authorities that is not simply a blind obedience to top-down laws and edicts; the importance of listening to and allowing the wisdom provided by the *sensus fidei* and *sensus fidelium* to nourish the life of the church; encountering reality and reading the signs of the times; a missionary discipleship marked by prophetic dialogue.[27] Austen Ivereigh, in his biography of Pope Francis, noted that Francis's formation "coincided with a period of epochal change in the church" and that the reform and far-reaching changes made by Vatican II were the greatest sources of inspiration for Pope Francis and a guiding teacher for his pontificate.[28] A few years back, before Pope Francis, in the introduction to a volume on Vatican II, Matthew Lamb and Matthew Levering asked the fundamental question: "What does it mean to implement Vatican II 'in faithful continuity with the two millennial tradition of the church' and thereby for it to serve as a 'compass' to guide us at the dawn of the third millennium?"[29] In other words, how can the unfinished business of Vatican II be continued by the church today and how has it continued in Pope Francis?[30]

One important truth that has emerged in the course of the church's history is that there is no metanarrative of Vatican II, just as there is no single narrative of Catholicism. Thus, the implementation of Vatican II that I see in Pope Francis is not the assumption of any particular form or model, but the opening of all the models of the church to a new hermeneutics of inclusion. In other words, Pope Francis has located the mission and identity of the church within a wider theological hermeneutics which places the mission of God as primary. A poor and merciful church is capable of being formed in this mission of God through a movement into history in a culture of encounter that leads to the light and the beautiful Christian way. Hinze's prophetic discernment or the church with a big ear in Uzukwu's ecclesiology[31] are not some sets of rules and patterns that define a system of being and acting in the lives of Christians and in the church. Rather, prophetic discernment, as Pope Francis shows, involves moments in illuminative ecclesiology—accountability, accompaniment, vulnerable

---

[27]Ibid., xviii–xix.

[28]Austen Ivereigh, *The Great Reformer: Francis and the Making of a Radical Pope* (New York: Henry Holt, 2014), 57.

[29]Matthew L. Lamb and Matthew Levering, Introduction to *Vatican II: Renewal with Tradition*, ed. Matthew L. Lamb and Matthew Levering (Oxford: Oxford University Press, 2008), 5.

[30]This is the title of an ecclesiological study by Paul Lakeland, *A Council That Will Never End: Lumen Gentium and the Church Today* (Collegeville, MN: Liturgical Press, 2013). See also Stephen Schloesser, "Reproach vs. Rapprochement: Historical Preconditions of a Paradigm Shift in the Reform of Vatican II," in *50 Years on: Probing the Riches of Vatican II*, ed. David G. Schultenover (Collegeville, MN: Liturgical Press, 2015), xi–xv.

[31]Elochukwu Uzukwu, *A Listening Church: Autonomy and Communion in African Churches* (Maryknoll, NY: Orbis Books, 1996), 149.

mission, and transformation—which bring the light of truth, grace, and life to the people of God. The realization of Vatican II in Pope Francis's ministry can be seen only through the theological aesthetics of form and being that are prior gifts to humanity, and realized in the church through attention to the concrete human experience and historical contexts and locations. Seeing the pattern of these movements is possible if the church is rooted in its primordial experience as emerging from God and from love and moving toward the effulgence of this gift of life and grace assisted by the Holy Spirit.

Becoming part of this illuminative church, which is a movement from one degree of glory to another through attention to the conditions of people in their search for God, requires a loosening of unwieldy structures of authority, a widening of the dialogue in the church-in-the-world, a commitment to social justice and a dynamic social mission, and a serious and sincere involvement of the laity, especially women, in every level of leadership and ministry in the church. The acceptance of the prior light as a gift that is present in the world and the openness to seeing this light in the most unseemly sites are innovations Pope Francis has brought to Catholicism. Pope John Paul's rallying call when he became pope was "do not be afraid"; however, the church under him moved to a more authoritarian and centrist notion of truth while pastoral plans and priorities were set for the whole church through curial manualism.

As a special pastoral assistant to the Nigerian bishops in 2000, I was quite surprised at the intimidating heaps of documents that came from Rome to local churches, all filled with instructions and guidelines. It was quite overwhelming. Pope Francis has taken John Paul II's rallying cry to heart. This is why he was not afraid to touch Muslims, to speak freely on topics and themes on the faith because Pope Francis believes that the Holy Spirit is able to reveal the truth through direct encounters rather than through filtered, redacted comments parsed ad nauseam that often speak of institutional protectionism rather than the fresh water that comes from the Spring of life. Therefore, the reform of Vatican II that Pope Francis has embarked on is more a redesigning of the process of proclamation and witnessing in the church, which has the capacity of revolutionizing everything in the church and freeing the church from ecclesial transcendentalism and triumphalism of any kind. This way, the church can be and see the light in the world and in its inner life. In this kind of church, all are fully attuned to the movement of the Spirit in history. As a result of this process, the light of Christ both in the world and in the church and the mutual exchange of light can become foundational theological aesthetics and heuristic structures for entering into the mysteries of God, of suffering, pain, wounds, and redemption in order to experience the light of salvation in the world. The church is mediator of this light rather than its moderator operating through a central command station in Rome.

My contention is that we cannot understand the new ecclesiological model that Pope Francis has introduced in the church today without appreciating how they have roots in the reform and spirit of Vatican II. By the same token, we cannot develop practices for living the message of Pope Francis in Africa and in the world church without seeing the connection between what we are being called to do in our church today and what the fathers of the council called us to embrace in order to meet the spiritual and material hunger of the people of our times. These practices of a poor and merciful church, when we study its foundations and enter into the mystery of how God reveals the light of love and grace in history, have deep roots in the grassroots approach to evangelization of the Lord Jesus, the examples of the early church, and the lives and examples of the saints and the church through the ages. This message is particularly important in the realization of the renewal called for by Vatican II in Africa through the inspiration of Pope Francis.

In his introduction to the magisterial study of Alfred Guy Bwidi Kitambala, *The Bishops of Africa and the Second Vatican Council: Participation, Contribution and Application of the Synod of Bishops of 1994*, Fidel Gonzales Fernandez makes the following important points: First, the Second Vatican Council and the first African Synod constitute the greatest ecclesial events that have significantly reshaped the face of the young African churches south of the Sahara. Second, one cannot fully understand the challenges and prospects of the church in Africa today without understanding the limited participation of African delegates and the state of the African hierarchy at the time of the council. Furthermore, one cannot fully apprehend the inspiration and dynamism of African Catholic churches and the propositions of the two subsequent African synods without an appreciation of Africa's reception of Vatican II documents and teaching.[32] Jean-Paul Messina argues that the lack of adequate representation of Africa at Vatican II was the natural consequence of the colonial nature of the church in Africa at that time. The African church at the time of the council was largely controlled and run from Rome with Western missionaries managing most of the dioceses, parishes, seminaries, and church establishments in Africa. Messina notes further that Africa was not really central to the discussion and decisions of the council. The indigenous African bishops at

---

[32]See Bwidi Kitambala, *Les evêques d'Afrique et le Concile Vatican II: Participation, contribution et application du synode des evêques de 1994* (Paris: L'Harmattan, 2010), 14.

the council, for example, did not have a common agenda because they did not have at that time any continental episcopal structure for articulating common concerns and pastoral programs.[33]

In addition, Africa did not have any influential theologian who could act as a theological adviser to the African bishops. The only Catholic university existing then was L'Université de Lovanium (Congo-Leopoldville in present day Democratic Republic of Congo), which was established in 1954. When the list of experts at the council was published on September 29, 1962, in the *Osservatore Romano*, there was only one African from Egypt on the list of 201 *periti*. There were, for instance, 165 theologians for Western Europe alone, 14 for Eastern Europe, 11 for the United States, and 4 for Canada. The 276 African fathers at the council were assigned Marie-Dominique Chenu, Joseph Greco, and Michel Cancouët, among others, who worked with particular regional blocs of African bishops.[34]

Despite these limitations, Vatican II has borne immense fruits in Africa. There have emerged in Africa many theological, ecclesial, liturgical, and pastoral traditions that reflect African priorities and responses to the challenges of evangelization and the specific needs of faith and culture in Africa. Among many other positive consequences of Vatican II in Africa are the development and renewal of African theologies and the emergence of truly indigenous African Catholic churches. In addition, Vatican II led to the translation of liturgical and canonical texts from Latin into indigenous languages, the adoption of African arts and customs in the liturgy and in church architecture, and the indigenization of the clergy, religious life, and sacramental life. Vatican II also led to a greater openness in Africa to the active participation of the laity in church life. Africa has witnessed since Vatican II a renewed commitment to the social mission of the church and a greater appreciation and familiarity with Catholic social teaching. All these have resulted in a strong movement in Africa toward the inculturation of the gospel.

According to John Baur, the emerging commitment of the African churches was the need for

> the local church to find its identity. A widely shared conviction emerged that congenial African structures have to be built up from the grassroots of village churches and small church communities. Together with their ecclesial self-consciousness, African church leaders professed indepen-

---

[33]Jean-Paul Messina, *Evêques Africains au Concile Vatican II (1959–1965)* (Paris: Karthala-UCAC), 25.

[34]Kitambala, *Les evêques d'Afrique*, 160–64; See also Daniel Moulinet, ed., *Michel Cancouët: L'Afrique au Concile Journal d'un Expert* (Rennes, France: Presses Universitaires de Rennes, 2010), 10.

dence from their governments and found the courage to exercise their prophetic role in the face of the prevailing evils in state and society.[35]

The liturgical renewal called for by Vatican II and its joyful implementation in Africa led to the approval of the Roman Missal for the Dioceses of Zaire on April 30, 1988, and there were other experimental missals.[36]

One positive effect of Vatican II globally is the emergence of theological creativity in world Catholicism. It is not simply that theologians were developing theologies of inculturation and liberation; rather, they were rediscovering new dimensions of the faith and culture, and new answers and new questions to the challenges of living faithfully and creatively in a world of social change.[37] As I argued in my essays for CNN and CTV, at the commencement of the papacy of Pope Francis:

> In terms of concrete actions, I am hoping that the next pope should not become a slave to one idea or a single narrative of Catholicism, but should be someone who understands the beauty and richness of diversity and pluralism within the oneness of the Catholic family. If the Christian God is a community of diversity with a rich unity of relationship and oneness of being, the church which is built on this image, should model its life, teaching, and action on recognizing and celebrating the dignity of differences without sacrificing its true identity. The next pope should be someone who has the capacity to listen, who is wise with a strong spiritual depth, and who will lead both from the head, but above all from the heart. Catholicism suffers when it essentializes what it means to be Catholic or interprets as normative those traditions, laws, or structures that are the product of historical exigencies, cultural factors, and human attempts in the past to meet the challenges of a bygone age. Each generation of Catholics must dig deep into the forces of its history, privileging the resources within the times, and tapping into the rich positive Christian traditions of the past, to meet the new challenges of the present.[38]

---

[35]John Baur, *2000 Years of Christianity in Africa: An African Church History*, ed. Silvano Borruso, 2nd ed. (Nairobi: Paulines Publications Africa, 2009), 387.

[36]Ibid., 388.

[37]For a history of these developments see the articles in the collected volume, Giuseppe Alberigo and Alphonse Ngindu Mushete, eds., *Towards the African Synod* (London: SCM Press, 1991). See also Tharcisse T. Tshibangu, *Le Concile Vatican II et L'Eglise Africaine: Mise en oevure du concile dans l'Eglise d'Afrique (1960–2010)* (Paris: Editions Karthala, 2010), 71–100. See also Maura Browne, ed., *African Synod: Documents, Reflections, Perspectives* (Maryknoll, NY: Orbis Books, 1996).

[38]Stan Chu Ilo, "What Happens in the Catholic Church Matters to Everyone," CTV News, March 13, 2013, www.ctvnews.ca.

The illuminative church of Pope Francis has been marked with these signs of diversity, dialogue, healthy debates, deepening of the spiritual and moral life, and a dynamic structure that makes possible the healthy exercise of the freedom of the Spirit in the church.

In this regard, his illuminative ecclesiology helps the church move away from a stifling uniformity, to a diversity that respects the new narratives of faith emerging in places such as Brazil, Mexico, Kenya, Nigeria, and India, as well as the renewal of faith happening in Nairobi, Taize, Lyon, Cebu, Rimini, and many unheralded but flourishing parishes throughout the world. The future of the church will be constructed through a learning church that is at home in the world, with women, LGBTQ, the poor, and those on the margins. It will be a church that searches for the hidden light of Christ in their places of exile from the heart of society and the church. It is a church that must embrace cultural traditions as a friend and not as a foe. That does not mean that the Catholic Church should embrace all the social experimentations in the modern world; there is need for the kind of discernment proposed in *Amoris Laetitia* in choosing the illuminative path that leads to the light of Christ. However, it means that the church must appreciate and respond to the deeper concerns of social change and social movements in the world. There is a convergence of values in the world today in terms of what is needed for human and cosmic flourishing. Pope Francis has invited the church today and into the future to wholeheartedly embrace global conversations at all levels for the promotion of human rights, for concerted global actions against climate change, for the removal of all discriminatory laws and prejudices against people the world over on account of sex, race, gender, sexuality, religion, ethnicity, economic, and social conditions. These are new realities that the church of today and of the future must embrace in order to become part of the renewal of creation in the search for the illuminative path that brings healing for wounded souls, hope for the despairing, and light in the darkness.

The new voices in African theology today demonstrate that African Christianity has its own unique identity and mission that needs to be rediscovered, celebrated, and embraced in the world church. They are also showing that Africa has much to give to the world church through its own unique history, spirituality, moral universe, and contextual appropriation of the Christian faith. African theologians are developing relevant theologies that are illuminative of the actual faith of Africans and painting the portrait of new images and models of African ecclesiology. This is an approach that images the church as the family of God as a model of the signs of the new reign of God in Africa in the narratives of faith of ordinary Africans, who are the salt and light in the world. They demonstrate the strong affirmation and practices of faith and hope in the daily commitments and sacrifices of African Christians.

One may note the fact that the riches of Vatican II are yet to be fully explored and that the recommendations of the two African synods on evangelization, dialogue, reconciliation, inculturation, means of social communication, proclamation, justice, and peace are yet to be fully appropriated in African theologies and pastoral life. There are present in Africa today strong theological traditions and ecclesial structures capable of being harvested in developing theologies of transformation and ecclesial practices. These theologies, spiritualities, and ecclesial initiatives in Africa can be further developed through the impetus given to local churches, popular piety, and the social mission of the church in the illuminative ecclesiology of Pope Francis. These theologies must be nourished by a theological aesthetics of beauty and light through the praxis of an illuminative church.

SALT OF THE EARTH, LIGHT OF THE WORLD, AND HOPE FOR THE FUTURE

I understand the disappointment you experienced with the papal (and larger) politics among your colleagues. There are a great many church leaders in the U.S. that rode a wave of superiority (and smugness) when John Paul II and Benedict XVI were at their peak, and they're now engaged in varying degrees of foot-dragging or opposition while hoping eagerly for a new conclave sooner rather than later. Whether or not Francis's vision gains traction among the current leaders, he is doing us all a great service by seeding the soil with dreams, theological insights, ideas and convictions that we can utilize for decades to come. These will allow people to keep his sort of vision alive even if pushed back into marginality within the church, and indeed a more robust version of the Gospel is usually a marginal presence in many of the pristine quarters of the church. If nothing else, frustrations like the ones you encountered head-on remind us that what we do had best not rise and fall on the vagaries of the papacy and its courtiers.

The above quote by Professor Michael Budde, a senior research professor at the Center for World Catholicism at DePaul University, Chicago, was a reply to my email to him about the frustration I felt after attending an international conference on the future of Catholic theology in Africa in April 2017. This was a gathering of all the important church leaders and theologians from Africa, including some of the senior members of the hierarchy in Rome and in many important dioceses in Africa. Also in attendance were most of the African professors at the Roman universities and the most influential African theologians from different parts of the world. I was frustrated because I did not see in our discussions any clear agenda for the future of Catholic theologies in Africa and how to implement the proposals from the two African synods, which were Africa's versions of how to implement Vatican II in Africa. Most significantly, for me, was also the absence of the voice of Pope Francis or his teaching in most of the presentations. There is a feeling in some quarters, even among colleagues who teach in the papal universities and priests and bishops who work at the Vatican, that Pope Francis is a passing phase or a temporary distraction that will fade away as soon as his papacy ends. I have heard some important figures in the church speak as if Pope Francis is only an ecclesial version of liberal thinking that has no future in the church.

I also noticed that the Pope Francis effect that I have witnessed in my work with the poor in five African countries, has not gained traction among rank-and-file African Catholic theologians and pastors. However, this is not a reality peculiar to Africa; this is a perennial challenge that the church must address in the future: the disconnect between theology and life, and the gulf between the teaching and beliefs and practices of the Catholic Church and what the people in the pews actually practice and how they live. If this gap continues to widen, the church will become increasingly irrelevant to their lives, and they will seek other forms of validation and legitimacy for their lives and choices in other places or simply turn their back on God and the church. There is a growth in the Catholic population in the Global South, but this growth is also happening at the same time when the new evangelical and Protestant churches are growing and drawing their membership from disenchanted Catholics who are looking for "more" from the liturgy and from the church beyond rituals, devotions, and five-minute homilies. They are also looking for vibrant parish communities and local dioceses where the dynamism of faith and effective and transformative pastoral ministry speak to the deepest hunger of their souls. Today's Catholics are looking for faith communities where they feel a sense of belonging to something bigger than themselves and bigger than a pastor or a bishop or even a pope.

The future of Catholicism will be determined not simply by what Pope Francis has done, but really by what happens in our local communities of faith, and how faith can become part of people's lives in many societies where there is a dualism between faith and life which has led to one-dimensional Christianity. This future will be constructed through an affirmation of the beauty in people, cultures, and in our world at a time when people are no longer seeing clearly the glory of God in the historical process, which has been dictated by subjugation of the poor and the weak, and unequal power relations among nations, in our churches, among sexes, and among peoples.

This future must be built by everyone. Catholicism has been shaped by a rich history. This is like a palace to the church where it feels comfortable, but it is also like a prison in which it feels isolated.

When Catholicism lives fully its universal identity, there is a divine fruitfulness and dynamism that brings light in the world. It is like being in a palace where everyone is at home, feels a sense of welcome, and where there is a mutual sharing of gifts and charism and a willingness to embrace the gifts and service of everyone. It is to put it simply, a Eucharistic experience where there is unity, harmony, sharing, grace, and thanksgiving. The Eucharist is the principle of otherness and unity as Tillard writes:

> At its source, the Christian way of life is radically, in virtue of God's very self, the absolute negation of any form of self-sufficiency, of any sort of self-absorption. The relationship to the other—this other who is first of all God, but God grasped within the unity between brothers and sisters in Christ Jesus—is intrinsic to the Christian way of life. It constitutes it. Where the communion of Christ Jesus is not present, the Christian way of being is absent. What we are speaking about is communion (1 Cor 1:9), not absorption, because freedom is at the very core of this process of salvation.[39]

However, the church can become self-absorbed in its ancient history and traditions. When this happens, it becomes a prison where the structures are obstacles to the movement of the Spirit. When this occurs, what we see in the church are the cultural relics of Christendom that are passed on as traditions. The relics of Christendom in Catholicism still retain a commanding force in many contexts of church life in those settings where church leaders have a monolithic notion of faith and ecclesial life, and where there is a project to calcify within the structure of faith, authority, and ministry a particular historically dominant sociological form of the church.[40] Pope Francis has begun the razing of the last relics of the bastions of Christendom in Roman Catholicism through a movement whose directions still remain unclear to many.

This is a movement led by the Holy Spirit, which has been present in the church since the time of the Lord Jesus, who commanded his followers

---

[39]J.-M.-R. Tillard, *Flesh of the Church, Flesh of Christ: At the Source of the Ecclesiology of Communion*, trans. Madeleine Beaumont (Collegeville, MN: Liturgical Press, 2001), 3–4.

[40]On the challenges that this model of understanding catholicity poses to the church today and into the future, especially how it suppresses local initiatives and stifles creativity in the church, see Richard Gaillardetz, *Ecclesiology for a Global Church: A People Called and Sent* (Maryknoll, NY: Orbis Books, 2011), 42. See also Joseph A. Komonchak, "Modernity and the Construction of Roman Catholicism," *Cristianesimo nella Storia* 18 (1997): 353–85. See also Massimo Faggioli, *A Council for the Global Church: Receiving Vatican II in History* (Minneapolis: Fortress Press, 2015), 292–305.

to be the salt of the earth and the light of the world. The sad fact is that we have been led by history into falsely believing that the church is about us, the systems and structures, the elegance of our architecture, and the solidity of our institutions and structures of authority. Ecclesiology has been built around how these structures should operate and work better to bring about the will of God for the church. However, illuminative ecclesiology in Pope Francis reverses everything by saying that who the church is can best be answered by where the church is. It is in that moment of encounter that God's light is found, and this happens everywhere and cannot be restricted or controlled through a Roman command center or a rigid structure. This kind of approach furnishes the theological aesthetics that should form the standard and measure of our ecclesiologies and the practices, priorities, and mission of the church. This is how we can build up the church of God as the new people of God on a mission.

Sister Rosemary Nyirumbe is often referred to as Africa's Mother Teresa because of the work she is doing saving the lives of thousands of young girls kidnapped by Joseph Kony's Lord's Resistance Army (LRA) in Northern Uganda. She is one of my heroes and a giant light bearer. It is fitting that I use her witnessing and proclamation of the Word of God to conclude this book. Sister Rosemary met Pope Francis in 2017 and was moved by that experience. She told me of her meeting with the pope in these words:

> It was such a moving moment. He knew about my work and was happy to receive my book, *Sewing Hope*. He gave me a wonderful embrace and a kiss. He gave me a new definition of church because he told me that I am building God's church at St. Monica's where hundreds of these rescued girls have found a home filled with love.[41]

Indeed, wherever there is a genuine culture of contact, we are building God's church. Wherever God's church is being built after the mind of Jesus Christ, there is always a light, an illuminative path, and a way of beauty. This can happen through popes, priests, bishops, religious, and lay members of Christ's faithful; it happens in many hidden parts of the world. There is a light in the human heart, waiting to be born in the womb of love, through the tenderness of the church, our Mother. Everyone is called to be that light so that the church of Christ can be the salt of the earth and the light of the world.

---

[41]See Reggie Whitten, *Sewing Hope: Joseph Kony Tore These Girls Lives Apart: Can She Stitch Them Back Together* (Oklahoma City: Dust Jacket Press, 2013). See also www.sewinghope.com.

Index